VISIONS
AND
REVISIONS
Critical Reading and Writing

Harvey Minkoff

Evelyn B. Melamed

Hunter College

Prentice Hall, Englewood Cliffs, New Jersey 07632

Library of Congress Cataloging-in-Publication Data

Minkoff, Harvey
    Visions and revisions: critical reading and writing/Harvey
Minkoff, Evelyn B. Melamed.
        p.   cm.
    ISBN 0-13-949884-2
        1. English language—Rhetoric. 2. College readers. 3. Readers—
United States. 4. United States—Civilization. I. Melamed,
Evelyn B. II. Title.
PE1408.M563 1990
808′.0427—dc20   89-26436
                                                            CIP

Editorial/production supervision: *Carole Brown*
Interior design: *Meryl Poweski*
Cover design: *Meryl Poweski*
Manufacturing buyer: *Mary Ann Gloriande*

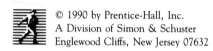 © 1990 by Prentice-Hall, Inc.
A Division of Simon & Schuster
Englewood Cliffs, New Jersey 07632

Printed in the United States of America
10 9 8 7 6 5 4 3 2 1

ISBN 0-13-949884-2

Prentice-Hall International (UK) Limited, *London*
Prentice-Hall of Australia Pty. Limited, *Sydney*
Prentice-Hall Canada Inc., *Toronto*
Prentice-Hall Hispanoamericana, S.A., *Mexico*
Prentice-Hall of India Private Limited, *New Delhi*
Prentice-Hall of Japan, Inc., *Tokyo*
Simon & Schuster Asia Pte. Ltd., *Singapore*
Editora Prentice-Hall do Brasil, Ltda., *Rio de Janeiro*

For Dinah and Jackie

Democratic nations care but little for what has been,
but they are haunted by visions of what will be.

Alexis de Tocqueville
Democracy in America

There will be time . . .
. . . for a hundred visions and revisions. . . .

T.S. Eliot
"The Love Song of J. Alfred Prufrock"

CONTENTS

Chapter Two
Re-Vision I: Critical Reading   31

What Makes Mario Run?   40

> "Do his old-fashioned Roman Catholicism and upright honor have
> an edge of sanctimony and priggishness? . . . Does his heritage as
> an immigrant's son make him thin-skinned and over-
> sensitive? . . . "

Essays for Critical Reading   62

TV Children Not Real, Study Charges   63

> "Children are white, rich and live with a divorced mother who
> has a satisfying full-time career in business. . . . "

SUSAN SCHERREIK: Lehman Professor Examines Role of Ethnic Identity 65

> ". . . how people feel about themselves is affected by their cultural
> background."

WASHINGTON IRVING: Traits of Indian Character   69

> "The rights of the savage have seldom been properly appreciated
> or respected by the white man."

FREDERICK JACKSON TURNER: The Significance of the Frontier in
American History   73

> "The existence of an area of free land . . . and the advance of
> American settlement westward, explain American development."

Making Connections   78

Chapter Three
Re-Vision II: Using Sources   87

PART TWO
ESSAY STRATEGIES *155*

Chapter Four
Structuring the Objective Essay *157*

". . . mothers of America—you, who have learned, by the cradles
of your own children, to love and feel for all mankind—by the
sacred love you bear your child; by your joy in his beautiful,
spotless infancy; by the motherly pity and tenderness with which
you guide his growing years. . . . I beseech you, pity those mothers
that are constantly made childless by the American slave-trade."

"Under a government which imprisons any unjustly, the true place
for a just man is also a prison."

"But do the people want good government? . . . Isn't our corrupt
government, after all, representative?"

"We have listened too long to the courtly muses of Europe."

Chapter Eight
Researched Writing

". . . while the law makers were deeply concerned with the
mental, moral, and physical quality of immigrants, there developed
as time went on an even greater concern as to the fundamental
racial character of the constantly increasing numbers who came."

TO THE
INSTRUCTOR

At the heart of good writing is a person saying something to another person. While this simple statement may sound like a truism, all three of its elements have been overlooked in composition classes at one time or another. Writing involves a person, a human being with opinions, one whose vision of the world is shaped by personal experience. This person has something to say that only he or she can say, not merely a rehash of clichés or other people's opinions. And this person tells his or her idea to another person, who perhaps has different opinions shaped by different experiences.

At one extreme, the wish to remove the threat presented by a blank sheet of paper has led teachers to declare that anyone can write, inadvertently fostering the belief that unexamined bias and informed opinion are equally valid. At the other extreme, attempting to wean students from the overly personal "What I Did Last Summer" essay has led teachers to ban the word *I* and the phrase *in my opinion*—as if objectivity is the absence of opinion.

A middle ground, however, exists between personal writing with no knowledge and impersonal writing with no personality. Good writers treat the reader to the joy of watching an intelligent person use his or her experience to come to terms with important ideas in an analytical way.

This text takes for granted the importance of teaching writing as a process. However, writing is more than its process. Writing requires having something to say; and this comes from information. The beginning of knowledge is knowing what others have said—the great thinkers, the influential ideas. But there comes a time when critical mass is reached and new knowledge explodes.

We have seen this mental fusion light up the faces of students who suddenly understood something about themselves they had never understood before. And we ourselves have been enlightened by the insights of students whose world view is very different from our own.

In our courses—as reflected in this book—we strive to make students part of the intellectual discourse that shapes our country and world, while not creating clones of ourselves. This is done through teaching students *how* to think, not *what* to think.

· ABOUT THIS BOOK

The Introduction explains how this book produces the results we have just outlined. In summary:

- "Re-vision"—the process of looking again at our ideas—is central to intellectual growth, not just to writing. Students begin by writing from personal experience but then revise—"re-see"—their essays in light of reading selections.
- Major historical and literary documents show how America has revised its view of itself over the centuries; sample essays show students engaging similar issues as they write, read, and revise what they have written.
- Reading selections and writing assignments are totally integrated. "Making Connections" questions in each chapter ask students to connect new ideas to previous readings and essay topics in order to generate class discussions and new topics.
- Questions after the reading selections stress previewing, call attention to significant passages, and ask students how they would use this new information.
- Short exercises give practice in applying such techniques as identifying details, connecting ideas, and analyzing logical relationships.

· ACKNOWLEDGMENTS

We wish to thank all those whose cooperation allowed us to write this book:

The students, both named and anonymous, at Hunter College and Iona College who have let us reprint their essays and share their sometimes intimate thoughts with a larger audience than they had intended.

The teachers and graduate students, and especially the participants of the Iona College Writing Institute, who used our material during its evolution and improved it with their critiques.

The authors and unsung editors of union and professional publications who generously shared their work, in particular John M. Barry of the AFL-CIO, Ted Bleeker and Thomas Y. Hobart of the New York State United Teachers, Elizabeth McPike and Albert Shanker of the American Federation of Teachers, Gerald Ratliff of *Communication Quarterly*, Carol Sims of the Professional Staff Congress/CUNY, Joseph Tarantola of the *Empire State Investigator*, and Bernard Wax of the American Jewish Historical Society.

The librarians and staff at the Hunter College and Mahopac libraries whose expertise made our work immeasurably easier, with special thanks to Julio Hernandez-Delgado, Suzanne Siegel, Jean-Jaques Strayer, Sarah Watstein, and Joseph Weiss of Hunter College; and Maria Brech, Susan Garry, Ping Foo, Liz Krieger, and Betty Trzaska of Mahopac.

The writing teachers who read the various versions of the manuscript and made helpful suggestions: Sara Burroughs, Northwestern State University of Louisiana; Susanna Defever, St. Clair County Community College; Nancy MacKenzie, Mankato State University; Raymond T. MacKenzie, Mankato State University; Berwyn Moore, Gannon University; and Peter Burton Ross, University of the District of Columbia.

Our editors at Prentice Hall: Phil Miller, Nancy Perry, and Kate Morgan, for their good counsel.

Irene Moran for her loving care of our children.

And finally, our children, Dinah and Jackie, for reminding us of our priorities.

TO THE STUDENT

This book will help you become a personal but objective writer. You will begin by writing about your personal experience, but you will then read what others have experienced. Based on this new information you will revise, or reconsider, your original essay. In this way you will build the kind of "knowledge base" that allows educated people to analyze their personal experiences in a way that is relevant to others as well.

Too often, students remove themselves and their opinions from their writing—they present lifeless summaries of conventional wisdom or common prejudices; they write what they hope the instructor wants to read. But more than anything, teachers want to read lively, engaging essays that reward the time spent grading them. Teachers who have to read fifty or a hundred papers are thrilled to discover a creative or thoughtful mind, especially if the essay makes them see familiar texts or ideas in a new light.

Ignorance is not creative and thoughtful. Believing something because you never bothered to analyze it is death to your essay. The reader will turn away with disdain. On the other hand, showing that you have thought about important issues—their history, consequences, controversies—will impress even the reader who disagrees with your conclusions.

Gaining the kind of knowledge we are describing takes effort. But the benefits extend far beyond your composition course. More valuable even than writing skills, this book will involve you in a process of intellectual growth that we are convinced will make you a wiser, better person.

· ABOUT THIS BOOK

The Introduction explains how this book produces the results we have just outlined. In summary:

- "Re-vision"—the process of looking again at our ideas—is central to intellectual growth, not just to writing. Students begin by writing from personal experience but then revise—"re-see"—their essays in light of reading selections.

- Major historical and literary documents show how America has revised its view of itself over the centuries; sample essays show students engaging similar issues as they write, read, and revise what they have written.

- Reading selections and writing assignments are totally integrated. "Making Connections" questions in each chapter ask students to connect new ideas to previous readings and essay topics in order to generate class discussions and new topics.

- Questions after the reading selections stress previewing, call attention to significant passages, and ask students how they would use this new information.

- Short exercises give practice in applying such techniques as identifying details, connecting ideas, and analyzing logical relationships.

I·N·T·R·O·D·U·C·T·I·O·N

CRITICAL READING AND WRITING

· WRITING TO LEARN

"How do you know what you think until you see what you've said?" With these words, which he adapted from the author E. M. Forster, a professor of ours used to encourage students to talk in class. Many students, of course, hesitate to take part in discussions because they are unsure of their knowledge; they don't want to make foolish mistakes or to be accused of shooting their mouths off. Almost everyone has hidden behind the excuse "I know the answer, but I can't explain it." Yet the truth is that if you can't put it into words, you don't know it.

Paradoxically, however, one way to learn something is by trying to explain it. As every teacher knows, nothing is as clear as the book or theory or problem that we have had to explain to a class. The very act of talking in front of people makes us ask questions, see possibilities, discover insights. Sometimes we go to class with a prepared lecture. But far more often we are armed only with a list of points we intend to cover; then, as the discussion unfolds, we decide what order to use, which ideas to stress, when to move on. And frequently in the midst of all this, an insight flashes before us to clarify what we thought we knew all along.

The same is true of writers. News reporters are noted for their ability to compose at their typewriters in the race against deadlines. They write as fast as they can type, seldom looking back, only occasionally making changes. But reporters sadly admit that they write for the wastebasket: "Today's story wraps tomorrow's garbage," in the words of an editor at a newspaper where we once worked. In contrast, thoughtful writing is approached more carefully. Even newspaper columns and editorials, which suffer the same brief life as news stories, involve more planning, more false starts, more crumpling of paper. The writer may know the general point to be made, but how it finally emerges is a surprise. On occasion the point itself may change as the essay evolves—because writing is a way of learning.

The need to put ideas down on paper forces us to confront our inner selves. We must examine our opinions and analyze our knowledge. In the process we may discover that we don't understand some subjects—even ourselves—as well as we had thought. Perhaps we may even realize, to our horror, that a cherished opinion is nothing but a baseless prejudice that ought to be discarded. Thus, as you learn to write, you will find that you are also learning through writing.

· CRITICAL THINKING

In a sense, the world is a chaos of individual facts, until our critical faculty imposes system. The meaning of events is not "out there" waiting to be discovered. It is inside us, waiting to be created. The analytical mind classifies, organizes, and interprets events to make them meaningful. Faced with the same situation, you may see a challenge where someone else sees a problem.

In popular usage the word *critical* commonly means "in the habit of finding fault" or "always showing disapproval"—as when parents are critical of their children's behavior or friends. But it also means "able to evaluate and form judgments" and in this usage it is related to the movie critic, literary criticism, and critiques. When we urge you to develop the habit of critical thinking, we are suggesting that you

- ask questions,
- weigh evidence,
- look for assumptions and biases,
- analyze reasoning and logic,
- evaluate opinions,
- judge generalizations,
- draw conclusions,
- suggest alternatives.

And, most of all, you should try to make connections between new information and what you already know and believe.

· READING FOR WRITING

One way to develop the habit of critical thinking is to read a lot and write about what you have read—as this text asks you to do. Reading and writing are not two skills, but two sides of the same coin. All good writers are avid readers first, and experiencing the decisions that go into writing makes the writer a more sensitive reader. As you will see in this book, good readers try to reconstruct and evaluate the writer's thought process; they ask, "Why is this here? What does it add?" Good writers try to see their own work as a reader would. They try to predict what the reader will want to know or may find troublesome, and they avoid raising expectations that will not be met.

Reading and writing are not passive experiences. Good readers do not simply accept what they read. They bring their own backgrounds and knowledge to the text so that they form expectations as they read. This approach to reading explains why teachers can often tell you that what you wrote is probably not what you meant. For their part, good writers lead the reader along by creating expectations and fulfilling them. They do not merely repeat what they have read or what someone else has told them. Rather, they use their own experiences for examples, explanations, insights. They see the world through their own filter. They make the reader want to know what they, not someone else, has to say about a topic. Through this type of active involvement, the mature reader/ writer experiences the world through the text and uses it to discover his or her own feelings and beliefs. In particular, evaluating the thoughts of others and trying to put our own views into words helps us move from unexamined prejudices to informed opinions.

· MAKING CONNECTIONS
THROUGH READING AND WRITING

So that you can see how reading and writing are ways to discover what you think, the reading passages and writing assignments in this text concentrate on one broad topic. Any topic would do, but we have chosen the American experience because of its interest and importance.

Like every person, you are unique. But you are also part of a social context. What is called *national character* is the product of a people's history, culture, and beliefs. Not everyone in a country shares the national character, of course. But in our own way, each of us is affected by it.

Some of the reading selections in this book assume that the American experience is the property of white male Protestants from western Europe. Others concentrate on women, minorities, and the disenfranchised. Some praise the melting pot ideal. Others attack it. Some are legal or philosophical classics that shaped America. Others are attempts by students to find their place in our society. Some will confirm your beliefs. Others will challenge them. And you, in turn, will attack some of the selections and draw on others for support.

You will explore aspects of the American experience through essays, news stories, editorials, speeches, reports, and legal documents. Issues such as ideals and values, ethnicity and assimilation, racial and sexual stereotypes, and the roles of the media and education reappear and intersect. As an alert reader and viewer you will want to see connections between a selection on cultural stereotypes and one about television commercials, and you will also want to weigh their relevance to what you already know about racism and sexism, or to your beliefs about the role of the media in our society. In the early chapters of this text we will help you by calling things to your attention and asking questions for you. Then, one by one, the prompts will disappear, until, by the end of the semester, you will be on your way to becoming a mature reader/writer on your own.

As such, you should not be satisfied just to know what an author says or to write a superficial paper for an assignment. You will want to understand where this new information fits into what you heard yesterday or learned in a different course. You will want to consider, for example, whether a profile of an Italian-American politician in New York helps you make sense of ethnic relations in your community. You will want to search your own experience to see if it confirms or contradicts what you have read, and you will want to hear what other students say about their own experiences. When you do this, reading selections and writing assignments—whether in history, sociology, science, or the arts— will be real sources of information for you to confront and to incorporate into your mental world.

· INVENTION: FROM READING TO WRITING

A practical value of always making connections between new information and old is that it provides a solution to that tormenting question "What should I write about?" The key to invention—the process of finding something to say in an essay—is knowledge.

Obviously, no textbook can include every aspect of a topic as rich as the American experience. You should view the reading selections and essay topics as starting points for exploration, not as the sum of what you should know. If you read about the image of women on television, you may choose to explore the image of Catholics in the movies or Arabs in newspapers. If you read something you disagree with, then evaluate, attack, and disprove it. In fact, if the way we phrase questions implies a value system that offends you, attack it and defend your own.

When you work conscientiously at clarifying your views through reading and writing, you will have something to say. For those times when you may have trouble writing about an assigned theme or focusing on a precise topic, this text will show you how to use prewriting techniques like free writing, brainstorming, issue trees, and peer critiquing for getting your intellectual adrenaline flowing. But in general you will find that learning how to make connections between reading passages and writing assignments will remove the terror once posed by a blank sheet of paper staring up at you. When you have information, the problem is in organizing it, not in filling a page with words.

· WRITING STRATEGIES

Organization is largely strategy. In putting together an essay, as in building a better mousetrap, "right" is what works. This book shows you some conventional ways of organizing an essay because experience has proven that they do the job of conveying your meaning clearly. But from the very start you will be developing your own "voice"—a style of vocabulary and sentence structure that reflects your personality. You will therefore modify these conventions to suit that voice. Thus, you will notice that many of the essays included in this book do not rigidly follow the format of introduction-development-conclusion that you have probably learned already and will be seeing again here. But conventions can be bent only so far before you lose your credibility with the reader, so how much liberty to take with them is another aspect of strategy that you will have to consider.

The best way to understand writing strategies is by exploiting the connection between reading and writing. As a writer who must weigh your own choice of words, you become a reader who draws inferences from someone else's choices. As a writer who must present the world through your own filter, you become a reader who can recognize a different filter. As a writer who must decide what to include in your own essay, you become a reader who will recognize when vital information has been omitted from what you read or see on television. And, of course, when you connect what you experience in one place with what you learn in another, when you approach reading as a source of ideas for writing, you become a person with something worthwhile to say.

You create worthwhile writing when you engage the world as yourself. For instance, in order to appreciate how a writer creates meaning from separate facts, you are asked to show the logical connection that you see in sets of ideas. You will find, however, that this exercise, like others in the text, does not have only one right answer. Each writer sees the world in his or her own way. Your answers may differ from ours but they are no less valid—when they accurately convey your worldview.

Similarly, there are conventions for the overall presentation, and choosing among them is also part of a writer's strategy. In the conventions of written English an author who writes about medicine in a popular magazine has a different purpose and thus needs a different presentation from one who writes in a professional journal. So too, an author who writes a comparison/contrast essay has a different point of view from one who writes an essay of persuasion. We therefore examine the major types of organization—such as comparison, evaluation, persuasion—to see how these rhetorical modes serve an author's purpose.

· RE-VISION

You will experience how reading and writing create knowledge through a technique which we call "re-vision." When kept distinct from rewriting or correcting errors, re-vision is a method of doing what the term originally meant: "seeing again." Re-vision means going back to what you have already written and looking at it with new eyes, re-seeing it in the light of new experience and new information. In fact, re-vision is not limited to writing. Constantly reexamining earlier opinions is central to intellectual growth.

The writing suggestions in this text begin with personal experience. Almost immediately, however, you will read something that makes you see this experience in a new way, and then you will write another essay in which you reconsider your experience. Perhaps you will analyze it, or evaluate it, or compare it to something. You are still unique, and your experience is still your own. But you will be applying your unique voice as a writer to topics other than yourself, for purposes other than talking about yourself. You will be telling the reader something about the American experience that only you are in a position to write.

The structure of this book exemplifies such revision. Many reading selections, discussion questions, and writing assignments refer to earlier ones, and even the presentation of the writing process is recursive. For instance, the conventions of the library paper, presented in Chapter 8, are an advanced version of using sources, introduced in Chapter 3. And throughout, examples which are discussed in the text are drawn from the reading selections.

· FEATURES OF THIS BOOK

Several features of *Visions and Revisions* will help you become the kind of mature reader/writer we have been describing.

We have already mentioned that there are exercises to help you experience how a writer creates meaning and that later writing assignments are revisions of earlier ones.

In addition, three types of questions follow the reading selections. One group, called Facts, asks for background information and content in order to help you understand the selection in terms of its time, place, and purpose. Such questions should become an automatic part of your reading and are soon phased out. A second group, Significance, asks you to explain passages from the selections. In the early chapters we present quotations for you to discuss; in the later chapters you choose and explain the passages that you believe are most significant. The group of questions labeled Future Use asks you to summarize what you have learned and think about the importance of the reading to your life and work. The information in turn becomes the key to the section entitled Making Connections, which asks you to go beyond the essay—to explore its larger implications, to connect it to other selections, to rethink your own opinions and experiences, to become a critical reader, writer, and thinker. Finally, a section of Additional Essays for Discussion challenges you to apply your critical skills without the guidance of the questions we have just described.

As these exercises and the organization of this book suggest, writing is not a linear or isolated skill. It is a cumulative, even circular, process that simultaneously draws on and contributes to your knowledge and experience. From the moment you approach a topic, you must be searching for your voice. As you find your voice, your thoughts mature. As you grow, your voice changes. Your goal, therefore, must be to go beyond the individual skills—to use them for creating your personal visions and re-visions.

VISIONS AND RE-VISIONS

VISIONS
From Thought
to Personal Essay

To write an essay, you must have something to say. So the first question to ask is, "What do I know well enough to write about?" A major problem, of course, is that what you know may not be what the teacher has asked you to discuss. You are in school, after all, to learn things that you don't already know. This is clearly the situation in a history or philosophy course when you are asked to write about a specific event or theory, such as the underlying causes of the Vietnam War or Plato's theory of ideas. In cases like these you will obviously have to find a source of information.

But a good essay is more than just facts. When the purpose of an assignment is to see if you have read a particular book or article, then summarizing the bare facts is adequate. However, in other kinds of writing, both in school and out, your job is to tell the readers something they don't already know, preferably something only you can tell them. This means that in addition to the facts, the essay also expresses the experience and point of view of a writer with a unique background who is addressing a particular audience. That is why three historians telling about the American role in Southeast Asia may tell three entirely different stories: Because of their different backgrounds and intended audiences, one may emphasize the need to stop communist expansion, another may deplore imperialist intervention, and the third may see a clash of cultures. It is not the case that one of them is right and the others are wrong, nor that one is telling the truth and the others are lying. They are each interpreting events; all three are looking at the same objective facts but seeing them through the filters of their own experience. You can learn to do this also.

· WRITING FROM PERSONAL EXPERIENCE

What do you know well enough to write about? What you know best is yourself, but your own experience is not necessarily what other people want to hear about. On the other hand, people do want to know why your experiences have caused you to see the world in a particular way. They want to know how someone from a particular background—which may be very different from their own—interprets the same events that they see through their own filter. Most important of all, readers want to see that the writer has actually thought about his or her experiences in some mature, analytical way, and is not just repeating clichés and platitudes.

· THINKING ABOUT A TOPIC

The first thing to remember is that you are unique. Only you have your specific parents, home, features, personality, and particular experiences. Despite your unique qualities, however, you did not grow up on a deserted island. That is what the philosopher Benedict Spinoza meant when he said, "Man is a social animal" and what the poet John Donne meant by "No man is an island." Things happen in the world that affect you, but they affect you in a specific way because you are yourself and not someone else. To take one example, the potato famine in Ireland during the late nineteenth century caused massive immigration to the United States, yet not everyone left Ireland. In some cases whole villages moved to the new land together, while in others, families split apart, with only the youngest or oldest sons leaving. Why? Why didn't all people react in the same way to the same situation? The answer, of course, is that individuals respond to the same situation in different ways. The stimulus is there, but it is experienced by particular men and women, each with a unique makeup. In other words, every person is both unique and part of a larger social context. Although we as individuals must make many decisions about how to live our lives, our choices are influenced by the very fact that we were born male or female into a specific family in a specific group at a specific time in a specific place.

The interplay of personal uniqueness and outside events can supply raw material for informative, worthwhile, and interesting essays, as you will now see.

WRITING ASSIGNMENT: The Personal Experience Essay

Choose a person that you know well enough to write about, and by using the techniques outlined in the rest of this chapter, try to show how an important action or decision by this person either:

1. is influenced by or

2. has moved away from

the values of his or her group, time, or place.

· GETTING STARTED

How do you go about writing a personal experience essay? You should not expect simply to sit down and turn out an attractive piece of work. Before anything resembling an essay appears, there are helpful techniques of **prewriting** —steps that you take before you write the first draft.

To begin, let's again return to the question at the beginning of this chapter: What do you know well enough to write about? You have been asked to write about how a specific person reached an important decision or why he or she undertook an important action. Who among your acquaintances has made important decisions or done important things? What kinds of decisions or actions? What made them important? Do you know the reasons behind these decisions or actions?

Brainstorming

Many students find it helpful to spend a few minutes just throwing ideas around before starting to write. This technique is called **brainstorming,** and it can be done individually, in small groups, or with the entire class participating. The following lists the responses of a typical small group session working on the question "What are important actions or decisions?"

"Getting married."

"Getting divorced."

"Breaking up with my boyfriend."

"Going to college."

"Dropping out of high school."

"Returning to school after ten years."

"Getting your own apartment."

"Moving to a new city."

"Coming to America."

"Who made these decisions?"

"My father immigrated from Greece."

"My sister just divorced this real slob."

"A friend of my mother's started her own business."

"I just returned to school."

"Why?"

"I wanted a better job."

"To earn more money?"

"No. I was making good money. I didn't like the work I was doing."

"What do you want to do?"

"I'm not sure yet."

"That's not so good."

"Do you know why you're here?"

"Sure."

"You're good. I don't."

"I don't know why I left home."

"Then think about it."

And so it goes. Nothing has to be resolved, but brainstorming gives you ideas about possible topics for an essay. Whether you brainstorm out loud in a group or quietly in your head or on a piece of paper, the next step is to start writing.

Free Writing

Some writers can sit down and turn out an essay. But many prefer to begin with a few minutes of **free writing,** a technique in which they write down thoughts that suggest themselves through free association. In free writing you don't worry about what you are going to say, or about how you are going to say it, because you don't know these things yet, and won't know them until you have done some initial experimenting. In addition, you don't worry about spelling or grammar or sentence structure. All of these mechanical considerations don't become important until you are ready to show your work to readers. For the present topic—how a specific person came to an important decision—you just choose a person who seems like a possible candidate: yourself, one of your parents, a close friend. Then start writing.

Here is an example of free writing that one student produced in about fifteen minutes:

```
Why am I in college? Did I really make a decision
to go or was it just expected of me. My father always
spoke about how I had to do something with my life and it
always seems like he took college for granted. He
```

didn't like my friends because they goofed around in
high school and he was always saying how they wouldn't
be accepted into any college and would make a mess of
their lives. They wouldn't get decent jobs and would
turn out to be bums. Does everyone who doesn't go to
college turn out to be a bum. My father didn't go to
college. Does he think he's a bum? Is he unhappy with
his life? Am I going to college because he couldn't? Is
he concerned about me or himself? What do I want? I
don't know what I want to major in so its not as if I'm
here because I always knew I wanted to be a doctor or
engineer or something like that. Sure I want to make
money. But there are other ways. Do I want to work in an
office? What jobs are there for college grads anyway.
Lots of them are driving cabs. And what about my sisters. They didn't go to college and theyre pretty well
off. They got married and live in nice houses in the
suburbs. They don't even have to work. Maybe I should
find a rich girl and marry her. Then I won't have to
worry about getting a job. But with girls its different. They don't have to support a wife and kids. And
besides, I'm the oldest son so I'll have to take care of
mom and dad when theyre old just like my father did. I
guess its easier if your a girl.

If you were the writer of the foregoing sample, what should you do next? You
have something on paper, but it certainly isn't an essay. There are scattered

ideas, some real emotion, and a serious question about what you want from life. One way to proceed is to try to sort all of this out by yourself.

Issue Trees

One method of sorting through preliminary ideas is to create an **issue tree.** To do this, go through your free writing from beginning to end and list the ideas that appear.

```
I'm in college

my father took it for granted

he thinks my friends are bums

he wants me to get a decent job

he didn't go to college

is he unhappy with his life?

am I in college to please him?

I don't want to be a doctor or engineer

there are other ways to make money

my sisters didn't go to college

they got married and don't work

I could marry a rich girl

girls don't have to support a family

I'll have to care for my parents when they're old
```

Then sort the ideas into groups.

people	choices	results
me	college	decent job
my father	job	unhappy
my friends	marriage	bums
my sisters		confused
		money

As they now stand, the three groups are simply three sets of ideas. They are not connected to each other in any way. It often helps if you arrange the groups like the branches of a tree.

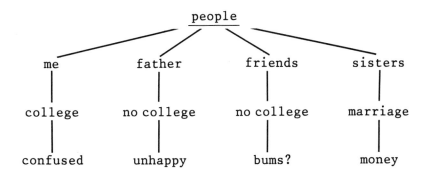

The tree does not use all the ideas listed and also may not capture what the student is trying to say, because the piece of writing is not clearly thought out. It is only the beginning of an essay and still needs to go through drafting and revising.

Peer Critiquing

As you gain more experience in writing you will be able to evaluate and rework your essays on your own, but at this stage in your development as a writer, it would be a good idea to show your ideas to a friend or classmate and get some feedback, using a strategy called **peer critiquing.** You should write down the comments of peers so that you can think about them later.

A friend or classmate—that is, a peer—who reads your passage of free writing has to understand what he or she is looking at and being asked to do. You want useful advice about the direction the paper should take, not a list of your errors in spelling and grammar. You want a critique, some constructive criticism. For this reason, it is worthwhile to remember what we said earlier: Readers want to learn something from your essay, preferably something only you can teach them. Therefore, the peer reading your free writing should try to answer the following questions:

What did I find interesting?
What does it look like I can learn from this?
What insights caught my attention?
What sentence or section seemed best?
What sentence or section seemed weakest?
What parts would I like to see explained more?

What parts should be omitted?
What parts seemed real?
What parts seemed phony?
What parts did the author really care about?
What parts seemed worth writing an essay about?
What idea held the whole piece together?
What was the most important idea?
What idea might tie the different points together?

Here are some of the comments that were generated by asking the preceding questions about the free-writing sample.

There is real insight in the suggestion that your father may be unhappy with his life and hoping to relive it through you. Are there other examples that make you believe this?

What does your father do? Why couldn't he go to college? Is education one of his values? For example, does he read a lot or watch documentaries on TV? Or does he see college as merely a practical step toward financial success?

You seem angry about being pressured into going to college. Is that how you really feel? What would you be doing if you weren't in college? Did you have other plans which your parents overruled?

Are you serious about marrying a rich girl and not having to work, or was that just a joke? If it's a joke leave it out; if you mean it, explain it further. Are you jealous of your sisters? Why weren't they pressured into going to college?

· DRAFTING THE ESSAY

After your reader has made comments, you will have a clearer sense of what you know that someone may want to read about. You will then be able to think about focusing on a particular point and developing it into a first draft of a paper about how a person was influenced by or moved beyond his or her family, time, and place.

A **draft** is an attempt to impose structure on the ideas that you have been generating. Like free writing, a first draft will have false starts and dead ends. But whereas these problems may be left in free writing—which is, after all, for your own use—they must be removed from a draft. A first draft is the bridge between prewriting techniques and a finished essay. It is the first step in the writing process that actually looks like an essay.

To create a first draft, study the comments that your peers have made in order to find a topic that is both interesting and productive. In the case of our free-writing sample, the peer critiques made four observations. One showed interest in the possibility that the writer's father was reliving his life through his son and requested more examples. Another asked for clarification about the father's attitudes toward education and college. The third asked whether the writer was angry about being in college and what he would rather be doing. The last wanted to know why the writer's sisters were treated differently from him.

Thinking about the four seemingly different points, the student discovered one factor that held them together: his Greek heritage. He therefore focused on his background in the introduction and then, in the following paragraphs, tried to show how the other aspects of his life were shaped by this one powerful influence. Based on the peer critiques, he found a central focus and wrote the following first draft:

1   Being the only son in a Greek-American family has been a mixed bag for me. On the one hand, I am what you might call the apple of my father's eye since I will be carrying on the family name. But I also feel a lot of pressure that I don't think my sisters have.

2   My father came to America with his mother in 1952 when he was 17 years old. Though he was a good student and his family wanted him to go to college, his father was killed during the Greek civil war and his mother

came to America to live with her father's sister, who
was married to a man who owned a grocery store in Brooklyn. My father worked in the store during the day and
went to school in the evening to learn English. After
one year he was drafted into the army, where he learned
most of his English, so his way of talking is a little
rough, even though he reads the New York Times every
day and watches a lot of talk shows on public
television.

3   When I was born my parents were very happy to have
a son because they already had two daughters, which is
not so valuable in Greek culture. My father was determined to make me proud to be Greek and even sent me to a
Greek-American school to learn the language and history of my heritage. He is still always telling me that
Greeks gave civilization to the world and we should be
proud of that. My sisters, though, went to regular public school. He was also angry when I came home with
friends who weren't Greek and he was always saying that
I had better marry a Greek girl.

4   In high school my favorite subject was shop. I
consider myself a pretty good carpenter and also like
to fool around with machines and gizmos. I wanted to go
to Brooklyn Tech, but my father wasn't too thrilled
with that idea. He thought that college was the only
place for a descendant of the Greeks. Even though I told

him that a good carpenter makes more money than a lot of college graduates he said that you can have money and still be a bum. He thinks that I should go to college to learn as much as I can and then afterwards worry about making a living. So I guess I can make him happy and still be a carpenter when I graduate.

5   As I said at the beginning, being an only son to my father is a mixed bag.

In the first draft, each paragraph answers questions from the peer critiques in terms of the writer's Greek heritage. The second paragraph addresses the questions about the student's father, in particular why he didn't go to college and whether his attitude toward education is strictly practical. We learn that a family tragedy in Greece kept the father from going to college as he had planned, but that he still reads a lot and watches educational shows on television. The third paragraph addresses the questions about the writer's attitudes toward his sisters: Since they were not valued as much as he was—being the only son—they went to public school while he went to a Greek-American school. The fourth paragraph addresses the questions about the writer's own plans: He enjoys carpentry, had wanted to go to a technical school, and agreed to go to college in order to please his father, who believed a Greek should go to college. For whatever reason, he does not address the questions about whether his father is reliving life through him.

· REVISING YOUR ESSAY: A NEVER-ENDING PROCESS

The essay we just read has many attractive features. It introduces us to an engaging personality and the writer's ambivalent relationship with a difficult, but sympathetic, father. The writer tempers his displeasure toward his father with understanding and accepts his predicament with resigned humor. The essay is also reasonably organized and coherent. But it is not a finished product.

What we have is a first draft that can benefit from the same questions we asked about the free writing: What is the most interesting part? What can we learn from this writer? What parts are worth developing further? But since we are now reading something with an essay structure—which was not the case with the free writing—we can ask questions about the organization also:

What is the point of the essay? Why is the writer telling us this? What is the idea that holds the essay together?

What is the purpose of the first paragraph? Does the opening catch our interest and make us want to continue? How does it prepare us for what we found in the rest of the essay?

What is the point of each example or story? Why is each example where it is? Why aren't there additional examples, or fewer ones?

How does the essay flow from one idea to the next? Are the ideas connected logically? What is the point of each paragraph? Why are the paragraphs arranged in this particular sequence?

Why does the essay end the way it does? Is this how we thought it would end? Is the ending justified by what went before, or does it seem tacked on as an afterthought? Does it resolve the discussion or raise new questions? Does the ending satisfy us or make us feel cheated?

As the writer considers the results of the self-analysis or peer critiquing, a second draft will emerge, and perhaps a third and fourth. At some point, of course, the essay must be submitted. But even then we would be wrong to think of it as finished, complete, ready to be filed. Just as a graduation ceremony is called *commencement*—the beginning of the rest of your life—a personal essay deserves to grow through the kind of re-vision we discussed in the introduction. The insights in the essay can deepen and broaden as the writer learns more about the world and himself. There is the germ of an idea here that is worth coming back to, either as another assignment or as something to mull over in private. By turning the original free writing into the essay we read, the writer took a jumble of emotions and imposed system on them; he made unspoken thoughts and gnawing doubts into the beginning of insight and self-knowledge. The more he reads and hears with a critical mind, the more his knowledge will blossom.

· EXPANDING THE PERSONAL ESSAY: EXPLAINING YOUR OPINIONS

We said earlier that a critical mind is able to evaluate and form judgments by asking questions, weighing evidence, analyzing reasoning, drawing conclusions, and making connections among ideas. One area where we see the blossoming of a critical mind is in opinions. We all have opinions, and in a free country we are allowed to say them out loud without fear of punishment. Not all opinions, however, are intelligent or based on firm foundations. A major benefit of critical reading and writing is that it teaches us to think about our opinions—how we arrived at them, why we keep them, whether we should change them.

WRITING ASSIGNMENT: The Personal Opinion Essay

We have already seen that one topic you know enough to write about is yourself, and certainly you can write about your opinions. But it is a little harder if you try to explain them. So now do the following:

1. Describe an advertisement you do not like;
2. explain why you dislike it;
3. figure out the audience it is aimed at; and
4. create an alternative ad aimed at you.

Here is one response to the assignment, written by a student who asked that her name not be used:

IS WISK A FEMALE OR MALE PRODUCT?

1   Although Wisk is a successful product in that it removes stains from clothing, it fails to impress me because of its advertisement. Wisk commercials imply that Wisk does not apply to both sexes. Wisk is a unisex product that should address females and males.

2   The setting of this specific Wisk commercial is in a couple's bedroom. The man approaches the woman with a shirt in his hand and asks why his shirt is dirty. She explains that there was another laundry product on sale so she decided to try it, instead of using Wisk. They immediately go to their laundry room to rewash his shirt. After some time, the couple is in their bedroom and the man asks for a clean shirt. Unfortunately the laundry is not yet in the wash; therefore, her response is to let him wash the laundry and use Wisk. He wants to

discuss this further and she lightly pushes the full
laundry basket, with the Wisk on top, toward him. He
slowly walks backward, continuing with his objection
which is, "No, I will not do the laundry." At the end of
the commercial, they are still attempting to
compromise.

3   This advertisement is offensive. I feel that the
advertisement is targeting the female population. The
assumption is that males do not do laundry because it is
the female's responsibility. Since most females must
work in order to survive or assist with the family's
support, the household responsibilities should have
some balance. This advertisement cannot apply to me
because I work two jobs and go to school at night. With
my busy schedule, it is essential that both partners
must share the chores equally. Besides illustrating
sexist responsibilities, notice which shirt is dirty.
In all Wisk commercials, the man's shirt is the dirty
one and there is always a woman to get it clean. The
obvious implication is that males either notice the
ring around the collar or they are too ignorant to
operate a washing machine. In either case, these advertisements mock the male intelligence and therefore
they offend not only females, but to some degree males
also.

4   This advertisement can avoid sexual discrimina-

tion with some alteration. For example, have the man doing the laundry and noticing the ring around the collar. Or noticing a stain on a woman's collar. Restricting the female to pouring Wisk and pushing the right buttons on a washing machine is offensive to me. Especially when all Wisk commercials use this particular scene. They should also omit the entire compromise scene because that would eliminate further discrimination. If the roles of the man and woman could alternate, then the advertisements could become more pleasing to me and probably to other women.

5   In conclusion, this specific Wisk commercial illustrates a sexist model of female responsibilities. Also it demonstrates a lack of intelligence on the male's part. However, with a few alterations this now offensive commercial can become pleasing. Since Wisk is an effective product, a few alterations are worthwhile in improving the underlying message.

· EXPANDING THE PERSONAL ESSAY: INCORPORATING YOUR OBSERVATIONS

As the preceding essay illustrates, the critical mind looks at the surrounding world carefully and thoughtfully. In fact, people with critical minds are hard to fool because they analyze everything they see and hear. They look beneath the surface. They ask the same kinds of questions about everything that you are learning to ask about essays:

Why are you telling me this?
How did you get from one idea to the next?

Why is this here?

Is your conclusion justified by your examples?

Does this resolve the issue or raise more questions?

WRITING ASSIGNMENT: Sharpening Your Observation Skills

To sharpen your skills of observation, do this: Choose a group that you know well—for example, teenagers, women, athletes, southerners, Irish Catholics, blue-collar workers—and analyze how the group you have chosen is portrayed on television.

Here is what one student wrote in response to this assignment:

ITALIAN-AMERICAN STEREOTYPES ON TV

by Paulette Racanelli

1   Various dialects are used on TV to "sell" products and characters, and producers depend on the viewer's prejudices against or identification with certain ethnic groups for success in this approach. In the case of Italian-Americans, this has led to reinforcing a negative stereotype.

2   Since the use of dialect is a means of manipulating the viewer's attitude, accents are used primarily to show the authenticity of products. Unfortunately, however, an ethnic "caste system" results from this method of advertising. Individual ethnic groups will only be seen engaging in certain activities or using particular products. The success of the commercials depends on the viewer's familiarity with products and his ability to associate these products with specific

groups. Therefore, the use of language encourages stereotyping, and sponsors benefit through societal prejudices and attitudes.

3   An example of manipulation through stereotyping is the use of Italian-American dialect, specifically the Brooklyn inflection, in various spaghetti sauce commercials. "Dick and Zesty" Ragu is a prepared sauce which is commercialized by individuals speaking with this dialect. Since Italians are noted for their culinary expertise, the predictable response of the viewer would be "If Italians are using Ragu it must be great sauce."

4   The Prince Spaghetti commercial is also interesting. The narrator speaks as the viewer is taken into an Italian-American kitchen of the north end of Boston. One may get the impression that a sociological study is taking place. A boy's mother calls from a window, "Ant-a-nee" with an Italian inflection. The narrator, speaking without a distinguishable dialect or accent, takes the viewer on an investigation of the Italian-American kitchen. Again, based on their prejudicial attitude regarding Italian cooking, the viewers are manipulated into believing Prince Spaghetti is special.

5   Because of this attitude towards Italian-American cooking, Italians are rarely taken out of the kit-

chen, though one might find an Italian-American selling transmissions for Lee Myles. Here, the Brooklyn-Italian inflection is used to appeal to a "blue-collar" population. It is direct but friendly and "down to earth."

6   Television shows "sell" characters through the same use of dialect. Arthur Fonzarelli, better known as "The Fonz," is a major character in "Happy Days." He is a high school dropout with "street smarts." Again, we find a Brooklyn dialect not present in any of the other characters on the show except for Fonzie's younger cousin, though the area in which Fonzie supposedly lives is over five hundred miles from Brooklyn. However, the viewer is convinced of the authenticity of the "Fonz" because Italian-Americans are often stereotyped as low academic achievers who speak with a particular New York dialect even if they live in Kansas.

7   Through dialect, television commercials exploit the Italian-American stereotype and in no way glamorize or elevate the Italian-American image.

CHECKLIST FOR CRITIQUING PERSONAL WRITING

For free writing and essays ask
  What did I find interesting?
  What does it look like I can learn from this?
  What insights caught my attention?
  What sentence or section seemed best?

What sentence or section seemed weakest?
What parts would I like to see explained more?
What parts should be omitted?
What parts seemed real?
What parts seemed phony?
What parts did the author really care about?
What parts seemed worth writing an essay about?
What idea held the whole piece together?
What was the most important idea?
What idea might tie the different points together?

For essays ask

What is the point of the essay? Why is the writer telling us this? What is the idea that holds the essay together?

What is the purpose of the first paragraph? Does the opening catch our interest and make us want to continue? How does it prepare us for what we found in the rest of the essay?

What is the point of each example or story? Why is each example where it is? Why aren't there additional examples, or fewer ones?

How does the essay flow from one idea to the next? Are the ideas connected logically? What is the point of each paragraph? Why are the paragraphs arranged in this particular sequence?

Why does the essay end the way it does? Is this how we thought it would end? Is the ending justified by what went before, or does it seem tacked on as an afterthought? Does it resolve the discussion or raise new questions? Does the ending satisfy us or make us feel cheated?

WRITING ASSIGNMENT: From Thought to Personal Essay

If you have not been doing each step as we have spoken about it, let's go back to the beginning and work through the whole process. How long this takes will vary, depending on whether each step is done in class or at home. But however the scheduling is arranged, choose one of the topics listed and follow the process from brainstorming through free writing, issue trees, peer critiquing, and drafting to finished essay.

1. Choose a person that you know well enough to write about and show how an action or decision by this person either
   a. was influenced by or
   b. has moved away from
   the values of his or her group, time, or place.
2. a. Describe an advertisement you don't like;
   b. explain why you dislike it;

    c. figure out the audience it is aimed at; and

    d. create an alternative ad aimed at you.

3. Choose a group that you know well enough to write about—for example, teenagers, women, athletes, southerners, Irish Catholics, blue-collar workers—and discuss the way the group you have chosen is portrayed in television commercials. Be sure to include whether you feel the treatment of the group is accurate.

C·H·A·P·T·E·R   T·W·O

RE-VISION I
Critical Reading

As the previous chapter implied, if a paper was worth writing in the first place it may never really be finished. You may get it into polished form and either decide to or have to hand it in for a grade. But if the topic engaged your interest and if writing about it brought you satisfying insights, then it is a likely target for **re-vision.**

Students usually think of revision as either punishment or compulsion: Their paper has come back covered with red ink and they now must correct the errors or write what the teacher wants to see. Neither option is what we mean by revision. We distinguish three types of rewriting. **Proofreading** requires looking for and correcting mistakes in spelling, punctuation, grammar, and other aspects of mechanics; when a teacher draws a line between two verbs and writes "tense" in the margin of your paper, you are being told to correct an error in the consistency or sequence of verb forms. **Editing** involves judgment, rather than detecting mechanical errors; a teacher or friend might suggest that you reconsider a particular choice of words or rearrange the order of ideas in a paragraph. In contrast, **revision,** as the components *re* and *vision* indicate, is an attempt to see the topic again—to have a re-vision, a return look with new eyes. It does not imply that you have made mistakes. An essay can be perfectly fine and you may still want to revise it.

Why would you want to change a good essay? There are two practical reasons: (1) you have changed, and (2) your purpose has changed. We will discuss the first reason in this chapter, and the second in Chapter 3.

31

· HOW READING CHANGES YOU

What do we mean by saying that you have changed? Because you are in college you will learn things that you did not know last year or last week; unless you intend to disregard this new information, it will make you take another look at many of your previous opinions. Based on your new experience and knowledge, you may change some of your previous views, or—if you do not totally reject them—you may modify or revise them. Even if everything you learn reinforces your earlier opinions, you will now want to revise your defense of those views by incorporating the new facts as additional evidence or by citing an authority you did not know before.

For example, imagine the reaction of the student who wrote about going to college to please his father if he came upon the following paragraph, which appeared in a *New York Times* article entitled "The Guerrilla Network":

> [Some] guerrilla leaders almost appear to have been raised to join rebel ranks. Plutarco Hernandez Sancho . . . was one of the top Sandinista military commanders in the revolt against the Nicaraguan dictator Anastasio Somoza Debayle. Mr. Hernandez's family was active in the Communist Party in Costa Rica—his father was a Congressman—and Mr. Hernandez remembers a childhood filled with political meetings and demonstrations. "I never had any doubt that I would be a revolutionary fighter," he says. His cousin . . . is the leader of a guerrilla faction, the Armed Forces of National Resistance, in El Salvador.

At the very least, the student who wrote that paper we discussed in Chapter 1 will have a good example to include in a revised paper on how people are shaped by their parents or home life. At best, he will experience a rush of recognition at how other people's lives parallel his own in general framework, even when the details are different.

This book attempts to make a new you in just this way. Everything you are asked to read or write is connected to everything else either vertically or horizontally; either you are going deeper into a topic, or you are exploring how it intersects something else—even when your topic is the influence of your heritage and the new article is about guerrilla networks. Thus, revision is the key to the writing process. When we asked you to describe a personal experience, it was because you will fit this personal story into a larger, more universal, framework. If your family or cultural background affected you, you are not the only one to whom this has happened. If you experienced family pressure because you are the eldest son, someone else felt pressure for being the youngest daughter, or black, or Chinese.

For reading to be valuable, it must be done carefully, thoughtfully, actively. It requires that you identify the facts, understand the significance that the author gives to them, and determine how you can use your new knowledge. Such reading demands effort. The nineteenth-century naturalist and philosopher Henry David Thoreau was correct when he said, "To read well will task the reader more than any exercise. . . . It requires a training such as the athletes underwent."

As with mastering gymnastics or baseball or other athletic skills, training in reading begins with understanding the basics.

· WHO? WHAT? WHERE? WHEN? WHY? HOW?

Every sentence, paragraph, essay, or story has a main idea, a central point that the author wants to make. There may be several less important points, a few examples, and some supporting details, but the main idea is the focus: It holds the work together. Everything revolves around the main idea and develops out of it.

First a good reader tries to identify the main idea, because it will help him or her understand the function of the remaining material. Therefore, as soon as good readers start reading they ask:

What is the point?
Where is this going?

Of course, just as a writer doesn't always know at the start where an essay will lead, readers don't immediately know the main idea. But once they think they know what it is, they use it to find the meaning of what follows. As they read, they constantly ask how each new point relates back to what they consider to be the main idea. They ask the same kinds of questions you used for critiquing:

Why is this here?
What does it add?
How does it fit in?

Everything in a well-written work must support, clarify, or qualify the main idea. If each new point relates to the main idea as you read, then you are interpreting the work properly. In contrast, if each new point does not fall into place, then either you have not focused on the right idea or the essay is not well written.

Whenever we read, we want to find answers to six basic questions: Who? What? Where? When? Why? How? The answer to Who? and What?—that is, "Who did what?"—is generally the main idea. Answers to the other questions are supporting details. It is important to realize, however, that words which are not part of the main idea cannot simply be ignored. A careful writer never includes anything that has no purpose, so a careful reader never ignores anything, even if it is less significant than the main idea.

EXERCISE: Finding the Main Idea

Underline (or highlight) the main idea—who did what—in each of the following sentences. To experience the way many good readers take notes, you may also want to write the main idea in the margin or in your notebook.

Adapted from "The Significance of the Frontier in American History" by Frederick Jackson Turner (1893)

1. The frontier promoted the formation of a composite nationality for the American people.
2. The coast was preponderantly English, but the later tides of continental immigration flowed across to the free lands.
3. This was the case from the early colonial days.
4. The Scotch-Irish and the Palatine Germans, or "Pennsylvania Dutch," furnished the dominant element in the stock of the colonial frontier.
5. With these people were also the freed indented servants, or redemptioners, who at the expiration of their time of service passed to the frontier.
6. Very generally these redemptioners were of non-English stock.
7. In the crucible of the frontier the immigrants were Americanized, liberated, and fused into a mixed race, English in neither nationality nor characteristics.
8. The process has gone on from the early days to our own.

· IDENTIFYING SUPPORTING DETAILS

As we have just seen, when underlining or highlighting, we want the main idea to stand out. But everything in a well-written sentence, paragraph, or essay is important, even if it is not the main idea. The main idea holds the unit together, but the supporting details make the main idea meaningful.

Imagine, for example, that a friend telephoned and said, "Get over here right away. They're giving away free stereos." All sorts of questions would flash through your mind: Where? When? Why? How do I get one? In the same way, when people with critical minds hear a statement or generalization they want to know the basis for it. They want to know where, when, why, and how it applies:

Where is this true? Is it true in all places, or only in specific ones?

When is this true? Is this something new, or has it always been true?

Why is this true? What evidence can you present to make me believe this? How is this true? What process, coincidence, or series of events caused this?

Obviously, in a sentence like

My father came to America from Greece in 1952 when he was 17 years old.

the phrases *from Greece, in 1952,* and *17 years old* are important to the student's essay. They supply the details that give significance to the "who" and "what."

Another kind of detail answers the question "Which one?" Such details limit the size of a group by stating the traits that identify specific members of a large class. Sometimes this limitation involves nothing more than placing one word next to another. For example, in the phrase "television commercials" the word *television* limits the large class *commercials* to those which appear on television. Details can also create subgroups that are defined by their place and time: Brown vs. the Board of Education *of Topeka,* the Civil Rights Act *of 1964.*

Details of where, when, why, and how may also apply to the main idea as a whole, not just to an individual word:

Wisk commercials *on television* offend women. (where)
By *1890* the American frontier had disappeared. (when)
Immigrants went West *for free land.* (why)
She had washed the shirt *with a bargain brand.* (how)

Supporting details that show place, time, reason, and manner often contain special signals:

Showing place: where, anywhere, everywhere, wherever.

Showing time: after, before, while, until, since, when, whenever, as, as soon as, as long as, just as.

Showing reason: because, since, so that, in order to, in order that, insofar as, due to the fact that.

Showing manner: with, in accordance with, in the way that, just as.

Thus, in the sentence

Whenever I come home with friends who aren't Greek my father gets angry at me.

the main idea is "My father gets angry (at me)."

"Whenever I come home with friends who aren't Greek" answers the question "when?"

And in the sentence

Men do not do laundry because it is women's responsibility.

the main idea is "Men do not do laundry." "Because it is women's responsibility" answers the question "why?"

Essential and Nonessential Details

We have already mentioned that every word is important. Sometimes every word is also essential: Leaving out a word will change the truth of the statement.

The distinction between essential and nonessential details is a vital element of good writing. The sentence

Immigrants in cities where there is high unemployment suffer discrimination.

cannot be reduced to "Immigrants suffer discrimination." The detail of place is essential to the writer's meaning: As it is written, the sentence is commenting on the situation only in certain cities. A careful reader knows that the detail is essential because it is not set off by commas. In contrast, the sentence

Immigrants in cities where there is high unemployment suffer discrimination.

means that in all cities immigrants suffer discrimination, and, by the way, there is high unemployment in cities.

The words *who, what,* and *which* share this characteristic. The sentence

Laundry commercials which show women catering to men are offensive.

means that only these specific laundry commercials are offensive. But the sentence

Laundry commercials, which show women catering to men, are offensive.

means that all laundry commercials are offensive, and, in addition, they all show women catering to men.

Needless to say, supporting details must be written carefully and read thoughtfully.

EXERCISE: Identifying Supporting Details

For each sentence underline or highlight the main idea—that is, who and what. Then answer where, when, why, and how. Not all of the information is in all the sentences. Be sure to distinguish essential details from nonessential ones.

From "Traits of Indian Character"
by Washington Irving (1819)

1. The current opinion of the Indian character is too apt to be formed from the miserable hordes which infest the frontiers, and hang on the skirts of the settlements.

2. These are too commonly composed of degenerate beings, corrupted and enfeebled by the vices of society, without being benefited by its civilization.

3. That proud independence, which formed the main pillar of savage virtue, has been shaken down, and the whole moral fabric lies in ruin.

4. Their spirits are humiliated and debased by a sense of inferiority, and their native courage cowed and daunted by the superior knowledge and power of their enlightened neighbors.

5. Society has advanced upon them like one of those withering airs that will sometimes breed desolation over a whole region of fertility.

6. It has driven before it the animals of the chase, who fly from the sound of the axe and the smoke of the settlement, and seek refuge in the depths of remoter forests and yet untrodden wilds.

7. Thus do we too often find the Indians on our frontiers to be the mere wrecks and remnants of once powerful tribes, who have lingered in the vicinity of the settlements, and sunk into precarious and vagabond existence.

· READING WITH PURPOSE

As important as the main idea and supporting details are, there is more to reading than finding such facts. A reader must also understand how the writer uses facts, since not everyone will give them the same significance.

Consider your own experience as a writer. Let's say that after writing your essay for the assignment in the last chapter, you came across the magazine article "What Makes Mario Run?" (pp. 40–44). Just glancing at the title and subheadings tells you that it is about how Gov. Mario Cuomo of New York is influenced by his Italian heritage and Catholic religion. Obviously, if you wrote about how a particular person was influenced by his or her background, the article promises to be useful: It will probably contain material about Cuomo's attitude toward his family and commitment to religious values which you will be able to show is either similar to or different from your subject's behavior. In fact, as you will see when you read it, the article is a perfect illustration of the assignment itself, since it analyzes how in some ways Cuomo is the product of his time and place and how in other ways he has moved beyond them.

But if you have chosen one of the other topics, the article will have a different significance for you. If you are exploring how television portrays a particular group, you may want to consider whether the television image of Italian-Americans or working-class New Yorkers coincides with the image in the article; then you can compare and contrast your findings in this case to the treatment of the group you have chosen. Or, if you are discussing an advertisement you don't like, you may want to consider what forces in your own life influenced your values and therefore explain your attitude toward the ad.

The authors of the article faced similar choices and decisions. They interviewed a number of people and then interpreted the information they had collected. It is quite possible that the significance they saw in an anecdote is different from the significance intended by the person who told the story. And the authors' interpretation of the significance may differ from yours. At every step, readers and writers use their own experiences and insights to give significance to facts. As a reader/writer, you must understand how an author uses facts and then determine how you want to use both the facts and the author's interpretation.

Therefore, when you approach an article like "What Makes Mario Run?" you have a specific reason for wanting to read it carefully. You don't know exactly what you will find, but you know more or less what you are looking for. How do you approach the article?

Previewing

We have already noted that teachers can often tell you what you intended to say because they form expectations as they read and try to predict where an essay is going. For good readers, the previewing process starts even before the actual reading; when approaching an article, for example, they will ask,

Who is the author?
What are the author's qualifications?
When and why was this written?
What type of article is this?
What kind of publication was it in?
What is the significance of the title?
What do the subheadings or boxed quotations call attention to?

They may even quickly skim parts of the content in order to get their bearings.

Previewing the article about Mario Cuomo, we would note that it was written by a team of reporters and that it appeared in *Newsweek*. The authors are unfamiliar to us, but they are clearly reporters for *Newsweek*. The article appeared in March 1986, when, as the first few lines tell us, Cuomo was a leading prospect to be the presidential candidate of the Democratic party. It is a type of journalistic essay called a *profile;* that is, it portrays and analyzes a person through interviews and anecdotes. *Newsweek* is a weekly newsmagazine aimed at a general audience; it specializes in short pieces that summarize and interpret events; it also carries longer pieces that explore issues of immediate concern. The title "What Makes Mario Run?" seems to be a play on the word *run:* What makes him "tick" and what makes him seek elected office? There are two subheadings, suggesting that the article contains two major divisions—one dealing with "The Italian-American" and the other with "The Catholic." Finally, the sub-subhead (called in journalism a drop head) of the first section calls our attention to "immigrant's son," "pride and exuberance," and "ethnic wound," and the drop head of the second section tells us that "Cuomo preaches values as part of his politics" but that he also "quarrels . . . with his cardinal."

Underlining and Taking Notes

Guided by your purpose in reading the article and a general sense of what you are looking at, you now read the text carefully, underlining (or highlighting) sentences, phrases, and words that

capture the author's point,

serve your purpose,

require further study.

If you underline sparingly—that is, only the significant sentences in a paragraph, only the main idea and key details in a sentence—you will have to be more thoughtful and will therefore learn more than if you simply underline everything or paint the page yellow.

In addition, you should write comments in the margin that

state the significance of the highlighted parts,

show the logic of the passage,

give your reactions,

explain difficult points,

suggest how you might use this information.

In this way, when you want to use the passage at a later time you will remember what you had in mind—and you will also be able to compare your previous reaction to your current one.

Now read "What Makes Mario Run?" and see how applying the techniques we have outlined produces material for a revision of your essay. After you have read through the article and formed your own opinions, you can look at our comments, which begin on page 44. Needless to say, you should read the article more than once. All our comments did not come from the first reading.

WHAT MAKES MARIO RUN?

by David Gelman and Kenneth L. Woodward
with Vincent Coppola and Peter McKillop
(*Newsweek*, March 24, 1986)

1   He might. Or he might not.

2   So Mario Cuomo insists: as of now, he has no plans to run for president. And Cuomo is a truthful man. But the mere possibility that the New York governor might head the Democratic ticket in 1988 has pols in both parties sniffing the air and launching pre-emptive strikes. . . . He is the most interesting and complex figure among the hopefuls, the one man nearly everybody wants to know more about.

3   He is undeniably tough, intelligent, competitive, honest. But does his combativeness shade into hot-tempered vindictiveness? Do his old-fashioned Roman Catholicism and upright honor have an edge of sanctimony and priggishness? Is he a hard worker or a workaholic who can't delegate? Does his heritage as an immigrant's son make him thin-skinned and oversensitive to fancied slights? Will his quick wit and lawyerly love of debate lead him into blunders? And can his vision of the nation as a family really be translated into a political agenda to start the next decade?

4   Cuomo has supplied many of his own answers in an extraordinary pair of published diaries. . . . But the enigma remains. There is no single key to Mario Cuomo, in the diaries or anywhere else.

THE ITALIAN-AMERICAN
The immigrant's son has pride and exuberance—
and the ethnic wound of slights long gone

5   "Let me tell you a speech I made and I'm very proud of it. Nobody heard it." Mario Cuomo, his pouched, mortician's eyes twinkling, his athletic, six-foot frame fairly bursting across his office desk at Manhattan's World Trade Center, was recalling a lost but cherished moment in the 1982 gubernatorial primary campaign:

6   "Nineteen eighty-two, the end of the campaign, we wind up on Arthur Avenue in the Bronx. Incredibly beautiful place. All Italian . . . *And I said all the right things.* I have got my beautiful Sicilian wife and, hey, I mean it is terrific. All you have to do is press the button and they were going to explode. And then I said, 'Look, we're Italian, we're very proud of it . . . Wouldn't it be great if those of us who remember being called guineas and wops and dagos will now stop talking about people as spics and niggers? Wouldn't it be terrible if we did to the people that came after us

what we think some people did to us? . . .' It was very well received, *very* well received."

7   It is all there, the passionate, humanist conviction along with the lawyer's calculation—the shrewd awareness that he has said "all the right things." In Mario Cuomo, the two are not so much contradictory as intriguingly intertwined. So, too, are other oddly assorted traits: the combativeness learned on the playing fields of his native Queens, N.Y., and the detachment that brought him his first fame as an arbitrator of neighborhood disputes. . . .

8   In spite of his denials, the ethnic wound is there too; Cuomo has often told how he was refused entry to the best law firms because of his working-class Italian background, although he dismisses, with a characteristic effusion, any suggestion of lingering resentment: "I mean, I'm not maybe a typical case, but life has been so good to me and my family . . . The idea of resenting anything makes me feel so guilty that it worries me. I mean, look what I've got."

9   Life *has* been good to him. Born under the dark star of the Depression of 1932, he came of age in a postwar America rejoicing in its sense of might and mission. The country's mythology was working. Cuomo's father, Andrea, could offer his three children the example of an unschooled immigrant laborer who worked his way up from digging sewers to the proprietorship of a small grocery store in the polyglot Queens neighborhood of South Jamaica. It was a household, Cuomo's brother Frank remembers, where the idea of family was sacrosanct and work was something you did seven days a week. "He was our role model: 'You no fool with girls. You don't hurt anybody.' He was a Catholic, family-type guy."

10   Cuomo went to St. John's Prep in Brooklyn, to St. John's University and later its law school. For four years he juggled commuting to St. John's and playing basketball and sandlot baseball for Joe Austin's Celtics. "The center of our universe was sports, particularly baseball," says Vinny Vane, a teammate who hasn't seen Cuomo in at least 25 years. . . .

11   It was at St. John's that Cuomo met and married Matilda Raffa, a student in the teacher-education program. According to friends, she was the only real girlfriend Mario ever had. "He was not as aggressive in that arena as he was in sports," says Vane. His other arena was the street corner at Tiedermann's Ice Cream Parlor on Jamaica Avenue. From the end of grammar school through college, Mario and his buddies hung out there, hassling one another, arguing baseball. As much as anything, the street-corner jousting quickened his debating skills. "Mario was our designated lawyer," Vane recalls.

12   He was also the group's flaming liberal—even then a believer in unions and "the people"—and its most serious student, sharing first-place honors in his law-school graduating class. In 1956 Cuomo got a clerkship with a

New York State Court of Appeals judge. But despite that prestigious reference, he was turned down by the leading Manhattan law firms. "One of them came right out and told him they didn't hire Italians," says Fabian Palomino. . . . Cuomo landed with a Brooklyn firm. Over 17 years he worked his way up to senior partner, distinguishing himself in appellate work. Always, he made time for pro bono criminal defense, which he seemed to view as an obligation of Catholic conscience as well as an expression of solidarity with the underdog.

13   By then, the Cuomos had five children and a modest Cape Cod house in Holliswood, Queens—built for them by Mario's father—where they continued to live until they moved to the governor's mansion. Matilda, a slender, comely woman, had quit her job as a grammar-school teacher and settled into the traditional role of homemaker and community do-gooder. The couple have taken only a single weeklong vacation in Rome since they married. But Mario almost always manages to set aside some weekend time for the children, relaxing with a round of basketball at the hoop attached to the garage. . . .

14   There are, in any case, at least three Cuomos for the public to judge. There is the hothead, who last December blundered into an awkward debate with reporters over the existence of the "Mafia." There is the somberly reflective diarist, forever questioning his achievements. . . . And there is the exuberant, irrepressible winner, celebrating his good fortune for the benefit of an interviewer last week, and implying he doesn't need anything more out of life: "I mean, look at what I've got . . . These kids are so nice, they are so perfect. But Matilda. [And] my mother! My mother forget about . . . I could write volumes about her. I am the governor of the State of New York, having a wonderful time."

THE CATHOLIC
Cuomo preaches values as part of his politics
—and often quarrels publicly with his cardinal

15   Not since Eugene McCarthy's moral crusade for the presidency in 1968 has a political leader been so intellectually, self-consciously, even aggressively Roman Catholic as Mario Matthew Cuomo. And, paradoxically, no Roman Catholic politician—including John F. Kennedy—has done more to make the American Catholic bishops rethink the church's relationship to political issues.

16   Kennedy was Harvard, money and youth. Irish by birth and just Catholic enough to make his religion a troubling issue in 1960. He deftly defused it by declaring he would not as president take direction from his church. McCarthy went a step further by demonstrating that his Midwestern Catholicism was progressive—even radical—on issues like Vietnam. Now comes Cuomo from Queens borough, New York City, proudly ethnic in

ways the patrician Kennedys never were and scrupulously Catholic in a manner alien to Midwesterners like McCarthy. But in his home town, Cuomo is confronted with Cardinal John J. O'Connor, whose instinct for politics is as pronounced as the governor's penchant for theological disputation. Each man has become a cross for the other to bear.

17   Cuomo is old enough to relish immigrant American Catholicism with its hushed Latin liturgy, neighborhood parishes and prickly consciences fine-tuned by zealous priests and nuns. But he is also young enough to appreciate the release that came with Vatican Council II. In parochial school, Cuomo's Italian sensibility was outfitted by parochial-school nuns with an Irish conscience, and the tension between the two is evident in the published diary of his campaign for governor. "The whole religious experience of Catholics like myself in that time and place," he writes, "painted for us a world of moral pitfalls that needed to be avoided in order to earn an eternal peace." In conversation, that becomes a joke: "I mean, you're supposed to be unhappy!" Cuomo's turning point as a Catholic came in the early '60s when he first read "The Divine Milieu," a mystical meditation by the Jesuit paleontologist Pierre Teilhard de Chardin, which convinced Cuomo that Christians were called to embrace the world, not mistrust it. "We never heard that at St. John's Prep," he says of his Catholic high school.

18   Even so, Cuomo retained so many scruples about entering the messy world of politics that he sought the advice of Brooklyn's Bishop Francis Mugavero before agreeing to run for mayor of New York in 1977. The bishop told him that politics needs men of sound values, and ever since Cuomo has preached values as part of his politics. "What I believe as a Christian is totally compatible with what I believe as a Democrat," Cuomo insists. "Take the Sermon on the Mount. You could write a pretty good platform out of that, and it wouldn't have a single proscription in it."

19   In his own political sermons, Cuomo stresses love rather than prohibition, compassion rather than exclusion—and backs them up with tough political judgments: last week he endorsed New York City's proposed gay-rights bill against O'Connor's opposition. The two men remain at a cordial distance, but Cuomo considers O'Connor the nation's "most important cardinal"—a judgment that only a Catholic from New York would make.

20   Indeed, it was O'Connor who inadvertently helped propel Cuomo into his role as this decade's most influential Catholic politician. During the 1984 presidential campaign, O'Connor told reporters that he personally could not see "how a Catholic in good conscience can vote for a candidate who supports abortion." The archbishop's remark seemed aimed at vice presidential candidate Geraldine Ferraro, but it was Cuomo who was sufficiently offended to offer extended public rebuttal. He had been an altar boy and had graduated from St. John's University and its law school. Now,

after two decades of service to Catholic institutions, of attending mass and of raising five children in the faith, he found that the archbishop was questioning his Catholicism.

21   The issue was fully joined three months later when Cuomo went to the University of Notre Dame to deliver what he called the most important speech of his political life. He said he personally opposed abortion but that as a public servant he could not impose his personal morality on others. Lacking a public consensus to the contrary, he said, he must uphold the law.

22   After the speech, Notre Dame president Theodore M. Hesburgh proposed that 10 American Catholic politicians meet privately with an equal number of bishops to discuss the issues Cuomo had raised. Cuomo was willing but found little support among his peers, and at least two cardinals—O'Connor and Boston's conservative Archbishop Bernard Law—caustically rejected the idea.

23   Father Hesburgh believes that Cuomo the Catholic politician must be understood "in the context of New York State, New York City and The New York Times; if he came from a prairie state, his personal and public stands on abortion might be more congruent." Cuomo disagrees. He believes that his views on abortion will be affirmed in the next presidential election, no matter who runs. He also thinks that publication of the Catholic bishops' pastoral letter on the American economy—which he supports—will help end what he calls the Republicans' six years of saying, "We can't take care of all those poor people." That's Cuomo's way of relating religion to politics. But the governor has yet to test whether it will play to a wider audience in which New York is just another state.

Now that you have read and commented on the article, compare your responses to ours. Did you see the same structure that we did? Did you find the same sections significant? Did you note ways to use the article in a revision of your previous essay(s)?

WHAT MAKES MARIO RUN?

by David Gelman and Kenneth L. Woodward with Vincent Coppola and Peter McKillop (Newsweek, March 24, 1986)

run:
1) "tick"
2) seek office

1   He might. Or he might not.

irony? an echo of "Brutus is an honorable man"?

put-down?

reason for article (1)

2   So Mario Cuomo insists: as of now, he has no plans to run for president. And Cuomo is a truthful man. But the mere possibility that the New York governor might head the Democratic ticket in 1988 has pols in both parties sniffing the air and launching pre-emptive strikes. . . . He is the most interesting and complex figure among the hopefuls, the one man nearly everybody wants to know more about.

3   He is undeniably tough, intelligent, competitive, honest. [But does his combativeness shade into hot-tempered vindictiveness? Do his old-fashioned Roman Catholicism and upright honor have an edge of sanctimony and priggishness? Is he a hard worker or a workaholic who can't delegate? Does his heritage as an immigrant's son make him thin-skinned and over-sensitive to fancied slights? Will his quick wit and lawyerly love of debate lead him into blunders? And can his vision of the nation as a family really be translated into a political agenda to start the next decade?]

questions the article will define answer define

useful info: Catholic, Italian, values family

4   Cuomo has supplied many of his own answers in an extraordinary pair of published diaries. . . . But the enigma remains. There is no single key to Mario Cuomo, in the diaries or anywhere else.

key: answers are elusive (2)

Part I

THE ITALIAN-AMERICAN

ethnic pride and wound

The immigrant's son has pride and exuberance—and the ethnic wound of slights long gone

5   "Let me tell you a speech I made and I'm very proud of it. Nobody heard it." Mario Cuomo, his pouched, mortician's eyes twinkling, his athletic, six-foot frame fairly bursting across his office desk at Manhattan's World Trade Center, was recalling a lost but cherished moment in the 1982 gubernatorial primary campaign:

6   "Nineteen eighty-two, the end of the campaign, we wind up on Arthur Avenue in the Bronx. Incredibly beautiful place. All Italian . . . *And I said all the right things*. I have got my beautiful Sicilian wife and, hey, I mean it is terrific. All you have to do is press the button and they were going to explode. And then I said, 'Look, we're Italian, we're very proud of it . . . Wouldn't it be great if those of us who remember being called guineas and wops and dagos will now stop talking about people as spics and niggers? Wouldn't it be terrible if we did to the people that came after us what we think some people did to us? . . .' It was very well received, *very* well received."

ethnic pride (1)

(2)

personal suffering taught compassion (3)

7   It is all there, the passionate, humanist conviction along with the lawyer's calculation—the shrewd awareness that he has said "all the right things." In Mario Cuomo, the two are not so much contradictory as intriguingly intertwined.

blend of define conviction, define shrewdness

So, too, are other oddly assorted traits: the combativeness learned on the playing fields of his native Queens, N.Y., and the detachment that brought him his first fame as an arbitrator of neighborhood disputes. . . .

ethnic   (4)
wound:
rejected by
law firms

define

8   In spite of his denials, the ethnic wound is there too; Cuomo has often told how he was refused entry to the best law firms because of his working-class Italian background, although he dismisses, with a characteristic effusion, any suggestion of lingering resentment: "I mean, I'm not maybe a typical case, but life has been so good to me and my family . . . The idea of resenting anything makes me feel so guilty that it worries me. I mean, look what I've got."

grew up in
time of (5)
optimism

define

9   Life has been good to him. [Born under the dark star of the Depression in 1932, he came of age in a postwar America rejoicing in its sense of might and mission. The country's mythology was working. Cuomo's father, Andrea, could offer his three children the example of an unschooled immigrant laborer who worked his way up from digging sewers to the proprietorship of a small grocery store in the polyglot Queens neighborhood of South Jamaica.] It was a household, Cuomo's brother Frank remembers, where the

father was   define
role model

family (6)
values

idea of family was sacrosanct and work was something you did seven days a week. "He was our role model: 'You no fool with girls. You don't hurt anybody.' He was a Catholic, family-type guy."

10   Cuomo went to St. John's Prep in Brooklyn, to St. John's University and later its law school. For four years he juggled commuting to St. John's and playing basketball and sandlot baseball for Joe Austin's Celtics. "The center of our universe was sports, particularly baseball," says Vinny Vane, a teammate who hasn't seen Cuomo in at least 25 years. . . .

wife was a
teacher

11   It was at St. John's that Cuomo met and married Matilda Raffa, a student in the teacher-education program. According to friends, she was the only real girlfriend Mario ever had. "He was not as aggressive in that arena as he was in sports," says Vane. His other arena was the street corner at Tiedermann's Ice Cream Parlor on Jamaica Avenue. From the end of grammar school through college, Mario and his buddies hung out there, hassling one another, arguing baseball. As much as anything, the street-corner jousting quickened his debating skills. "Mario was our designated lawyer," Vane recalls.

like designated
hitter

always liberal	12 (7)	He was also the group's flaming liberal—even then a believer in unions and "the people"—and its most serious student, sharing first-place honors in his law-school graduating class. In 1956 Cuomo got a clerkship with a New York State Court of Appeals judge. But despite that prestigious reference, he was turned down by the leading Man-
rejected for being Italian		hattan law firms. "One of them came right out and told him they didn't hire Italians," says Fabian Palomino. . . . Cuomo landed with a Brooklyn firm. Over 17 years he worked his way up to senior partner, distinguishing himself
define	(8)	in appellate work. [Always, he made time for pro bono criminal defense, which he seemed to view as an obligation
sides with underdog		of Catholic conscience as well as an expression of solidarity with the underdog.]
	13	By then, the Cuomos had five children and a modest Cape Cod house in Holliswood, Queens—built for them by Mario's father—where they continued to live until they
wife follows traditional Italian role	(9)	moved to the governor's mansion. Matilda, a slender, comely woman, had quit her job as a grammar-school teacher and settled into the traditional role of homemaker and community do-gooder. The couple have taken only a single weeklong vacation in Rome since they married. But
time with children	(10)	Mario almost always manages to set aside some weekend time for the children, relaxing with a round of basketball at the hoop attached to the garage. . . .
	14	There are, in any case, at least three Cuomos for the public to judge. There is the ① hothead, who last December
enigma remains: 1) hothead 2) somber 3) exuberant	(11)	blundered into an awkward debate with reporters over the existence of the "Mafia." There is the ② somberly reflective diarist, forever questioning his achievements. . . . And there is the ③ exuberant, irrepressible winner, celebrating his good fortune for the benefit of an interviewer last week, and implying he doesn't need anything more out of life: "I
values his family	(12)	mean, look at what I've got . . . These kids are so nice, they are so perfect. But Matilda. [And] my mother! My mother forget about . . . I could write volumes about her. I am the governor of the State of New York, having a wonderful time."

THE CATHOLIC

Part II	
preaches values but disagrees with church	Cuomo preaches values as part of his politics—and often quarrels publicly with his cardinal

15   Not since Eugene McCarthy's moral crusade for the presidency in 1968 has a political leader been so <u>intellectually, self-consciously, even aggressively Roman Catholic</u> as Mario Matthew Cuomo. And, paradoxically, no Roman Catholic politician—including John F. Kennedy—has done more to make the American Catholic bishops rethink the church's relationship to political issues.

3 Catholic politicians reflect their time and place (1)

16   <u>Kennedy was Harvard, money and youth.</u> Irish by birth and just⎮Catholic <u>enough</u> to make his religion a troubling issue in 1960. He⟨deftly⟩defused it by declaring he would not as president take direction from his church. <u>McCarthy went a step further by demonstrating that his Midwestern Catholicism was progressive</u>—even radical—on issues like Vietnam. Now comes <u>Cuomo</u> from Queens borough, New York City, <u>proudly ethnic⎮</u> in ways the⟨patrician⟩Kennedys never were and ⎮scrupulously Catholic in a manner alien to Midwesterners like McCarthy. But in his home town, Cuomo is confronted with Cardinal John J. O'Connor, whose <u>instinct</u> for politics is as pronounced as the governor's⟨penchant⟩for⟨theological disputation.⟩ Each man has become a cross for the other to bear.

Kennedy: rich, not very religious — define

McCarthy: Midwestern radical

Cuomo: ethnic, religious — define

define

17   Cuomo is old enough to relish immigrant American Catholicism with its hushed Latin liturgy, neighborhood parishes and prickly consciences fine-tuned by zealous priests and nuns. But he is also young enough to appreciate the release that came with <u>Vatican Council II.</u> In parochial school, Cuomo's <u>Italian sensibility</u> was outfitted by parochial-school <u>nuns</u>⎮with an Irish conscience, and the <u>tension between the two</u> is evident in the published diary of his campaign for governor. "The whole religious experience of Catholics like myself in that time and place," he writes, "painted for us a world of moral pitfalls that needed to be avoided in order to earn an eternal peace." In conversation, that becomes a joke: "I mean, <u>you're supposed to be unhappy!</u>" Cuomo's turning point as a Catholic came in the early '60s when he first read "The Divine ⟨Milieu⟩" a mystical meditation by the Jesuit paleontologist Pierre Teilhard de Chardin, which convinced Cuomo that Christians were called to embrace the world, not mistrust it. "We never heard that at St. John's Prep," he says of his Catholic high school.

what was Vatican II? (2)

what is difference between Irish and Italian Catholicism? Is Irish more strict, less happy?

define

18   Even so, Cuomo retained so many scruples about enter-

bishop says
to enter   (3)
politics:
needs people
with values

Sermon on   (4)
Mount as
platform   define
                19
                (5)
conflict
with church
over gays

                20

conflict
over   (6)
abortion

politician
can't impose
own morality

                21

                22

ing the messy world of politics that <u>he sought the advice of</u>
<u>Brooklyn's Bishop Francis Mugavero before agreeing to run</u>
<u>for mayor</u> of New York in 1977. The <u>bishop told him that</u>
<u>politics needs men of sound values</u>, and ever since Cuomo
has preached values as part of his politics. "<u>What I believe</u>
<u>as a Christian is totally compatible with what I believe as</u>
<u>a Democrat</u>," Cuomo insists. "Take the <u>Sermon on the</u>
<u>Mount</u>. You could write <u>a pretty good platform</u> out of that,
and it wouldn't have a single (proscription) in it."

In his own political sermons, Cuomo stresses love rather
than prohibition, <u>compassion rather than exclusion</u>—and
backs them up with <u>tough political judgments</u>: last week <u>he</u>
<u>endorsed New York City's proposed gay-rights bill against</u>
<u>O'Connor's opposition</u>. The two men remain at a cordial
distance, but Cuomo considers O'Connor the nation's
"most important cardinal"—a judgment that only a Catholic from New York would make.

Indeed, it was O'Connor who inadvertently helped propel Cuomo into his role as this decade's most influential
Catholic politician. During the 1984 presidential campaign, <u>O'Connor told reporters</u> that he personally <u>could</u>
<u>not see</u> "<u>how a Catholic in good conscience can vote for a</u>
<u>candidate who supports abortion</u>." The archbishop's remark
seemed aimed at vice presidential candidate Geraldine Ferraro, but it was <u>Cuomo</u> who was sufficiently offended to
offer <u>extended public</u> rebuttal. He had been an altar boy
and had graduated from St. John's University and its law
school. Now, after two decades of service to Catholic institutions, of attending mass and of raising five children in
the faith, he found that the archbishop was questioning his
Catholicism.

The issue was fully joined three months later when
Cuomo went to the University of Notre Dame to deliver
what he called the most important speech of his political
life. He said he personally opposed abortion but that <u>as a</u>
<u>public servant he could not impose his personal morality on</u>
<u>others</u>. Lacking a public consensus to the contrary, he said,
he must uphold the law.

After the speech, Notre Dame president Theodore M.
Hesburgh proposed that 10 American Catholic politicians
meet privately with an equal number of bishops to discuss
the issues Cuomo had raised. Cuomo was willing but found

little support among his peers, and at least two cardinals—
O'Connor and Boston's conservative Archbishop Bernard
Law—caustically rejected the idea.

good conclusion: Cuomo in his time and place 23   Father Hesburgh believes that Cuomo the Catholic politician must be understood "in the context of New York
State, New York City and The New York Times; if he came
from a prairie state, his personal and public stands on abor-
define tion might be more congruent." Cuomo disagrees. He believes that his views on abortion will be affirmed in the
next presidential election, no matter who runs. He also
what did this letter say? thinks that publication of the Catholic bishops' pastoral
letter on the American economy—which he supports—
will help end what he calls the Republicans' six years of
saying, "We can't take care of all those poor people." That's
Cuomo's way of relating religion to politics. But the gover-
is he too "New York"? nor has yet to test whether it will play to a wider audience
in which New York is just another state.

Either while reading or when organizing your notes, you have to look up the
words you are unsure of. It is a good idea to collect unfamiliar words in a specific
place—for example, on the last few pages of a notebook—for study and reference. Remember also that familiar words can have more than one meaning, and
the definition you already know may not fit the context. With this caution in
mind, make sure you can explain how the following words are being used in the
article. The number in parentheses after each word refers to the paragraph where
the word appears.

calculation (7)
congruent (23)
conviction (7)
deftly (16)
effusion (8)
humanist (7)
milieu (17)
patrician (16)
penchant (16)
polyglot (9)
priggishness (3)
pro bono (12)

proscription (18)

sacrosanct (9)

sanctimony (3)

theological disputation (16)

vindictiveness (3)

Condensing

Now that you have read the article carefully a few times, you want to condense, or summarize, it. As you saw when underlining, a whole paragraph can be
captured in a few words taken from separate sentences. For example, the reason
that *Newsweek* commissioned and published the article is stated in the last
sentence of the second paragraph. But it is pointless to underline the whole
paragraph or even the whole sentence. The words we want are "[He is the] one
man everybody wants to know more about." Similarly, Frank Cuomo's characterization of his father does not require the whole quotation "He was our role
model: 'You no fool with girls. You don't hurt anybody.' He was a Catholic,
family-type guy." The idea can be captured in the words: "our role model . . . a
Catholic, family-type guy."

Now that you have read the article and want to summarize it, you should try
to do something similar, that is, paraphrase everything into your own words
except for the essential phrases like "Catholic, family-type guy." One possible
summary of the article follows:

> The two main forces in Cuomo's character are his Italian heritage and
> his Catholic faith. His role model was his father, "a Catholic, family-type
> guy." Cuomo suffered discrimination as an Italian, being called offensive
> names and being rejected by law firms. But this led to compassion for
> others who suffer discrimination. He believes his faith shaped his liberal
> politics: He believes the Sermon on the Mount is a good platform to run
> on. Though he considers himself a good Catholic, he opposes Church
> positions on gay rights and abortion. He is the product of New York
> liberalism.

Outlining

As we read the article we underlined sections that we considered important.
If we examine the highlighted sections we will find that some are more important than others. They are more general, in the sense that saying them automatically includes the others. In fact, most of the underlined sections seem to be

examples or details that support the more general statements. In other words, we can distinguish the article's main ideas from the supporting ideas.

As we have already said, every well-written essay has a main idea that the author wants to convey and that holds the work together. So as you reach each new thought, try to see how it is connected to the main idea, and, in turn, use it to make certain that you have correctly identified the main idea.

Let's look at the points we numbered in the margin of the article and see how outlining works.

1. one man everybody wants to know more about

2. enigma remains, no single key

Part I: The Italian-American

1. Incredibly beautiful place. All Italian.

2. "we're Italian, we're very proud of it."

3. "Wouldn't it be terrible if we did to the people that came after us what we think some people did to us?"

4. the ethnic wound is there

5. he came of age in a postwar America rejoicing in its sense of might and mission.

6. "our role model: a Catholic, family-type guy."

7. the group's flaming liberal—a believer in unions and "the people"

8. pro bono criminal defense

9. Matilda quit her job, settled into traditional role

10. weekend time for children

11. three Cuomos

    a. hothead

    b. somberly reflective diarist

    c. exuberant, irrepressible winner

12. "look at what I've got . . . These kids are so nice"

Part II: The Catholic

1. self-consciously, aggressively Catholic

2. McCarthy, Kennedy, Cuomo

3. Italian sensibility vs. nuns with Irish conscience

4. sought the advice of bishop

5. "What I believe as a Christian is totally compatible with what I believe as a Democrat."

6. compassion rather than exclusion

7. could not see "how a Catholic can vote for a candidate who supports abortion."

Conclusion:

"New York State, New York City, The New York Times"

Our previewing had already told us that the article was organized into two parts, "The Italian-American" and "The Catholic," so as we read we made one set of numbers for the first part and a new set for the second. We also noticed two important points even before we reached Part I, and we recognized a clever turn of phrase in the concluding paragraph. Therefore, as we read we could see that the article had an introduction, a two-part body, and a conclusion.

As experienced readers, we expected a statement of the main idea—also called the **thesis statement**—somewhere in the first few paragraphs of an article this long. We found two possibilities: "one man everybody wants to know more about" and "enigma remains, no single key." Our guess—or theory, or hypothesis—is that the first is the reason that *Newsweek* chose to run the piece, and the second was what the reporters found. The second was therefore our choice for the main idea, and was supported by the two-part structure of the article: If understanding Cuomo requires examining two formative influences, the ethnic and the religious, then, in fact, there is "no single key."

Just as the article as a whole has a thesis statement, each of the two parts has its own as well. In an essay, such a statement would usually be a sentence, generally in an early paragraph. But the conventions of a journalistic profile are somewhat different: The main idea of Part I is stated in the subhead "The immigrant's son has pride and exuberance—and the ethnic wound of slights long gone." As we suggested when we underlined, the key words are "immigrant's son," "pride" and "ethnic wound," and are the points that hold together and are supported by the anecdotes and quotations that follow. If we now divide the twelve entries in Part I under these three key word headings, we get the following outline:

Part I: The Italian-American

    immigrant's son

- "our role model: a Catholic, family-type guy."
- Matilda quit her job, settled into traditional role
- weekend time for children
- "look at what I've got . . . These kids are so nice"

    pride

- Incredibly beautiful place. All Italian.
- "we're Italian, we're very proud of it."

- he came of age in a postwar America rejoicing in its
  sense of might and mission.

ethnic wound

- "Wouldn't it be terrible if we did to the people that
  came after us what we think some people did to us?"
- the ethnic wound is there
- the group's flaming liberal—a believer in unions
  and "the people"
- pro bono criminal defense

And we are left with the conclusion for this section:

three Cuomos

- hothead
- somberly reflective diarist
- exuberant, irrepressible winner

The thesis statement of Part II is likewise in its subhead, the key words being "preaches values" and "quarrels with cardinal." Dividing the seven quotations from this section under these two key word headings, we have the following outline:

Part II: The Catholic

preaches values

- self-consciously, aggressively Catholic
- sought the advice of bishop

- "What I believe as a Christian is totally compatible
  with what I believe as a Democrat."
- compassion rather than exclusion

<u>quarrels with cardinal</u>
- could not see "how a Catholic can vote for a candidate who supports abortion."
- Italian sensibility vs. nuns with Irish conscience

The contrast in the role of religion in the politics of Kennedy, McCarthy, and
Cuomo is the introduction to the last section and illustrates how Cuomo is
different from the two other recent Catholic presidential candidates. The clever
remark about New York State, New York City, and The New York Times restates
the contrast and concludes the profile.

Without worrying at the moment about correct form, our outline now looks
like this:

<u>Introduction</u>
- one man everybody wants to know more about
- enigma remains; no single key

<u>Part I: The Italian-American</u>

<u>immigrant's son</u>
- "our role model: a Catholic, family-type guy."
- Matilda quit her job, settled into traditional role
- weekend time for children
- "look at what I've got . . . These kids are so nice"

pride

- "Incredibly beautiful place. All Italian."

- "we're Italian, we're very proud of it."

- he came of age in a postwar America rejoicing in its
  sense of might and mission.

ethnic wound

- "Wouldn't it be terrible if we did to the people that
  came after us what we think some people did to us?"

- the ethnic wound is there

- the group's flaming liberal—a believer in unions
  and "the people"

- pro bono criminal defense

conclusion of section

three Cuomos

- hothead

- somberly reflective diarist

- exuberant, irrepressible winner

Part II: The Catholic

introduction to section

religion and politics of Kennedy, McCarthy, Cuomo

preaches values

- self-consciously, aggressively Catholic

- sought the advice of bishop
- "What I believe as a Christian is totally compatible with what I believe as a Democrat."
- compassion rather than exclusion

quarrels with cardinal

- could not see "how a Catholic can vote for a candidate who supports abortion."
- Italian sensibility vs. nuns with Irish conscience

Conclusion

Cuomo is product of "New York State, New York City, The New York Times"

An outline like the preceding one is very useful for determining whether you understand the point of what you are reading; it is almost indispensable when you want to review something several weeks or months later. In addition, outlining helps you follow the structure of the essay. For example, the outline shows that items are not presented group by group according to a system of logical classification. Instead, they are strung together by speaker, time and place, or loose association. This technique is common in journalism, but is avoided in academic essays, as we will see in Chapter 4.

Evaluating

The last step in reading is evaluating—that is, putting a value on both the material you have read and its usefulness to you. In other words, you analyze how well the article fulfilled its purpose, whether it was well written, whether it seemed authoritative. You also decide how you might use it in your own writing, if at all.

In evaluating a piece of writing, a careful reader will always ask,

What is the overall point?
How is this point conveyed?
What are the secondary or supporting points?

In considering whether the piece is well written, you should look at each sentence, paragraph, anecdote, and quotation and be able to explain,

Why is this passage included?
Why is it in this particular place?
What does it add to the whole?

When judging whether it is authoritative, you should ask,

Is the author a recognized authority?
Is the evidence from authoritative sources?
Is the evidence convincing?
Is the author's use of the evidence reasonable?

When weighing the usefulness of the piece to your own writing, you should ask,

Do I agree with this?
If not, can I refute it?
Are there particularly good examples?
Is there a striking turn of phrase?

In the case of "What Makes Mario Run?" the overall point is that Cuomo is a complex person who is the product of his Italian heritage and Catholic religion. The point is conveyed through quotations from his published diaries and from interviews with him, through illustrative anecdotes about his life and career, and through interviews with people who have known him in various contexts.

To see how we arrived at our conclusions, we can look at a few of the passages which we had highlighted in the article:

"Wouldn't it be terrible if we did to the people that came after us what we think some people did to us?"

The quotation shows that Cuomo suffered because of his ethnic background. It opens the section called "The Italian-American" by showing him sharing a common experience with an Italian audience. It is significant because while some people might seek revenge, Cuomo seems to have learned compassion from his suffering.

Born under the dark star of the Depression in 1932, he came of age in a postwar America rejoicing in its sense of might and mission. The country's mythology was working.

During Cuomo's formative years the United States went from the depths of the Great Depression to the heights of being the world's superpower after World War II. It was a time of great optimism and accomplishment: America had a mission to bring peace and prosperity to a war-torn world. Cuomo's liberal politics still reflect this kind of mission. His belief that life can improve for the "nation-family" seems to be based on the experience of his own family.

> "He was our role model: 'You no fool with girls. You don't hurt anybody.' He was a Catholic, family-type guy."

His father was an immigrant from Italy who worked hard and instilled family values in his sons: the idea of not hurting anyone, of not fooling around with girls. This was the role model that Cuomo seems to have copied in his own family life. In this respect he is the product of his upbringing.

> "What I believe as a Christian is totally compatible with what I believe as a Democrat," Cuomo insists. "Take the Sermon on the Mount. You could write a pretty good platform out of that."

The quotation shows the influence of Cuomo's religion. He went to Catholic schools and accepts most of what he was taught. He asked a bishop for advice before entering politics, and he tries to incorporate his values into his public life. Here he is saying that his liberalism is rooted in his religion. This statement is significant because it is followed immediately by incidents in which Cuomo opposes official Catholic policy.

> Father Hesburgh believes that Cuomo the Catholic politician must be understood "in the context of New York State, New York City and The New York Times; if he came from a prairie state, his personal and public stands on abortion might be more congruent."

The quotation is an excellent conclusion to the article because it sums up how Cuomo is a product of his time and place: His politics and his religion both reflect the realities of New York liberalism. Father Hesburgh believes that if Cuomo were from "Middle America" he would be more conservative.

Obviously, the article contains a lot of information that would be usable in an essay about how people are influenced by their time and place or about how they form their values. It could also serve as an example in a paper about how the media portray people of various backgrounds and classes; for example, the authors contrast the "characteristic effusion" of Italians to the strictness of Irish nuns, and describe Matilda Cuomo as "a slender, comely woman" who "settled into the traditional role of homemaker and community do-gooder." Exactly how you choose to use this information is, of course, up to you and will reflect your own personality. It should also take into account your purpose in writing, which is the topic of the next chapter.

CHECKLIST FOR CRITICAL READING

Critical reading includes finding facts, understanding the significance that the authors give to the facts, and determining how you might use what you have read. It consists of a series of interlocking activities: previewing, underlining and taking notes, condensing, outlining, and evaluating. Within each step there are questions to ask or guidelines to follow.

When previewing ask

Who is the author?
What are the author's qualifications?
When and why was this written?
What type of writing is it?
What kind of publication was it in?
What is the significance of the title?
What do the headings or other graphics call attention to?

Underline (or highlight) phrases and passages that

capture the author's point
serve your purpose in reading and writing
require further study

Write notes that

state the significance of the underlining (or highlighting)
show the logic of the passage
give your reactions
explain difficult points
suggest how you might use this information

Condense

the essay into a brief summary
the thesis statement into a short title
significant passages into a few key words

Outline the work by listing

the thesis statement
subheads of major divisions
secondary thesis statements
topic sentences
important supporting details

Evaluate
the meaning by asking

What is the overall point?
How is this point conveyed?
What are the secondary or supporting points?

the organization by asking

> Why is this passage included?
> Why is it in this particular place?
> What does it add to the whole?

the authority by asking

> Is the author a recognized authority?
> Is the evidence from authoritative sources?
> Is the evidence convincing?
> Is the logic valid?
> Is the author's use of the evidence reasonable?

the usefulness to you by asking

> Do I agree with this?
> If not, can I refute it?
> Are there particularly good examples?
> Is there a striking turn of phrase?
> What have I learned from this?
> How is this connected to other topics?

· ESSAYS FOR CRITICAL READING

Practice the skills you have just learned as you read the following selections. Underline, take notes, and, in particular, look for information that will help you revise your previous essay(s).

The questions after each selection are divided into categories solely for convenience. Careful reading, of course, is more than the sum of isolated skills; you will therefore want to move back and forth among the categories as you consider and clarify specific points.

The following article appeared during 1986 in Local 44 News, *the newspaper of a union affiliated with the AFL-CIO. It is part of a series dealing with television presentations of workers, women, minorities, and other groups. As is common with news stories, the author is not named.*

TV CHILDREN NOT REAL, STUDY CHARGES

1   Children are white, rich and live with a divorced mother who has a satisfying full-time career in business, but no trouble with arranging for child care, reconciling home and job, or meeting the bills. This, at least, is what you would believe if you got your information by watching television, charges the National Commission of Working Women.

2   In addition, a study for the Commission found, on prime-time network programs racial discrimination is rare and problems of bigotry are resolved by the last commercial, since children are noble, resourceful and fully competent to run their lives with only minimal adult intervention.

3   According to the study, 23 prime-time programs during the 1984–85 season featured children as regulars—equally divided between boys and girls, but 80% white. Only four of these shows—that is, 1 in 6—had the children living with both parents, in contrast to the real national proportion of 4 in 5. Only one show had black children living with both parents, and two shows had black children with white guardians. In all three of these shows, however, the adults were clearly well-to-do financially, while in reality half of all black children in the U.S. live in poverty.

4   "American viewers deserve more than repetitious portrayals of affluent families where the mothers work as corporate presidents and oil tycoons," charged Commission chairman Alexis Herman. But George Schweitzer of CBS disagreed. "Comedy can't be expected to reflect the harshness of reality," he claimed. "Comedy is there to give us relief from it."

Reprinted by permission.

VOCABULARY

Explain what the following words mean in the article:
affluent (4)
reconciling (1)
resolved (2)

FACTS

What type of article is this? What are the author's qualifications for writing it? Where does the author get the information in this article?

What kind of publication was this article in? What significance, if any, does this have?

Why do you think this article was written? Do you think the author approached the subject with an open mind? Why or why not? How extensive were the author's sources? How balanced?

When was the article written? Is it up to date?

What is the main idea of this article? What is the significance of the title? What is the thesis statement? What are the secondary points, if any?

What evidence supports the main idea? What is the source of this evidence? Is this source trustworthy?

The article summarizes a survey. What was the nature of the survey? Why do you think it was undertaken? Do you agree with its findings? Can you present evidence to support or refute the findings? How would you collect such evidence?

SIGNIFICANCE

Explain the significance of the following quotations to the point or structure of the article:

". . . a divorced mother who has a satisfying full-time career in business, but no trouble with arranging for child care, reconciling home and job, or meeting the bills."

"This, as least, is what you would believe if you got your information by watching television, charges the National Commission of Working Women."

". . . children are noble, resourceful and fully competent to run their lives with only minimal adult intervention."

"Only four of these shows—that is, 1 in 6—had the children living with both parents, in contrast to the real national proportion of 4 in 5. Only one show had black children living with both parents, and two shows had black children with white guardians."

"But George Schweitzer of CBS disagreed. 'Comedy can't be expected to reflect the harshness of reality,' he claimed. 'Comedy is there to give us relief from it.'"

FUTURE USE

Briefly summarize the article.

Outline the structure and main points.

What information in this article is relevant to your essay(s)? How could you use this information?

The following article appeared in 1985 in Clarion, *the newspaper of the Professional Staff Congress, the teachers' union at the City University of New York. Lehman College is a branch of the university.*

LEHMAN PROFESSOR EXAMINES ROLE OF ETHNIC IDENTITY
by Susan Scherreik

1   Like many youngsters of immigrant parents, Lehman College professor Anthony Patti grew up at the crossroads of two cultures.

2   At school, he learned to perfect his English by writing reports on his favorite sports stars, Lou Gehrig and Knute Rockne, and then followed their example by playing on baseball and football teams. At home, in his Italian neighborhood in the Bronx, however, he was taught to appreciate the operas of Puccini and not to stray far from home.

3   "The only way an Italian-American would follow the advice, 'Go West, young man,' would be by taking his entire family with him," joked Dr. Patti as he he pointed out the confusion he and other Italian-Americans feel when they try to reconcile the value Americans place on individualism with Italian family loyalty. These contradictions—and the personal problems they cause—prompted his recent research project on Italian-American identity, said Dr. Patti, who is chairman of the Department of Secondary, Adult and Business Education in Lehman's Division of Professional Studies.

4   Funded by a $32,000 grant from the now-defunct Italian-American Institute to Foster Higher Education, the project he conducted with Dr. Aileen Riotto Sirey, director of the National Institute for the Psychotherapies, and graduate student Lisa Mann used ethnotherapy—short-term group therapy that focuses on ethnic identity—to help 27 participating Italian-Americans develop pride in their cultural heritage and, as a consequence, a better self-image.

5   But most important, according to Dr. Patti, the study's outcome underscored the important role ethnicity plays in human development, helping to shape personality as well as educational and career goals.

6   "Our study implied that how people feel about themselves is affected by their cultural background," said Dr. Patti. Yet until recently, he added, educators and psychotherapists have paid little attention to the ethnic background of students and patients. In fact, his study using ethnotherapy to explore Italian-American identity is the only project of its kind on this ethnic group, he said.

7   Although the project focused on Italian-Americans, the same ethnotherapy techniques can be used to learn more about all ethnic populations, said Dr. Patti, who is currently seeking funds to conduct similar research on black and Hispanic identity. Information collected from such research, he continued, can

be utilized by therapists to better counsel patients and by educators to develop new ways to motivate students.

8   "This is a new way of looking at people's problems and a way of extracting information on what affects student learning," he explained.

9   The study itself was partly motivated by the State Legislature's concern that not enough Italian-Americans continued their education after high school. In 1981 it created the Italian-American Institute to Foster Higher Education to examine the problem. As one of those selected to participate in the institute, Dr. Patti said these concerns prompted him to contact Dr. Sirey who had a similar interest in exploring Italian-American identity.

10   Their research supported the view that because education is not highly valued at home, traditionally only a small percentage of Italian-Americans have attended college. Noting that many of the participants in the study said their parents gave them little encouragement to pursue education for its own sake, Dr. Patti attributed this attitude to a belief among southern Italian peasants that practical skills are far more essential to survival than intellectual achievement.

11   Their study also found that even those group participants who were several generations removed from the Old World held beliefs rooted in rural Italy, suggesting that a distinct ethnic approach to life is communicated from one generation to the next, Dr. Patti reported.

12   The project began by recruiting men and women of various ages and professions, primarily through Italian-American organizations. By volunteering for the study, the participants comprised a self-selected group which felt the desire to reconnect with their ethnic heritage, Dr. Patti explained. Many, who were second and third generation Americans, had shown a previous interest in their ethnicity. The majority worked in professional, managerial or self-employed positions. Seventy-eight percent were college graduates and 56 percent of those held advanced degrees.

13   Patti and Sirey divided the participants into three groups which discussed the pros and cons of being Italian-Americans during their sessions. They pinpointed areas of personal conflict and explored how their identity was tied to the White Anglo-Saxon Protestant ideal.

14   Many admitted they had mixed feelings about their backgrounds and had experienced confusion as a result. "My father tried not to be Italian but was. He created a vacuum in me: I don't know who I am," said one 35-year-old male participant who is quoted in the recently published report on the study.

15   The sessions consisted of three distinct phases, Dr. Patti said. At first, participants explored their identity in terms of stereotypes, recounting incidents of prejudices. The group then used this knowledge to gain a deeper understanding of their feelings. In the final phase, they were led through exercises to integrate their new sense of pride into their lives.

16   In a survey comparing the participants' attitudes before and after therapy

sessions, the majority indicated they had developed a more positive attitude about themselves and their heritage. For example, prior to the therapy sessions, only 37 percent agreed with the statement: "The public schools should teach more about the contributions of people of Italian heritage to America." But in the after-sessions survey, 69 percent agreed with the statement.

17   Moreover, in a follow-up study a year later, most of the participants reported that the ethnotherapy experience continued to have a positive impact on their lives.

18   In addition to the report, two videotapes of ethnotherapy sessions that can be used as training and information films in educational and clinical settings were produced.

19   Dr. Patti said that he has now begun to focus on ethnic identity in his human behavior courses and hopes that his efforts will add to the growing awareness of the needs of students based on their ethnic backgrounds.

From the Clarion, published by the Professional Staff Congress/CUNY. Reprinted by permission.

VOCABULARY

Explain what the following words mean in the article:
attributed (10)
defunct (4)
ethnicity (5)
ethnotherapy (4)
individualism (3)

FACTS

What type of article is this? What are the author's qualifications for writing it? Where does the author get the information in this article?

What kind of publication was this article in? What significance, if any, does this have?

Why do you think this article was written? How extensive were the author's sources?

When was the article written? Is it up to date?

What is the main idea of this article? What is the significance of the title? What is the thesis statement? What are the secondary points, if any?

The article describes a project. What was the nature of the project? How many people took part? What kind of people? How were they chosen? Why did they take part? What personality traits did they share? How representative were they of their ethnic group? What generalizations can be drawn from their experience?

Why was the project undertaken? What were the initial findings? What were the results? Can you present similar (or different) findings and results from your own experience?

SIGNIFICANCE

Explain the significance of the following quotations to the point or structure of the article:

"'The only way an Italian-American would follow the advice, "Go West, young man," would be by taking his entire family with him,' joked Dr. Patti as he pointed out the confusion he and other Italian-Americans feel when they try to reconcile the value Americans place on individualism with Italian family loyalty."

". . . according to Dr. Patti, the study's outcome underscored the important role ethnicity plays in human development, helping to shape personality as well as educational and career goals."

"Although the project focused on Italian-Americans, the same ethnotherapy techniques can be used to learn more about all ethnic populations, said Dr. Patti, who is currently seeking funds to conduct similar research on black and Hispanic identity."

"Their research supported the view that because education is not highly valued at home, traditionally only a small percentage of Italian-Americans have attended college."

"Their study also found that even those group participants who were several generations removed from the Old World held beliefs rooted in rural Italy. . . ."

"They pinpointed areas of personal conflict and explored how their identity was tied to the White Anglo-Saxon Protestant ideal."

FUTURE USE

Briefly summarize the article.

Outline the structure and main points.

What information in this article is relevant to your essay(s)? How could you use this information?

Washington Irving was the first American writer with an international reputation. At a time when the new nation was ridiculed by Europeans as brutish and uncultured, Irving showed audiences that education, taste, and wit existed on both sides of the Atlantic Ocean. The Sketch Book, which includes short stories like "The Legend of Sleepy Hollow" and "Rip Van Winkle" as well as essays, was written while Irving was in England representing his brothers' hardware-importing company.

From TRAITS OF INDIAN CHARACTER in *THE SKETCH BOOK* by Washington Irving (1819)

1   There is something in the character and habits of the North American savage, taken in connection with the scenery over which he is accustomed to range, its vast lakes, boundless forests, majestic rivers, and trackless plains, that is, to my mind, wonderfully striking and sublime. He is formed for the wilderness, as the Arab is for the desert. His nature is stern, simple, and enduring; fitted to grapple with difficulties, and to support privations. There seems but little soil in his heart for the support of the kindly virtues; and yet, if we would but take the trouble to penetrate through the proud stoicism and habitual taciturnity, which lock up his character from casual observation, we should find him linked to his fellow-man of civilized life by more of those sympathies and affections than are usually ascribed to him.

2   It has been the lot of the unfortunate aborigines of America, in the early periods of colonization, to be doubly wronged by the white men. They have been dispossessed of their hereditary possessions by mercenary and frequently wanton warfare; and their characters have been traduced by bigoted and interested writers. The colonist often treated them like beasts of the forest; and the author has endeavored to justify him in his outrages. The former found it easier to exterminate than to civilize; the latter, to vilify than to discriminate. The appellations of savage and pagan were deemed sufficient to sanction the hostilities of both; and thus the poor wanderers of the forest were persecuted and defamed, not because they were guilty, but because they were ignorant.

3   The rights of the savage have seldom been properly appreciated or respected by the white man. In peace he has too often been the dupe of artful traffic; in war he has been regarded as a ferocious animal, whose life or death was a question of mere precaution and convenience. Man is cruelly wasteful of life when his own safety is endangered, and he is sheltered by impunity; and little mercy is to be expected from him when he feels the sting of the reptile and is conscious of the power to destroy.

4   The same prejudices, which were indulged thus early, exist in common circulation at the present day. Certain learned societies have, it is true, with
laudable diligence, endeavored to investigate and record the real characters and
manners of the Indian tribes; the American government, too, has wisely and
humanely exerted itself to inculcate a friendly and forbearing spirit toward them,
and to protect them from fraud and injustice. The current opinion of the Indian
character, however, is too apt to be formed from the miserable hordes which
infest the frontiers, and hang on the skirts of the settlements. These are too
commonly composed of degenerate beings, corrupted and enfeebled by the vices
of society, without being benefited by its civilization. That proud independence,
which formed the main pillar of savage virtue, has been shaken down, and the
whole moral fabric lies in ruins. Their spirits are humiliated and debased by a
sense of inferiority, and their native courage cowed and daunted by the superior
knowledge and power of their enlightened neighbors. Society has advanced
upon them like one of those withering airs that will sometimes breed desolation
over a whole region of fertility. It has enervated their strength, multiplied their
diseases, and superinduced upon their original barbarity the low vices of artificial
life. It has given them a thousand superfluous wants, whilst it has diminished
their means of mere existence. It has driven before it the animals of the chase,
who fly from the sound of the axe and the smoke of the settlement, and seek
refuge in the depths of remoter forests and yet untrodden wilds. Thus do we too
often find the Indians on our frontiers to be the mere wrecks and remnants of
once powerful tribes, who have lingered in the vicinity of the settlements, and
sunk into precarious and vagabond existence. Poverty, repining, and hopeless
poverty, a canker of the mind unknown in savage life, corrodes their spirits, and
blights every free and noble quality of their natures. . . .

5   In discussing the savage character, writers have been too prone to indulge in
vulgar prejudice and passionate exaggeration, instead of the candid temper of
true philosophy. They have not sufficiently considered the peculiar circumstances in which the Indians have been placed, and the peculiar principles under
which they have been educated. No being acts more rigidly from rule than the
Indian. His whole conduct is regulated according to some general maxims early
implanted in his mind. The moral laws that govern him are, to be sure, but few;
but then he conforms to them all. The white man abounds in laws of religion,
morals, and manners, but how many does he violate?

VOCABULARY

Explain what the following words mean in the essay:
aborigines (2)
airs (4)
appellation (2)
artful traffic (3)
endeavored (2)

enervated (4)
enfeebled (4)
impunity (3)
inculcate (4)
interested (2)
laudable (4)
mercenary (2)
privations (1)
sanction (2)
stoicism (1)
sublime (1)
taciturnity (1)
temper (5)
traduced (2)
vulgar (5)
wanton (2)

FACTS

What type of essay is this? What are the author's qualifications for writing it? Where does the author get his information?

What kind of book was this essay in? Why do you think the book was written?

What is the main idea of this essay? What is the significance of the title? What is the thesis statement? What are the secondary points, if any?

The essay describes a situation. What was the nature of the situation? When was the essay written? Was the situation still true fifty years later? Is it true now? Can you think of other situations that either support or contradict the author's point?

Why do you think this essay was written? Who is the intended audience? What is the audience looking for when reading this essay?

SIGNIFICANCE

Explain the significance of the following quotations to the point or structure of the essay:

"He is formed for the wilderness, as the Arab is for the desert. His nature is stern, simple, and enduring; fitted to grapple with difficulties, and to support privations."

". . . if we would but take the trouble to penetrate through the proud stoicism and habitual taciturnity, which lock up his character from casual observation, we should find him linked to his fellow-man of civilized life by more of those sympathies and affections than are usually ascribed to him."

"They have been dispossessed of their hereditary possessions by mercenary and frequently wanton warfare; and their characters have been traduced by bigoted and interested writers. The colonist often treated them like beasts of the forest; and the author has endeavored to justify him in his outrages."

"The rights of the savage have seldom been properly appreciated or respected by the white man."

". . . the American government, too, has wisely and humanely exerted itself to inculcate a friendly and forbearing spirit toward them, and to protect them from fraud and injustice."

"The current opinion of the Indian character, however, is too apt to be formed from the miserable hordes which infest the frontiers, and hang on the skirts of the settlements."

"That proud independence, which formed the main pillar of savage virtue, has been shaken down, and the whole moral fabric lies in ruins."

"It has given them a thousand superfluous wants, whilst it has diminished their means of mere existence."

"The moral laws that govern him are, to be sure, but few; but then he conforms to them all. The white man abounds in laws of religion, morals, and manners, but how many does he violate?"

FUTURE USE

Briefly summarize the essay.

Outline the structure and main points.

What information from this essay is relevant to your essay(s)? How could you use this information?

Nations, like people, have values that are influenced by their experiences. In this famous essay, originally a lecture to the American Historical Association in 1893, Frederick Jackson Turner, then a teacher at the University of Wisconsin, explained how he believed American character and institutions were shaped. In his view, the major influence was the continuous movement of civilization from East to West, into a seemingly endless expanse of land, challenge, and promise.

From THE SIGNIFICANCE OF THE FRONTIER IN AMERICAN HISTORY
by Frederick Jackson Turner

1   Up to our own day American history has been in a large degree the history of the colonization of the Great West. The existence of an area of free land, its continuous recession, and the advance of American settlement westward, explain American development.

2   Behind institutions, behind constitutional forms and modifications, lie the vital forces that call these organs into life and shape them to meet changing conditions. The peculiarity of American institutions is the fact that they have been compelled to adapt themselves to the changes of an expanding people—to the changes involved in crossing a continent, in winning a wilderness, and in developing at each area of this progress out of the primitive economic and political conditions of the frontier into the complexity of city life. Said Calhoun in 1817, "We are great, and rapidly—I was about to say fearfully—growing!" So saying, he touched the distinguishing feature of American life. All peoples show development; the germ theory of politics has been sufficiently emphasized. In the case of most nations, however, the development has occurred in a limited area; and if the nation has expanded, it has met other growing peoples whom it has conquered. But in the case of the United States we have a different phenomenon. Limiting our attention to the Atlantic coast, we have the familiar phenomenon of the evolution of institutions in a limited area, such as the rise of representative government; the differentiation of simple colonial governments into complex organs; the progress from primitive industrial society, without division of labor, up to manufacturing civilization. But we have in addition to this a recurrence of the process of evolution in each western area reached in the process of expansion. Thus American development has exhibited not merely advance along a single line, but a return to primitive conditions on a continually advancing frontier line, and a new development for that area. American social development has been continually beginning over again on the frontier. This perennial rebirth, this fluidity of American life, this expansion westward with its new opportunities, its continuous touch with the simplicity of primitive society, furnish the forces dominating American character. The true point of view in the history of this nation is not the Atlantic coast; it is the Great West. . . .

3   Our early history is the study of European germs developing in an American environment. Too exclusive attention has been paid by institutional students to the Germanic origins, too little to the American factors. The frontier is the line of most rapid and effective Americanization. The wilderness masters the colonist. It finds him a European in dress, industries, tools, modes of travel, and thought. It takes him from the railroad car and puts him in the birch canoe. It strips off the garments of civilization and arrays him in the hunting shirt and the moccasin. It puts him in the log cabin of the Cherokee and Iroquois and runs an Indian palisade around him. Before long he has gone to planting Indian corn and plowing with a sharp stick; he shouts the war cry and takes the scalp in orthodox Indian fashion. In short, at the frontier the environment is at first too strong for the man. He must accept the conditions which it furnishes, or perish, and so he fits himself into the Indian clearings and follows the Indian trails. Little by little he transforms the wilderness, but the outcome is not the old Europe, not simply the development of Germanic germs. . . . Here is a new product that is American. . . .

4   The United States lies like a huge page in the history of society. Line by line as we read this continental page from West to East we find the record of social evolution. It begins with the Indians and the hunters; it goes on to tell of the disintegration of savagery by the entrance of the trader, the pathfinder of civilization; we read the annals of the pastoral stage in ranch life; the exploitation of the soil by the raising of unrotated crops of corn and wheat in sparsely settled farming communities; the intensive culture of the denser farm settlement; and finally the manufacturing organization with city and factory system. . . .

5   The Atlantic frontier was compounded of fisherman, fur-trader, miner, cattle-raiser, and farmer. Excepting the fisherman, each type of industry was on the march toward the West, impelled by an irresistible attraction. Each passed in successive waves across the continent. Stand at Cumberland Gap and watch the procession of civilization, marching single file—the buffalo following the trail to the salt springs, the Indian, the fur-trader and hunter, the cattle-raiser, the pioneer farmer—and the frontier has passed by. Stand at South Pass in the Rockies a century later and see the same procession with wider intervals between. The unequal rate of advance compels us to distinguish the frontier into the trader's frontier, the rancher's frontier, or the miner's frontier, and the farmer's frontier. . . .

6   Having now roughly outlined the various kinds of frontiers, . . . we may next inquire what were the influences on the East and on the Old World. A rapid enumeration of some of the more noteworthy effects is all that I have time for.

7   First, we note that the frontier promoted the formation of a composite nationality for the American people. The coast was preponderantly English, but the later tides of continental immigration flowed across to the free lands. This was the case from the early colonial days. The Scotch-Irish and the Palatine Germans, or "Pennsylvania Dutch," furnished the dominant element in the

stock of the colonial frontier. With these people were also the freed indented servants, or redemptioners, who at the expiration of their time of service passed to the frontier. Governor Spotswood of Virginia writes in 1717, "The inhabitants of our frontiers are composed generally of such as have been transported hither as servants, and, being out of their time, settle themselves where land is to be taken up and that will produce the necessaries of life with little labor." Very generally these redemptioners were of non-English stock. In the crucible of the frontier the immigrants were Americanized, liberated, and fused into a mixed race, English in neither nationality nor characteristics. The process has gone on from early days to our own. Burke and other writers in the middle of the eighteenth century believed Pennsylvania was "threatened with the danger of being wholly foreign in language, manners, and perhaps even inclinations." The German and Scotch-Irish elements of the South were only less great. In the middle of the present century the German element in Wisconsin was already so considerable that leading publicists looked to the creation of a German state out of the commonwealth by concentrating their colonization. Such examples teach us to beware of misinterpreting the fact that there is a common English speech in America into a belief that the stock is also English. . . .

8   It was this nationalizing tendency of the West that transformed the democracy of Jefferson into the national republicanism of Monroe and the democracy of Andrew Jackson. The West of the War of 1812, the West of Clay, and Benton and Harrison, and Andrew Jackson, shut off by the Middle States and the mountains from the coast sections, had a solidarity of its own, with national tendencies. On the tide of the Father of Waters, North and South met and mingled into a nation. Interstate migration went steadily on—a process of cross-fertilization of ideas and institutions. The fierce struggle of the sections over slavery on the western frontier does not diminish the truth of this statement; it proves the truth of it. Slavery was a sectional trait that would not down, but in the West it could not remain sectional. It was the greatest of frontiersmen who declared: "I believe this Government can not endure permanently half slave and half free. It will become all of one thing or all of the other." Nothing works for nationalism like intercourse within the nation. Mobility of population is death to localism, and the western frontier worked irresistibly in unsettling population. The effect reached back from the frontier and affected profoundly the Atlantic coast and even the Old World.

9   But the most important effect of the frontier has been in the promotion of democracy here and in Europe. The frontier is productive of individualism. Complex society is precipitated by the wilderness into a kind of primitive organization based on the family. The tendency is anti-social. It produces antipathy to control, and particularly to direct control. The tax-gatherer is viewed as a representative of oppression. Prof. Osgood, in an able article, has pointed out how the frontier conditions prevalent in the colonies are important factors in the explanation of the American Revolution, where individual liberty was some-

times confused with absence of all effective government. The same conditions aid in explaining the difficulty of instituting a strong government in the period of the confederacy. The frontier individualism has from the beginning promoted democracy. . . .

10   From the conditions of frontier life came intellectual traits of profound importance. The works of travelers along each frontier from colonial days onward describe certain common traits, and these traits have, while softening down, still persisted as survivals in the place of their origin, even when a higher social organization succeeded. The result is that to the frontier the American intellect owes its striking characteristics. That coarseness and strength combined with acuteness and inquisitiveness; that practical, inventive turn of mind, quick to find expedients; that masterful grasp of material things, lacking in the artistic but powerful to effect great ends; that restless, nervous energy; that dominant individualism, working for good and for evil, and withal that buoyancy and exuberance which comes with freedom—these are traits of the frontier, or traits called out elsewhere because of the existence of the frontier. . . .

VOCABULARY

Explain what the following words mean in the essay:
acuteness (10)
annals (4)
antipathy (9)
arrays (3)
composite (7)
crucible (7)
expedients (10)
germ theory (2)
impelled (5)
indented (7)
institutional students (3)
palisade (3)
pastoral (4)
perennial (2)
precipitated (9)
recession (1)
succeeded (10)
successive (5)
withal (10)

FACTS

What type of essay is this? What are the author's qualifications for writing it? Where does the author get his information?

What is the main idea of this essay? What is the significance of the title? What is the thesis statement? What are the secondary points, if any?

The essay describes a situation. What is the nature of the situation? When was the essay written? Is the situation still true today? Can you think of evidence that either supports or contradicts the author's point?

Why do you think this essay was written? Who is the intended audience? What is the audience looking for in this essay?

SIGNIFICANCE

Explain the significance of the following quotations to the point or structure of the essay:

"The existence of an area of free land, its continuous recession, and the advance of American settlement westward, explain American development."

"American social development has been continually beginning over again on the frontier. This perennial rebirth, this fluidity of American life, this expansion westward with its new opportunities, its continuous touch with the simplicity of primitive society, furnish the forces dominating American character."

"The wilderness masters the colonist. It finds him a European. . . . It strips off the garments of civilization and arrays him in the hunting shirt and the moccasin."

"The United States lies like a huge page in the history of society. Line by line as we read this continental page from West to East we find the record of social evolution."

". . . the frontier promoted the formation of a composite nationality for the American people. The coast was preponderantly English, but the later tides of continental immigration flowed across to the free lands."

"In the crucible of the frontier the immigrants were Americanized, liberated, and fused into a mixed race, English in neither nationality nor characteristics."

"It was this nationalizing tendency of the West that transformed the democracy of Jefferson into the national republicanism of Monroe and the democracy of Andrew Jackson."

"Interstate migration went steadily on—a process of cross-fertilization of ideas and institutions."

"Nothing works for nationalism like intercourse within the nation. Mobility of population is death to localism, and the western frontier worked irresistibly in unsettling population."

"But the most important effect of the frontier has been in the promotion of democracy here and in Europe. The frontier is productive of individualism."

". . . the frontier conditions prevalent in the colonies are important factors in the explanation of the American Revolution, where individual liberty was sometimes confused with absence of all effective government."

"From the conditions of frontier life came intellectual traits of profound importance. . . . and these traits have, while softening down, still persisted as survivals in the place of their origin, even when a higher social organization succeeded. The result is that to the frontier the American intellect owes its striking characteristics."

FUTURE USE

Briefly summarize the essay.
Outline the structure and main points.
What information in this essay is relevant to your essay(s)? How could you use this information?

· MAKING CONNECTIONS

Critical readers increase their knowledge and insight not just by understanding what someone else has written but also by connecting every new idea to what they already know and believe.

Prepare responses to the following discussion topics. The questions in each section are meant to stimulate your thoughts, not to elicit one- or two-word answers.

1. What similarities are there between "TV Children Not Real" (p. 63) and "Italian-American Stereotypes on TV" (p. 26)? What differences? According to the news story, is the portrayal of children positive or negative? What about the portrayal of Italian-Americans? Do the authors of the two articles agree or disagree about the accuracy of television images? Explain whether stereotypes have to be negative to be offensive. What essay topic(s) could incorporate information from both articles?

2. What relevance does Prof. Patti's study (p. 65) have to "Italian-American Stereotypes on TV"? Do his findings support or contradict the television image? Explain whether a stereotype can be accurate. How does this issue relate to the discussion in the *Newsweek* article of Governor Cuomo's "ethnic wound"? What essay topic(s) could incorporate information from these three sources?

3. What is Washington Irving's (p. 69) belief about the news media of his time? Does he think that Indians are portrayed accurately? What does he feel motivates writers to distort the truth? Does he think readers are being manipulated or given what they want? How are these questions about Washington Irving relevant to the discussion about the image of children on television? To the image of Italian-Americans? What essay topic(s) could incorporate information from these sources?

4. What does Turner (p. 73) believe shaped American character and institutions? Does Dr. Patti's study support or contradict this view? What part does Turner believe the Indians played in shaping America? How is the television and movie portrayal of the Old West similar to or different from Turner's? How does the Hollywood image of Indians compare to Irving's? What essay topic(s) could incorporate information from these sources?

· ADDITIONAL ESSAYS FOR DISCUSSION

At the beginning of the chapter we pointed out the importance of previewing, of learning something about the author, date, purpose, and source of what you read; and we have supplied this information for the four selections given earlier. Usually, however, you must infer on your own such things as the author's purpose in writing and the significance of the date and publication source. Therefore, we have not previewed the essays in the following section for you. It is your responsibility as a mature reader to gather the background knowledge that you need in order to understand these selections.

From *THE AUTOBIOGRAPHY OF BENJAMIN FRANKLIN* (1771)

Dear Son,

1   I have ever had a Pleasure in obtaining any little Anecdotes of my Ancestors. You may remember the Enquiries I made among the Remains of my Relations when you were with me in England; and the Journey I took for that purpose. Now imagining it may be equally agreeable to you to know the Circumstances of my Life, many of which you are yet unacquainted with; and expecting a Weeks uninterrupted Leisure in my present Country Retirement, I sit down to write them for you. To which I have besides some other Inducements. Having emerg'd from the Poverty and Obscurity in which I was born and bred, to a State of Affluence and some Degree of Reputation in the World, and having gone so far thro' Life with a considerable Share of Felicity, the conducing Means I made use of, which, with the Blessing of God, so well succeeded, my Posterity may like to know, as they may find some of them suitable to their own Situations, and therefore fit to be imitated. That Felicity, when I reflected on it, has induc'd me sometimes to say, that were it offer'd to my Choice, I should have no Objection to a Repetition of the same Life from its Beginning, only asking the Advantage Authors have in a second Edition to correct some Faults of the first. So would I if I might, besides correcting the Faults, change some sinister Accidents and Events of it for others more favourable, but tho' this were deny'd, I should still accept the Offer. However, since such a Repetition is not to be expected, the next Thing most like living one's Life over again, seems to be a *Recollection* of that Life; and to make that Recollection as durable as possible, the putting it down in Writing. Hereby, too, I shall indulge the Inclination so natural in old Men, to be talking of themselves and their own past Actions, and I shall indulge it, without being troublesome to others who thro' respect to Age might think themselves oblig'd to give me a Hearing, since this may be read or not as any one pleases. And lastly, (I may as well confess it, since my Denial of it will be believ'd by no body) perhaps I shall a good deal gratify my own *Vanity.* . . .

2   The Notes one of my Uncles (who had the same kind of Curiosity in collecting Family Anecdotes) once put into my Hands, furnish'd me with several Particulars relating to our Ancestors. From these Notes I learnt that the Family had liv'd in the same Village, Ecton in Northamptonshire, for 300 Years, and how much longer he knew not (perhaps from the Time when the Name *Franklin* that before was the Name of an Order of People, was assum'd by them for a Surname, when others took Surnames all over the Kingdom), on a Freehold of about 30 Acres, aided by the Smith's Business which had continued in the Family till his Time, the eldest Son being always bred to that Business. A Custom which he and my Father both followed as to their eldest Sons. When I search'd the Register at Ecton, I found an Account of their Births, Marriages and

Burials, from the year 1555 only, there being no Register kept in that Parish at any time preceding. By that Register I perceiv'd that I was the youngest Son of the youngest Son for 5 Generations back. . . .

3   This obscure Family of ours was early in the Reformation, and continu'd Protestants thro' the Reign of Queen Mary, when they were sometimes in Danger of Trouble on Account of their Zeal against Popery. They had got an English Bible, and to conceal and secure it, it was fastned open with Tapes under and within the Frame of a Joint Stool. When my Great Great Grandfather read in it to his Family, he turn'd up the Joint Stool upon his Knees, turning over the Leaves then under the Tapes. One of the Children stood at the Door to give Notice if he saw the Apparitor coming, who was an Officer of the Spiritual Court. In that Case the Stool was turn'd down again upon its feet, when the Bible remain'd conceal'd under it as before. The anecdote I had from my Uncle Benjamin. The Family continu'd all of the Church of England till about the End of Charles the 2ds Reign, when some of the Ministers that had been outed for Nonconformity, holding Conventicles in Northamptonshire, Benjamin and Josiah adher'd to them, and so continu'd all their Lives. The rest of the Family remain'd with the Episcopal Church.

4   Josiah, my Father, married young, and carried his Wife with three Children unto New England, about 1682. The Conventicles having been forbidden by Law, and frequently disturbed, induced some considerable Men of his Acquaintance to remove to that Country, and he was prevail'd with to accompany them thither, where they expected to enjoy their Mode of Religion with Freedom. By the same Wife he had 4 Children more born there, and by a second Wife ten more, in all 17, of which I remember 13 sitting at one time at his Table, who all grew up to be Men and Women, and married. I was the youngest Son and the youngest Child but two, and was born in Boston, N. England.

5   My Mother the 2d Wife was Abiah Folger, a Daughter of Peter Folger, one of the first Settlers of New England, of whom honourable mention is made by Cotton Mather, in his Church History of that Country, (entitled Magnalia Christi Americana) as a *godly learned Englishman*, if I remember the words rightly. I have heard that he wrote sundry small occasional Pieces, but only one of them was printed which I saw now many Years since. It was written in 1675, in the homespun Verse of that Time and People, and address'd to those then concern'd in the Government there. It was in favour of Liberty of Conscience, and in behalf of the Baptists, Quakers, and other Sectaries, that had been under Persecution; ascribing the Indian Wars and other Distresses, that had befallen the Country to that Persecution, as so many Judgments of God, to punish so heinous an Offence; and exhorting a Repeal of those uncharitable Laws. . . .

6   My elder Brothers were all put Apprentices to different Trades. I was put to the Grammar School at Eight Years of Age, my Father intending to devote me as the Tithe of his Sons to the Service of the Church. My early Readiness in learning to read (which must have been very early, as I do not remember when I

could not read) and the Opinion of all his Friends that I should certainly make a good Scholar, encourag'd him in this Purpose of his. My Uncle Benjamin too approv'd of it, and propos'd to give me all his Shorthand Volumes of Sermons I suppose as a Stock to set up with, if I would learn his Character. I continu'd however at the Grammar School not quite one Year, tho' in that time I had risen gradually from the Middle of the Class of that Year to be the Head of it, and farther was remov'd into the next Class above it, in order to go with that into the third at the End of the Year. But my Father in the mean time, from a View of the Expence of a College Education which, having so large a Family, he could not well afford, and the mean Living many so educated were afterwards able to obtain, Reasons that he gave to his Friends in my Hearing, altered his first Intention, took me from the Grammar School, and sent me to a School for Writing and Arithmetic kept by a then famous Man, Mr. Geo. Brownell, very successful in his Profession generally, and that by mild encouraging Methods. Under him I acquired fair Writing pretty soon, but I fail'd in the Arithmetic, and made no Progress in it.

7   At Ten Years old, I was taken home to assist my Father in his Business, which was that of a Tallow Chandler and Sope-Boiler. A Business he was not bred to, but had assumed on his Arrival in New England and on finding his Dying Trade would not maintain his Family, being in little Request. Accordingly I was employed in cutting Wick for the Candles, filling the Dipping Mold, and the Molds for cast Candles, attending the Shop, going of Errands, &c. I dislik'd the Trade and had a strong Inclination for the Sea; but my Father declar'd against it; however, living near the Water, I was much in and about it, learnt early to swim well, and to manage Boats, and when in a Boat or Canoe with other Boys I was commonly allow'd to govern, especially in any case of Difficulty; and upon other Occasions I was generally a Leader among the Boys, and sometimes led them into Scrapes, of which I will mention one Instance, as it shows an early projecting public Spirit, tho' not then justly conducted. There was a Salt Marsh that bounded part of the Mill Pond, on the Edge of which at Highwater, we us'd to stand to fish for Minews. By much Trampling, we had made it a mere Quagmire. My Proposal was to build a Wharf there fit for us to stand upon, and I show'd my Comrades a large Heap of Stones which were intended for a new House near the Marsh, and which would very well suit our Purpose. Accordingly in the Evening when the Workmen were gone, I assembled a Number of my Playfellows, and working with them diligently like so many Emmets, sometimes two or three to a Stone, we brought them all away and built our little Wharff. The next Morning the Workmen were surpriz'd at Missing the Stones; which were found in our Wharff; Enquiry was made after the Removers; we were discovered and complain'd of; several of us were corrected by our Fathers; and tho' I pleaded the Usefulness of the Work, mine convinc'd me that nothing was useful which was not honest.

8   I think you may like to know Something of his Person and Character. He had

an excellent Constitution of Body, was of middle Stature, but well set and very strong. He was ingenious, could draw prettily, was skill'd a little in Music and had a clear pleasing Voice, so that when he play'd Psalm Tunes on his Violin and sung withal as he sometimes did in an Evening after the Business of the Day was over, it was extreamly agreable to hear. He had a mechanical Genius too, and on occasion was very handy in the Use of other Tradesmen's Tools. But his great Excellence lay in a sound Understanding, and solid Judgment in prudential Matters, both in private and publick Affairs. In the latter indeed he was never employed, the numerous Family he had to educate and the straitness of his Circumstances, keeping him close to his Trade, but I remember well his being frequently visited by leading People, who consulted him for his Opinion in Affairs of the Town or of the Church he belong'd to and show'd a good deal of Respect for his Judgment and Advice. He was also much consulted by private Persons about their Affairs when any Difficulty occur'd, and frequently chosen an Arbitrator between contending Parties. At his Table he lik'd to have as often as he could, some sensible Friend or Neighbour, to converse with, and always took care to start some ingenious or useful Topic for Discourse, which might tend to improve the Minds of his Children. By this means he turn'd our Attention to what was good, just, and prudent in the Conduct of Life; and little or no Notice was ever taken of what related to the Victuals on the Table, whether it was well or ill drest, in or out of season, of good or bad flavour, preferable or inferior to this or that other thing of the kind; so that I was bro't up in such a perfect Inattention to those Matters as to be quite Indifferent what kind of Food was set before me; and so unobservant of it, that to this Day, if I am ask'd I can scarce tell, a few Hours after Dinner, what I din'd upon. This has been a Convenience to me in travelling, where my Companions have been sometimes very unhappy for want of a suitable Gratification of their more delicate because better instructed Tastes and Appetites. . . .

From NARRATIVE OF THE LIFE OF FREDERICK DOUGLASS
by Frederick Douglass (1845)

1   I was born in Tuckahoe, near Hillsborough, and about twelve miles from Easton, in Talbot county, Maryland. I have no accurate knowledge of my age, never having seen any authentic record containing it. By far the larger part of the slaves know as little of their ages as horses know of theirs, and it is the wish of most masters within my knowledge to keep their slaves thus ignorant. I do not remember to have ever met a slave who could tell of his birthday. They seldom come nearer to it than planting-time, harvest-time, cherry-time, spring-time, or fall-time. A want of information concerning my own was a source of unhappiness to me even during childhood. The white children could tell their ages. I could not tell why I ought to be deprived of the same privilege. I was not allowed to make any inquiries of my master concerning it. He deemed all such inquiries on the part of a slave improper and impertinent, and evidence of a restless spirit. The nearest estimate I can give makes me now between twenty-seven and twenty-eight years of age. I come to this, from hearing my master say, some time during 1835, I was about seventeen years old.

2   My mother was named Harriet Bailey. She was the daughter of Isaac and Betsey Bailey, both colored, and quite dark. My mother was of a darker complexion than either my grandmother or grandfather.

3   My father was a white man. He was admitted to be such by all I ever heard speak of my parentage. The opinion was also whispered that my master was my father; but of the correctness of this opinion, I know nothing; the means of knowing was withheld from me. My mother and I were separated when I was but an infant—before I knew her as my mother. It is a common custom, in the part of Maryland from which I ran away, to part children from their mothers at a very early age. Frequently, before the child has reached its twelfth month, its mother is taken from it, and hired out on some farm a considerable distance off, and the child is placed under the care of an old woman, too old for field labor. For what this separation is done, I do not know, unless it be to hinder the development of the child's affection toward its mother, and to blunt and destroy the natural affection of the mother for the child. This is the inevitable result.

4   I never saw my mother, to know her as such, more than four or five times in my life; and each of these times was very short in duration, and at night. She was hired by a Mr. Stewart, who lived about twelve miles from my home. She made her journeys to see me in the night, travelling the whole distance on foot, after the performance of her day's work. She was a field hand, and a whipping is the penalty of not being in the field at sunrise, unless a slave has special permission from his or her master to the contrary—a permission which they seldom get, and one that gives to him that gives it the proud name of being a kind master. I do

not recollect of ever seeing my mother by the light of day. She was with me in the night. She would lie down with me, and get me to sleep, but long before I waked she was gone. Very little communication ever took place between us. Death soon ended what little we could have while she lived, and with it her hardships and suffering. She died when I was about seven years old, on one of my master's farms, near Lee's Mill. I was not allowed to be present during her illness, at her death, or burial. She was gone long before I knew any thing about it. Never having enjoyed, to any considerable extent, her soothing presence, her tender and watchful care, I received the tidings of her death with much the same emotions I should have probably felt at the death of a stranger.

5   Called thus suddenly away, she left me without the slightest intimation of who my father was. The whisper that my master was my father, may or may not be true; and, true or false, it is of but little consequence to my purpose whilst the fact remains, in all its glaring odiousness, that slaveholders have ordained, and by law established, that the children of slave women shall in all cases follow the condition of their mothers; and this is done too obviously to administer to their own lusts, and make a gratification of their wicked desires profitable as well as pleasurable; for by this cunning arrangement, the slaveholder, in cases not a few, sustains to his slaves the double relation of master and father.

6   I know of such cases; and it is worthy of remark that such slaves invariably suffer greater hardships, and have more to contend with, than others. They are, in the first place, a constant offence to their mistress. She is ever disposed to find fault with them; they can seldom do any thing to please her; she is never better pleased than when she sees them under the lash, especially when she suspects her husband of showing to his mulatto children favors which he withholds from his black slaves. The master is frequently compelled to sell this class of his slaves, out of deference to the feelings of his white wife; and, cruel as the deed may strike any one to be, for a man to sell his own children to human flesh-mongers, it is often the dictate of humanity for him to do so; for, unless he does this, he must not only whip them himself, but must stand by and see one white son tie up his brother, of but few shades darker complexion than himself, and ply the gory lash to his naked back; and if he lisp one word of disapproval, it is set down to his parental partiality, and only makes a bad matter worse, both for himself and the slave whom he would protect and defend.

7   Every year brings with it multitudes of this class of slaves. It was doubtless in consequence of a knowledge of this fact, that one great statesman of the south predicted the downfall of slavery by the inevitable laws of population. Whether this prophecy is ever fulfilled or not, it is nevertheless plain that a very different-looking class of people are springing up at the south, and are now held in slavery, from those originally brought to this country from Africa; and if their increase will do no other good, it will do away the force of the argument, that God cursed Ham, and therefore American slavery is right. If the lineal descendants of Ham are alone to be scripturally enslaved, it is certain that slavery at the south must

soon become unscriptural; for thousands are ushered into the world, annually, who, like myself, owe their existence to white fathers, and those fathers most frequently their own masters.

WRITING ASSIGNMENTS

1. If in Chapter 1 you wrote about a person's motivation for a decision or an action, now use the article "What Makes Mario Run?" as a model or source of inspiration to describe the influence(s) that shaped your subject. The decision or action in your first paper should be one example, but find others that illustrate the same influence(s) or that show additional influences in this person's life.

2. If in Chapter 1 you wrote about an advertisement you don't like, now try to explain the basis for your opinion in the context of the influences that have shaped your values.

3. If in Chapter 1 you wrote about how the media portray a particular group, now use some of the reading selections in this chapter as models or sources of inspiration in order to place your original examples in a larger context.

4. Write an essay on one of the topics you (or the class) developed during the discussion for Making Connections.

5. Write an essay on one of the topics that emerged during the discussion of the autobiographies of Franklin and Douglass.

C·H·A·P·T·E·R   T·H·R·E·E

RE-VISION II
Using Sources

In Chapter 2 we spoke about revising an essay because you have changed. In this chapter we will discuss the second reason for re-vision: because your purpose for writing the essay has changed.

Imagine that for the assignment in Chapter 1, about how our choices are often influenced by our family or the time and place we live, you wrote the perceptive and moving paper about how your decision to go to college was made to please your father. The class liked it; the teacher liked it; you felt it was among the best things you had ever written. Now imagine that another assignment is to compare and contrast the values in two cultures. You have already done a good paper on one aspect of your own culture, namely its attitude toward education. So, instead of starting all over again and looking for two new aspects of two new cultures, you would be well advised to compare the attitude toward education in a different culture to the situation in yours. Of course, you can't simply lift the entire original paper and drop it into the new one. The purpose of the new essay is different, the focus must be different, perhaps even the course and teacher are different. But you can certainly revise large parts of the first paper for use in the second.

· REVISING TO REFLECT A NEW PURPOSE

To see how an earlier paper may be incorporated into a later one, consider the following essay, which originally appeared as an installment in a newspaper column called "Watching Your Language."

THE IMPORTANCE OF BODY LANGUAGE

1   "When I served overseas, I really saw for the first time that the important thing isn't what you say, but how you say it." That was how a detective friend of mine described learning one of the basic tools of police investigation. And the lesson he learned is one that anthropologists and linguists emphasize again and again.

2   We all know that in some cultures people shake hands when they greet each other; in others, they bow; and in still others, they hug and kiss. But what is called *body language* is so much a part of us, it's actually often overlooked. For example, everyone decides whether to believe what someone else says in terms of how he says it. Does he look me straight in the eye? Does he cringe or avoid answering certain questions? Does he "seem sincere"? But body language can cause real problems to someone who doesn't realize that each culture uses different gestures, postures and facial expressions.

3   In his popular book *Body Language*, Julius Fast tells the story of a Puerto Rican girl in a New York City high school who was suspected of trouble-making and suspended. Though she had denied any wrong-doing, the principal didn't believe her. "It was simply her attitude," he explained. As he said, "There was something sly and suspicious about her. She wouldn't meet my eye. She wouldn't look at me." It was only after neighborhood parents protested, that the principal reopened the investigation and found out from a teacher who was familiar with the culture that a nice Puerto Rican girl doesn't look directly at an adult. To do so would indicate boldness and disrespect. What the principal had taken for slyness, based on the behavior of white, middle-class Americans with English-speaking backgrounds, was actually good breeding in a different culture.

4   Similar misunderstandings arise from the way different societies treat the distance between people. Anthropologists have pointed out that people of North European heritage tend to avoid bodily contact even with friends, and certainly with mere acquaintances. People from Mediterranean and Latin American countries, on the other hand, touch each other quite a lot. Therefore, it's possible that in conversation, it may look like a Latino is chasing an Anglo all over the room. The Latino, trying to communicate friendship, will keep moving closer and closer. The Anglo, very probably seeing this as pushiness, will keep backing away—which the Latino will in turn interpret as coldness.

5   Obviously, a great deal is going on when people talk. And only a part of it—perhaps really a small part—is in the words themselves. And when the parties are from different cultures, there's the strong possibility of misunderstanding. As my detective friend told me: Whatever an investigator learns about someone else's culture will make him a better investigator. And the lesson he learned is equally true for all of us.

As you no doubt saw, the preceding essay focuses on body language, specifically how it "can cause real problems to someone who doesn't realize that each culture uses different gestures, postures, and facial expressions." The opening quotation from the unnamed detective friend is in the nature of a personal testimonial. Even though the writer's friend is a police officer and his experience occurred while he was a soldier serving overseas, there is no implication here that the audience is limited to detectives or members of the armed forces. Rather, the experience is presented as a single instance of a more general situation; it is similar, for example, to appearances of satisfied customers in TV commercials. In fact, the column appeared in general interest newspapers throughout the country and the author's intended audience is all people. As the last sentence says, ". . . the lesson he learned is equally true for all of us."

On another occasion, however, the same author was asked by his detective friend—Joseph Tarantola, president of the New York State District Attorney Investigators—to write an article for the association's newspaper, *The Empire State Investigator,* explaining why it would be beneficial for detectives to take inservice seminars in foreign languages and cultures, and why it would be worthwhile for their departments to pay for such courses. Now the name of the speaker in the opening paragraph is important, the audience is quite specific, and the focus of the essay includes, but is not limited to, body language.

When you read the following essay, look carefully at how almost the entire column on body language has been incorporated, but within this larger focus and for a more specific audience.

WHY POLICE CAN'T TRUST INTERPRETERS
by Harvey Minkoff

1   "When I served overseas, I really saw for the first time that the important thing isn't what you say, but how you say it. That was when I started thinking about how different cultures do things differently."

2   The speaker is Joseph Tarantola, president of the New York State District Attorney Investigators, and he is explaining why he believes investigators and other law enforcement officials should try to become familiar with foreign languages and the cultures of other people. And he is touching upon an issue that many scholars who have studied the subject would agree with.

3   People tend to believe that if they do not understand another language, all they have to do is get an interpreter. They do not realize that while the interpreter may give them the general sense of what the person is saying, a great deal is always lost. This is because it is very rare for two words in different languages to have exactly the same meaning and use—in other words to be equal to each other.

4   Take, for example the English word *box.* We all know what a box is in

its most general use. As any dictionary will tell us, it is "a receptacle of firm material with four sides, a top and bottom." But how does it differ from a bin, carton, case, chest and crate? In English, we can talk about a box of cigarettes, a carton of cigarettes, and a case of cigarettes. And in this instance (as I could have said, in this case), the boxes go into a carton, and the cartons go into a case. But when we speak of a milk box and a milk carton we are speaking about the same thing, and using *box* and *carton* interchangeably.

5   This has obvious implications for an investigator. If a witness says he saw a suspect steal a box of cigarettes, it might be on his person. Not so with a case of cigarettes. Similarly, if someone says that the crime weapon was thrown into a crate, the investigator will look for a particular type of box. The clues here are in the choice of words, even if the witness did not consciously think about them. And the investigator who knows English will find leads that the witness did not know he was giving.

6   In contrast, now consider what happens when the investigator does not speak the language and is dependent on an interpreter. Let's say there has been a fight in a school and someone has been injured. A Spanish speaking witness says that he saw the suspect grab the victim by the *brazo* and pull him across a *pupitre*. The interpreter, in all honesty, says that the suspect grabbed the victim by the *arm* and pulled him across a *desk*. The investigator thinks he has a picture of what occurred and works from this assumption. Unfortunately, the investigator does not know that the interpreter has had to make two assumptions of his own.

7   First, Spanish *brazo* is a more general word than English *arm*. In English the arm stops at the wrist, but in Spanish *brazo* can also correspond to English *hand*. Thus, Spanish *dar el brazo* (literally "give the arm") corresponds to English "lend a hand." And *volverse con los brazos cruzados* corresponds to "return emptyhanded." In other words, the interpreter said *arm* because that is the most common meaning for *brazo*. But the victim might have been pulled by the wrist or hand.

8   Second, English *desk* is a more general word than Spanish *pupitre*. In English, both students and teachers sit at desks. But in Spanish, only a student's desk is a *pupitre*.

9   The point is that the investigator is missing information because it is getting lost in translation. At every step of the way, the interpreter has had to make decisions that have a direct bearing on the investigator's evidence. But the investigator has no way of knowing this and probably would never even think to ask.

10   And there is even more to the problem than just losing meaning in translation. As Mr. Tarantola's observation implies, if you are not actually talking to the person, you can miss all the meaning that is conveyed through "body language."

11   Every investigator knows that how much credence we give to what someone says is directly related to how he says it. Does he look me straight in the eye? Does he seem to cringe when asked certain questions? Does he "seem sincere"?

12   But body language can cause real problems to an investigator who does not realize that each culture uses different gestures, postures, and facial expressions.

13   In his popular book *Body Language* Julius Fast tells the story of a Puerto Rican in a New York City high school who was suspected of trouble-making and suspended. Though she had denied any wrong-doing the principal did not believe her. "It was simply her attitude," he said. "There was something sly and suspicious about her. She wouldn't meet my eye. She wouldn't look at me."

14   It was only later, after neighborhood parents protested, that the principal reopened the investigation and found out from a teacher who was familiar with Puerto Rican customs that in their culture a nice girl does not look directly at an adult. To do so would indicate boldness and disrespect. What the principal, using the standards of white, middle-class Americans, had taken for slyness was actually good breeding in a different culture.

15   Similar misunderstandings arise from the way different societies treat the space between two people talking. As anthropologists Edward and Mildred Hall point out in an article called "The Sounds of Silence," people of North European heritage tend to avoid bodily contact with friends and, certainly, with mere acquaintances. People from Mediterranean and Latin American countries, on the other hand, touch each other a lot. Therefore, it is quite possible that a conversation between a Latino and an Anglo may look like the former is chasing the latter all over the room. The Latino, trying to communicate friendship, will keep moving closer. The Anglo, very probably seeing this as pushiness, will keep backing away—which the Latino will in turn interpret as coldness.

16   Obviously, there is a great deal going on when people talk. And only a part—perhaps really a small part—is in the actual words. This is always true, but when the parties are from different cultures and speaking different languages there is the possibility of severe handicaps for an investigation.

17   As Mr. Tarantola says, "Investigators may not become fluent in a foreign language. But whatever they learn about someone else's language and culture will certainly make them better investigators."

As you probably realized, what was the main point in the first essay is one example of a larger point in the second. Body language was the topic of the first essay; in the second, the topic is how "different cultures do things differently" and body language is Part II of the essay. This contrast is clearly seen when the two essays are outlined. The first essay can be outlined like this:

Body Language

Not what you say, but how you say it
Part I:
    Definition of "body language"
Part II: Examples
    1. looking directly at person
    2. standing close or far away
Conclusion:
    "Equally true for all of us."

In contrast, the second essay can be outlined this way:

Problems with Interpreters

Different cultures do things differently
Part I: Translation Problems
    1. "box"
        a. not same as carton, case, etc.
        b. implication for investigator
    2. "arm" and "desk"
        a. not same as *brazo* and *pupitre*
        b. implication for investigator
Part II: Body Language Problems
    1. looking directly at person
        a. innocent person falsely suspected
        b. implication for investigator
    2. standing close or far
Conclusion:
    Implication for investigator

The outlines also show the different purposes of the two essays, in particular that everything in the second essay is presented in terms of its implication for an investigator. This difference is further proven when we notice how several sentences in the two versions are very similar except that the first essay uses a universal word and the second essay uses one with a narrow reference. For example, the first essay says, "*Everyone* decides whether to believe what some-one else says in terms of how he says it." In contrast, the second essay says, "*Every investigator* knows that how much credence we give to what someone says is directly related to how he says it." Again, the first essay says, "Body language can cause real problems for *someone* who doesn't realize that each culture uses different gestures, postures and facial expressions." The second essay has the same sentence with the word *someone* changed to *an investigator*. And, of course, the conclusion of the first essay is universal: "The lesson he learned is equally true for all of us." But the conclusion of the second essay is limited to investigators: "Whatever they learn about someone else's language and culture will certainly make them *better investigators.*"

· FROM PERSONAL EXPERIENCE TO INFORMED OPINION

The essays you have been writing so far have been *subjective,* meaning that their major concern has been personal—either you or your opinion. The kind of writing that you will most often be asked to produce in school and at work is *objective,* that is, based on observable facts presented without bias.

You should also understand that objective writing is not necessarily impersonal, and bias is not the same as informed opinion. It is entirely acceptable to use the word *I* or the expression *in my opinion* in objective writing; and these personal usages are generally preferable to transparent third-person references like *this writer believes* or bloodless passives like *it is widely thought.* But such references should be limited, because you and your opinion are not the focus of the essay. On the other hand, how you arrived at an opinion is a valid focus for an objective essay. There is a distinction between bias and opinion. A bias is an attitude or position that you already have even before you look at the facts, or perhaps hang on to in spite of facts to the contrary. An informed opinion is a position that you arrive at after you have collected and studied evidence. In numerous cases when we develop informed opinions we overturn our previous biases. The process is certainly something that a writer can describe in an objective essay.

The essence of an objective essay is that it goes beyond the writer and offers something substantial to the reader. How you arrived at a particular opinion can help the reader do the same. How you overcame an obstacle can be an inspiration to the reader. How you, given your background, interpret an event gives the reader from a different background insights into other cultures and value systems. Such objectivity grows from careful analysis of your experience in light of additional evidence. Your experience guides your interpretation of the outside world, and evidence from the outside world helps you understand your experiences. As we said in Chapter 1, readers want to see that the writer has thought about his or her experience in a mature way and is not just repeating clichés or biases.

One way that a personal experience or anecdote can become the basis for an objective essay is illustrated in the following editorial, which appeared in the newspaper of a police officers' association. The essay begins with a story, but the story is not the main point. Rather, it is a strategy for engaging the reader's interest so that a larger point can be made—a point that includes the specific event in the story, interprets it from a particular point of view, and draws a universal conclusion. As you read the essay, notice how the personal references include the reader, instead of focusing attention on the writer. Notice, too, how the writer's point of view is central to his interpretation of the event. And, finally, notice how the main point goes far beyond the limited events of the opening anecdote.

1   The other day a 70-year-old friend of ours came out of his house just in time to see two teenagers steal the hubcaps from his car and run down the street. He chased them for a block, until he saw two policemen, to whom he outlined the situation. The officers quickly grabbed the two youths and their loot. But when our friend asked for his hubcaps, he was told they would have to be held as evidence. Our friend explained that he didn't intend to press charges, but was told that he would still have to come to the police station to reclaim his property. Once there, a sergeant tried to convince him to press charges. Our friend still refused, and after several hours of delays and paperwork—during which he was repeatedly urged to press charges—he received his hubcaps. As he was leaving, the sergeant said, "We can't do anything to stop crime if honest citizens won't help us."

2   "I realize," our friend told us afterwards, "that the delay and inconvenience were part of a ploy to get me to bring charges. And I don't hold it against the police because they can't do their job if people like me don't cooperate. But I'm also on the spot. I have to live here, and those kids have friends. If I make trouble for them, they'll break my windows, or push me down the stairs, or hurt my wife. And what can the police do—give me a bodyguard because my hubcaps were stolen?"

3   This story haunts us because it captures the human side of our present law enforcement predicament. It is easy to condemn the "good citizens" who don't want to get involved. But the sad reality is that law-abiding citizens are, in fact, at the mercy of criminals. Stores charge *us* extra to cover losses from shoplifting. We pay extra for coverage so that *we* won't suffer if our car is hit by an uninsured driver. And *we* pay for rehabilitation programs so that *we* won't have to pay more for jails.

4   The real paradox of law enforcement is that it isn't meant to be enforcement. Law is a social contract. And no number of police can enforce compliance if enough people refuse to agree on their own. It is simply not possible to assign a police officer to protect every piece of property that can be stolen or every person who can be victimized. And it is simply too expensive to imprison every petty crook and delinquent.

5   Democratic societies have always been hostage to their worst element whenever moral persuasion has failed. And that is what we are experienc-

ing in this country. So in the long run, whether we like it or not, we are involved. And we are already losing. And we can't do much about it unless there is a major change in the moral tone of society.

In addition to being a touching human interest story, the opening of the editorial is effective because it creates a tension between the point the old man is making and the response we expect from the writer. The old man is telling how he was subtly harassed by the police but stood firm and refused to give in. Harassed how? Give in to what? After all, the police were trying to persuade him to file charges against thieves who had victimized him. Yet he refuses because he is afraid of further trouble, and he knows that the police cannot protect him. In a sense, then, he wins his confrontation with the police by giving up the larger fight against crime. But the writer of the editorial is a police officer writing in a police newspaper. How, we wonder, will he interpret these events? Will he side with his friend or with his fellow officers? Will he condemn his friend for refusing to be a responsible citizen, or will he scold the officers for harassing the victim of a crime? He does neither. Through the use of the first-person pronouns *we* and *us* in the third paragraph he includes the police and the crime victim in the same category: *We*—meaning all law-abiding citizens—are at the mercy of criminals. A solution is hard to find, he says, because law in a democracy is supposed to evolve by social agreement; it is not imposed by the police. The police cannot force the old man to press charges any more than they can protect every item of value. Democratic law is a social contract. When a society loses its moral basis, he says, we all become victims—old men, police officers, everyone. Thus, the personal anecdote at the beginning becomes the basis for constructing a universal main idea at the end.

· USING SOURCES

But how did the writer arrive at his opinion? Where did he get the idea that law is a social contract and that law in a democracy is based on moral persuasion? Of course, these could be ideas he developed on his own. But, as a matter of fact, they are not. These are central concepts in the political theories of the Founding Fathers of the United States; they, in turn, read them in the works of philosophers like John Locke. For example, in *Two Treatises on Government*, written in 1690, John Locke says,

> . . . because no political society can . . . subsist without having in itself the power to preserve the property, and . . . punish the offenses of all those of that society, there, and there only, is political society, where every one of its members hath quitted this natural power, [and] resigned it up into the hands of the community. . . .

Men being . . . by nature all free, equal, and independent, no one can
be put out of this estate, and subjected to the political power of another,
without his own consent, which is done by agreeing with other men to
join and unite into a community for their comfort, safety, and peaceable
living one amongst another. . . . And so whoever has the legislative or
supreme power of any commonwealth is bound to govern by established
standing laws, promulgated and known to the people . . . and upright
judges, who are to decide controversies by those laws. . . .

The political ideas that Locke presents here are among the "self-evident"
truths of the Declaration of Independence:

We hold these truths to be self-evident: that all men are created equal; that
they are endowed by their Creator with certain inalienable rights; . . . that
to secure these rights, governments are instituted among men, deriving
their just powers from the consent of the governed. . . .

Obviously, these ideas are neither necessarily self-evident nor truths in all other
times and places, or under all other forms of government. But they are accepted
in the United States now and are part of the store of knowledge of educated
people—even people who may not be able to identify John Locke or the source
of the quotations. The writer of the editorial has learned and absorbed these
concepts and phrases. He has made them part of his own system of values and
assumes that his readers have done the same. Because the ideas belong to the
public domain, he can allude to them without using quotation marks or citing
his source.

Clearly, you will have to consider your purpose in using a source, as well as
the choice of paraphrasing or quoting, and the mechanics of acknowledging
sources.

Your Purpose in Using Sources

We have already seen one way to use a source: You can summarize it, as we
did in Chapter 2 with the article about Mario Cuomo. Such a summary would
serve your purpose if a teacher were merely checking whether you had read the
assignment. Assuming the question was "Briefly summarize 'What Makes Mario
Run?'" an acceptable answer would be as follows:

```
The two main forces in Cuomo's character are his

Italian heritage and his Catholic faith. His role model

was his father, "a Catholic, family-type guy." Cuomo
```

suffered discrimination as an Italian, being called
offensive names and being rejected by law firms. But
this led to compassion for others who suffer discrimination. He believes his faith shaped his liberal politics: he believes the Sermon on the Mount is a good
platform to run on. Though he considers himself a good
Catholic, he opposes Church positions on gay rights and
abortion. He is the product of New York liberalism.

If, on the other hand, you were asked to incorporate parts of the article into your own essay, you could not just insert the summary. You would have to consider the purpose of your paper and find the aspects of the article that fit your purpose.

For example, if you are told "Compare and contrast your own life to Mario Cuomo's," your paper can very well be an item-by-item comparison and contrast of the two of you. You might begin by making two parallel columns labeled "me" and "Mario Cuomo" and filling in corresponding points about the two of you. For Cuomo's column, the outline that you made when you read the article will be very valuable. From the outline on pages 56–57, for instance, we can enter the following points on our list:

Me   Mario Cuomo

                              Italian-American

                              immigrant's son

                              role model is father

                              wife quit her job, settled

                                into traditional role

                              weekend time for children

                              ethnic pride

                              Italian and proud of it

<u>Me</u>   <u>Mario Cuomo</u>

                              ethnic wound

                              suffered because he is

                                 Italian

                              learned compassion from

                                 that

                              group's flaming liberal

                              believer in unions and "the

                                 people"

                              pro bono criminal defense

                              Catholic

                              preaches values

                              self-consciously,

                                 aggressively Catholic

                              religion is compatible with

                                 politics

                              quarrels with cardinal

                              supports abortion

                              Italian vs. Irish

                                 Catholic

Now try to fill in your own column. First see how many aspects of your life correspond—either positively or negatively—to items in the "Mario Cuomo" column. Then add important points about yourself that do not correspond to entries in the other column. Of course, you are the one to determine what is important for your purpose. But you do not want an essay that goes on and on like this: "Mario Cuomo and I are very different. He is in his fifties; I am nineteen. He is six-feet tall; I am five-foot-seven. He is governor of New York; I am a college student." However, such information could become important— and even a clever opening strategy—if you immediately add: "Still and all, in the really important things we are very similar. He and I both value our families and try to live by our religion."

When you have made your list of items, you have the raw material for a paper comparing and contrasting your life with Mario Cuomo's. A point-by-point comparison and contrast is one way to proceed, but it is not the best. A better approach is to form a generalization that gives shape to the comparison/contrast and holds the items together. In the following essay, for example, even though the point-by-point pattern is apparent, the student has taken a cue from the class discussion and shaped a main idea to impose order on the comparison/contrast.

THE GOVERNOR AND ME

by Barbara Ryan

1   Ethnicity, family, and faith are issues we can all relate to in varying degrees. We are all part of a social context. Although each one of us makes decisions about how to live our lives, these decisions, to some extent, are influenced by our family background, our faith, and the place and time we grew up.

2   Family values influence us in certain ways. After reading "What Makes Mario Run?" (Newsweek, March 24, 1986), especially the section called "The Italian-American," I came to the conclusion that Gov. Mario Cuomo was very much influenced by his family. He held both his mother and father in high esteem. Like his father, the governor believes that the family is

sacred. Matilda Cuomo, like Mario's mother, stayed home to raise the children and to do charity work. Like his father, Governor Cuomo believes work is extremely important, but he always manages to find time to spend with his children, who he thinks are "perfect."

3   The governor's brother, Frank, remembers some advice their father gave them: "You no fool with girls. You don't hurt anybody." Governor Cuomo still follows this advice. He was raised with these values and he still holds them.

4   Like the governor, I am also greatly influenced by my family. In our home, "family" was and still is everything. Growing up, my brother and I quickly learned the value of a good education. Because of the war and the Depression, neither of my parents had the opportunity to get an education. In our family, a good education was and still is considered essential. My father always encouraged us to learn something, any- thing, no matter where we were. It is for this reason that I vowed to take at least one course per year in a subject which I found stimulating, even if it is out- side my major.

5   Like Andrea Cuomo, my father believes that hard work is good for you and should be done seven days a week. My father lived through the Depression and experienced the horrors of Hitler's concentration camps. Recently,

he confided to me that no matter how much money he makes
in his business, he's always afraid that he will someday
find himself with nothing to eat and no place to live.
When he talks about his and his brother's experience in
the concentration camp, he still cries. Like many other
survivors, he never gave up hope. In some ways these
experiences strengthened him. I, like the governor,
look at my father as a role model. Sometimes, when I feel
like I'll never be able to accomplish anything I think of
my father and it helps me to go on.

6   People are influenced by their faith in varying
degrees. The governor is still influenced by his religion. He was born and raised in the Catholic Church.
He was an altar boy and he attended Catholic schools.
He also raised his five children in the Catholic
faith. "What I believe as a Christian is totally compatible with what I believe as a Democrat," he says.
Obviously, the governor's faith influences his politics. Although his political position may sometimes
conflict with his beliefs as a Christian, he maintains,
according to what the article says, that "as a public
servant he could not impose his personal morality on
others." For example, he is personally against abortion, but as a public servant he does not impose this
belief on others.

7   I, too, was born and raised a Catholic. I attended

Sunday school and parochial school. I attended religion class twice a week when I was in grammar school. I remember Father John telling us that thinking a bad thought was equivalent to committing a sin. I was terrified. For years I thought I was damned. I completely agree with the governor's statement that the experience of Catholics "painted for us a world of moral pitfalls that needed to be avoided in order to earn an eternal peace." I remember how terrified I felt when I made the decision to go to Bronx Science. Most of my friends were going to Catholic high schools. Public schools, we were told, had drug and discipline problems.

8   Unlike the governor, I no longer practice my faith the way I used to, nor do I know the Bible as well as he does. I still believe in God and I think about my faith every day. I even hope I will go back some day. For, like the governor, my faith had a positive influence on my career. In religion class and at home we were always taught to help people who were less fortunate than we were. We were taught to give of ourselves unconditionally. I chose to go into such a giving profession.

9   I believe it is fair to say that we have all experienced prejudice in one way or another. Governor Cuomo was refused entry into prestigious law firms because he came from a working-class Italian family. He

says that he feels no resentment and does not want others
to suffer the way he suffered. In a speech he gave to an
Italian community in the Bronx during the 1983 gubernatorial primary campaign, he told them: "Wouldn't it
be terrible if we did to the people that came after us
what we think some people did to us?"

10   My father, like the governor, was called different names. People made fun of his accent and name. He
told me that this made him work twice as hard. America
had so many opportunities, he was grateful. I am not so
magnanimous. I resent people who made fun of him, and I
still feel animosity toward the Germans because they
hurt my father and uncle.

11   In conclusion, I would say that I have a great
deal in common with the governor. I, like the governor,
will always be influenced by my family's values. When I
have children I will teach them the importance of respect, education, manners, and the church. I, like the
governor, believe that my faith was a positive influence on my career. I am not as religious as he is, but I
believe in God and I still pray. Unlike the governor, I
feel resentment for those who hurt my family.

In addition to the main idea that the writer keeps returning to, the essay
makes good use of the *Newsweek* article. It is especially clear that the student
searched for apt quotations and tried to weave them into the fabric of her essay.
Still, as we said, the essay is essentially an item-by-item comparison/contrast.

Your use of the article would be quite different if the assignment did not require, or lend itself to, a comparison/contrast. The following essay is responding to these instructions: "Read 'What Makes Mario Run?' and then discuss how people are influenced by their families, time, and place. You may want to focus on yourself, a friend, Mario Cuomo, or more than one person." Although less blatantly autobiographical than the previous essay, it is in a sense more personal, more like a private meditation. Rather than write a comparison/contrast, the student has focused on one significant idea and then sought examples from a wide range of sources to illustrate it.

A BELIEF IN THINGS UNSEEN

by Patricia Cleary Graham

1   It was a belief in things unseen which led Abraham
to the crest of a hill, knife in hand, to offer his son
Isaac as a holocaust to the Lord. It was a belief in
things unseen that led a people to wander the deserts
of Sinai for forty years in search of a land flowing
with milk and honey. It was a belief in things unseen
that caused a Franciscan monk at Auschwitz to point
his feet in death's direction so that another man
might live. And it is the same belief in things unseen
which calls men and women, even today, to live their
lives, either publicly or privately, in ways that are
guided by that same kind of trust in something or Someone greater than themselves. This faith may for some
have little or nothing to do with organized religion;
for others like Mario Cuomo and me, it was born of an
upbringing suffused by teachings and traditions that

are almost two thousand years old with roots that
reach back even further in time. We are both Roman
Catholics. And, as such, the belief we share has influenced the meaning we have placed in our own lives—the
kind of education we have received, the career choices
we have made, the social consciousness we have developed—all because we believe, and live out those beliefs as we do.

2   Sixteen to eighteen years of Catholic school education have left us with what I believe is a sense of
the importance of our roles as individuals in the
human family, the general scheme of things. The conviction that one person _can_ make a difference is what
the nuns and priests attempted to impress upon us during all of those years. Consequently, we were taught
the obligations of a Catholic conscience: honesty,
with ourselves and others, industry, self-control, humility, faithfulness, solidarity with the poor, a hunger and thirst for justice, along with the idea that
these were realities to be lived, not just pious notions to be memorized. More important, we were taught
something which has since fallen out of favor in most
circles—a sense of sin, the realization that human
nature left to itself is, at best, weak and limited, and
at worst, capable of the cruelest kinds of brutality
and evil.

3   With this kind of educational philosophy as both
a starting point and sustaining force, our career
choices were made, almost, it seems, as public exten-
sions of our very personal beliefs. Any profession
with ties to social action would have appealed to
Cuomo——medicine, education, health administration.
That he chose the law stems from what Newsweek refers
to as his attitude of combative detachment which
goes back to his childhood. It is the law and politics
which best suit his personality, upbringing, and
temperament.

4   Similarly, teaching, a career with a strong social orientation, is the profession I have ultimately
chosen. The idea that I don't live just for myself, that
my life can make a difference——the belief taught by the
nuns I knew and embodied in their own life choice——
evidently made a deep impression on me. Medicine or the
law would also have interested me; they still do. But as
a girl growing up during the sixties, my career choices
were limited, even more so than Cuomo's. His restraints
were ethnic while mine were biological. Lacking strong
role models other than my female teachers, I chose
teaching.

5   What each of us has done in our respective professions——the ways in which Cuomo has lived out his life
in the law and politics and I mine as a teacher——is a
direct result of our beliefs as Catholics. His guilt

over resenting anything because his life has been so
good, his liberal political stance, his commitment to
pro bono work, his lack of interest in making "big"
money, his solidarity with the underdog, his desire to
bring a strong sense of values and ethics into the
political arena, all stem from his idealism and
belief.

6   And as for me, my teaching career, my liberal
political affiliations, my choice of a marriage partner who shares the same religious values and beliefs
and ethnic background as I, and my desire to bring a
love of knowledge, respect for moral values, and desire
for excellence to my students are, like Cuomo's, tied
directly to my beliefs and the strong sense of social
responsibility that stems from those beliefs.

7   Cuomo's life and mine have been influenced by the
same spiritual beliefs and moral values. While there
are contrasts and variations which make us quite different, the mark this belief has made on each of us is
quite evident. We are living our lives, making our
choices and choosing our destinies and will, in all
probability, continue to do so because of our shared
belief in things unseen.

Unlike the first essay, "The Governor and Me," Graham's essay does not
make the comparison of Cuomo and the writer the center of attention, and
there are almost no contrasts between them. Instead, the focus is on a larger,
even towering, issue—"the belief in things unseen." Now, Cuomo and the

writer become examples, along with Abraham, Isaac, the Israelites, and the Franciscan monk, of people guided by religious faith. Family, ethnicity, and direct references to the article play a much smaller part here than in the first essay.

The next essay, by another student in the same class, is in response to the same assignment. It does not focus as strongly on a general thesis, and in this respect is more autobiographical, like the first one. The strength of this selection is in the role played by the author's personality. As we have said several times already, what makes an essay exciting for a reader is discovering an interesting person interpreting the facts from a point of view that differs from his or her own. Like the last example, this is an engaging essay. You will see for yourself how different the two essays are.

ME AND MARIO

by Lucretia DeVito O'Connor

1   I was born five years into the second half of the 20th century to a father whose parents migrated from Italy and to a mother whose ancestors arrived in Massachusetts with the Mayflower. Unlike Mario Cuomo, I am only half Italian; my other half is English. But like Cuomo, I've been considered and called an Italian since I was in fourth grade. It is obviously the brown hair, brown eyes, and the vowel at the end of my (maiden) name. I never minded being called an Italian. I have always loved everything about Italy and Italians: the food, the wine, the country, the people, the art. I could go on forever. And I have always called people racial or ethnic names——sometimes to hurt, other times to joke. It is no big deal. But I always felt sorry for my mother. She had pretty green eyes, ash-blond hair, skin which

tanned biscuit brown rather than olive (as in oil)
brown like mine, and she was as smart as can be. People
tend to ignore the fact that everyone has had a mother
who is responsible for 50% of their blood, etc. People
tend to listen to everyone's last name and forget the
rest.

2   Anyway, my Wasp mother did not practice religion.
I believe at one time her ancestors practiced Quakerism
or Shakerism or some other 'ism', but religion was not
prevalent in her life. But Dad was born and baptized
Catholic, and, like 99.5% of the Catholics that I know,
has been to church only on occasion, to receive a few
sacraments and then a few other times just for the hell
of it. But——like a Catholic——Dad had to put his eight
children through the religious ringer he himself went
through. Waspy Mom made no fuss as far as I know. Because
I was compelled to attend Catholic schools for 11½
years, compelled to wear uniforms, compelled to attend
9 a.m. mass on Sundays, compelled to receive sacraments
which I never understood, I became a nonreligious, non-
church-going nun-hater. Unlike Cuomo, a Catholic upbringing did not favorably impress me; it scarred me for
life. I will never raise my children as Catholics. I do
not listen to Cardinal O'Connor and don't know the
present Pope's name.

3   A similarity in my and Cuomo's life is that he and

my father are attorneys. The difference, however, is
the fact that my father did not wait around to be rejected from law firms who have prejudices toward Italians; he started his own firm. Like Cuomo's dad, mine
was a role model in our family. But he said—without an
accent—"You better not fool around with boys or I'll
break their heads." He is a father of five girls.

4   My mother was a role model too, to both the girls
and boys in my family. She was as intelligent, as powerful, as loving, and as important as my father. Cuomo
doesn't seem to consider women in his life as worth
much. I hardly heard mention of his mother. Did he have
a sister? An aunt? And he mentioned his wife only in
terms of physical appearance and as one who quit work
for her family. Unlike Cuomo's marriage to Matilda, my
father married my mother—who continued being herself, refusing to "settle into" anything—because he
loved her for the person she was. He expected nothing
more; he wanted nothing else. He did not marry my
mother because she was waiting for someone to sweep her
off her feet so she can become a community do-gooder
moron.

5   Obviously my upbringing has influenced the way I
am now. Like Cuomo, I have learned certain values and
morals which I either deny or utilize today. The family
was/is an important figure in Cuomo's life. It is in

mine too, but not in the same way. Dad did not belittle the girls. Mom was not subservient. The girls went to college if they wanted to. The boys did too. In my own family, my husband is not the sole breadwinner, nor is he under the assumption that we will have 17 children which I will be able to care for when I quit work and settle into the traditional anything. My Catholic up-bringing was a disaster; as an adult I reject Catholi-cism and absolutely will not insult my own children by forcing the religion on them.

6   One issue we do agree on is abortion. Though I personally disapprove of it, I believe the choice should be up to women. However, if Cuomo is so "Catho-lic," can he really go against O'Connor——his god——and approve of abortion? Obviously he is more political-minded than Catholic-minded.

7   As far as politics, I truly believe that what knowledge and beliefs I have today are a direct result of my parents' open discussion on politics. I do not believe my successes or failures are resultant of my religious rejection or the fact that my mom was a Wasp, my dad is Italian and I married an Irishman. Of course my successes and failures in life can be attributed, in part, to the values I've learned from my parents. But, I cannot say that because I hung out on the corner of Main & Elm discussing sports or because I was smacked around

by nuns or named after an English ancestor, that I have

learned nothing new and rejected all other possible

influences. I haven't, I don't, I won't. I feel sorry

for Mario; I think he is wrapped up in politics and

pleasing other people. There are loads of people in the

world with different faiths and beliefs. Having only

taken one week-long vacation, how can he possibly learn

about or know different cultures, different people? He

has been living a sheltered life. Wake up Mario, this

is 1987.

Using Sources as Inspiration

A source can also serve as a model or inspiration. You might read something that fascinates you so much you try to imitate it; an article might set you thinking about a topic for the first time or in a new way.

In this passage from his *Autobiography*, Benjamin Franklin explains how he learned the craft that made him famous.

> About this time I met with an odd volume of the *Spectator*. . . . I bought it, read it over and over, and was much delighted with it. I thought the writing excellent, and wished if possible to imitate it. With that view, I took some of the papers, and making short hints of the sentiment in each sentence, laid them by a few days, and then without looking at the book, tried to complete the papers again, by expressing each hinted sentiment at length and as fully as it had been expressed before, in any suitable words, that should come to hand.
>
> Then I compared my *Spectator* with the original, discovered some of my faults and corrected them. . . . I also sometimes jumbled my collections of hints into confusion, and after some weeks endeavored to reduce them again into the best order, before I began to form sentences, and complete the paper. This was to teach me method in the arrangement of thoughts. By comparing my work afterwards with the original, I discovered many faults and amended them; but I sometimes had the pleasure of fancying that in certain particulars of small import, I had been lucky enough to improve the method or the language and this encouraged me to think I might possibly in time come to be a tolerable English writer. . . .

In addition to serving as a model of organization and style, an article may inspire you to think along new lines. Thus, rather than compare and contrast himself and Cuomo, the student writer of the next essay chose to examine the part his own values play in his life.

MY WORK AND VALUES

by Brian Larsen

1   My current job allows me to live my life according to the values I believe in as well as providing security and benefits for my family.

2   I feel good about working for Northern Telecom because we provide products and services that benefit both business and private individuals. We don't pollute the environment, our employees are treated with respect, and they are compensated for their efforts.

3   Since my promotion to management I have assumed many responsibilities, not only for my own work, but also for a staff of five subordinates. I'm learning how to use management techniques to accomplish tasks and achieve company goals. For instance, there is a fine line between delegating work and dumping it, between leadership and dictatorship. These areas create a challenge for me which is what makes work interesting. Other aspects of my work that coincide with my values are the fact that my opinion and judgment are considered valuable, teamwork is stressed, and I can set a career path that is unlimited.

4   The quality of life that my family enjoys as a result of my job is very important to me. I earn enough money to allow my wife to stay home and raise our children, rather than sending them to a baby sitter. We have seen them grow and develop in their early years, which we feel will benefit them throughout their lives. If I have to travel out of town, it is rare that I will have to stay away more than one night. Usually we manage to have dinner together in the evenings as well.

5   I do have dreams and aspirations that are not connected with Northern Telecom. However, it is hard to break away from the security and family life that this job offers. Finishing my college degree is also important, and since the company pays tuition for me I enjoy this advantage as well.

6   In this essay I've tried to show some similarities in my life and work as compared with Cuomo and the way he approaches life. Personal values play an important part in our happiness, goals, and achievement. Providing for a family, helping others, and working hard can be very satisfying.

Using Sources to Revise an Essay

Finally, you might be told to use a source in order to revise—or rethink—a previous essay. You have written your personal response to a question, or given your personal view of an issue, and now you are being asked to look again at your work in light of this new information, additional stimulus, or supporting (or contradictory) evidence. For example: "In Chapter 1 you were asked to write an essay illustrating how a decision or action of a particular person was influenced by or has moved away from the values of his or her group, time, and place. Revise that essay in light of 'What Makes Mario Run?' You may find support for your views in the article, you may wish to change your position because of contrary evidence, or you may decide to distinguish between Cuomo's experience and the experience of your subject."

Here is the essay of the young man whose Greek heritage forced him to go to college.

1   It seems that one way or another your past catches up to you. Though I am from an irreligious (or a-religious) Greek background and Mario Cuomo is from a religious Italian Catholic background, we are both shaped by our fathers. He, though, seems less angry about it than I am.

2   Being the only son in a Greek-American family, I am what you might call the apple of my father's eye since I will be carrying on the family name. But I also feel a lot of pressure that I don't think my sisters have. It seems to me that Cuomo also felt a hand in his back pushing him to live his life by his father's dreams.

3   My father came to America with his mother in 1952 when he was 17 years old. Though he was a good student and his family wanted him to go to college, his father was killed during the Greek civil war and his mother came to America to live with her father's sister. My father worked in his aunt's store during the day and went to school in the evening to learn English. After one year he was drafted into the army, where he learned

most of his English, so his way of talking is a little
rough. But he reads the <u>New York Times</u> every day and
watches a lot of talk shows on public television.
Cuomo's father also did not have much education and
worked as a laborer when he came to this country. He
must have respected education because he seems to have
supported Mario and maybe also his brother in school.

4   When I was born my parents were very happy to have
a son because they already had two daughters, which is
not so valuable in Greek culture. Girls don't seem to be
such a big shake in Cuomo's family either. The article
doesn't say if he has any sisters, and his wife gets
about two sentences, basically to say that she gave up
her job to become a traditional Italian housewife.

5   My father was determined to make me proud to be
Greek and even sent me to a Greek-American school to
learn the language and history of my heritage. He is
still always telling me that Greeks gave civilization
to the world and we should be proud of that. My sisters,
though, went to regular public school. He was also angry when I came home with friends who weren't Greek and
he was always saying that I had better marry a Greek
girl. Cuomo seems to have the kind of ethnic pride that
my father wants me to have, but it looks like he got his
with less hassle. He absorbed his family's pride without having it shoved down his throat. Maybe that is why
he is less resentful than I am.

6   In high school my favorite subject was shop. I consider myself a pretty good carpenter and also like to fool around with machines and gizmos. I wanted to go to Brooklyn Tech, but my father wasn't too thrilled with that idea. He thought that college was the only place for a descendant of the Greeks. It is not clear from the article whether Mario Cuomo would have become a lawyer if he hadn't gotten hit by a bean ball, but it seems as if his interest in sports was like carpentry for me.

7   Finally, if my father has a religion you would have to say it is Greekism. He worships Greek ideas and the Greek contribution to the world. And that is how he wants me to guide my life. So in a way, I was brought up in my father's religion like Cuomo. But I am not happy about it the way he is.

8   Was it a Greek who said "The apple doesn't fall far from the tree"?

Quoting and Paraphrasing Sources

When using sources in your writing, you must show which ideas are your own and which belong to someone else. This is true whether you quote the exact words or change them.

The simplest way to give credit to your source is to mention it in the sentence with the information.

According to the article "What Makes Mario Run?" (<u>Newsweek</u>, March 24, 1986), Governor Cuomo was very much influenced by his family.

In our example the name of the article and the magazine it appeared in are both right there for the reader to see. And unless you are told not to follow this style, it is the one we recommend. (For those times when you will need to include them, notes and bibliography are explained in Chapter 8.)

In the discussion of critical reading we suggested that you summarize the main point(s) of what you read and underline key words and striking phrases. This is also how you should approach the choice of whether to quote or paraphrase. **Quote** the exact words in the source for those ideas the author has captured in a few brilliant words that you cannot hope to summarize or improve. **Paraphrase** —that is, put into your own words—everything else.

The following passage has a good mix between paraphrase and quotation:

According to "What Makes Mario Run?," the two main
forces in Governor Cuomo's life are his Italian heritage and Catholic faith. His role model was his father,
whom Frank Cuomo calls "a Catholic, family-type guy."
And the governor tries to follow this lead. But, he
opposes Church positions on gay rights and abortion,
perhaps because he is from the liberal East Coast. As
the president of Notre Dame said, Governor Cuomo has to
be seen "in the context of New York State, New York
City, and The New York Times."

The summary shows that the writer has understood the article, and the two direct quotations are short and striking: It would be pointless to try to paraphrase the first, and impossible to capture the wit of the second in different words.

In contrast, the next passage is a cut and paste pastiche that tells the experienced reader that the writer has not absorbed, or even thought much about, the article:

In describing Governor Cuomo, the article "What Makes
Mario Run?" says "the immigrant's son has pride and
exuberance--and the ethnic wound of slights long gone"

and "Cuomo preaches values as part of his politics—and
often quarrels openly with his cardinal." The governor's father "could offer his three children the example of an unschooled immigrant laborer who worked his
way up from digging sewers to the proprietorship of a
small grocery store in the polyglot Queens neighborhood
of South Jamaica." And as for religion, "not since
Eugene McCarthy's moral crusade for the presidency in
1968 has a political leader been so intellectually,
self-consciously, even aggressively Roman Catholic as
Mario Matthew Cuomo."

CHECKLIST FOR QUOTING AND PARAPHRASING

Since quotations should contain only what is essential to your point, they have to be crafted. Quotations must fit into your sentence as if they were your own words, but they must also follow the original wording exactly. Since this takes some doing, here are a few pointers.

1. Use double quotation marks at the beginning and end of any words that you take from a source.

The article calls Cuomo "proudly ethnic."

2. Use a comma to separate the source from a quoted sentence.

As Cuomo told the reporter, "What I believe as a
Christian is totally compatible with what I believe as
a Democrat."

3. Use a colon to make a quotation more emphatic or to introduce a long quotation.

Cuomo says: "What I believe as a Christian is totally compatible with what I believe as a Democrat."

4. Indent, without quotation marks, quotations longer than five lines or fifty words—if you absolutely must use such a long passage.

In discussing the relation of Cuomo's Catholicism to his politics, "What Makes Mario Run?" says:

> Not since Eugene McCarthy's moral crusade for the presidency in 1968 has a political leader been so intellectually, self-consciously, even aggressively Catholic as Mario Matthew Cuomo. And, paradoxically, no Roman Catholic politician—including John F. Kennedy—has done more to make the American Catholic bishops rethink the church's relationship to political issues.

And this seems like a good place to begin an investigation of religion in American politics.

5. Structure your sentence so that it accommodates the quotation smoothly.

His role model was his father, whom Frank Cuomo calls "a Catholic, family-type guy."

6. Use three spaced periods to show ellipsis—that is, omitted words—in the body of the quotation.

Frank Cuomo says, "He was our role model: . . . a
Catholic, family-type guy."

7. Use four spaced periods to indicate ellipsis at the end of a quoted sentence, or the omission of an entire intervening sentence.

The authors conclude, "There are, in any case, at
least three Cuomos. . . . There is the hothead. . . . the
somberly reflective diarist. . . . the exuberant irrepressible winner. . . ."

8. Use square brackets to indicate an addition to or change in the quotation.

The bishop told him [Cuomo] that politics needs
men of sound values.
The bishop told [Cuomo] that politics needs men
of sound values. (The original has "him.")
Speaking of his father, Frank Cuomo says that
"[h]e was our role model. (The original has "He.")

9. Use parentheses after the quotation to indicate a change within the quotation.

The article contrasts the "proudly ethnic"
Cuomo with the "patrician Kennedys" (emphasis added).

10. Put a comma or period required by your sentence inside the quotation marks.

While the article calls Cuomo "proudly ethnic," it labels the Kennedys as "patrician."

11. Put all other punctuation required by your sentence outside the quotation marks.

Why would the article call Cuomo "proudly ethnic"?

The Kennedys were, indeed, "patrician"!

12. Omit your own punctuation when the sentence ends with punctuation in the quotation.

A good source for understanding Cuomo is the article "What Makes Mario Run?"

13. Avoid sentence organizations that require strings of end punctuation.

Is a good source for understanding Cuomo the article "What Makes Mario Run?"?

14. Use single quotation marks to indicate a quotation within the quotation.

Despite their disagreements, "Cuomo considers O'Connor the nation's 'most important cardinal.'"

· ESSAYS FOR CRITICAL READING

Al Seton, a retired commander, served in the Pacific during World War II. He was the youngest officer commissioned from the ranks of the regular navy during the war. For many years he wrote a newspaper column about the experiences of servicemen and veterans.

MEMORIES OF IWO JIMA
by Al Seton

1   Thirty-five years ago, a young U.S. Marine fighting desperately in the toughest scrap in the Corps' history made a promise: If he lived through the war, he would return to this spot—Iwo Jima—to honor and pay tribute to his enemy—the 23,000 magnificent, stubborn, brave, crafty and heroic Japanese troops defending with their lives every inch of this tiny, miserable volcanic island just 750 miles from Tokyo. By the time the battle was over twenty-six days later, all but 200 of these elite Japanese defenders were dead, at a cost of 20,196 U.S. casualties.

2   Now at 3 P.M. on February 19, 1980, that former Marine, Charles Early, a lawyer in Sarasota, Florida, stood atop Mount Suribachi to fulfill that battlefield promise. Standing in ranks before him were thirteen other veterans of that heroic struggle, seven Americans and six Japanese. And before the week was over, by this simple act, he had changed the hearts and minds of the Japanese people.

3   Our Marines who made the landing are, of course, heroes today, and the picture of the flag raising on Mount Suribachi during the assault, taken by Associated Press photographer Joe Rosenthal, will memorialize the U.S. Marines on Iwo Jima through eternity. But for the Japanese defenders at the reunion, the situation at home was completely different. For centuries the Japanese people were taught that to die for the emperor was the highest act of man, and to be taken prisoner was the most disgraceful. Japanese survivors of any battle which Imperial forces lost were outcasts, a shame to their families. As a result, these six survivors and their comrades had lived since the war in disgrace. They kept silent about the battles they had fought and the awards they had won. They "could not walk in the sun."

4   But the visit of Charles Early and the seven other Americans to pay tribute to the Iwo Jima defenders—which went virtually unnoticed in the U.S.—attracted the sympathetic attention of the Japanese press, radio and television. There was saturation coverage throughout Japan—all lauding the courageous

Reprinted by permission of Empire State Investigator.

soldiers. For the first time the Japanese public learned of the five surviving defenders who have been coming to Iwo every year since Japan regained the island in 1968, to spend their month vacation searching for remains and possessions of their buddies. Speaking for them at the ceremony was Captain Abe Takeo, now 67, a former mortar company commander who was wounded 27 times in the four weeks of battle.

5   And there was Sergeant Uribayshi, wounded four times, who said a few words of commemoration in Japanese, followed by a prayer and the laying of a wreath on an American memorial. Uribayshi's nose had been burned off by a flame thrower on Iwo and he was fitted out with another one through plastic surgery in the United States. He is no longer all Japanese, he now jokes, because "my nose was made in America."

6   When the American group returned to Japan they were guests at a luncheon given by 28 Japanese survivors of Iwo Jima. The Japanese press was there. That night, another group of Japanese gave a dinner for the Americans. At each function the Japanese stressed how this visit by Americans had, overnight, changed the lives of their veterans—making the survivors of their defeat into national heroes.

VOCABULARY

Explain what the following words mean in the article:
crafty (1)
function (6)
lauding (4)
saturation (4)
tribute (4)
virtually (4)

FACTS

What type of article is this? What are the author's qualifications for writing it? Where does the author get the information in this article?

What kind of publication was this article in? What significance, if any, does this have?

Why do you think the column was written? How extensive were the author's sources?

What is the main idea of the column? What is the significance of the title? What is the thesis statement? What are the secondary points, if any?

The column describes two events. What was the nature of the earlier event? When did it occur? How many people took part? What kind of people? What personality traits did they share? How did their personalities differ? What generalizations does the author make about these people?

What was the nature of the later event? When did it occur? How many people took part? What kind of people? What traits did they share? How did their lives compare? What generalizations does the author make about these people?

When was this column written? Do you think the later event could have occurred twenty years sooner? Do you think the author's attitude would have been the same twenty years ago?

What situations can you present that are similar to or different from the main point of this column?

SIGNIFICANCE

Explain the significance of the following quotations to the point or structure of the article:

". . . his enemy—the 23,000 magnificent, stubborn, brave, crafty and heroic Japanese troops defending with their lives every inch of this tiny, miserable volcanic island . . ."

"By the time the battle was over twenty-six days later, all but 200 of these elite Japanese defenders were dead, at a cost of 20,196 U.S. casualties."

"And before the week was over, by this simple act, he had changed the hearts and minds of the Japanese people."

"Our Marines who made the landing are, of course, heroes today, and the picture of the flag raising on Mount Suribachi during the assault . . . will memorialize the U.S. Marines on Iwo Jima through eternity."

"For centuries the Japanese people were taught that to die for the emperor was the highest act of man, and to be taken prisoner was the most disgraceful."

". . . the visit of Charles Early and the seven other Americans to pay tribute to the Iwo Jima defenders—which went virtually unnoticed in the U.S.— attracted the sympathetic attention of the Japanese press, radio and television."

FUTURE USE

Briefly summarize the article.

Outline the structure and main points.

What information in this column is relevant to your essay(s)? How could you use this information?

Thomas Y. Hobart is president of New York State United Teachers. This column appeared in the union's newspaper, New York Teacher, *in 1982.*

SCHOOLS MUST TEACH VALUES
by Thomas Y. Hobart, Jr.

1   During the past several years, there has been an increasing interest in teaching values in the public schools. The latest Gallup Poll of the Public's Attitudes Toward the Public Schools shows that 70 percent of Americans favor instruction in the schools which would deal with values and ethical behavior. Only 17 percent oppose such instruction. A related response shows that 62 percent of those polled believe that "not enough attention" is given in the schools to developing students' moral and ethical character.

2   The belief that moral values should be taught in the schools is as old as the nation itself. Thomas Jefferson argued that an educational system should fortify citizens with moral strength to resist the enemies of liberty. In early writings, Benjamin Franklin supported the study of ethics in the curriculum of the schools of Pennsylvania.

3   During the past quarter century, however, many schools have adopted a values clarification approach where there is no absolute right or wrong, but choices are relative to the situation. Indeed, the tenor of the times led to values and morality being constantly debated, questioned and revised.

4   Since the public schools have had, until recent years, a long history of moral instruction, and since a large majority of persons seem to favor such instruction in the schools, the only area of controversy appears to be how that instruction should be carried out. There has been widespread disagreement in the schools on what should be taught, how it should be taught and/or whether it should be taught in public schools in the first place.

5   One such discussion is currently taking place in Illinois, where Donald G. Gill, the state superintendent of education, has shelved, at least temporarily, a plan to teach values in the public schools. Some members of the state board had been publicly critical of the superintendent's initiative.

6   It is more than coincidental that the decline in public confidence in our schools has coincided with a lessening in the emphasis on values education. Values such as honesty, integrity, responsibility, hard work, courage, and compassion have ceased to be guiding principles in too many of our schools. They have been replaced by a type of situational ethics or moral relativism.

7   The problem that this approach causes for our schools is enormous. Parents raised during a period when correct behavior was definable have not accepted a

From the New York Teacher. *Reprinted with permission.*

system in which their children are allowed to decide on the rightness or wrongness of an act based on the circumstances surrounding that act.

8   Likewise, students who do not know or are not taught to know that certain actions are right and others wrong find it most difficult to conform to established standards of conduct. Clearly, this relativistic approach is one of the major problems schools have had in maintaining strong discipline. The lack of discipline remains, as it has been for the past several years, the primary concern of persons surveyed in the Gallup Poll.

9   I believe that men and women who enter teaching do so with the idea of shaping the character of future generations. Today, in the face of difficult and, often, dangerous conditions, teachers continue to use their ingenuity and skills to positively affect the character of every student who enters their classroom.

10   Inability to emphasize in our schools the importance of values and morality in society could lead to disastrous results. Past failures in this regard are one of the most important reasons for the growth of fundamentalist Christian schools and for the growth of the pro-tuition tax credit lobby.

11   Most importantly, our democratic form of government rests on certain values basic to individual rights and the rule of law. Democracies cannot rely on force or intimidation to enforce laws or to bring about the cooperation or participation of their citizens. If our schools fail to live up to their responsibility to develop citizens as well as to educate, the future of our democracy may well be at stake.

VOCABULARY

Explain what the following words mean in the article:
ingenuity (9)
integrity (6)
moral relativism (6)
shelved (5)
tenor (3)

FACTS

What type of article is this? What are the author's qualifications for writing it? Where does the author get the information in this article?

What kind of publication was this article in? What significance, if any, does this have?

Why do you think the column was written? How extensive were the author's sources?

When was the column written? Is it up to date?

What is the main idea of the column? What is the significance of the title? What is the thesis statement? What are the secondary points, if any?

The column describes an opinion poll. What was the nature of the poll? When did it occur? What were the findings?

The column mentions an event in Illinois. What was the nature of the event? When did it occur? What was its significance?

What situations can you present that either support or contradict the main point of this column?

SIGNIFICANCE

Explain the significance of the following quotations to the point or structure of the article:

"Thomas Jefferson argued that an educational system should fortify citizens with moral strength to resist the enemies of liberty. In early writings, Benjamin Franklin supported the study of ethics in the curriculum of the schools of Pennsylvania."

"Indeed, the tenor of the times led to values and morality being constantly debated, questioned and revised."

"There has been widespread disagreement in the schools on what should be taught, how it should be taught and/or whether it should be taught in public schools in the first place."

"It is more than coincidental that the decline in public confidence in our schools has coincided with a lessening in the emphasis on values education. Values such as honesty, integrity, responsibility, hard work, courage, and compassion have ceased to be guiding principles in too many of our schools."

"Parents raised during a period when correct behavior was definable have not accepted a system in which their children are allowed to decide on the rightness or wrongness of an act based on the circumstances surrounding that act."

"I believe that men and women who enter teaching do so with the idea of shaping the character of future generations."

". . . our democratic form of government rests on certain values basic to individual rights and the rule of law. Democracies cannot rely on force or intimidation to enforce laws or to bring about the cooperation or participation of their citizens."

FUTURE USE

Briefly summarize the article.

Outline the structure and main points.

What information in this column is relevant to your essays(s)? How could you use this information?

The next selection is from an article that appeared in Communication Quarterly *in 1983. Articles in the journal are written by and aimed at professionals in the field of communications, including teachers, students, and people in the media.*

From CLASSISM, SEXISM, RACISM AND THE SITUATION COMEDY
by K. Edgington

1   Television transmits values and shapes attitudes and behaviors. The National Institute of Mental Health's report on the subject, released in May 1982, concludes that exposure to violence on the tube produces aggressive behavior among young viewers, from pre-schoolers to teenagers; that heavy viewing may lead youngsters to "accept violence as normal"; and that adult's perceptions of the world as violent relate to viewing habits. The report's findings indicate, then, that adults as well as children are influenced by what they watch. Furthermore, the study establishes a relationship between television and behavior which extends beyond aggression and aggressive response: *Repeated exposure to a given set of values will eventually ingrain that set of values in an audience.*

2   Clearly, television's capacity to mold attitudes and behaviors requires that we examine carefully the values which TV projects. We need to determine to what extent television exposes and helps to expel harmful myths and negative stereotypes within our culture and to what extent television reinforces and perpetuates discrimination and prejudices. . . .

3   The comedy of the sitcom relies on stereotype and disparagement. Each character represents a group and is defined largely by stereotypical traits associated with that group. The "humor" occurs when the character, because of one or more of his/her assigned traits, is made to appear ridiculous. The disparagement attributes a negative value to the trait and ultimately to the group defined by that trait. In order to find the situation amusing, the audience must accept—if only temporarily—this devaluation. . . .

4   To appreciate how heavily situation comedies apply stereotypes requires extensive examination of individual series. The following case study of *Gilligan's Island* demonstrates how classism, sexism, and racism form the basis of the program. . . .

5   The situation on which the series depends, seven people shipwrecked on a tropical island, limits direction of the plot to rescue and survival; settings, for the most part, must be restricted to the island; and the isolation of the group prohibits the introduction of other characters on any regular basis. Given these restrictions, the approaches used to discuss one episode can be applied to any

other, and conclusions drawn about a single show generally will hold true for the others. Furthermore, because *Gilligan's Island* follows strictly the formula of the sitcom genre, the critical analysis used can be applied with little modification to other sitcoms.

6   In this series, the stranded group of seven forms its own society which serves as a microcosm preserving the values of American culture: money, prestige, privilege, and white male supremacy. Therefore, the comic elements must turn on the antithetical, i.e., lack or absence of money, prestige, privilege, maleness, or whiteness.

7   Comedy of this type requires a stratified social structure to establish "prestige" groups and "butt" groups. Consequently, the characters are arranged in a patriarchal hierarchy reflecting class differences. This structure can easily be discerned by examining the character's names and activities.

8   At the pinnacle sits Thurston Howell III, who holds the position of authority because of his wealth, education, and heritage. The *III* informs the viewer that Mr. Howell ranks above the nouveau riche; he is an heir of the ruling class. Accordingly, he is addressed as "Mr. Howell" by the others—with the exception of his wife, who calls him "Thurston, Dear." Mr. Howell's primary activity consists of sipping exotic drinks from coconut shells, reclining on a settee, and overseeing the labors of the group.

9   Mrs. Howell is also of prime stock. Her first name appears to be "Lovey," but only Mr. Howell uses this expression. To the others, she is "Mrs. Howell," and her title suggests that her status and identity rely on her relationship to her husband. Lovey's main responsibility is to assure the comfort of Mr. Howell: She serves the drinks. But Mrs. Howell, being a woman, must be included in women's work. Although spared most of the cooking and scrubbing, she fulfills her domestic role by supervising the work of the "girls."

10   The Professor is known only as "the Professor." Because the group's survival rests on his knowledge and intelligence, he occupies a position of authority and assumes most of the decision-making power. However, his research is "financed" by the Howells, whose abundant possessions, recovered from the wreck, furnish him with most of his materials.

11   Like the Professor, the Skipper is called by his professional title. As a property-owner—of the wrecked ship—he commands some respect. But his power is as defunct as his boat. (Note, the Skipper is not called "Captain.") He functions as a foreman and gives orders to his crew, Gilligan, and the "girls."

12   "Gilligan" appears to be a surname, but the first mate and title character is never addressed as "Mr." Gilligan serves as the group's common laborer although his slight build renders him unsuitable for the heavy chores he is assigned. In keeping with the stereotype of the blue-collar worker, Gilligan isn't too bright.

13   Ginger, one of the "girls," provides the series with a sex object. A Hollywood starlet, Ginger wears evening gowns, frets over her appearance, and carries out those tasks least likely to result in a broken fingernail or snagged nylon.

14   Offsetting Ginger's "spice," Mary Ann, a wholesome farm girl from the Midwest, is "everything nice." But, lacking Ginger's beauty and possessing neither status nor valuable skill, Mary Ann is relegated to domestic duties and spends much of her time cooking meals, doing laundry, and tidying the huts.

15   Thus, classism and sexism form the basis of the social structure from which the comic situation draws its material. Money/ownership of property and education/profession determine the hierarchy for the males. Women's positions are assigned in accordance with attachment to men; the "unattached" women occupy the lowest stratum.

16   Additionally, racism appears. Implicit racism derives from the all-white composition of the main characters; however, overt prejudice surfaces in episodes which introduce nonwhites. On occasion, dark-skinned savages invade the island, threaten to devour the men, and carry off the women. A similar situation occurs when a Japanese soldier, unaware that World War II has ended, captures the island and imprisons its inhabitants. In each case, nonwhites pose a threat to the white society; predictably, the "superior" intelligence of the white males prevails and disaster is averted. . . .

17   Although the female characters are spared pratfalls and immersion in goo, the women become sources of humor through their "feminine weaknesses." Mrs. Howell, Ginger, and Mary Ann are frequently sent shrieking in terror across the island, frightened by the sudden appearance of the muck-covered Gilligan after one of his many mishaps. As the fear of the women is offered for enjoyment, the audience is again reminded of the women's inability to function in a crisis. Likewise, the women's over-concern with trifles provides comic relief while reinforcing the myth that women are capable of thinking only on a trivial level. Faced with a life-threatening upheaval of the elements, Mrs. Howell laments that she has nothing suitable to wear to a storm shelter, Ginger complains that her nail polish won't dry in the torrential rains, and Mary Ann fears that the thunderclaps will cause her pineapple-coconut cake to fall.

18   . . . [A]nother very common plot involves change or disruption of the structure. Of course, only members of the lower echelons desire change in status, and at the climax of such episodes, the errant soul returns to his or her proper position. Mary Ann covets Ginger's beauty, Mrs. Howell aspires to a successful theatrical career, or Ginger seeks the sophistication of the Howells or the intelligence of the Professor. (Nobody, of course, wants to be Mary Ann.) In these episodes, the group unites to convince the misguided woman that she should be content to be herself, accept her limitations, and stay in her proper place.

19   However, the plots in which Gilligan attempts to "prove his manhood" through acts of heroism take on a different twist: The other characters join forces to assist Gilligan in his quest and stage incidents which will permit him to exercise some macho daring-do [sic]. Gilligan bungles the set up job but is finally able to demonstrate his true courage when a real, unexpected danger confronts the group.

20   Two observations can be made: First, the group supports attempts by the male

character to enhance self-esteem but discourages the female attempting to improve her self-image. Second, the male is able to achieve self-recognition and acceptance independently, through his own actions, whereas the female must be forcefully disabused by the others of her delusions.

21   Program after program confirms these observations: Male rationality triumphs over female irrationality; the group directs its efforts toward preserving the existent patriarchal hierarchy, which is threatened when a woman desires change in status. The comic elements of the series rest on a value system immersed in classism, sexism, and racism; the "humor" of the program degrades the working class, women, and minorities; such degradation trades on misconceptions and myths, the established negative stereotypes. . . .

22   . . . To bring about necessary change in programming, we must expose the myths, misrepresentations, and negative stereotypes which television conveys, and we must apply pressure to the networks to alter what they air. But first, we must increase our own awareness of the attitudes toward class, sex, and race which underlie major series. This is a beginning.

VOCABULARY

Explain what the following words mean in the article:
antithetical (6)
classism (15)
devaluation (3)
disparagement (3)
echelons (18)
errant (18)
genre (5)
hierarchy (15)
microcosm (6)
nouveau riche (8)
overt (16)
patriarchal (7)
perceptions (1)
relegated (14)
sitcom (3)

FACTS

What type of article is this? Where does the author get the information in this article? How extensive are the author's sources?

What kind of publication was this article in? What significance, if any, does this have?

Why do you think the article was written? Do you think the author (whose first name is given as K.) is a man or woman? Why do you think this? What is the significance of your answer to this question?

What is the main idea of the article? What is the significance of the title? What is the thesis statement?

The article briefly mentions events from a television show. What do you think the plots of these episodes were?

When was this article written? When was the show it discusses televised? Is the article up to date?

What television shows can you present that are either similar to or different from the show described in this article?

SIGNIFICANCE

Explain the significance of the following quotations to the point or structure of the article:

". . . television's capacity to mold attitudes and behaviors requires that we examine carefully the values which TV projects."

"The comedy of the sitcom relies on stereotype and disparagement. Each character represents a group and is defined largely by stereotypical traits associated with that group."

"The following case study of *Gilligan's Island* demonstrates how classism, sexism, and racism form the basis of the program."

"Mr. Howell's primary activity consists of sipping exotic drinks from coconut shells, reclining on a settee, and overseeing the labors of the group."

"To the others, she is 'Mrs. Howell,' and her title suggests that her status and identity rely on her relationship to her husband."

"Ginger, one of the 'girls,' provides the series with a sex object."

". . . lacking Ginger's beauty and possessing neither status nor valuable skill, Mary Ann is relegated to domestic duties. . . ."

"Money/ownership of property and education/profession determine the hierarchy for the males. Women's positions are assigned in accordance with attachment to men. . . ."

"Faced with a life-threatening upheaval of the elements, Mrs. Howell laments that she has nothing suitable to wear to a storm shelter, Ginger complains that her nail polish won't dry in the torrential rains, and Mary Ann fears that the thunderclaps will cause her pineapple-coconut cake to fall."

"In these episodes, the group unites to convince the misguided woman that she should be content to be herself, accept her limitations, and stay in her proper place."

FUTURE USE

Briefly summarize the article.

Outline the structure and main points.

What information in this article is relevant to your essay(s)? How could you use this information?

Thorstein Veblen was one of the founders of the modern scientific study of economics. As a professor at the University of Chicago, Stanford University, and the New School for Social Research, he helped extend the Darwinian theory of evolution to the social sciences. In The Theory of the Leisure Class, *published in 1899, he introduced the term* conspicuous consumption *as a label for "consumption as evidence of wealth," tracing this behavior from hunting and gathering cultures to industrialized nations. It begins, he writes, in the belief that "unproductive consumption of goods is honorable, primarily as a mark of prowess and a perquisite of human dignity; secondarily, it becomes substantially honorable in itself, especially the consumption of the more desirable things."*

From *THE THEORY OF THE LEISURE CLASS* by Thorstein Veblen

1   Conspicuous consumption of valuable goods is a means of reputability to the gentleman of leisure. As wealth accumulates on his hands, his own unaided effort will not avail to sufficiently put his opulence in evidence by this method. The aid of friends and competitors is therefore brought in by resorting to the giving of valuable presents and expensive feasts and entertainments. Presents and feasts had probably another origin than that of naive ostentation, but they acquired their utility for this purpose very early, and they have retained that character to the present. . . .

2   . . . [L]ower grades, especially the impecunious, or marginal, gentlemen of leisure, affiliate themselves by a system of dependence or fealty to the great ones; by so doing they gain an increment of repute, or of the means with which to lead a life of leisure, from their patron. They become his courtiers or retainers, servants; and being fed and countenanced by their patron they are indices of his rank and vicarious consumers of his superfluous wealth. . . .

3   With the disappearance of servitude, the number of vicarious consumers attached to any one gentlemen tends, on the whole, to decrease. The like is of course true, and perhaps in a still higher degree, of the number of dependents who perform vicarious leisure for him. In a general way, though not wholly nor consistently, these two groups coincide. The dependent who was first delegated for these duties was the wife, or the chief wife; and, as would be expected, in the later development of the institution, when the number of persons by whom these duties are customarily performed gradually narrows, the wife remains the last. In the higher grades of society a large volume of both these kinds of service is required; and here the wife is of course assisted by a more or less numerous corps of menials. But as we descend the social scale, the point is presently reached where the duties of vicarious leisure and consumption devolve upon the

wife alone. In the communities of the Western culture, this point is at present found among the lower middle class.

4   And here occurs a curious inversion. It is a fact of common observation that in this lower middle class there is no pretence of leisure on the part of the head of the household. Through force of circumstances it has fallen into disuse. But the middle-class wife still carries on the business of vicarious leisure, for the good name of the household and its master. In descending the social scale in any modern industrial community, the primary fact—the conspicuous leisure of the master of the household—disappears at a relatively high point. The head of the middle-class household has been reduced by economic circumstances to turn his hand to gaining a livelihood by occupations which often partake largely of the character of industry, as in the case of the ordinary businessman of today. But the derivative fact—the vicarious leisure and consumption rendered by the wife, and the auxiliary vicarious performances of leisure by menials—remains in vogue as a conventionality which the demands of reputability will not suffer to be slighted. It is by no means an uncommon spectacle to find a man applying himself to work with the utmost assiduity, in order that his wife may in due form render for him that degree of vicarious leisure which the common sense of the time demands.

5   The leisure rendered by the wife in such cases is, of course, not a simple manifestation of idleness or indolence. It almost invariably occurs disguised under some form of work or household duties or social amenities, which prove on analysis to serve little or no ulterior end beyond showing that she does not and need not occupy herself with anything that is gainful or that is of substantial use. . . . If beauty or comfort is achieved—and it is a more or less fortuitous circumstance if they are—they must be achieved by means and methods that commend themselves to the great economic law of wasted effort. The more reputable, "presentable" portion of middle-class household paraphernalia are, on the one hand, items of conspicuous consumption, and on the other hand, apparatus for putting in evidence the vicarious leisure rendered by the house-wife.

6   The requirement of vicarious consumption at the hands of the wife continues in force even at a lower point in the pecuniary scale than the requirement of vicarious leisure. At a point below which little if any pretence of wasted effort, in ceremonial cleanness and the like, is observable, and where there is assuredly no conscious attempt at ostensible leisure, decency still requires the wife to consume some goods conspicuously for the reputability of the household and its head. So that, as the latter-day outcome of this evolution of an archaic institution, the wife, who was at the outset the drudge and chattel of the man, both in fact and in theory—the producer of goods for him to consume—has become the ceremonial consumer of goods which he produces. But she still quite unmistakably remains his chattel in theory; for the habitual rendering of vicarious leisure and consumption is the abiding mark of the unfree servant.

VOCABULARY

Explain what the following words mean in the selection:
amenities (5)
assiduity (4)
chattel (6)
commend (5)
common sense (4)
conspicuous (1)
conventionality (4)
countenanced (2)
devolve (3)
fealty (2)
fortuitous (5)
impecunious (2)
increment (2)
indices (2)
industry (4)
menials (3)
naive ostentation (1)
ostensible (6)
pecuniary (6)
reputability (1)
suffer (4)
vicarious (2)
vogue (4)

FACTS

What type of selection is this? Where does the author get his information? How extensive are his sources?

What kind of publication is this selection from? What significance, if any, does this have?

What is the main idea of the selection? What is the significance of the title? What is the thesis statement?

The selection describes the behavior of "gentlemen of leisure" who have no money. What do they do? What similar situation(s) can you add?

The selection describes the activities of a wife. From what social level? Ethnic background? Nationality?

When was this study written? In what ways is the situation similar today? Different?

What experience(s) do you have that can either support or contradict the author's point?

SIGNIFICANCE

Explain the significance of the following quotations to the point or structure of the selection:

"Conspicuous consumption of valuable goods is a means of reputability to the gentleman of leisure."

"They become his courtiers or retainers, servants; and being fed and countenanced by their patron they are indices of his rank and vicarious consumers of his superfluous wealth. . . ."

"The dependent who was first delegated for these duties was the wife, or the chief wife; and, as would be expected, in the later development of the institution, when the number of persons by whom these duties are customarily performed gradually narrows, the wife remains the last."

". . . in this lower middle class there is no pretence of leisure on the part of the head of the household. Through force of circumstances it has fallen into disuse. But the middle-class wife still carries on the business of vicarious leisure, for the good name of the household and its master."

"The more reputable, 'presentable' portion of middle-class household paraphernalia are, on the one hand, items of conspicuous consumption, and on the other hand, apparatus for putting in evidence the vicarious leisure rendered by the housewife."

". . . decency still requires the wife to consume some goods conspicuously for the reputability of the household and its head."

"But she still quite unmistakably remains his chattel in theory; for the habitual rendering of vicarious leisure and consumption is the abiding mark of the unfree servant."

FUTURE USE

Briefly summarize the selection.

Outline the structure and main points.

What information in this selection is relevant to your essay(s)? How could you use this information?

· MAKING CONNECTIONS

Prepare responses to the following discussion topics. The questions are meant to stimulate your thoughts, not to elicit one- or two-word answers.

1. What similarities are there between "Memories of Iwo Jima" (p. 123) and "Traits of Indian Character" (p. 69)? What differences? What is the attitude in the former toward the Japanese and in the latter toward Indi-

ans? Are these the attitudes that were popular at the time? Are the descriptions of the Japanese and Indians in these essays more accurate, less accurate, or about as accurate as the popular image? What elements of stereotype can you find in these descriptions? What makes a description into a stereotype? Are the attitudes more favorable, less favorable, or about as favorable as the popular attitudes? What is the relationship, if any, between attitude and stereotype? What essay topic(s) could incorporate information from these sources? What essay topic(s) could incorporate information from these sources and from the articles about Italian-Americans?

2. What similarities are there between "Classism, Sexism, Racism and the Situation Comedy" (p. 129) and "TV Children Not Real" (p. 63)? What differences? What does each article say about the accuracy of the facts that television includes? What does each article say about the attitude toward the subject conveyed by the television image? What do you think would satisfy the authors of these articles: more accurate information or more sympathetic portraits, or both? Can you think of examples where a group demanded a less accurate but more sympathetic media image? A more accurate but less sympathetic image? What essay topic(s) could incorporate information from these sources? What essay topic(s) could incorporate information from these sources and from the articles about the Italian-Americans, Indians, and Japanese?

3. "TV Children Not Real" (p. 63) quotes a spokesman from CBS as saying, "Comedy can't be expected to reflect the harshness of reality." What do you think? Are stereotypes a necessary part of comedy? What answer is given in "Classism, Sexism, Racism and the Situation Comedy" (p. 129)? What should be the practice in other types of entertainment, for example, dramas? Do the villains on crime shows reflect the ethnic and racial composition of the whole population? Should they? Do newscasts concentrate on crime (or accomplishments) by some groups but not others? How does "What Makes Mario Run?" (p. 40) include or address stereotypes? What essay topic(s) could explore these questions? What essay topic(s) could explore these questions by incorporating information from the selections you have been reading?

4. According to "Schools Must Teach Values" (p. 126), where do children learn honesty, integrity, compassion, and other desirable behaviors? How does someone "teach" values? What is the meaning of the expression "Do what I say, not what I do"? Who determines, or should determine, which values to teach? Which do you think is more important in teaching values, the home or school? Can you name an attitude you learned at home that conflicts with the values taught (or learned) in school? What can or should be done if home values conflict with values taught in school? What part does television play in teaching values? Do children

learn from the actions and attitudes they see on television? Can you name an attitude you learned from television rather than from home or school? What essay topic(s) could explore these questions? What essay topic(s) could explore these questions by incorporating information from the selections you have been reading about the values of different groups and the images conveyed by television?

5. According to *The Theory of the Leisure Class* (p. 134), how are values transmitted? Where do they come from? What happens to values that no longer "make sense"? How is this theory of values similar to or different from the position taken in "Schools Must Teach Values" (p. 126)? To the position in "The Significance of the Frontier" (p. 73)? To the view in "What Makes Mario Run?" (p. 40)? To the findings in Dr. Patti's study (p. 65)? What values are reflected in television commercials? Are they the kind of attitudes that we want to teach? Do commercials support or contradict the theory of conspicuous consumption? Now that most women work outside the home, what will happen to conspicuous consumption? Will it disappear or be transferred to pets, children, or something else?

· ADDITIONAL ESSAYS FOR DISCUSSION

From *THE SCARLET LETTER*
by Nathaniel Hawthorne (1850)

1   This old town of Salem—my native place, though I have dwelt much away from it, both in boyhood and maturer years—possesses, or did possess, a hold on my affections, the force of which I have never realized, during my seasons of actual residence here. Indeed, so far as its physical aspect is concerned, with its flat, unvaried surface, covered chiefly with wooden houses, few or none of which pretend to architectural beauty,—its irregularity, which is neither picturesque nor quaint, but only tame—its long and lazy street lounging wearisomely through the whole extent of the peninsula, with Gallows Hill and New Guinea at one end, and a view of the almshouse at the other,—such being the features of my native town, it would be quite as reasonable to form a sentimental attachment to a disarranged checker-board. And yet, though invariably happiest elsewhere, there is within me a feeling for old Salem, which, in lack of a better phrase, I must be content to call affection. The sentiment is probably assignable to the deep and aged roots which my family has struck into the soil. It is now nearly two centuries and a quarter since the original Briton, the earliest emigrant of my name, made his appearance in the wild and forest-bordered settlement, which has since become a city. And here his descendants have been born and died, and have mingled their earthly substance with the soil, until no small portion of it must necessarily be akin to the mortal frame wherewith, for a little while, I walk the streets. In part, therefore, the attachment which I speak of is the mere sensuous sympathy of dust for dust. Few of my countrymen can know what it is; nor, as frequent transplantation is perhaps better for the stock, need they consider it desirable to know.

2   But the sentiment has likewise its moral quality. The figure of that first ancestor, invested by family tradition with a dim and dusky grandeur, was present to my boyish imagination, as far back as I can remember. It still haunts me, and induces a sort of home-feeling with the past, which I scarcely claim in reference to the present phase of the town. I seem to have a stronger claim to a residence here on account of this grave, bearded, sable-cloaked and steeple-crowned progenitor,—who came so early, with his Bible, and his sword, and trode the unworn street with such a stately port, and made so large a figure, as a man of war and peace,—a stronger claim than for myself, whose name is seldom heard and my face hardly known. He was a soldier, legislator, judge; he was a ruler in the Church; he had all the Puritanic traits, both good and evil. He was likewise a bitter persecutor, as witness the Quakers, who have remembered him in their histories, and relate an incident of his hard severity towards a woman of their sect, which will last longer, it is to be feared, than any record of his better

deeds, although these were many. His son, too, inherited the persecuting spirit, and made himself so conspicuous in the martyrdom of the witches, that their blood may fairly be said to have left a stain upon him. So deep a stain, indeed, that his old dry bones, in the Charter Street burial-ground, must still retain it, if they have not crumbled utterly to dust! I know not whether these ancestors of mine bethought themselves to repent, and ask pardon of Heaven for their cruelties; or whether they are now groaning under the heavy consequences of them, in another state of being. At all events, I, the present writer, as their representative, hereby take shame upon myself for their sakes, and pray that any curse incurred by them—as I have heard, and as the dreary and unprosperous condition of the race, for many a long year back, would argue to exist—may be now and henceforth removed.

3   Doubtless, however, either of these stern and black-browed Puritans would have thought it quite a sufficient retribution for his sins, that, after so long a lapse of years, the old trunk of the family tree, with so much venerable moss upon it, should have borne, as its topmost bough, an idler like myself. No aim, that I have ever cherished, would they recognize as laudable; no success of mine—if my life, beyond its domestic scope, had ever been brightened by success—would they deem otherwise than worthless, if not positively disgraceful. "What is he?" murmurs one gray shadow of my forefathers to the other. "A writer of story-books! What kind of a business in life,—what mode of glorifying God, or being serviceable to mankind in his day and generation,— may that be? Why, the degenerate fellow might as well have been a fiddler!" Such are the compliments bandied between my great-grandsires and myself, across the gulf of time! And yet, let them scorn me as they will, strong traits of their nature have intertwined themselves with mine.

4   Planted deep, in the town's earliest infancy and childhood, by these two earnest and energetic men, the race has ever since subsisted here; always, too, in respectability; never, so far as I have known, disgraced by a single unworthy member; but seldom or never, on the other hand, after the first two generations, performing any memorable deed, or so much as putting forward a claim to public notice. Gradually, they have sunk almost out of sight; as old houses, here and there about the streets, get covered half-way to the eaves by the accumulation of new soil. From father to son, for above a hundred years, they followed the sea; a gray-headed shipmaster, in each generation, retiring from the quarter-deck to the homestead, while a boy of fourteen took the hereditary place before the mast, confronting the salt spray and the gale, which had blustered against his sire and grandsire. The boy, also, in due time, passed from the forecastle to the cabin, spent a tempestuous manhood, and returned from his world-wanderings, to grow old, and die, and mingle his dust with the natal earth. This long connection of a family with one spot, as its place of birth and burial, creates a kindred between the human being and the locality, quite independent of any charm in the scenery or moral circumstances that surround him. It is not love,

but instinct. The new inhabitant—who came himself from a foreign land, or whose father or grandfather came—has little claim to be called a Salemite; he has no conception of the oysterlike tenacity with which an old settler, over whom his third century is creeping, clings to the spot where his successive generations have been imbedded. It is no matter that the place is joyless for him; that he is weary of the old wooden houses, the mud and dust, the dead level of site and sentiment, the chill east wind, and the chillest of social atmospheres,—all these, and whatever faults besides he may see or imagine, are nothing to the purpose. The spell survives, and just as powerfully as if the natal spot were an earthly paradise. So has it been in my case. I felt it almost as a destiny to make Salem my home; so that the mould of features and cast of character which had all along been familiar here,—ever, as one representative of the race lay down in his grave, another assuming, as it were, his sentry-march along the main street,—might still in my little day be seen and recognized in the old town. Nevertheless, this very sentiment is an evidence that the connection, which has become an unhealthy one, should at last be severed. Human nature will not flourish, any more than a potato, if it be planted and replanted, for too long a series of generations, in the same worn-out soil. My children have had other birthplaces, and, so far as their fortunes may be within my control, shall strike their roots into unaccustomed earth. . . .

From 1745–1755: THE COMBATANTS
in *FRANCE AND ENGLAND*
IN NORTH AMERICA
by Francis Parkman (1884)

1   The French claimed all America, from the Alleghanies to the Rocky Mountains, and from Mexico and Florida to the North Pole, except only the ill-defined possessions of the English on the borders of Hudson Bay; and to these vast regions, with adjacent islands, they gave the general name of New France. They controlled the highways of the continent, for they held its two great rivers. First, they had seized the St. Lawrence, and then planted themselves at the mouth of the Mississippi. Canada at the north, and Louisiana at the south, were the keys of a boundless interior, rich with incalculable possibilities. The English colonies, ranged along the Atlantic coast, had no royal road to the great inland, and were, in a manner, shut between the mountains and the sea. At the middle of the century they numbered in all, from Georgia to Maine, about eleven hundred and sixty thousand white inhabitants. By the census of 1754 Canada had but fifty-five thousand. Add those of Louisiana and Acadia, and the whole white population under the French flag might be something more than eighty thousand. Here is an enormous disparity; and hence it has been argued that the success of the English colonies and the failure of the French was not due to difference of religious and political systems, but simply to numerical preponderance. But this preponderance itself grew out of a difference of systems. We have said before, and it cannot be said too often, that in making Canada a citadel of the state religion,—a holy of holies of exclusive Roman Catholic orthodoxy,—the clerical monitors of the Crown robbed their country of a trans-Atlantic empire. New France could not grow with a priest on guard at the gate to let in none but such as pleased him. One of the ablest of Canadian governors, La Galissonière, seeing the feebleness of the colony compared with the vastness of its claims, advised the King to send ten thousand peasants to occupy the valley of the Ohio, and hold back the British swarm that was just then pushing its advance-guard over the Alleghanies. It needed no effort of the King to people his waste domain, not with ten thousand peasants, but with twenty times ten thousand Frenchmen of every station,—the most industrious, most instructed, most disciplined by adversity and capable of self-rule, that the country could boast. While La Galissonière was asking for colonists, the agents of the Crown, set on by priestly fanaticism, or designing selfishness masked with fanaticism, were pouring volleys of musketry into Huguenot congregations, imprisoning for life those innocent of all but their faith,—the men in the galleys, the women in the pestiferous dungeons of Aigues Mortes,—hanging their ministers, kidnapping their children, and reviving, in short, the dragonnades. Now, as in the past century, many of the victims escaped to the British colonies, and became a part

of them. The Huguenots would have hailed as a boon the permission to emigrate under the fleur-de-lis, and build up a Protestant France in the valleys of the West. It would have been a bane of absolutism, but a national glory; would have set bounds to English colonization, and changed the face of the continent. The opportunity was spurned. The dominant Church clung to its policy of rule and ruin. France built its best colony on a principle of exclusion, and failed; England reversed the system, and succeeded. . . .

2   The thirteen British colonies were alike, insomuch as they all had representative governments, and a basis of English law. But the differences among them were great. Some were purely English; others were made up of various races, though the Anglo-Saxon was always predominant. Some had one prevailing religious creed; others had many creeds. Some had charters, and some had not. In most cases the governor was appointed by the Crown; in Pennsylvania and Maryland he was appointed by a feudal proprietor, and in Connecticut and Rhode Island he was chosen by the people. The differences of disposition and character were still greater than those of form.

3   The four northern colonies, known collectively as New England, were an exception to the general rule of diversity. The smallest, Rhode Island, had features all its own; but the rest were substantially one in nature and origin. The principal among them, Massachusetts, may serve as the type of all. It was a mosaic of little village republics, firmly cemented together, and formed into a single body politic through representatives sent to the "General Court" at Boston. Its government, originally theocratic, now tended to democracy, ballasted as yet by strong traditions of respect for established worth and ability, as well as by the influence of certain families prominent in affairs for generations. Yet there were no distinct class-lines, and popular power, like popular education, was widely diffused. Practically Massachusetts was almost independent of the mother-country. Its people were purely English, of sound yeoman stock, with an abundant leaven drawn from the best of the Puritan gentry; but their original character had been somewhat modified by changed conditions of life. A harsh and exacting creed, with its stiff formalism and its prohibition of wholesome recreation; excess in the pursuit of gain,—the only resource left to energies robbed of their natural play; the struggle for existence on a hard and barren soil; and the isolation of a narrow village life,—joined to produce, in the meaner sort, qualities which were unpleasant, and sometimes repulsive. Puritanism was not an unmixed blessing. Its view of human nature was dark, and its attitude towards it one of repression. It strove to crush out not only what is evil, but much that is innocent and salutary. Human nature so treated will take its revenge, and for every vice that it loses find another instead. Nevertheless, while New England Puritanism bore its peculiar crop of faults, it produced also many good and sound fruits. An uncommon vigor, joined to the hardy virtues of a masculine race, marked the New England type. The sinews, it is true, were hardened at the expense of blood and flesh,—and this literally as well as figur-

atively; but the staple of character was a sturdy conscientiousness, an undespairing courage, patriotism, public spirit, sagacity, and a strong good sense. A great change, both for better and for worse, has since come over it, due largely to reaction against the unnatural rigors of the past. That mixture, which is now too common, of cool emotions with excitable brains, was then rarely seen. The New England colonies abounded in high examples of public and private virtue, though not always under the most prepossessing forms. They were conspicuous, moreover, for intellectual activity, and were by no means without intellectual eminence. Massachusetts had produced at least two men whose fame had crossed the sea,—Edwards, who out of the grim theology of Calvin mounted to sublime heights of mystical speculation; and Franklin, famous already by his discoveries in electricity. On the other hand, there were few genuine New Englanders who, however personally modest, could divest themselves of the notion that they belonged to a people in an especial manner the object of divine approval; and this self-righteousness, along with certain other traits, failed to commend the Puritan colonies to the favor of their fellows. Then, as now, New England was best known to her neighbors by her worst side.

4   In one point, however, she found general applause. She was regarded as the most military among the British colonies. This reputation was well founded, and is easily explained. More than all the rest, she lay open to attack. The long waving line of the New England border, with its lonely hamlets and scattered farms, extended from the Kennebec to beyond the Connecticut, and was everywhere vulnerable to the guns and tomahawks of the neighboring French and their savage allies. The colonies towards the south had thus far been safe from danger. New York alone was within striking distance of the Canadian war-parties. That province then consisted of a line of settlements up the Hudson and the Mohawk, and was little exposed to attack except at its northern end, which was guarded by the fortified town of Albany, with its outlying posts, and by the friendly and warlike Mohawks, whose "castles" were close at hand. Thus New England had borne the heaviest brunt of the preceding wars, not only by the forest, but also by the sea; for the French of Acadia and Cape Breton confronted her coast, and she was often at blows with them. Fighting had been a necessity with her, and she had met the emergency after a method extremely defective, but the best that circumstances would permit. Having no trained officers and no disciplined soldiers, and being too poor to maintain either, she borrowed her warriors from the workshop and the plough, and officered them with lawyers, merchants, mechanics, or farmers. To compare them with good regular troops would be folly; but they did, on the whole, better than could have been expected, and in the last war achieved the brilliant success of the capture of Louisbourg. This exploit, due partly to native hardihood and partly to good luck, greatly enhanced the military repute of New England, or rather was one of the chief sources of it.

5   The great colony of Virginia stood in strong contrast to New England. In

both the population was English; but the one was Puritan with Roundhead traditions, and the other, so far as concerned its governing class, Anglican with Cavalier traditions. In the one, every man, woman, and child could read and write; in the other, Sir William Berkeley once thanked God that there were no free schools, and no prospect of any for a century. The hope had found fruition. The lower classes of Virginia were as untaught as the warmest friend of popular ignorance could wish. New England had a native literature more than respectable under the circumstances, while Virginia had none; numerous industries, while Virginia was all agriculture, with but a single crop; a homogeneous society and a democratic spirit, while her rival was an aristocracy. Virginian society was distinctly stratified. On the lowest level were the negro slaves, nearly as numerous as all the rest together; next, the indented servants and the poor whites, of low origin, good-humored, but boisterous, and sometimes vicious; next, the small and despised class of tradesmen and mechanics; next, the farmers and lesser planters, who were mainly of good English stock, and who merged insensibly into the ruling class of the great landowners. It was these last who represented the colony and made the laws. They may be described as English country squires transplanted to a warm climate and turned slave-masters. They sustained their position by entails, and constantly undermined it by the reckless profusion which ruined them at last. Many of them were well born, with an immense pride of descent, increased by the habit of domination. Indolent and energetic by turns; rich in natural gifts and often poor in book-learning, though some, in the lack of good teaching at home, had been bred in the English universities; high-spirited, generous to a fault; keeping open house in their capacious mansions, among vast tobacco-fields and toiling negroes, and living in a rude pomp where the fashions of St. James were somewhat oddly grafted on the roughness of the plantation,—what they wanted in schooling was supplied by an education which books alone would have been impotent to give, the education which came with the possession and exercise of political power, and the sense of a position to maintain, joined to a bold spirit of independence and a patriotic attachment to the Old Dominion. They were few in number; they raced, gambled, drank, and swore; they did everything that in Puritan eyes was most reprehensible; and in the day of need they gave the United Colonies a body of statesmen and orators which had no equal on the continent. A vigorous aristocracy favors the growth of personal eminence, even in those who are not of it, but only near it.

6   The essential antagonism of Virginia and New England was afterwards to become, and to remain for a century, an element of the first influence in American history. Each might have learned much from the other; but neither did so till, at last, the strife of their contending principles shook the continent. Pennsylvania differed widely from both. She was a conglomerate of creeds and races,—English, Irish, Germans, Dutch, and Swedes; Quakers, Lutherans, Presbyterians, Romanists, Moravians, and a variety of nondescript sects. The

Quakers prevailed in the eastern districts; quiet, industrious, virtuous, and serenely obstinate. The Germans were strongest towards the centre of the colony, and were chiefly peasants; successful farmers, but dull, ignorant, and superstitious. Towards the west were the Irish, of whom some were Celts, always quarrelling with their German neighbors, who detested them; but the greater part were Protestants of Scotch descent, from Ulster; a vigorous border population. Virginia and New England had each a strong distinctive character. Pennsylvania, with her heterogeneous population, had none but that which she owed to the sober neutral tints of Quaker existence. A more thriving colony there was not on the continent. Life, if monotonous, was smooth and contented. Trade and the arts grew. Philadelphia, next to Boston, was the largest town in British America; and was, moreover, the intellectual centre of the middle and southern colonies. Unfortunately, for her credit in the approaching war, the Quaker influence made Pennsylvania non-combatant. Politically, too, she was an anomaly; for, though utterly unfeudal in disposition and character, she was under feudal superiors in the persons of the representatives of William Penn, the original grantee.

7   New York had not as yet reached the relative prominence which her geographical position and inherent strength afterwards gave her. The English, joined to the Dutch, the original settlers, were the dominant population; but a half-score of other languages were spoken in the province, the chief among them being that of the Huguenot French in the southern parts, and that of the Germans on the Mohawk. In religion, the province was divided between the Anglican Church, with government support and popular dislike, and numerous dissenting sects, chiefly Lutherans, Independents, Presbyterians, and members of the Dutch Reformed Church. The little city of New York, like its great successor, was the most cosmopolitan place on the continent, and probably the gayest. It had, in abundance, balls, concerts, theatricals, and evening clubs, with plentiful dances and other amusements for the poorer classes. Thither in the winter months came the great hereditary proprietors on the Hudson; for the old Dutch feudality still held its own, and the manors of Van Renselaer, Cortland, and Livingston, with their seigniorial privileges, and the great estates and numerous tenantry of the Schuylers and other leading families, formed the basis of an aristocracy, some of whose members had done good service to the province, and were destined to do more. Pennsylvania was feudal in form, and not in spirit; Virginia in spirit, and not in form; New England in neither; and New York largely in both. This social crystallization had, it is true, many opponents. In politics, as in religion, there were sharp antagonisms and frequent quarrels. They centred in the city; for in the well-stocked dwellings of the Dutch farmers along the Hudson there reigned a tranquil and prosperous routine; and the Dutch border town of Albany had not its like in America for unruffled conservatism and quaint picturesqueness.

8   Of the other colonies, the briefest mention will suffice: New Jersey, with its

wholesome population of farmers; tobacco-growing Maryland, which, but for its proprietary government and numerous Roman Catholics, might pass for another Virginia, inferior in growth, and less decisive in features; Delaware, a modest appendage of Pennsylvania; wild and rude North Carolina; and, farther on, South Carolina and Georgia, too remote from the seat of war to take a noteworthy part in it. The attitude of these various colonies towards each other is hardly conceivable to an American of the present time. They had no political tie except a common allegiance to the British Crown. Communication between them was difficult and slow, by rough roads traced often through primeval forests. Between some of them there was less of sympathy than of jealousy kindled by conflicting interests or perpetual disputes concerning boundaries. The patriotism of the colonist was bounded by the lines of his government, except in the compact and kindred colonies of New England, which were socially united, though politically distinct. The country of the New Yorker was New York, and the country of the Virginian was Virginia. The New England colonies had once confederated; but, kindred as they were, they had long ago dropped apart. William Penn proposed a plan of colonial union wholly fruitless. James II. tried to unite all the northern colonies under one government; but the attempt came to naught. Each stood aloof, jealously independent. At rare intervals, under the pressure of an emergency, some of them would try to act in concert; and, except in New England, the results had been most discouraging. Nor was it this segregation only that unfitted them for war. They were all subject to popular legislatures, through whom alone money and men could be raised; and these elective bodies were sometimes factious and selfish, and not always either farsighted or reasonable. Moreover, they were in a state of ceaseless friction with their governors, who represented the king, or, what was worse, the feudal proprietary. These disputes, though varying in intensity, were found everywhere except in the two small colonies which chose their own governors; and they were premonitions of the movement towards independence which ended in the war of Revolution. . . .

9   Divided in government; divided in origin, feelings, and principles; jealous of each other, jealous of the Crown; the people at war with the executive, and, by the fermentation of internal politics, blinded to an outward danger that seemed remote and vague,—such were the conditions under which the British colonies drifted into a war that was to decide the fate of the continent.

10   This war was the strife of a united and concentred few against a divided and discordant many. It was the strife, too, of the past against the future; of the old against the new; of moral and intellectual torpor against moral and intellectual life; of barren absolutism against a liberty, crude, incoherent, and chaotic, yet full of prolific vitality.

Note: The numerous suspension points (. . .) are part of Whitman's style and do not indicate omissions.

From LEAVES OF GRASS
by Walt Whitman (1855)

1   The Americans of all nations at any time upon the earth have probably the fullest poetical nature. The United States themselves are essentially the greatest poem. In the history of the earth hitherto the largest and most stirring appear tame and orderly to their ampler largeness and stir. Here at last is something in the doings of man that corresponds with the broadcast doings of the day and night. Here is not merely a nation but a teeming nation of nations. Here is action untied from strings necessarily blind to particulars and details magnificently moving in vast masses. Here is the hospitality which forever indicates heroes. . . . Here are the roughs and beards and space and ruggedness and nonchalance that the soul loves. Here the performance disdaining the trivial unapproached in the tremendous audacity of its crowds and groupings and the push of its perspective spreads with crampless and flowing breadth and showers its prolific and splendid extravagance. One sees it must indeed own the riches of the summer and winter, and need never be bankrupt while corn grows from the ground or the orchards drop apples or the bays contain fish or men beget children upon women.

2   Other states indicate themselves in their deputies . . . but the genius of the United States is not best or most in its executives or legislatures, nor in its ambassadors or authors or colleges or churches or parlors, nor even in its newspapers or inventors . . . but always most in the common people. Their manners speech dress friendships—the freshness and candor of their physiognomy—the picturesque looseness of their carriage . . . their deathless attachment to freedom—their aversion to anything indecorous or soft or mean—the practical acknowledgment of the citizens of one state by the citizens of all other states— the fierceness of their roused resentment—their curiosity and welcome of novelty—their self-esteem and wonderful sympathy—their susceptibility to a slight— the air they have of persons who never knew how it felt to stand in the presence of superiors—the fluency of their speech—their delight in music, the sure symptom of manly tenderness and native elegance of soul . . . their good temper and openhandedness—the terrible significance of their elections—the President's taking off his hat to them not they to him—these too are unrhymed poetry. It awaits the gigantic and generous treatment worthy of it.

3   The largeness of nature of the nation were monstrous without a corresponding largeness and generosity of the spirit of the citizen. Not nature nor swarming states nor streets and steamships nor prosperous business nor farms nor capital nor learning may suffice for the ideal of man . . . nor suffice the poet. No

reminiscences may suffice either. A live nation can always cut a deep mark and can have the best authority the cheapest . . . namely from its own soul. This is the sum of the profitable uses of individuals or states and of present action and grandeur and of the subjects of poets.—As if it were necessary to trot back generation after generation to the eastern records! As if the beauty and sacredness of the demonstrable must fall behind that of the mythical! As if men do not make their mark out of any times! As if the opening of the western continent by discovery and what has transpired since in North and South America were less than the small theatre of the antique or the aimless sleepwalking of the middle ages! The pride of the United States leaves the wealth and finesse of the cities and all returns of commerce and agriculture and all the magnitude of geography or shows of exterior victory to enjoy the breed of fullsized men or one fullsized man unconquerable and simple.

4   The American poets are to enclose old and new for America is the race of races. Of them a bard is to be commensurate with a people. To him the other continents arrive as contributions . . . he gives them reception for their sake and his own sake. His spirit responds to his country's spirit . . . he incarnates its geography and natural life and rivers and lakes. Mississippi with annual freshets and changing chutes, Missouri and Columbia and Ohio and Saint Lawrence with the falls and beautiful masculine Hudson, do not embouchure where they spend themselves more than they embouchure into him. The blue breadth over the inland sea of Virginia and Maryland and the sea off Massachusetts and Maine and over Manhattan bay and over Champlain and Erie and over Ontario and Huron and Michigan and Superior, and over the Texan and Mexican and Floridian and Cuban seas and over the seas off California and Oregon, is not tallied by the blue breadth of the waters below more than the breadth of above and below is tallied by him. When the long Atlantic coast stretches longer and the Pacific coast stretches longer he easily stretches with them north or south. He spans between them also from east to west and reflects what is between them. On him rise solid growths that offset the growths of pine and cedar and hemlock and liveoak and locust and chestnut and cypress and hickory and limetree and cottonwood and tuliptree and cactus and wildvine and tamarind and persimmon . . . and tangles as tangled as any canebrake or swamp . . . and forests coated with transparent ice and icicles hanging from the boughs and crackling in the wind . . . and sides and peaks of mountains . . . and pasturage sweet and free as savannah or upland or prairie . . . with flights and songs and screams that answer those of the wildpigeon and highhold and orchard-oriole and coot and surf-duck and redshouldered-hawk and fish-hawk and white-ibis and indian-hen and cat-owl and water-pheasant and qua-bird and pied-sheldrake and blackbird and mockingbird and buzzard and condor and night-heron and eagle. To him the hereditary countenance descends both mother's and father's. To him enter the essences of the real things and past and present events—of the enormous diversity of temperature and agriculture and mines—the tribes of red aborigines—the weatherbeaten vessels entering new

ports or making landings on rocky coasts—the first settlements north or south—the rapid stature and muscle—the haughty defiance of '76, and the war and peace and formation of the constitution . . . the union always surrounded by blatherers and always calm and impregnable—the perpetual coming of immigrants—the wharfhem'd cities and superior marine—the unsurveyed interior—the loghouses and clearings and wild animals and hunters and trappers . . . the free commerce—the fisheries and whaling and gold-digging—the endless gestation of new states—the convening of Congress every December, the members duly coming up from all climates and the uttermost parts . . . the noble character of the young mechanics and of all free American workmen and workwomen . . . the general ardor and friendliness and enterprise—the perfect equality of the female with the male . . . the large amativeness—the fluid movement of the population—the factories and mercantile life and laborsaving machinery—the Yankee swap—the New-York firemen and the target excursion—the southern plantation life—the character of the northeast and of the northwest and southwest—slavery and the tremulous spreading of hands to protect it, and the stern opposition to it which shall never cease till it ceases or the speaking of tongues and the moving of lips cease. For such the expression of the American poet is to be transcendent and new. It is to be indirect and not direct or descriptive or epic. Its quality goes through these to much more. Let the age and wars of other nations be chanted and their eras and characters be illustrated and that finish the verse. Not so the great psalm of the republic. Here the theme is creative and has vista. Here comes one among the wellbeloved stonecutters and plans with decision and science and sees the solid and beautiful forms of the future where there are now no solid forms.

5   Of all nations the United States with veins full of poetical stuff most need poets and will doubtless have the greatest and use them the greatest. Their Presidents shall not be their common referee so much as their poets shall. Of all mankind the great poet is the equable man. Not in him but off from him things are grotesque or eccentric or fail of their sanity. Nothing out of its place is good and nothing in its place is bad. He bestows on every object or quality its fit proportions neither more nor less. He is the arbiter of the diverse and he is the key. He is the equalizer of his age and land . . . he supplies what wants supplying and checks what wants checking. If peace is the routine out of him speaks the spirit of peace, large, rich, thrifty, building vast and populous cities, encouraging agriculture and the arts and commerce—lighting the study of man, the soul, immortality—federal, state or municipal government, marriage, health, free-trade, intertravel by land and sea . . . nothing too close, nothing too far off . . . the stars not too far off. In war he is the most deadly force of the war. Who recruits him recruits horse and foot . . . he fetches parks of artillery the best that engineer ever knew. If the time becomes slothful and heavy he knows know to arouse it . . . he can make every word he speaks draw blood. Whatever stagnates in the flat of custom or obedience or legislation he never stagnates. Obedience does not master him, he masters it. High up out of reach he stands

turning a concentrated light . . . he turns the pivot with his finger . . . he baffles the swiftest runners as he stands and easily overtakes and envelops them. The time straying toward infidelity and confections and persiflage he withholds by his steady faith . . . he spreads out his dishes . . . he offers the sweet firmfibred meat that grows men and women. His brain is the ultimate brain. He is no arguer . . . he is judgment. He judges not as the judge judges but as the sun falling around a helpless thing. As he sees the farthest he has the most faith. His thoughts are the hymns of the praise of things. In the talk on the soul and eternity and God off of his equal plane he is silent. He sees eternity less like a play with a prologue and denouement . . . he sees eternity in men and women . . . he does not see men and women as dreams or dots. Faith is the antiseptic of the soul . . . it pervades the common people and preserves them . . . they never give up believing and expecting and trusting. There is that indescribable freshness and unconsciousness about an illiterate person that humbles and mocks the power of the noblest expressive genius. The poet sees for a certainty how one not a great artist may be just as sacred and perfect as the greatest artist. . . . The power to destroy or remould is freely used by him but never the power of attack. What is past is past. If he does not expose superior models and prove himself by every step he takes he is not what is wanted. The presence of the greatest poet conquers . . . not parleying or struggling or any prepared attempts. Now he has passed that way see after him! there is not left any vestige of despair or misanthropy or cunning or exclusiveness or the ignominy of a nativity or color or delusion of hell or the necessity of hell . . . and no man thenceforward shall be degraded for ignorance or weakness or sin.

WRITING ASSIGNMENTS

In the essay(s) you write on the following topics, be sure to summarize, paraphrase, or quote from the selections you have read in order to support, clarify, or find examples for your points.

1. If you have been writing about a person's motivation for a decision or action, enlarge the topic so that that person is now one example of a more general issue, for instance, the influence of family, the source of values, the conflict between home and school and television.

2. If you have been writing about an advertisement that offends your values, expand the essay to include where your values fit into the values of the larger society.

3. If you have been writing about how the media portray a certain group, expand the topic so the group in question becomes one example of a larger discussion, for instance, stereotypes in commercials, accuracy versus sympathy, the responsibility of the media.

4. If for your previous essays you have been exploring a single issue, combine that with another one to create a more general topic, for example, how

television commercials convey values through their portrayal of certain groups, or how your values motivated a particular action and your dislike of a specific commercial.

5. Write an essay about whether classic studies like "The Significance of the Frontier" or *The Theory of the Leisure Class,* written at the start of the twentieth century, still have anything to say to us about who we are.

6. Write an essay on one of the topics you (or the class) developed during the discussions for Making Connections.

7. Write an essay on a topic that emerged from the discussions of the selections by Hawthorne, Parkman, and Whitman.

ESSAY STRATEGIES

STRUCTURING THE OBJECTIVE ESSAY

As the preceding two chapters have shown, one difference between personal writing and objective writing is in what constitutes support. In a personal essay, anecdotes or statements of opinion are adequate. In **objective** writing, something else is needed as well. It is certainly all right for you to have opinions and to base them on personal experience, but you are also expected to look for support in other people's experiences, opinions, research, and writing.

Another difference between the two types of writing is in their organization. Essays that are required in most academic and business situations have a recognizable three-part structure: introduction, development, conclusion. As Mark Twain said, "First I tell them what I'm going to tell them. Then I tell them. Then I tell them I told them." This is not the only correct way to write an essay, and of course the introduction and conclusion are not as bald as Twain's joke implies. However, the three-part structure is the agreed upon, or conventional, way to write in certain circumstances. It constitutes an agreement between the reader and writer. The writer follows the conventions because the reader expects them, and not least important, following the conventions helps establish the writer's authority as someone who knows the rules of the game.

· THE FUNCTION OF THE MAIN IDEA

We said in Chapter 2 that a good reader asks, "Why is this here? What does it add?" That is, the reader tries to understand what every element in an essay contributes to the whole. This process succeeds only when the essay has a clear point or direction. In a serious conversation you don't want your friends to say they can't figure out what you're getting at; you also don't want that to happen in an essay. Needless to say, the whole process of free writing, drafting, critiquing, and revision implies that you don't always know at the beginning what your essay will look like at the end. By the time you pronounce the essay finished, however, it should certainly have a central focus or main idea. As we have already seen, everything must revolve around the main idea and develop out of it.

Skilled readers try to figure out the main idea as quickly as possible in order to help them interpret the remaining material. For example, knowing that the main idea in "What Makes Mario Run?" is that Cuomo is the product of two major influences allowed us to explain the significance of the passages we underlined. For this reason, good readers start looking for the main idea of an essay or paragraph immediately. Then, after forming a theory as to what it is, they use this possible main idea to understand what follows, and use what follows to test if this is, in fact, the main idea. As you have seen, if each new point supports, clarifies, qualifies, or adds to this suggested main idea, then it is probably correct; if each new idea does not fall into place in this way, the reader has probably misinterpreted the intent of the piece. Our whole discussion, however, presupposes that the essay is properly written.

As a writer, therefore, you must try to present your ideas in a way that meets expectations and makes the reader's job easy. During free writing and peer critiquing you are still searching for your ideas. Once you have decided what you want to say, you should organize your essay in a way that makes the main idea stand out and that clearly shows the relationship of each following point to the main idea. As a writer you should always put yourself in the position of your reader and ask whether what you are doing will be clear to someone else. You must always remember that when you are writing you have a wealth of background material in your mind, which you take for granted because you know what you intend to say. But the reader does not necessarily share this information, so it is your job to write what you want the reader to know. When you don't, when you make it unnecessarily hard to follow your thesis, the reader is likely to dismiss your ideas as disorganized or poorly thought out.

Although every sentence, paragraph, or essay must have a main idea, it may be located in a variety of places and dressed in a variety of ways. For example, we have already seen that in a personal profile in a newsmagazine, the main idea may appear in a subhead rather than in a paragraph. In the succeeding chapters we will read several *genres*—that is, types of writing—to see how the significant ideas of the past help us expand and mature our vision. But from this point onward we will concentrate on writing the conventional objective essay, also called the **expository** essay.

In contrast to the personal essay or profile, the expository essay generally has a thesis statement and paragraphs with topic sentences, and it carries on a silent dialogue with the reader. Let's examine each of its characteristics.

The Thesis Statement

In most well-written expository essays there is a straightforward statement of the main idea. Also called the **thesis statement,** it is usually stated in a single sentence, though it may sometimes be two or three sentences. It most often appears in the introduction of an essay, that is, in the first paragraph of a short essay or in the first few paragraphs of a longer work. However, it may also appear at the end, as a climactic conclusion.

The famous opening sentence of the Declaration of Independence contains a thesis statement:

> When in the course of human events it becomes necessary for one people to dissolve the political bands which have connected them with another, and to assume among the powers of the earth, the separate and equal station to which the Laws of Nature and of Nature's God entitle them, a decent respect to the opinions of mankind requires that they should declare the causes which impel them to the separation.

As part of our background knowledge, or previewing, of the Declaration of Independence we can note that many English colonists in America felt that they were not receiving the same rights as Englishmen in Great Britain. Escalating friction led to armed conflict, which broke out in April 1775. In the months that followed, the severity of the British response caused more and more colonists to believe that the rights they sought could be achieved only through independence. But there was no precedent for a colony to separate itself from a European power, and the Americans feared that other colonizing nations would side with Britain. The purpose of the Declaration of Independence of July 4, 1776, was to prove the legality of what the colonists were doing and to gain support from, rather than frighten, kings who themselves controlled colonial empires. The thesis statement, therefore, is "a decent respect (to the opinions of mankind) requires that they should declare the causes." In other words, the sentence tells the reader that what follows will be the colonists' reasons for renouncing allegiance to this specific king and empire.

Development and Conclusion

A thesis statement is a promise that more specific details will follow. In Mark Twain's formulation, the authors of the Declaration of Independence are telling the audience what they are going to tell them. Now, of course, they must tell them in the **development,** and then, in the **conclusion,** tell them they told them.

The second paragraph of the Declaration of Independence points back to the thesis statement by explaining the philosophical basis of the colonists' legal position: "We hold these truths to be self-evident" that people receive their rights from their Creator, that governments are made by men to serve them, and that it is the right of citizens to throw off a government that violates these "natural" laws. The third section, which makes up the bulk of the document, is a list of these violations—the actual reasons promised in the thesis statement: ". . . the present King of Great Britain . . . has refused . . . , forbidden . . . , obstructed . . . , plundered . . . , destroyed. . . ." The last paragraph is the logical conclusion: All of these reasons being true, therefore "these United Colonies are, and of Right ought to be free and independent states." Clearly, our theory about the thesis statement helped us understand the significance of each of the following parts, and the way each part fell into place proved that we had correctly identified the thesis statement and, in consequence, the point of the document.

Similarly, the thesis statement of "Italian-American Stereotypes on TV," a student paper which you read in Chapter 1 (p. 26), clarifies the following paragraphs and is in turn clarified by them.

In the first paragraph, each of the following three statements sounds like a possible thesis statement:

(1) Various dialects are used on TV to "sell" products and characters, (2) and producers depend on the viewer's prejudices against or identification with certain ethnic groups for success in this approach. (3) In the case of Italian-Americans, this has led to reinforcing a negative stereotype.

The first statement is a generalization about how speech patterns are used to "sell"—that is, gain acceptance for—products and characters. If it is the thesis statement we should expect the essay to show how a wide range of products and characters has gained acceptance through the use of distinctive speech patterns on TV. The second statement shifts the focus to how producers use attitudes which the viewers already have. If it is the thesis statement we should again expect an essay that covers many groups, but one that also shows that television follows, rather than creates, public opinion. The third statement is very specific: Italian-Americans are made to look bad because of how they speak. If it is the thesis statement we should expect the examples to be limited to Italian-Americans and to be unflattering. A skilled reader will theorize that this last choice is the most likely thesis because (1) it is most specific, suggesting it can be treated adequately in a short essay, and (2) it is not introduced by a phrase like "for example," which would have implied that it is only one illustration of the larger topic that will be presented.

The second paragraph elaborates on the first two points made in the first paragraph:

(1) Since the use of dialect is a means of manipulating the viewer's attitude, accents are used primarily to show the authenticity of products. (2)
Unfortunately, however, an ethnic "caste system"
results from this method of advertising. (3) Individual ethnic groups will only be seen engaging in
certain activities or using particular products. (4)
The success of the commercials depends on the viewer's
familiarity with products and his ability to associate
these products with specific groups. (5) Therefore,
the use of language encourages stereotyping and sponsors benefit through societal prejudices and
attitudes.

The paragraph explains the mechanism by which television uses society's exist-ing prejudices and attitudes about language to create a sense of authenticity. Since the paragraph does not specifically mention Italian-Americans, our choice of thesis statement seems weakened. But we might still be correct. The general mechanism described in this paragraph would apply to Italian-Americans as well as to any other group. If the essay is going to be about negative images of Italian-Americans, this paragraph may be a general explanation that will account for the specific charge.

That it is, in fact, about the Italian-American image becomes clear in the third and following paragraphs. Starting with "An example of manipulation through stereotyping is the use of Italian-American dialect" in the third paragraph, every paragraph until the conclusion gives examples of limiting or un-favorable images of Italian-Americans: They are cooks, auto mechanics, and high school dropouts. The conclusion clinches this understanding of the essay: "Through dialect, television commercials exploit the Italian-American stereotype and in no way glamorize or elevate the Italian-American image." The third statement of the first paragraph was the thesis statement and helped us explain the purpose of each succeeding idea and example.

Topic Sentences

Just as an essay has a main idea that holds its parts together, so does a paragraph. And just as the main idea of an essay is usually contained in a straightforward thesis statement, the main idea of a paragraph in an expository essay is in the **topic sentence.** Most often the topic sentence is the first sentence in a paragraph, or the second (as in this paragraph) or third (as in the next), when the first sentence acts as a bridge to a previous idea. But even more than the thesis statement, topic sentences have considerable freedom and may appear almost anywhere in a paragraph. Needless to say, the organization of a paragraph and the location of its topic sentence should be an aspect of your overall strategy in evolving and deciding exactly what it is you want to say.

We saw in Chapter 2 that a journalistic profile often hangs information on a hook provided by a speaker or situation. This is generally not the case in expository essays. Instead, an expository essay organizes examples, anecdotes, and quotations into paragraphs that are built on concepts. A well-written expository paragraph is built on one central point, and this main point is almost always contained in a clearly stated topic sentence. In most cases the topic sentence makes a general statement that the rest of the sentences in the paragraph explain, support, or elaborate on. When a point is not very complex, a single paragraph with a topic sentence and a few additional sentences may be all that is needed for an adequate treatment. In other cases, however, a complicated idea may require an essay with a number of paragraphs; in this case, each paragraph then deals with one aspect of the larger idea and contains a topic sentence stating what that aspect is.

To see how a topic sentence gives direction to the rest of its paragraph, let's examine the following passage from Henry Adams's *History of the United States of America during the Administrations of Thomas Jefferson:*

(1) Nothing was more elusive than the spirit of American democracy. (2) Jefferson, the literary representative of the class, spoke chiefly for the Virginians, and dreaded so greatly his own reputation as a visionary that he seldom or never uttered his whole thought. (3) Gallatin and Madison were still more cautious. (4) The press in no country could give shape to a mental condition so shadowy. (5) The people themselves, although mil-

lions in number, could not have expressed their finer instincts had they tried, and might not have recognized them if expressed by others.

Based on the definition that the topic sentence states the main idea of a paragraph and holds together its parts, we can conclude that the first sentence is the topic sentence: "Nothing was more elusive than the spirit of American democracy." The second sentence then explains that Thomas Jefferson, a gifted writer and leading supporter of the democratic movement, did not clarify its guiding spirit because he was afraid of being considered too visionary. The third sentence provides two more examples of men—Gallatin and Madison—who might have been expected to clarify the spirit of democracy but did not. The fourth sentence then says that the press could not be expected to explain something so difficult; it implies that the press did not do it. The last sentence says that the people themselves did not have the skill or intellectual power to explain what motivated them. Thus, every sentence from the second to the last points back to the generalization presented in the first sentence. This is a successful topic sentence.

The first sentence is also the topic sentence of the third paragraph of "Italian-American Stereotypes on TV":

(1) An example of manipulation through stereotyping is the use of Italian-American dialect, specifically the Brooklyn inflection, in various spaghetti sauce commercials. (2) "Dick and Zesty" Ragu is a prepared sauce which is commercialized by individuals speaking with this dialect. (3) Since Italians are noted for their culinary expertise, the predictable response of the viewer would be "If Italians are using Ragu it must be great sauce."

Having said in the two paragraphs we previously analyzed that television producers use viewer attitudes about speech patterns to assign ethnic groups to particular activities, the writer here offers the appearance of Italian-Americans in spaghetti sauce commercials as a concrete example of such manipulation. The second sentence illustrates how Italian-American speech is mimicked in the

Ragu commercial—"dick" instead of "thick," since this group is supposed to say "Dees, dem, and dose" instead of "these, them, and those." The third sentence explains how the viewer is manipulated into assuming the product is good because of preexisting beliefs about Italians and food. Here too, then, the topic sentence directs us to the main idea of the paragraph.

The Silent Dialogue Between Reader and Writer

We have already seen that a critical reader is an active participant, creating hypotheses, asking questions, predicting the direction of the essay. The good writer, therefore, tries to predict what the reader will want to know, in order to answer any questions or objections before they become distractions. Clearly, the interaction works both ways: The writer tries to predict the reader's questions, and the reader tries to reconstruct the writer's thought process. It is almost as if there were a silent dialogue between the two, as we can see by looking again at the paragraph by Henry Adams. The questions he assumes the reader will ask are in square brackets:

> Nothing was more elusive than the spirit of American democracy. [Why? Weren't the Founding Fathers political theorists?] Jefferson, the literary representative of the class, spoke chiefly for the Virginians, and dreaded so greatly his own reputation as a visionary that he seldom or never uttered his whole thought. [What about Madison and the "Federalist Papers"?] Gallatin and Madison were still more cautious. [Wasn't the colonial press in the forefront of the struggle?] The press in no country could give shape to a mental condition so shadowy. [Didn't the people themselves know what they were doing?] The people themselves, although millions in number, could not have expressed their finer instincts had they tried, and might not have recognized them if expressed by others.

We can also think in terms of the questions that a skilled reader asks—"Why is this here? What does this add?" Now, the reader's answers are in the brackets:

> Nothing was more elusive than the spirit of American democracy. [Now he'll prove that.] Jefferson, the literary representative of the class, spoke chiefly for the Virginians, and dreaded so greatly his own reputation as a visionary that he seldom or never uttered his whole thought. [That explains why one leader of the party didn't do it.] Gallatin and Madison were still more cautious. [That explains why these two leaders didn't do it.] The press in no country could give shape to a mental condition so shadowy. [That explains why this important group didn't do it.] The people themselves, although millions in number, could not have expressed their finer instincts had they tried, and might not have recognized them if expressed

by others. [That accounts for the people. I see he went from individuals to a group to the whole people—a climactic order.]

Of course, the reader reacts and asks questions simultaneously. Here, for example, are some implied questions and interpretations that guided the writer and reader through the third paragraph of "Italian-American Stereotypes on TV":

An example of manipulation through stereotyping is the use of Italian-American dialect, specifically the Brooklyn inflection, in various spaghetti sauce commercials. [This is a specific ethnic group that is stereotyped in the way described in the previous paragraph. Can you give me an example?] "Dick and Zesty" Ragu is a prepared sauce which is commercialized by individuals speaking with this dialect. [This commercial exploits the speech pattern of this group by using "dick" instead of "thick." But where is the manipulation?] Since Italians are noted for their culinary expertise, the predictable response of the viewer would be "If Italians are using Ragu it must be great sauce." [This is the manipulation that the writer objects to.]

Other Locations for the Topic Sentence

We have already said that the topic sentence does not have to be the first sentence in a paragraph, and we find other locations as we continue examining the two selections we have been reading. In the paragraphs we just analyzed, the writers make a general statement and then support it with specific examples. But a writer may also present a series of specifics and tie them together by drawing a conclusion, or the topic sentence can serve as the transition between two ideas.

By creating a hypothesis—a theory about what the topic sentence is—and using it while reading, skillful readers discover the writer's technique and become engaged in it. And by knowing that they are doing this, the writer can enter into a dialogue with the readers.

The following paragraph, which comes right after the one we just read from "Italian-American Stereotypes on TV," first lays out the details and then ends with a topic sentence which draws the conclusion the author wants us to see:

The Prince Spaghetti commercial is also interesting. The narrator speaks as the viewer is taken into an Italian-American kitchen of the north end of Boston. One may get the impression that a sociological study is taking place. A boy's mother calls from a window, "Ant-a-nee" with an Italian inflection. The narrator, speaking without a distinguishable dialect or accent, takes the viewer on an investigation of the Italian-American kitchen. Again, based on their prejudicial attitude regarding Italian cooking, the viewers are manipulated into believing Prince Spaghetti is special.

The following paragraph, which continues the earlier discussion of the elusiveness of the spirit of American democracy, uses the topic sentence to contrast the facts that begin the paragraph with the point Adams wants to make in the rest of the paragraph. For clarity, we have put the topic sentence in italics:

In the early days of colonization, every new settlement represented an idea and proclaimed a mission. Virginia was founded by a great, liberal movement aiming at the spread of English liberty and empire. The Pilgrims of Plymouth, the Puritans of Boston, the Quakers of Pennsylvania, all avowed a moral purpose, and began by making institutions that consciously reflected a moral idea. *No such character belonged to the colonization of 1800.* From Lake Erie to Florida, in long, unbroken line, pioneers were at work, cutting into the forests with the energy of so many beavers, and with no more express moral purpose than the beavers they drove away. The civilization they carried with them was rarely illumined by an idea; they sought room for no new truth, and aimed neither at creating, like the Puritans, a government of saints, nor, like the Quakers, one of love and peace; they left such experiments behind them, and wrestled only with the hardest problems of frontier life. No wonder that foreign observers, and even the educated, well-to-do Americans of the sea-coast, could seldom see anything to admire in the ignorance and brutality of frontiersmen, and should declare that virtue and wisdom no longer guided the United States! What they saw was not encouraging. To a new society, ignorant and semibarbarous, a mass of demagogues insisted on applying every stimulant that could inflame its worst appetites, while at the same instant taking away every influence that had hitherto helped to restrain its passions. Greed for wealth, lust for power, yearning for the blank void of savage freedom such as Indians and wolves delighted in,—these were the fires that flamed under the caldron of American society, in which, as conservatives believed, the old, well-proven, conservative crust of religion, government, family, and even common respect for age, education, and experience was rapidly melting away, and was indeed already broken into fragments, swept about by the seething mass of scum ever rising in greater quantities to the surface.

Using the Conventions to Clarify the Main Idea

Now that we know how a reader thinks while trying to understand what we have written, let's look at how a writer can improve an essay by making it clearer to the reader. The following essay was written by a student, Brian Larsen, for the assignment asking him to describe and analyze a commercial that he found unsuccessful:

First Draft:

1   The advertisement that bothers me most is the
McDonald's Mac Tonight campaign. The product is a hamburger, McDonald's "Big Mac." Basically, the ad shows
a man with a moonhead singing "Mac the Knife" while

hovering over the city. He's telling us to enjoy the great taste of "Dinner" at McDonald's tonight. It seems to me as if this commercial is aired on every television show I watch and now every time I see this guy the less likely I am to go to McDonald's.

2   Apparently the "Moonhead" is used to get your attention, which it does, but I fail to see the connection between this guy and the hamburgers. Seeing and hearing the same commercial many times a day will turn me away from a product rather than towards it. Also I don't consider eating at McDonald's to be a "dinner."

3   I think this commercial is targeting a youthful audience that is interested in gimmicks. This would be much more tolerable if the ads were less frequent. I like the music but not the visual, so when the ad is on the radio it seems more sensible.

This paper has some promising features: The student has definite opinions about what he likes and dislikes, and he also tries to explain who might like the aspects of the commercial that bother him, that is, who the intended audience could be.

But how many things bother him? Why? Are the faults he finds in the commercial all equally significant? Can they be corrected in a way that will satisfy him? The answers to these questions are not clear because when we, as careful readers, ask of each sentence in this essay, "Why is this here? What does this add?" our job is too hard. We have difficulty connecting everything to a thesis statement and topic sentences. The problems with the organization of this essay become especially clear if you try to outline it by using topic sentences and supporting details, as we did with "What Makes Mario Run?" in Chapter 2 (where we used the term *secondary thesis statement*).

Using our checklist for critiquing and critical reading, we might ask the following of the first paragraph:

What is the point (thesis) of this essay? Is it given in a thesis statement? Is there anything here that will help us understand or interpret what follows?

Does it tell us what idea holds the essay together?

What is the purpose of this paragraph? Is it introducing the essay as a whole?

Is it describing the commercial? Is it giving his reasons for not liking the commercial?

What is the significance of the man with a moonhead singing "Mac the Knife"?

Why is this information followed by a sentence telling us that this man wants us to "enjoy the great taste of 'Dinner' at McDonald's"? Why is "Dinner" in quotation marks?

Why is this followed by the complaint that the commercial appears too frequently?

This paragraph leaves us with many unanswered questions because it tries to do too much. It touches on, but does not explain, (1) the description of the commercial, (2) an implied problem with the word "dinner," (3) the frequency of the commercial. Of course, unanswered questions after the first paragraph of an essay are not a fatal problem—if they are eventually answered. Topic sentences serve a vital function in this respect: A skilled reader will immediately skim the next few paragraphs, looking for topic sentences that show whether these questions will be systematically addressed. But in this essay we do not find such topic sentences or answers.

The second paragraph does not have a topic sentence that holds together everything in the paragraph. Instead the paragraph has three sentences, one for each of the three questions that we were left with after the previous paragraph. The first sentence refers to the content of the commercial. The second repeats the student's dislike of constant repetition. And the third returns to the problem of "dinner." This last sentence, however, is the best in the paragraph because it adds the very important personal opinion that "I don't consider eating at McDonald's to be a 'dinner.'" We do not know the reason for this opinion, but we can now infer that the quotation marks are meant to indicate that "dinner" is not used literally or accurately in this commercial.

Similarly, the third paragraph begins by referring to the gimmick, then repeats the complaint about frequency, and finally adds a distinction between the annoying visual in the commercial and the acceptable music. This distinction, though, suggests that frequency in general may not bother the writer, only the frequency of a particular commercial that he does not like.

The objections we have listed were the problems raised by three of the student's classmates and the teacher during a group discussion of the essay. The student took notes during the critiquing process and then rewrote the essay.

Second Draft:

1   The advertisement that annoys me the most these days is McDonald's "Mac Tonight" campaign, promoting their basic menu of hamburgers and fries.

2   The ad shows a man with a moon-head playing a piano and singing a song which was originally called "Mac the Knife," while hovering over the city at night. The words have been changed to promote "Mac Tonight." He's telling us to enjoy the great taste of "dinner" at McDonald's which to me is a contradiction. I think of McDonald's as fast food, when you don't have time for a real dinner. As far as great taste goes the food is just something to ward off hunger. To me dinner is a time when my family sits down to a balanced meal in comfortable surroundings and our money is spent on good nutrition.

3   Apparently the moon-head is used to get your attention, which it does, but I fail to see the connection between this guy and hamburgers. I think this gimmick is targeted for teenagers because of his sunglasses and "cool" mannerisms. The song is an old Bobby Darin tune called "Mac the Knife" which may appeal to a generation now in their 30's and 40's. By using this combination the advertisers are hoping to reach a wider audience, and by promoting dinner they

hope to increase the frequency in which people go to eat there.

4   I like the music but not the visual, so when the ad comes on the radio it seems more sensible. The lyrics which have been chosen to go with the tune are tolerable but after seeing the TV ad you immediately think of this "Moonie." Also the ads are run too frequently for me, I don't like to have something repeated over and over as if to brainwash me that this is the greatest product.

5   In my opinion if the ad concentrated more on nutrition, variety of choice, and value I would be more motivated than with gimmicks. If they truly want to expand with dinner, have a real salad bar and specialties for dinner like they have for breakfast. Service is also something that should be stressed because that can bring satisfaction and repeat business.

The first paragraph has been reduced to one sentence. It tries to do much less than the first paragraph of the previous draft, but it does it successfully. This is a straightforward introduction to the content of the essay.

The second paragraph describes the commercial and gives the student's first reason for not liking it: A fast-food hamburger is not his idea of dinner. This paragraph also answers several of the questions raised about the first draft. A connection is drawn between "Mac the Knife" and "Mac Tonight," though it is not explained. The quotation marks on "dinner" are now clear. And the student has explained in some detail what part dinner plays in his family. Unfortunately, the paragraph still lacks a clear topic sentence because it has two separate parts: the description of the commercial and a reason for not liking it. Also, the student briefly shrugs off the claim that this food has "great taste." There is no arguing with taste, of course, and neither the claim nor his rejection of it can be defended objectively.

In the third paragraph the writer admits that he cannot see a connection between the moon-head and hamburgers, but he offers reasons for the other gimmicks in the commercial and choice of song. The gimmicks and the song appeal to two different groups, and after explaining them separately, the student pulls them together in the last sentence of the paragraph: "By using this combination the advertisers are hoping to reach a wider audience." This is the topic sentence of the third paragraph.

The fourth paragraph states the writer's distinction between his distaste for the visual and happiness with the music. But aside from simply saying that he likes one and not the other, there is no explanation. Apparently his inability to understand the connection between the moon-head and hamburgers grates on him whenever he sees the commercial. The final sentence in the paragraph repeats his complaint that the commercial appears too frequently.

The last paragraph is entirely new. Here the writer discusses what kind of advertisement would appeal to him. As he says in the first sentence, he is interested in nutrition, variety, and value, not gimmicks. This is the topic sentence of the paragraph; the paragraph is a climactic ending of the essay.

As the preceding comments show, the peer critique of the second draft noted its significant improvement over the first draft, and also pointed out some areas that readers still found problematic. Based on the discussion, the student rewrote the essay.

Third Draft:

1   The advertisement that annoys me the most these days is McDonald's' "Mac Tonight" campaign, promoting their basic menu of hamburgers and fries. The ad shows a man with a moon-head playing a piano and singing a song which was originally called "Mac the Knife," while hovering over the city at night. The lyrics of the song have been changed to "Mac Tonight," a play on words to turn the song into a product promotion.

2   The moon-head tells us to enjoy the great taste of "dinner" at McDonald's. To me this is a contradiction. I think of McDonald's as fast food, when you don't have time for a real dinner. My idea of dinner is a time when my family sits down to a balanced meal in comfortable surroundings and our money is spent on good nutrition.

3   Apparently the moon-head is used to get your attention, which it does, and to symbolize the night which would be dinner time. I think this gimmick is targeted for teenagers because of his sunglasses and "cool" mannerisms. The original "Mac the Knife" song was sung by Bobby Darin in the late 50's and was popular in the 60's, thereby appealing to a generation now in their 30's and 40's. By using this combination the advertisers are hoping to reach a wider audience, and by promoting dinner they hope to increase the frequency in which people go to eat there.

4   In my opinion if McDonald's concentrated more on nutrition, variety of choice, and value I would be more motivated to buy their products. If they truly want to expand with dinner, they should have a full salad bar and specialties for dinner like they have for breakfast. Service is also something that should be stressed because that can bring satisfaction and repeat business.

In this last version, the description of the advertisement has been moved to the first paragraph, immediately after its first mention in the topic sentence. The second paragraph can now concentrate on the student's first reason for not liking a commercial that calls fast-food hamburgers "dinner." As the topic sentence says, "To me this is a contradiction."

The third paragraph is substantially the same as in the previous draft, with one important difference. The writer has now included an analysis of the connection between the moon-head and the product: It is an attempt to link the hamburgers with evening and dinnertime.

The last paragraph is also substantially the same as in the previous draft, though it shifts the focus of the suggestion from the commercial to McDonald's itself. This change is an improvement, since the company, not the advertisement, would have to expand the menu.

Finally, it is interesting that two significant improvements are the result of omissions. In the second paragraph the writer has omitted the remark about the "great taste" of the food, perhaps because he could not support it objectively. The entire paragraph about the annoying frequency of the commercial has also been cut. In conference he explained that since constant repetition of any commercial annoys him, the complaint had nothing to do with this specific one.

The significant improvement of the third version over the original can be seen by making an outline with the topic sentences and supporting details:

Thesis: "Mac Tonight" ad annoys me

    1. "Dinner" is a contradiction.

        A. McDonald's is fast food.

        B. My idea is family, comfort, nutrition.

    2. They hope to reach wider audience.

        A. Gimmick for teenagers

        B. Music for 30's and 40's

    3. They should offer nutrition, variety, value.

        A. Better and varied choices

        B. Better service

CHECKLIST FOR EXPOSITORY ESSAYS

An expository essay has

introduction, development, conclusion
paragraphs organized around a single idea
thesis statement for main idea of essay
topic sentences for main idea of paragraphs

· ESSAYS FOR CRITICAL READING

Among the rights that Americans take for granted is freedom of speech. But from the earliest days of the nation, debate has raged over whether limits should be imposed. When Matthew Fraser, a student at Bethel High School in Washington, used a sexual metaphor as the basis for a speech to a school assembly, he was suspended. Fraser sued, and both the District Court and Court of Appeals ruled that his First Amendment rights had been violated. The school district appealed to the Supreme Court. Parts I and II of the court's opinion, which was written by Chief Justice Warren Burger, review the details of the case. Part III, given here, is the basis of the ruling. "Tinker's armband" refers to a case in which a student won the right to wear a black armband in school as a protest against the war in Vietnam; "Cohen's jacket" condemned the military draft in vulgar language.

BETHEL SCHOOL DISTRICT V. FRASER (1986)

1   The role and purpose of the American public school system was well described by two historians, saying "public education must prepare pupils for citizenship in the Republic. . . . It must inculcate the habits and manners of civility as values in themselves conducive to happiness and as indispensable to the practice of self-government in the community and the nation." C. Beard & M. Beard, New Basic History of the United States (1968). In *Ambach v. Norwick* (1979), we echoed the essence of this statement of the objectives of public education as the "inculcat[ion of] fundamental values necessary to the maintenance of a democratic political system."

2   These fundamental values of "habits and manners of civility" essential to a democratic society must, of course, include tolerance of divergent political and religious views, even when the views expressed may be unpopular. But these "fundamental values" must also take into account consideration of the sensibilities of others, and, in the case of a school, the sensibilities of fellow students. The undoubted freedom to advocate unpopular and controversial views in schools and classrooms must be balanced against the society's countervailing interest in teaching students the boundaries of socially appropriate behavior. Even the most heated political discourse in a democratic society requires consideration for the personal sensibilities of the other participants and audiences.

3   In our Nation's legislative halls, where some of the most vigorous political debates in our society are carried on, there are rules prohibiting the use of expressions offensive to other participants in the debate. The Manual of Parliamentary Practice, drafted by Thomas Jefferson and adopted by the House of Representatives to govern the proceedings in that body, prohibits the use of

"impertinent" speech during debate and likewise provides that "[n]o person is to use indecent language against the proceedings of the House." (Jefferson's Manual governs the House in all cases to which it applies.) The Rules of Debate applicable in the Senate likewise provide that a Senator may be called to order for imputing improper motives to another Senator or for referring offensively to any State. Senators have been censured for abusive language directed at other Senators. . . . Can it be that what is proscribed in the halls of Congress is beyond the reach of school officials to regulate?

4   The First Amendment guarantees wide freedom in matters of adult public discourse. A sharply divided Court upheld the right to express an antidraft viewpoint in a public place, albeit in terms highly offensive to most citizens. See *Cohen v. California* (1971). It does not follow, however, that simply because the use of an offensive form of expression may not be prohibited to adults making what the speaker considers a political point, that the same latitude must be permitted to children in a public school. In *New Jersey v. T.L.O.* (1985), we reaffirmed that the constitutional rights of students in public school are not automatically coextensive with the rights of adults in other settings. As cogently expressed by Judge Newman, "the First Amendment gives a high school student the classroom right to wear Tinker's armband, but not Cohen's jacket." *Thomas v. Board of Education*, Granville Central School Dist. (CA2 1979).

5   Surely it is a highly appropriate function of public school education to prohibit the use of vulgar and offensive terms in public discourse. Indeed, the "fundamental values necessary to the maintenance of a democratic political system" disfavor the use of terms of debate highly offensive or highly threatening to others. Nothing in the Constitution prohibits the states from insisting that certain modes of expression are inappropriate and subject to sanctions. The inculcation of these values is truly the "work of the schools." The determination of what manner of speech in the classroom or in school assembly is inappropriate properly rests with the school board.

6   The process of educating our youth for citizenship in public schools is not confined to books, the curriculum, and the civics class; schools must teach by example the shared values of a civilized social order. Consciously or otherwise, teachers—and indeed the older students—demonstrate the appropriate form of civil discourse and political expression by their conduct and deportment in and out of class. Inescapably, like parents, they are role models. The schools, as instruments of the state, may determine that the essential lessons of civil, mature conduct cannot be conveyed in a school that tolerates lewd, indecent, or offensive speech and conduct such as that indulged in by this confused boy.

7   The pervasive sexual innuendo in Fraser's speech was plainly offensive to both teachers and students—indeed to any mature person. By glorifying male sexuality, and in its verbal content, the speech was acutely insulting to teenage girl students. The speech could well be seriously damaging to its less mature audience, many of whom were only 14 years old and on the threshold of awareness

of human sexuality. Some students were reported as bewildered by the speech and the reaction of mimicry it provoked.

8   This Court's First Amendment jurisprudence has acknowledged limitations on the otherwise absolute interest of the speaker in reaching an unlimited audience where the speech is sexually explicit and the audience may include children. In *Ginsberg v. New York* (1968) this Court upheld a New York statute banning the sale of sexually oriented material to minors, even though the material in question was entitled to First Amendment protection with respect to adults. And in addressing the question whether the First Amendment places any limit on the authority of public schools to remove books from a public school library, all Members of the Court, otherwise sharply divided, acknowledged that the school board has the authority to remove books that are vulgar. *Board of Education v. Pico* (1982). These cases recognize the obvious concern on the part of parents, and school authorities acting *in loco parentis* to protect children—especially in a captive audience—from exposure to sexually explicit, indecent, or lewd speech.

9   We have also recognized an interest in protecting minors from exposure to vulgar and offensive spoken language. In FCC v. *Pacifica Foundation* (1978), we dealt with the power of the Federal Communications Commission to regulate a radio broadcast described as "indecent but not obscene." There the Court reviewed an administrative condemnation of the radio broadcast of a self-styled "humorist" who described his own performance as being in "the words you couldn't say on the public, ah, airwaves, um, the ones you definitely wouldn't say ever." The Commission concluded that "certain words depicted sexual and excretory activities in a patently offensive manner, [and] noted that they 'were broadcast at a time when children were undoubtedly in the audience.'" The Commission issued an order declaring that the radio station was guilty of broadcasting indecent language in violation of 18 U.S.C. §1464. The Court of Appeals set aside the Commission's determination, and we reversed, reinstating the Commission's citation of the station. We concluded that the broadcast was properly considered "obscene, indecent, or profane" within the meaning of the statute. The plurality opinion went on to reject the radio station's assertion of a First Amendment right to broadcast vulgarity:

> "These words offend for the same reasons that obscenity offends. Their place in the hierarchy of First Amendment values was aptly sketched by Mr. Justice Murphy when he said: '[S]uch utterances are no essential part of any exposition of ideas, and are of such slight social value as a step to truth that any benefit that may be derived from them is clearly outweighed by the social interest in order and morality.' *Chaplinsky v. New Hampshire* [1942]."

10   We hold that petitioner School District acted entirely within its permissible authority in imposing sanctions upon Fraser in response to his offensively lewd and indecent speech. Unlike the sanctions imposed on the students wearing armbands in *Tinker*, the penalties imposed in this case were unrelated to any

political viewpoint. The First Amendment does not prevent the school officials from determining that to permit a vulgar and lewd speech such as respondent's would undermine the school's basic educational mission. A high school assembly or classroom is no place for a sexually explicit monologue directed towards an unsuspecting audience of teenage students. Accordingly, it was perfectly appropriate for the school to disassociate itself to make the point to the pupils that vulgar speech and lewd conduct is wholly inconsistent with the "fundamental values" of public school education. Justice Black, dissenting in *Tinker*, made a point that is especially relevant in this case:

> I wish therefore, . . . to disclaim any purpose . . . to hold that the federal Constitution compels the teachers, parents and elected school officials to surrender control of the American public school system to public school students." . . .

11   The judgment of the Court of Appeals for the Ninth Circuit is reversed.

SIGNIFICANCE

Explain the significance of the following quotations to the point or structure of the selection:

". . . 'public education must prepare pupils for citizenship in the Republic. . . . It must inculcate the habits and manners of civility as values in themselves. . . .' "

"In our Nation's legislative halls, where some of the most vigorous political debates in our society are carried on, there are rules prohibiting the use of expressions offensive to other participants in the debate."

"The determination of what manner of speech in the classroom or in school assembly is inappropriate properly rests with the school board."

"The process of educating our youth for citizenship in public schools is not confined to books, the curriculum, and the civics class; schools must teach by example the shared values of a civilized social order."

"The speech could well be seriously damaging to its less mature audience. . . ."

FUTURE USE

What is the main point of this selection? What is the thesis statement?
What is the topic sentence and point of each paragraph?
Briefly summarize the selection.
Outline the structure and main points.
What information in this selection is relevant to your essay(s)? How could you use this information?

Andrew Carnegie immigrated to the United States from Scotland in 1848 at the age of 13. He worked in a cotton factory and telegraph office and for the railroad before starting his own iron company. By 1888 he owned steel mills, coalfields, a railroad, and a steamship line. When strikers at his plant in Homestead, Pennsylvania, fought a bloody battle with armed company guards in 1892, the state militia was called in and unionization of the steel industry was blocked for almost half a century. After creating U.S. Steel from his holdings in 1901, Carnegie retired and devoted himself to the public welfare. He established the Carnegie Foundation for the Advancement of Teaching and the Carnegie Institute of Technology, and supported Booker T. Washington's Tuskegee Institute, a black college.

In a famous essay, Carnegie proposed that men spend half their lives gaining wealth and half giving it away. The opening of the essay, reprinted here, gives his view of social organization in order to set the stage for his proposal.

From WEALTH
by Andrew Carnegie

1   The problem of our age is the proper administration of wealth, so that the ties of brotherhood may still bind together the rich and poor in harmonious relationship. The conditions of human life have not only been changed, but revolutionized, within the past few hundred years. In former days there was little difference between the dwelling, dress, food, and environment of the chief and those of his retainers. The Indians are to-day where civilized man then was. When visiting the Sioux, I was led to the wigwam of the chief. It was just like the others in external appearance, and even within the difference was trifling between it and those of the poorest of his braves. The contrast between the palace of the millionaire and the cottage of the laborer with us to-day measures the change which has come with civilization.

2   This change, however, is not to be deplored, but welcomed as highly beneficial. It is well, nay, essential for the progress of the race, that the houses of some should be homes for all that is highest and best in literature and the arts, and for all the refinements of civilization, rather than that none should be so. Much better this great irregularity than universal squalor. Without wealth there can be no Maecenas. The "good old times" were not good old times. Neither master nor servant was as well situated then as to-day. A relapse to old conditions would be disastrous to both—not the least so to him who serves—and would sweep away civilization with it. But whether the change be for good or ill, it is upon us, beyond our power to alter, and therefore to be accepted and made the best of. It is a waste of time to criticize the inevitable.

3   It is easy to see how the change has come. One illustration will serve for almost every phase of the cause. In the manufacture of products we have the

whole story. It applies to all combinations of human industry, as stimulated and enlarged by the inventions of this scientific age. Formerly articles were manufactured at the domestic hearth or in small shops which formed part of the household. The master and his apprentices worked side by side, the latter living with the master, and therefore subject to the same conditions. When these apprentices rose to be masters, there was little or no change in their mode of life, and they, in turn, educated in the same routine succeeding apprentices. There was, substantially, social equality, and even political equality, for those engaged in industrial pursuits had then little or no political voice in the State.

4   But the inevitable result of such a mode of manufacture was crude articles at high prices. To-day the world obtains commodities of excellent quality at prices which even the generation preceding this would have deemed incredible. In the commercial world similar causes have produced similar results, and the race is benefited thereby. The poor enjoy what the rich could not before afford. What were the luxuries have become the necessaries of life. The laborer has now more comforts than the farmer had a few generations ago. The farmer has more luxuries than the landlord had, and is more richly clad and better housed. The landlord has books and pictures rarer, and appointments more artistic, than the King could then obtain.

5   The price we pay for this salutary change is, no doubt, great. We assemble thousands of operatives in the factory, in the mine, and in the counting-house, of whom the employer can know little or nothing, and to whom the employer is little better than a myth. All intercourse between them is at an end. Rigid Castes are formed, and, as usual, mutual ignorance breeds mutual distrust. Each Caste is without sympathy for the other, and ready to credit anything disparaging in regard to it. Under the law of competition, the employer of thousands is forced into the strictest economies, among which the rates paid to labor figure prominently, and often there is friction between the employer and the employed, between capital and labor, between rich and poor. Human society loses homogeneity.

6   The price which society pays for the law of competition, like the price it pays for cheap comforts and luxuries, is also great; but the advantages of this law are also greater still, for it is to this law that we owe our wonderful material development, which brings improved conditions in its train. But, whether the law is benign or not, we must say of it, as we say of the change in the conditions of men to which we have referred: It is here, we cannot evade it; no substitutes for it have been found; and while the law may be sometimes hard for the individual, it is best for the race, because it insures the survival of the fittest in every department. We accept and welcome, therefore, as conditions to which we must accommodate ourselves, great inequality of environment, the concentration of business, industrial and commercial, in the hands of a few, and the law of competition between these, as being not only beneficial, but essential for the future progress of the race. Having accepted these, it follows that there must be

great scope for the exercise of special ability in the merchant and in the manu-facturer who has to conduct affairs upon a great scale. That this talent for organization and management is rare among men is proved by the fact that it invariably secures for its possessor enormous rewards, no matter where or under what laws or conditions. The experienced in affairs always rate the MAN whose services can be obtained as a partner as not only the first consideration, but such as to render the question of his capital scarcely worth considering, for such men soon create capital; while, without the special talent required, capital soon takes wings. Such men become interested in forms or corporations using millions; and estimating only simple interest to be made upon the capital invested, it is inevitable that their income must exceed their expenditures, and that they must accumulate wealth. Nor is there any middle ground which such men can occupy, because the great manufacturing or commercial concern which does not earn at least interest upon its capital soon becomes bankrupt. It must either go forward or fall behind: to stand still is impossible. It is a condition essential for its successful operation that it should be thus far profitable, and even that, in addition to interest on capital, it should make profit. It is a law, as certain as any of the others named, that men possessed of this peculiar talent for affairs, under the free play of economic forces, must, of necessity, soon be in receipt of more revenue than can be judiciously expended upon themselves; and this law is as beneficial for the race as the others.

7   Objections to the foundations upon which society is based are not in order, because the condition of the race is better with these than it has been with any others which have been tried. Of the effect of any new substitutes proposed we cannot be sure. The Socialist or Anarchist who seeks to overturn present condi-tions is to be regarded as attacking the foundation upon which civilization itself rests, for civilization took its start from the day that the capable, industrious workman said to his incompetent and lazy fellow, "If thou dost not sow, thou shalt not reap," and thus ended primitive Communism by separating the drones from the bees. One who studies this subject will soon be brought face to face with the conclusion that upon the sacredness of property civilization itself de-pends—the right of the laborer to his hundred dollars in the savings bank, and equally the legal right of the millionaire to his millions. To those who propose to substitute Communism for this intense Individualism the answer, therefore, is: The race has tried that. All progress from that barbarous day to the present time has resulted from its displacement. Not evil, but good, has come to the race from the accumulation of wealth by those who have the ability and energy that produce it.

8   But even if we admit for a moment that it might be better for the race to discard its present foundation, Individualism, that it is a nobler ideal that man should labor, not for himself alone, but in and for a brotherhood of his fellows, and share with them all in common, realizing Swedenborg's idea of Heaven,

where, as he says, the angels derive their happiness, not from laboring for self, but for each other—even admit all this, and a sufficient answer is, This is not evolution, but revolution. It necessitates the changing of human nature itself— a work of aeons, even if it were good to change it, which we cannot know. It is not practicable in our day or in our age. Even if desirable theoretically, it belongs to another and long-succeeding sociological stratum. Our duty is with what is practicable now; with the next step possible in our day and generation. It is criminal to waste our energies in endeavoring to uproot, when all we can profitably or possibly accomplish is to bend the universal tree of humanity a little in the direction most favorable to the production of good fruit under existing circumstances. We might as well urge the destruction of the highest existing type of man because he failed to reach our ideal as to favor the destruction of Individualism, Private Property, the Law of Accumulation of Wealth, and the Law of Competition; for these are the highest results of human experience, the soil in which society so far has produced the best fruit. Unequally or unjustly, perhaps, as these laws sometimes operate, and imperfect as they appear to the Idealist, they are, nevertheless, like the highest type of man, the best and most valuable of all that humanity has yet accomplished.

9   We start, then, with a condition of affairs under which the best interests of the race are promoted, but which inevitably gives wealth to the few. Thus far, accepting conditions as they exist, the situation can be surveyed and pro- nounced good. The question then arises—and, if the foregoing be correct, it is the only question with which we have to deal—What is the proper mode of administering wealth after the laws upon which civilization is founded have thrown it into the hands of the few? And it is of this great question that I believe I offer the true solution.

SIGNIFICANCE

Explain the significance of the following quotations to the point or structure of the selection:

"The problem of our age is the proper distribution of wealth, so that the ties of brotherhood may still bind together the rich and poor in harmonious relationship."

"The conditions of human life have not only been changed, but revolution- ized, within the past few hundred years."

"This change . . . is not to be deplored, but welcomed as highly beneficial."

"To-day the world obtains commodities of excellent quality at prices which even the generation preceding this would have deemed incredible."

"Under the law of competition, the employer of thousands is forced into the strictest economies, among which the rates paid to labor figure prominently, and often there is friction between the employer and the employed, between capital and labor, between rich and poor."

". . . while the law [of competition] may be sometimes hard for the individual, it is best for the race, because it insures the survival of the fittest in every department."

"Objections to the foundations upon which society is based are not in order, because the condition of the race is better with these than it has been with any others which have been tried."

". . . the only question with which we have to deal—What is the proper mode of administering wealth after the laws upon which civilization is founded have thrown it into the hands of the few?"

FUTURE USE

What is the main point of this selection? What is the thesis statement?
What is the topic sentence and point of each paragraph?
Briefly summarize the selection.
Outline the structure and main points.
What information in this selection is relevant to your essay(s)? How could you use this information?

The following selection is the introduction to "A Short History of American Labor," which was prepared by the AFL-CIO in honor of the 1981 centennial of the American labor movement.

AMERICAN LABOR'S SECOND CENTURY

1   This brief history of the 100 years of the modern trade union movement in the United States can only touch the high spots of activity and identify the principal trends of a "century of achievement." In such a condensation of history, episodes of importance and of great human drama must necessarily be discussed far too briefly, or in some cases relegated to a mere mention.

2   What is clearly evident, however, is that the working people of America have had to unite in struggle to achieve the gains that they have accumulated during this century. Improvements did not come easily. Organizing unions, winning the rights to representation, using the collective bargaining process as the core of their activities, struggling against bias and discrimination, the working men and women of America have built a trade union movement of formidable proportions.

3   Labor in America has correctly been described as a stabilizing force in the national economy and a bulwark of our democratic society. Furthermore, the gains that unions have been able to achieve have brought benefits, direct and indirect, to the public as a whole. It was labor, for example, that spearheaded the drive for public education for every child. The labor movement, indeed, has served as a force for American progress.

4   Now, in the 1980s, as the American trade union movement looks toward its second century, it takes pride in its first "century of achievement" as it recognizes a substantial list of goals yet to be achieved.

5   In this past century, American labor has played a central role in the elevation of the American standard of living. The benefits which unions have negotiated for their members are, in most cases, widespread in the economy and enjoyed by millions of our fellow citizens outside the labor movement. It is often hard to remember that what we take for granted—vacations with pay, pensions, health and welfare protection, grievance and arbitration procedures, holidays—never existed on any meaningful scale until unions fought and won them for working people.

6   Through these decades, the labor movement has constantly reached out to groups in the American society striving for their share of opportunity and rewards . . . to the blacks, the Hispanics and other minorities . . . to women striving for jobs and equal or comparable pay . . . to those who work for better

schools, for the freedom of speech, press and assembly guaranteed by the Bill of Rights . . . to those seeking to make our cities more livable or our rural recreation areas more available . . . to those seeking better health for infants and more secure status for the elderly.

7   Through these decades, in addition, the unions of America have functioned in an economy and a technology marked by awesome change. When the Federation of Organized Trades and Labor Unions gathered in convention in 1881, Edison had two years earlier invented the electric light, and the first telephone conversation had taken place just five years before. There were no autos, no airplanes, no radio, no television, no air conditioning, no computers or calculators, no electronic games. For our modest energy needs—coal, kerosene and candles—we were independently self-sufficient.

8   The labor movement has seen old industries die (horse-shoeing was once a major occupation) and new industries mature. The American workforce, once predominantly "blue collar," now finds "white collar" employees and the "grey collar" people of the service industries in a substantial majority.

9   The workforce in big mass production industries has contracted, and the new industries have required employees with different skills in different locations. Work once performed in the United States has been moved to other countries, often at wage levels far below the American standards. Multinational, conglomerate corporations have moved operations around the globe as if it were a mammoth chessboard. The once thriving U.S. merchant marine has shriveled.

10   A new kind of "growth industry"—consultants to management skilled in the use of every legal loophole that can frustrate union organizing, the winning of representation elections, or the negotiation of a fair and equitable collective bargaining agreement—has mushroomed in recent years, and threatens the stability of labor-management relationships. A group of organizations generally described as the "new right" enlist their followers in retrogressive crusades to develop an anti-union atmosphere in the nation, and to repeal or mutilate various social and economic programs that have brought a greater degree of security and peace of mind to the millions of American wage earners in the middle and lower economic brackets.

11   Resistance to modest proposals like the labor law reform bill of 1977, and the use of lie detectors and electronic surveillance in probing the attitudes and actions of employees are a reminder that opposition to unions, while changing in style from the practices of a few decades ago, is still alive and flourishing— often financed by corporate groups, trade associations and extremist ideologues.

12   Yet through this dizzying process of change, one need remains constant—the need for individual employees to enjoy their human rights and dignity, and to have the power to band together to achieve equal collective status in dealing with multi-million and multi-billion dollar corporations. In other words, there is no substitute for the labor union.

13   American labor's responsibility in its second century is to adjust to the new

conditions, so that it may achieve optimum ability to represent its members and contribute to the evolutionary progress of the American democratic society.

14   AFL-CIO President Lane Kirkland expressed that concept in his formal statement on labor's centennial in 1981:

"Labor has a unique role in strengthening contemporary American society and dealing adequately and forcefully with the challenge of the future.

"We shall rededicate ourselves to the sound principle of harnessing democratic tradition and trade union heritage with the necessity of reaching out for new and better ways to serve all working people and the entire nation."

SIGNIFICANCE

Explain the significance of the following quotations to the point or structure of the selection:

"Labor in America has correctly been described as a stabilizing force in the national economy."

"In this past century, American labor has played a central role in the elevation of the American standard of living."

". . . the labor movement has constantly reached out to groups in the American society striving for their share of opportunity and rewards."

"There were no autos, no airplanes, no radio, no television, no air conditioning, no computers or calculators, no electronic games."

"The once thriving U.S. merchant marine has shriveled."

". . . opposition to unions . . . is still alive and flourishing. . . ."

"AFL-CIO President Lane Kirkland expressed that concept in his formal statement on labor's centennial in 1981: 'Labor has a unique role in strengthening contemporary American society. . . .'"

FUTURE USE

What is the main point of this selection? What is the thesis statement?

What is the topic sentence and point of each paragraph?

Briefly summarize the selection.

Outline the structure and main points.

What information in this selection is relevant to your essay(s)? How could you use this information?

Michel-Guillaume Jean de Crèvecoeur emigrated from France to North America in
1754. After considerable travel, he became a citizen of the colony of New York in
1765, changing his name to Hector St. John. Unable to choose between his sympathy
for the patriots' views and his moral allegiance to the king during the Revolutionary
War, he returned to Europe. Letters from an American Farmer *appeared in London*
in 1782 and in Paris in 1784 and went through many editions. Letter III is the classic
description of America as a melting pot. Some editions make the title an exclamation;
others add a question mark.

WHAT IS AN AMERICAN
by Hector St. John de Crèvecoeur

1   . . . [W]hence came all these people? They are a mixture of English, Scotch,
Irish, French, Dutch, Germans, and Swedes. From this promiscuous breed, that
race now called Americans have arisen. The eastern provinces [New England]
must indeed be excepted, as being the unmixed descendants of Englishmen. I
have heard many wish that they had been more intermixed also: for my part, I
am no wisher, and think it much better as it has happened. They exhibit a most
conspicuous figure in this great and variegated picture; they too enter for a great
share in the pleasing perspective displayed in these thirteen provinces. I know it
is fashionable to reflect on them, but I respect them for what they have done; for
the accuracy and wisdom with which they have settled their territory, for the
decency of their manners; for their early love of letters; their ancient college
[Harvard], the first in this hemisphere; for their industry; which to me who am
but a farmer, is the criterion of everything. There never was a people, situated as
they are, who with so ungrateful a soil have done more in so short a time. Do
you think that the monarchical ingredients which are more prevalent in other
governments, have purged them from all foul stains? Their histories assert the
contrary.

2   In this great American asylum, the poor of Europe have by some means met
together, and in consequence of various causes; to what purpose should they ask
one another what countrymen they are? Alas, two thirds of them had no country. Can a wretch who wanders about, who works and starves, whose life is a
continual scene of sore affliction and pinching penury—can that man call
England or any other kingdom his country? A country that had no bread for
him, whose fields procured him no harvest, who met with nothing but the
frowns of the rich, the severity of the laws, with jails and punishments; who
owned not a single foot of the extensive surface of this planet? No! Urged by a
variety of motives, here they came. Every thing has tended to regenerate them:
new laws, a new mode of living, a new social system. Here they have become
men: in Europe they were as so many useless plants, wanting refreshing showers;

they withered, and were mowed down by want, hunger, and war. But now by the power of transplantation, like all other plants they have taken root and flourished. Formerly they were not numbered in any civil lists of their country, except in those of the poor; here they rank as citizens. By what invisible power has this surprising metamorphosis been performed? By that of the laws and that of their industry. The laws, the indulgent laws, protect them as they arrive, stamping on them the symbol of adoption; they receive ample rewards for their labours; these accumulated rewards procure them lands; those lands confer on them the title of freemen, and to that title every benefit is affixed which man can possibly require. This is the great operation daily performed by our laws. From whence proceed these laws? From our government. Whence the government? It is derived from the original genius and strong desire of the people ratified and confirmed by the crown. This is the great chain which links us all. . . .

3   What attachment can a poor European emigrant have for a country where he had nothing? The knowledge of the language, the love of a few kindred as poor as himself, were the only cords that tied him; his country is now that which gives him land, bread, protection and consequence. *Ubi panis ibi patria* ["Where bread is, there the homeland is"] is the motto of all emigrants. What then is the American, this new man? He is either an European, or the descendant of an European; hence the strange mixture of blood, which you will find in no other country. I could point out to you a family whose grandfather was an Englishman, whose wife was Dutch, whose son married a French woman, and whose present four sons have now four wives of different nations. He is an American, who, leaving behind him all his ancient prejudices and manners, receives new ones from the new mode of life he has embraced, the new government he obeys, and the new rank he holds. He becomes an American by being received in the broad lap of our great *Alma Mater* ["Nourishing Mother"]. Here individuals of all nations are melted into a new race of men, whose labours and posterity will one day cause great changes in the world. Americans are the western pilgrims, who are carrying along with them that great mass of arts, sciences, vigour, and industry which began long since in the east; they will finish the great circle. The Americans were once scattered all over Europe; here they are incorporated into one of the finest systems of population which has ever appeared, and which will hereafter become distinct by the power of the different climates they inhabit. The American ought therefore to love this country much better than that wherein he or his forefathers were born. Here the rewards of his industry follow with equal steps the progress of his labour; his labour is founded on the basis of nature, *self-interest*; can it want a stronger allurement? Wives and children, who before in vain demanded of him a morsel of bread, now, fat and frolicsome, gladly help their father to clear those fields whence exuberant crops are to rise to feed and to clothe them all; without any part being claimed, either by a despotic prince, a rich abbot, or a mighty lord. Here religion demands but little of him; a small voluntary salary to the minister, and gratitude to God; can he refuse these?

The American is a new man, who acts upon new principles; he must therefore entertain new ideas, and form new opinions. From involuntary idleness, servile dependence, penury, and useless labour, he has passed to toils of a very different nature, rewarded by ample subsistence.—This is an American.

SIGNIFICANCE

Explain the significance of the following quotations to the point or structure of the selection:

"They are a mixture of English, Scotch, Irish, French, Dutch, Germans, and Swedes. From this promiscuous breed, that race now called Americans have arisen."

"The eastern provinces must indeed be excepted, as being the unmixed descendants of Englishmen. I have heard many wish that they had been more intermixed also. . . ."

"In this great American asylum, the poor of Europe have by some means met together, and in consequence of various causes; to what purpose should they ask one another what countrymen they are?"

"Every thing has tended to regenerate them: new laws, a new mode of living, a new social system. Here they have become men: in Europe they were as so many useless plants, wanting refreshing showers; they withered, and were mowed down by want, hunger, and war."

"From whence proceed these laws? From our government. Whence the government? It is derived from the original genius and strong desire of the people ratified and confirmed by the crown. This is the great chain which links us all. . . ."

"What attachment can a poor European emigrant have for a country where he had nothing? The knowledge of the language, the love of a few kindred as poor as himself, were the only cords that tied him; his country is now that which gives him land, bread, protection and consequence."

"Here individuals of all nations are melted into a new race of men. . . ."

"Here the rewards of his industry follow with equal steps the progress of his labour; his labour is founded on the basis of nature, *self-interest*; can it want a stronger allurement?"

FUTURE USE

What is the main point of this selection? What is the thesis statement?

What is the topic sentence and point of each paragraph?

Briefly summarize the selection.

Outline the structure and main points.

What information in this selection is relevant to your essay(s)? How could you use this information?

· MAKING CONNECTIONS

Prepare responses to the following discussion topics. The questions are meant to stimulate thought, not to elicit one- or two-word answers.

1. According to *Bethel School District v. Fraser* (p. 176), what part does school play in transmitting values? Which values are the schools expected to transmit? Where do these values come from? How is the philosophy of the Supreme Court in this case similar to or different from the views in "Schools Must Teach Values"? Would it be possible or advisable to say that television or newspapers must teach values? Are there countries that expect this from their media? Whose values would be taught in such a situation? What would or should be done if the media did not teach the required values? Where do the people who object to stereotypes or unfavorable media portrayals fit into this discussion? What essay topic(s) could emerge from this discussion?

2. Do you think someone should be allowed to offend members of an audience by using obscene language? By making offensive comments about an individual? By ridiculing or stereotyping a group of people? Should freedom of speech be absolute or have limits? Would you distinguish between the freedom of speech of individuals and of the media? What does the fact that two courts ruled that the school had violated a student's freedom of speech say about the values of the United States? What other values does this country espouse? To what extent are these values actually practiced? What is the situation in other countries? Do other countries share the same values as this country? Do they live up to their values? What essay topic(s) could emerge from this discussion?

3. What are the values of the United States? Which of these are distinctly American? Which values that other people practice are not American values? Where do a society's values come from? How are they maintained? How and why do they change? Which reading selections address this question? What values do these selections say the United States espouses? Where do these sources say the values came from? What essay topic(s) could emerge from this discussion?

4. What is your image of a wealthy capitalist? Of a labor union? What are the television images? What experiences and information are the basis for your images? To what extent do your images and the television images agree or disagree with the self-images presented by Andrew Carnegie (p. 180) and the AFL-CIO (p. 185)? Do you think that Carnegie's defense of accumulating wealth is sincere or self-serving? What about organized labor's views of its contribution to American society? What evidence can

you bring to support or contradict these views? What essay topic(s) could emerge from this discussion?

5. What is the individualism which Carnegie discusses? What is the view of human nature that he says it implies? How are his views similar to or different from those of Turner (p. 73) and Crèvecoeur (p. 188)? What does Carnegie say anarchists, socialists, and communists must believe about human nature? Do you agree or disagree with this analysis? Why? On what does Carnegie base his belief about human nature? Is this the general American belief? What was the biblical view of human nature held by the Puritans? What was the view of the Founding Fathers? Do the events of the century since Carnegie wrote his essay support or contradict his views? What essay topic(s) could emerge from this discussion?

6. What does Crèvecoeur (p. 188) see as the greatest strength of America? What weakness does he say people find with New England? What do you think he would say about a third-generation Italian-American who still speaks Italian? Who is still a practicing Catholic? Who likes pasta? What do you think he would say about hyphenated labels like Italian-American? What values would he say should be taught in schools? Do you agree or disagree with him? Why? Do you think that he was right in seeing America as a melting pot? Should it be? What has changed since his time? What essay topic(s) could emerge from this discussion?

· ADDITIONAL ESSAYS FOR DISCUSSION

. . . THE AMERICAN SYSTEM
OF RUGGED INDIVIDUALISM . . .
From a speech by Herbert Hoover (1928)

1   After the war, when the Republican party assumed administration of the country, we were faced with the problem of determination of the very nature of our national life. During 150 years we have builded up a form of self-government and a social system which is peculiarly our own. It differs essentially from all others in the world. It is the American system. It is just as definite and positive a political and social system as has ever been developed on earth. It is founded upon a particular conception of self-government in which decentralized local responsibility is the very base. Further than this, it is founded upon the conception that only through ordered liberty, freedom and equal opportunity to the individual will his initiative and enterprise spur on the march of progress. And in our insistence upon equality of opportunity has our system advanced beyond all the world.

2   During the war we necessarily turned to the Government to solve every difficult economic problem. The Government having absorbed every energy of our people for war, there was no other solution. For the preservation of the State the Federal Government became a centralized despotism which undertook unprecedented responsibilities, assumed autocratic powers, and took over the business of citizens. To a large degree we regimented our whole people temporarily into a socialistic state. However justified in time of war if continued in peace time it would destroy not only our American system but with it our progress and freedom as well.

3   When the war closed, the most vital of all issues both in our own country and throughout the world was whether Governments should continue their wartime ownership and operation of many instrumentalities of production and distribution. We were challenged with a peace-time choice between the American system of rugged individualism and a European philosophy of diametrically opposed doctrines—doctrines of paternalism and state socialism. The acceptance of these ideas would have meant the destruction of self-government through centralization of government. It would have meant the undermining of the individual initiative and enterprise through which our people have grown to unparalleled greatness.

4   . . . . When the Republican Party came into full power it went at once resolutely back to our fundamental conception of the State and the rights and responsibilities of the individual. Thereby it restored confidence and hope in the American people, it freed and stimulated enterprise, it restored the Government to its position as an umpire instead of a player in the economic game. For these

reasons the American people have gone forward in progress while the rest of the world has halted, and some countries have even gone backwards. If anyone will study the causes of retarded recuperation in Europe, he will find much of it due to the stifling of private initiative on one hand, and overloading of the Government with business on the other.

5   There has been revived in this campaign, however, a series of proposals which, if adopted, would be a long step toward the abandonment of our American system and a surrender to the destructive operation of governmental conduct of commercial business. Because the country is faced with difficulty and doubt over certain national problems—that is, prohibition, farm relief and electrical power—our opponents propose that we must thrust government a long way into the businesses which give rise to these problems. In effect, they abandon the tenets of their own party and turn to State socialism as a solution for the difficulties presented by all three. It is proposed that we shall change from prohibition to the State purchase and sale of liquor. If their agricultural relief program means anything, it means that the Government shall directly or indirectly buy and sell and fix prices of agricultural products. And we are to go into the hydro-electric-power business. In other words, we are confronted with a huge program of government in business.

6   There is, therefore, submitted to the American people a question of fundamental principle. That is: shall we depart from the principles of our American political and economic system, upon which we have advanced beyond all the rest of the world, in order to adopt methods based on principles destructive of its very foundations? And I wish to emphasize the seriousness of these proposals. I wish to make my position clear; for this goes to the very roots of American life and progress.

7   I should like to state to you the effect that this projection of government in business would have upon our system of self-government and our economic system. That effect would reach to the daily life of every man and woman. It would impair the very basis of liberty and freedom not only for those left outside the fold of expanded bureaucracy but for those embraced within it. . . .

8   It is a false liberalism that interprets itself into the Government operation of commercial business. Every step of bureaucratizing of the business of our country poisons the very roots of liberalism—that is, political equality, free speech, free assembly, free press, and equality of opportunity. It is the road not to more liberty, but to less liberty. Liberalism should be found not striving to spread bureaucracy but striving to set bounds to it. True liberalism seeks all legitimate freedom, first in the confident belief that without such freedom the pursuit of all other blessings and benefits is vain. That belief is the foundation of all American progress, political as well as economic.

9   Liberalism is a force truly of the spirit, a force proceeding from the deep realization that economic freedom cannot be sacrificed if political freedom is to be preserved. Even if Governmental conduct of business could give us more

efficiency instead of less efficiency, the fundamental objection to it would remain unaltered and unabated. It would destroy political equality. It would increase rather than decrease abuse and corruption. It would stifle initiative and invention. It would undermine the development of leadership. It would cramp and cripple the mental and spiritual energies of our people. It would extinguish equality and opportunity. It would dry up the spirit of liberty and progress. For these reasons primarily it must be resisted. For a hundred and fifty years liberalism has found its true spirit in the American system, not in the European systems.

10   I do not wish to be misunderstood in this statement. . . . Nor do I wish to be misinterpreted as believing that the United States is free-for-all and devil-take-the-hindmost. The very essence of equality of opportunity and of American individualism is that there shall be no domination by any group or combination in this Republic, whether it be business or political. On the contrary, it demands economic justice as well as political and social justice. It is no system of laissez faire.

11   I feel deeply on this subject because during the war I had some practical experience with governmental operation and control. I have witnessed not only at home but abroad the many failures of Government in business. I have seen its tyrannies, its injustices, its destructions of self-government, its undermining of the very instincts which carry our people forward to progress. I have witnessed the lack of advance, the lowered standards of living, the depressed spirits of people working under such a system. My objection is based not upon theory or upon a failure to recognize wrong or abuse, but I know the adoption of such methods would strike at the very roots of American life and would destroy the very basis of American progress. . . .

12   And what have been the results of our American system? Our country has become the land of opportunity to those born without inheritance, not merely because of the wealth of its resources and industry, but because of this freedom of initiative and enterprise. Russia has natural resources equal to ours. Her people are equally industrious, but she has not had the blessings of 150 years of our form of government and of our social system.

13   By adherence to the principles of decentralized self-government, ordered liberty, equal opportunity, and freedom to the individual, our American experiment in human welfare has yielded a degree of well-being unparalleled in all the world. It has come nearer to the abolition of poverty, to the abolition of fear of want, than humanity has ever reached before. Progress of the past seven years is the proof of it. This alone furnishes the answer to our opponents who ask us to introduce destructive elements into the system by which this has been accomplished. . . .

From the Preface
to *THE LEATHER-STOCKING TALES*
by James Fenimore Cooper (1850)

1   This series of stories, which has obtained the name of "The Leather-Stocking Tales," has been written in a very desultory and inartificial manner. The order in which the several books appeared was essentially different from that in which they would have been presented to the world, had the regular course of their incidents been consulted. In "The Pioneers," the first of the series written, the Leather-Stocking is represented as already old, and driven from his early haunts in the forest, by the sound of the axe, and the smoke of the settler. "The Last of the Mohicans," the next book in the order of publication, carried the readers back to a much earlier period in the history of our hero, representing him as middle-aged, and in the fullest vigor of manhood. In "The Prairie," his career terminates, and he is laid in his grave. There, it was originally the intention to leave him, in the expectation that, as in the case of the human mass, he would soon be forgotten. But a latent regard for this character induced the author to resuscitate him in "The Pathfinder," a book that was not long after succeeded by "The Deerslayer," thus completing the series as it now exists. . . .

2   The author has often been asked if he had any original in his mind, for the character of Leather-Stocking. In a physical sense, different individuals known to the writer in early life, certainly presented themselves as models, through his recollections; but in a moral sense this man of the forest is purely a creation. The idea of delineating a character that possessed little of civilization but its highest principles as they are exhibited in the uneducated, and all of savage life that is not incompatible with these great rules of conduct, is perhaps natural to the situation in which Natty was placed. He is too proud of his origin to sink into the condition of the wild Indian, and too much a man of the woods not to imbibe as much as was at all desirable, from his friends and companions. In a moral point of view it was the intention to illustrate the effect of seed scattered by the way side. To use his own language, his "gifts" were "white gifts," and he was not disposed to bring on them discredit. On the other hand, removed from nearly all the temptations of civilized life, placed in the best associations of that which is deemed savage, and favorably disposed by nature to improve such advantages, it appeared to the writer that his hero was a fit subject to represent the better qualities of both conditions, without pushing either to extremes.

3   There was no violent stretch of the imagination, perhaps, in supposing one of civilized associations in childhood, retaining many of his earliest lessons amid the scenes of the forest. Had these early impressions, however, not been sustained by continued, though casual connexion with men of his own color, if not of his own caste, all our information goes to show he would soon have lost every

trace of his origin. It is believed that sufficient attention was paid to the particular circumstances in which this individual was placed to justify the picture of his qualities that has been drawn. The Delawares early attracted the attention of missionaries, and were a tribe unusually influenced by their precepts and example. In many instances they became Christians, and cases occurred in which their subsequent lives gave proof of the efficacy of the great moral changes that had taken place within them.

4   A leading character in a work of fiction has a fair right to the aid which can be obtained from a poetical view of the subject. It is in this view, rather than in one more strictly circumstantial, that Leather-Stocking has been drawn. The imagination has no great task in portraying to itself a being removed from the everyday inducements to err, which abound in civilized life, while he retains the best and simplest of his early impressions; who sees God in the forest; hears him in the winds; bows to him in the firmament that o'ercanopies all; submits to his sway in a humble belief of his justice and mercy; in a word, a being who finds the impress of the Deity in all the works of nature, without any of the blots produced by the expedients, and passion, and mistakes of man. This is the most that has been attempted in the character of Leather-Stocking. Had this been done without any of the drawbacks of humanity, the picture would have been, in all probability, more pleasing than just. In order to preserve the *vrai-semblable*, therefore, traits derived from the prejudices, tastes, and even the weaknesses of his youth, have been mixed up with these higher qualities and longings, in a way, it is hoped, to represent a reasonable picture of human nature, without offering to the spectator a "monster of goodness."

5   It has been objected to these books that they give a more favorable picture of the red man than he deserves. The writer apprehends that much of this objection arises from the habits of those who have made it. One of his critics, on the appearance of the first work in which Indian character was portrayed, objected that its "characters were Indians of the school of Heckewelder, rather than of the school of nature." These words quite probably contain the substance of the true answer to the objection. Heckewelder was an ardent, benevolent missionary, bent on the good of the red man, and seeing in him one who had the soul, reason, and characteristics of a fellow being. The critic is understood to have been a very distinguished agent of the government, one very familiar with Indians, as they are seen at the councils to treat for the sale of their lands, where little or none of their domestic qualities come in play, and where, indeed, their evil passions are known to have the fullest scope. As just would it be to draw conclusions of the general state of American society from the scenes of the capital, as to suppose that the negotiating of one of these treaties is a fair picture of Indian life.

6   It is the privilege of all writers of fiction, more particularly when their works aspire to the elevation of romances, to present the *beau-idéal* of their characters

to the reader. That it is which constitutes poetry, and to suppose that the red man is to be represented only in the squalid misery or in the degraded moral state that certainly more or less belongs to his condition, is, we apprehend, taking a very narrow view of an author's privileges. Such criticism would have deprived the world of even Homer.

From DEFINING SOCIALIST WOMANHOOD: THE WOMEN'S PAGE OF THE *JEWISH DAILY FORWARD* IN 1919
by Maxine S. Seller

1   In recent years, increased activity in the overlapping fields of ethnic history, women's history, and labor history has stimulated research about eastern European Jewish women who came to the United States at the turn of the century. Scholars have examined the public lives of these women as workers, suffragists, and socialists and their private lives as daughters, wives, and mothers using a variety of sources, including census data, autobiographies, novels, and oral histories. This study looks at immigrant Jewish women through another, heretofore virtually untapped, source, the women's page of the popular socialist paper, the *Jewish Daily Forward*. It examines the definition of socialist womanhood in the women's page of the *Forward* in 1919—in the aftermath of World War I and the Bolshevik Revolution and at the peak of the early twentieth-century feminist movement, when Jewish women were still immersed in a progressive working-class immigrant world but already on their way to Americanization and social mobility.

2   With a daily circulation approaching 200,000 the *Forward* in 1919 was one of the most important foreign language papers in the United States, the leading Yiddish newspaper in the world, and the voice of a vibrant left-wing working class Yiddish culture. Read by the apolitical as well as the political, the *Forward* was enormously influential. . . .

3   . . . . Like the rest of the *Forward*, the women's page wrestled with the contradictions of selling the socialist ideology of a class-conscious, oppressive Europe to Jewish immigrants in the United States, where social mobility seemed possible and many workers were less interested in abolishing capitalism than in joining the ranks of the capitalists.

4   Unlike the rest of the *Forward*, the women's page also wrestled with the contradictions between socialism and the interests of women. The staff were socialists, but some were also women (at least one—Dr. Esther Luria—was a feminist), and their intended audience, of course, was women. Yet as Mari Jo Buhl, Sally Miller, Mark Pittenger, and other scholars have pointed out, women were denied real power in the Socialist Party, and women's issues were not high among the Party's priorities. The views of the *Forward* were not identical with those of the Socialist Party. Nevertheless, the conflict between the interests of

the male-dominated workers' movement—including the trade unions as well as the Socialist Party—and the interests of women created problems for columnists defining the socialist woman.

5   Columnists who defined socialist womanhood on the women's page of the *Forward* were influenced by at least four ideological currents: socialism, the desire to help readers adjust to the United States, feminism, and, to a lesser extent and perhaps unconsciously, Jewish tradition. Because these ideological currents could conflict with as well as reinforce one another, the definition of socialist womanhood that they produced was not always consistent. Columnists' definition of ideal socialist womanhood did not spring entirely from ideological considerations, however. It also sprang from astute observation of their readers: immigrant women moving toward Americanization with multiple and not always compatible commitments to politics, work, and family. Thus reality interacted with ideology to enrich—and complicate—the columnists' definition of socialist womanhood.

6   Stimulated by the suffrage movement and by women's increasing participation in higher education and in the paid labor market, Americans at the turn of the century were examining and debating the woman question. Most women as well as men still subscribed to the nineteenth-century view that women were inherently different from men and thus destined for a separate sphere, for domestic rather than public life. Enamored of modern science, most socialists accepted the Darwinian view that women were lower on the evolutionary ladder than men, or, alternatively, that women had evolved differently from men because of their maternal roles and were therefore more conservative and altruistic. In either case, they concluded that women were adapted to home life but not to the political arena or the workplace.

7   The women's page of the socialist *Forward* did not agree. In 1919 at least half of the women's page was devoted to political and economic subjects, carrying the implicit message that the ideal socialist woman could and should participate in public life. The message was explicit as well as implicit; column after column urged women to take an active role in the workers' movement and the feminist cause and applauded their participation in the paid labor force.

8   In 1919 the women's page included a regular column of national and international news about women called "Notes from the Women's World" and many feature articles on suffrage, wages, and notable women, usually political or social activists. Obituaries praised women who had been active in the workers' movement in Europe and the United States, providing role models for women's political activism. Additional role models were provided by long and frequent articles on politically active women of the past. Jacob Padalier wrote about the medieval Johanna who supposedly served as Pope John VIII until pregnancy revealed that she was a woman. Moving from myth to history, he wrote about the women heroes of the French Revolution. Padalier's articles provided instruction as well as entertainment: they demonstrated that women could hold public

power and change the course of history. Padalier's articles also demonstrated the difficulties women faced in doing so. Women activists in the French Revolution, he pointed out, were opposed not only by aristocrats but also by fellow revolutionaries who did not want them in positions of influence.

9   Columnists' definition of the political arena as an appropriate place for women was unusual for a women's page. It reflected the political ferment of the post-World War I years and the labor-activist orientation of the paper and its editor. Equally important, it reflected the interests of the readers, many of whom in 1919 were deeply involved in political life. Extensive participation in political life continued a pattern begun in eastern Europe, where a conspicuous minority of Jewish women had been active in anti-tsarist revolutionary parties, trade unions, Zionism, and the socialist Bund. In the United States many more participated in massive garment industry strikes, in tenant and consumer actions, in school protests, and in the suffrage and socialist movements.

10   The ideal socialist woman was expected to focus her political energy on the workers' cause. Columnists assumed that their reader understood the general socialist outlook, if not the intricacies of dialectical materialism, and was in sympathy with it. Their columns frequently referred to capitalism negatively and the proletariat positively. Allusions to class conflict were rare, however, and muted by gender solidarity.

11   Despite his editorial support of the Bolshevik Revolution (later withdrawn), editor Cahan favored a democratic, gradualist approach to socialism in the United States as appropriate to what he considered a more open and less class-conscious society than Europe. Since Cahan's views dominated the paper, this was also the position taken by the women's page. The socialist woman was to strive for the cultural and personal growth of the individual worker as well as the economic advancement of the working class. She was to use peaceful, gradualist methods, such as trade unions and legislative activity, rather than revolutionary means to achieve her goals.

12   The transformation of European-style revolutionary socialism into political and cultural activity acceptable in the United States is clear in the life and writings of Dr. Esther Luria, whose columns appeared regularly on the women's page in 1919. A member of the socialist Bund in Warsaw, Luria was arrested several times for revolutionary activity in tsarist Russia and spent six years in exile in Siberia. Escaping to the United States in 1912, she turned from revolution to journalism, writing for the Yiddish edition of the International Ladies' Garment Workers' Union paper, *Justice;* the *Forward;* and other leftist Yiddish publications. Despite her revolutionary past, Luria recommended trade unionism, not Bolshevism, as the proper arena in which socialist women should work for change in the United States. Her definition of socialism was cultural as well as political and economic. She held up as models of socialist womanhood the women of the Ladies' Waist and Dressmakers Union, whose union wages enabled them to lead "an intelligent and cultured life."

13   The socialist woman, then, was defined as an avid and active trade unionist. Unlike Samuel Gompers, leader of the American Federation of Labor, columnists for the women's page did not consider socialism to be in opposition to trade unionism. Rather, the two were considered complementary means to the same end—the advancement of the individual worker and the working class—and trade unions were seen as especially appropriate to American conditions and Jewish immigrants' needs. . . .

14   Columnists were silent in 1919 about the discrimination women faced within the trade unions, even in unions representing predominantly female trades, although Jewish women had complained of this discrimination as early as the shirtwaist makers strike of 1909. They were silent, too, about the problematic status of women in the Socialist Party. In 1909 garment worker and socialist organizer Theresa Malkiel had complained that despite verbal support for women's rights, the Party expected women to wait quietly for progress and to advocate equality "everywhere except within the walls of their own homes." The Party's women's magazine, *Progressive Woman*, was discontinued in 1913, and its Women's National Committee was eliminated in 1915 during a period of financial and political retrenchment. Given the troubled history of women in the Socialist Party, it is not surprising that the *Forward's* ideal socialist woman participated in unions and legislative action but not, ironically, in the Socialist Party itself.

15   Columnists presented conflicting messages about the ideal socialist woman's participation in the workers' movement. They were enthusiastic about her involvement in trade unions and lobbying but silent about her involvement in the Socialist Party, celebratory about her leadership in revolutionary movements of the past but silent about problems of assuming leadership in their own day. Columnists expressed no ambivalence, however, about the socialist woman's participation in the women's suffrage movement, the great political battle of early twentieth-century feminism. The ideal socialist woman was defined as a suffragist and a feminist. Columnists wrote at length and with warm approval of the campaign to pass the Nineteenth Amendment and of the subsequent campaign to ratify it in the state legislatures. Regular columns in "Notes from the Women's World" and feature articles provided sophisticated political analysis of the progress of the amendment in the United States and applauded advances toward political equality in England, France, Italy, and India.

16   Nowhere did columnists on the women's page argue, as many of their American-born counterparts did, that women should have the ballot because they were morally superior to men and would purify the political arena, or that women needed the vote in order to pass Prohibition and thus protect the sanctity and sobriety of the home. Because columnists considered the desire to participate in politics normal rather than exceptional for eastern European Jewish women, they saw no need to justify it in terms of women's special mission. Indeed, the idea that women were essentially different from and morally superior to men and that

consequently they had a special moral mission in society—an idea widespread among American-born suffragists and antisuffragists—did not appear in any context on the women's page in 1919. Women were portrayed as neither better nor worse than men and more like them than different; women's suffrage was a question of simple social justice.

17   In one instance suffrage was portrayed as a means to another end. Citing shocking statistics on maternal deaths and infant mortality among blacks, "Notes from the Women's World" urged the states to remedy the situation by providing free doctors and nurses. To make this happen, said the columnist, women as well as workers must have political power. In this case women's suffrage, a feminist goal, was advocated as a means of realizing a socialist goal, government-sponsored medical care. Despite this exception, however, suffrage was generally viewed as an end rather than a means. Its correctness was considered self-evident and the support of readers, many of whom had been active in recent state suffrage campaigns, justifiably assumed.

18   The ideal socialist woman was expected to work not only for suffrage but also for the realization of feminism in many other areas. While middle class, American-born feminists focused their attention almost exclusively on suffrage in 1919, columnists of the women's page defined feminism in broader terms. They reminded readers that state laws discriminated against women in marriage, divorce, property and inheritance rights, and family life and warned that "these remainders from barbarism must be erased from all the law books." The socialist woman was advised of the importance of psychological as well as legal barriers to women's equality: "It will take time to uproot . . . [men's] prejudices about the 'weaker sex' and before women themselves will look upon themselves as completely equal in ability with the 'stronger sex.' " Finally the socialist woman, unlike many middle-class American feminists, was always to link political equality with economic equality: "There should be for equal work, equal pay. This is naturally of the greatest importance to working women."

19   The socialist woman, then, according to the columnists of the women's page, should be heavily involved in political life—in trade unionism and legislative activity and in suffrage and other feminist issues. She should also be an advocate for the interests of the oppressed, including blacks. At a time when much of the nation was indifferent to the worsening plight of blacks, the women's page informed women not only about the medical problems of black women and children but also about the loss of black voting rights in the South. "We have democracy in one part of the land but not in the other," wrote columnist Michael Zametkin. Black suffrage, like women's suffrage, was seen as simple social justice and therefore as an issue about which the socialist woman should be concerned.

20   The women's page did not limit the socialist women's involvement in the public sphere to political activity, however. The socialist woman was seen as a wage earner as well as a political activist. Column after column dealt with

woman as worker—her relationship with the boss and with her coworkers and her economic problems, especially the problem of low wages. . . .

21   Although it barely acknowledged the conflict between men and women in the Socialist Party and the trade unions, the women's page had a great deal to say about the conflict between men and women in the labor market. Recognizing that male workers (including socialists and unionists) often objected to female job competition in the workplace, columnists insisted that men must accept women's right to pursue their economic interests and to earn "equal pay for work of equal worth." The women's page did not share the widespread view that women should be at home rather than in the paid labor force, nor was the ideal socialist woman restricted to "female" occupations. On the contrary, Luria applauded the entry of women into a broad range of formerly male occupations during the recent war and predicted optimistically but inaccurately that the gains would be permanent. . . .

WRITING ASSIGNMENTS

Write an expository essay with an introduction, development, and conclusion about one of the following topics. Be sure to have a thesis statement and paragraphs focused on a topic sentence, and to summarize, paraphrase, or quote from the reading selections to develop your thesis. Feel free to draw from your earlier papers for "re-vision."

1. If you have been writing about the relationship of values to actions, now write an expository essay about the influence of family, the source of values, conflict between home and other sources of values, or "American" values.

2. If you have been writing about commercials and values, now write an expository essay about the relationship of your values to society's values or to the values on television.

3. If you have been writing about how the media portray groups, now write an expository essay about stereotypes in the media, accuracy versus sympathy, the responsibility of the media, or the question of regulating or censoring the media.

4. If you wrote about the significance of classic, but old, studies, now write an expository essay that expands your thesis to include the works of Carnegie and Crèvecoeur.

5. Write an expository essay on one of the topics developed during the discussions for Making Connections.

6. Write an expository essay on one of the topics that emerged from the discussions of Hoover, Cooper, and Seller.

7. An editorial in the *New York Times* attacks the television shows known as docudramas. "The license to fictionalize requires giving up the license to claim reality," the editorial says, adding, "'Fact-based drama' not only defrauds the news but assaults it, hit and run."

   Write an expository essay in which you discuss the question of reality versus fiction on television, in the movies, or in literature.

8. Harold Evans, editorial director of *U.S. News and World Report,* accuses television news of showing "what its cameras happen to have shot" rather than what is important. "The searchlight glares on the errors of the open societies," he believes, but overlooks "the hoodlums in the shadows," who don't allow reporters into their countries.

   Write an expository essay in which you discuss the contents of television news shows.

9. In *Miseducation: Preschoolers at Risk,* David Elkind argues that since women are no longer "the primary symbols of leisure-class status in middle-class families," parents now buy designer clothes for children and send toddlers to expensive nursery schools and play groups.

   Write an expository essay in which you discuss the current treatment of children.

C·H·A·P·T·E·R F·I·V·E

METHODS OF DEVELOPMENT

Your team loses to a rival you were expected to beat easily, and afterward you all sit around trying to figure out what went wrong. The stock market plunges, and television talk shows are filled with economists explaining what happened. A dark horse candidate wins the election, and next day all the newspapers in town have theories about how she did it. All of these situations are examples of **analysis**.

Almost everything you write for school or business will contain analysis. As we have seen, even a personal story should be more than a simple catalogue of events one after another. You tell a story because it has a point, and you include specific details and arrange them in a certain way to bring out the point you want your audience to see. Sometimes the analysis is the point of the essay; other times it is in the background, informing and shaping the paper.

When we analyze something, we look at its parts and explain how they add up to the whole. We may know the end product, and want to understand how the parts produced it, or we may know the input, and want to predict the outcome. We may know who and what, and have to explain why, or we may know what and how, and have to discover who.

Writers, like scientists and investigators, try to create a single generalization that explains many specifics. If a rare disease suddenly becomes widespread, researchers try to discover what all the victims have in common. Every detail of the victims' lives—age, sex, race, occupation, eating habits, lifestyle, place of residence, national origin—is compared in the hope that a single factor can be found that ties all the victims together. Most large issues must be approached in a similar way. You can write an essay describing a television program that you like, but a better paper would use the description in order to explain why you like the show. An essay can list and describe ten shows with black characters, but a more thoughtful paper would incorporate details into an explanation of how the shows are similar or different.

· GENERAL IDEAS AND SPECIFIC DETAILS

The main idea of an essay or book can usually be stated in a very general way: "Waves of immigration to America have created a multiethnic society." "Television depicts minorities in a demeaning manner." "Women are not taken seriously in politics." The general idea, however, must then be backed up by specifics—by supporting details. A paragraph contains supporting details in the several sentences that elaborate on the topic sentence. An essay contains even more supporting details in the paragraphs that fill out the thesis statement.

In many cases supporting details consist of specific examples. Imagine, for instance, that your friend says, "The new Reebok jogging shoes are fantastic." You haven't worn them yet, so you ask, "Why?" It would not be especially helpful if your friend answers, "Oh, I don't know. They just are." In contrast, a helpful answer might be, "They're made of a special synthetic that doesn't make your feet sweat. The innersole cushions your foot when you run. And there's a new ankle support that cuts down the chances of a bad sprain." In this case, the generalization is supported by meaningful specifics.

An essay works the same way. The strength of the general statement—the thesis or main idea—depends on the strength of the evidence behind it—the supporting details. As a reader you must pay close attention to details and be sure that you understand why they are significant, and as a writer you must supply the details that a reader will need in order to accept your point. The passage by Henry Adams which we looked at in the last chapter contains a generalization that is immediately supported by four specific examples.

> In the early days of colonization, every new settlement represented an idea and proclaimed a mission. [example 1] Virginia was founded by a great, liberal movement aiming at the spread of English liberty and empire. [example 2] The Pilgrims of Plymouth, [example 3] the Puritans of Boston, [example 4] the Quakers of Pennsylvania, all avowed a moral purpose, and began by making institutions that consciously reflected a moral idea.

Similarly, the second section of the Declaration of Independence has a generalization supported by a long series of specific examples.

> The history of the present King of Great Britain is a history of repeated injuries and usurpations, all having in direct object the establishment of

an absolute Tyranny over these States. To prove this, let Facts be submitted to a candid world.

[example 1] He has refused his Assent to Laws, the most wholesome and necessary for the public good.

[example 2] He has forbidden his Governors to pass laws of immediate and pressing importance, unless suspended in their operation till his Assent should be obtained; and when so suspended, he has utterly neglected to attend to them.

[example 3] He has refused to pass other Laws for the accommodation of large districts of people, unless those people would relinquish the right of Representation in the Legislature, a right inestimable to them and formidable to tyrants only.

[example 4. . . .]

The following description of New York City's Lower East Side is from *How the Other Half Lives,* which was written in 1902 by Jacob Riis, a Danish immigrant who pioneered photojournalism. As you read it, notice how Riis uses carefully chosen details to support the generalizations in the topic sentences.

It is said that nowhere in the world are so many people crowded together on a square mile as here. The average five-story tenement adds a story or two to its stature in Ludlow Street and an extra building on the rear lot, and yet the sign "To Let" is the rarest of all there. Here is one seven stories high. The sanitary policeman whose beat this is will tell you that this building here contains thirty-six families, but the term has a widely different meaning here and on the avenues. In this house, where a case of small-pox was reported, there were fifty-eight babies and thirty-eight children that were over five years of age. In Essex Street two small rooms in a six-story tenement were made to hold a "family" of father and mother, twelve children and six boarders. . . . These are samples of the packing of the population that has run up the record here to the rate of three hundred and thirty thousand per square mile. The densest crowding in Old London, I pointed out before, never got beyond a hundred and seventy-five thousand. . . .

. . . The homes of the Hebrew quarter are its workshops also. Reference will be made to the economic conditions under which they work in a succeeding chapter. Here we are concerned simply with the fact. You are made fully aware of it before you have travelled the length of a single block in any of these East Side streets, by the whir of a thousand sewing-machines, worked at high pressure from the earliest dawn till mind and muscle give out together. Every member of the family, from the youngest to the oldest, bears a hand, shut in the qualmy rooms, where meals are cooked and clothing washed and dried besides, the live-long day. It is not unusual to find a dozen persons—men, women, and children—at work in a single small room. The fact accounts for the contrast that strikes with wonder the observer who comes across from the Bend. Over there the entire population seems possessed of an uncontrollable impulse to get out into the street; here all its energies appear to be bent upon keeping in and away from it.

Showing Logical Relationships Between Ideas

Of course, there is more to analysis than simply listing an idea and examples. In most cases the writer has to collect and tie together facts that may not necessarily seem connected. Objects and events in the outside world do not come with explanations attached to them. In effect, the writer has to impose system on a chaos of specifics. In nature, for example, no two oak trees are exactly alike; yet we can ignore the individual differences and identify common traits that define the class *oak tree*. We can do the same for pine, maple, ash, birch, and others. We can even create a larger class called *tree*. Similarly, in sociology, psychology, or economics we can ignore the numerous differences among people and say that this or that trait which they share is the key motivation for a particular action. It is the writer who determines what to focus on and what to ignore. And, of course, several writers may disagree. One may argue that the motivating force in the life of a black woman lawyer is her race; another may think it is her sex; a third may say it is her career.

The most important part of reading an analysis is following the author's reasoning; the hardest part of writing one is making your reasoning clear to someone else. The reader has to know how the writer gets from one idea to the next, and how these ideas build up to the main idea that the writer wants him or her to accept. Fortunately for both reader and writer, English has words that signal the logical relationship that the author intends to make.

Sometimes signal words are not needed because the relationship between two ideas is obvious:

Passing the chemistry exam was essential.
They studied through the night.

The relationship here is causation (also called cause and effect or "the reason"): Because they had to do well, they studied. When a relationship is this obvious, we often omit the word *because*.

Many times, however, a relationship is not obvious, or the speaker or writer is setting up the audience for a shock:

I got an "A" on the chemistry final.
Nonetheless, I failed the course.

We would not expect someone to get an "A" on a final exam and still fail the course; the word *nonetheless* signals that the situation is the opposite of what we expected. In addition, the information raises many questions in our minds and ensures that we will listen to or read what follows. We want to understand what happened, and we assume that our friend or the writer has an interesting story to tell.

As we said earlier, the logical relationship is not "out there." The writer creates the relationship through the analysis. Read the next two sentences and decide what logical relationship you would make.

Man works from sun to sun.
Woman's work is never done.

Regardless of what this old proverb was supposed to mean or once meant, our students generally offer three interpretations.

Man works from sun to sun.
In contrast, woman's work is never done.
[Meaning: women work harder than men.]

Man works from sun to sun.
Similarly, woman's work is never done.
[Men and women work equally hard.]

Man works from sun to sun.
Therefore, woman's work is never done.
[Men quit and leave the work for women.]

Your own interpretation may have been one of the preceding, or it may have been different. But the important thing to remember is that other readers saw something in the two sentences that you did not. Not everyone sees the world the way you do. As a reader, you must look at the signals in order to see how the writer wants the ideas connected. As a writer, you cannot simply put ideas side by side; you must signal the relationship that you want the reader to see.

Transitional Phrases

Very often, logical relationships are signaled by **transitional phrases,** words that show how the writer intends to get from here to there. These phrases are the signals that create the bridge, or transition, from one idea to the next.

Transitional phrases show place, time, similarity, contrast, condition, and causation; for example:

Showing place: where, anywhere, everywhere
Showing time: after, before, while

Showing similarity: just as, also, similarly
Showing contrast: although, even if, nonetheless
Showing condition: if, unless, whether
Showing causation: because, since, so that

Of course, the words in each group are not interchangeable. First of all, *after* and *before*, for instance, obviously do not mean the same thing, though they both show time. Second, transitional phrases fall into two groups on the basis of how they serve the writer's needs.

The two groups have differing emphasis. For example, an author can write

Although I got an "A" on the exam, I failed the course.

or

I got an "A" on the exam. Nonetheless I failed the course.

In a sense, we can say that both alternatives mean the same thing. But in a significant way they convey different messages. The first version has one sentence, with a comma between the two ideas; the relationship of the ideas comes to us as a unit. In contrast, the reader of the second version sees a sentence ending with a period and mentally pauses for a moment. But then he or she sees another sentence, with the second idea—the shocker. In this way the author has created a close, flowing relationship in the first version, and a jolting effect in the second.

The difference in effect is also reinforced by the contrasting types of organization. A word like *nonetheless* is always part of the second idea, and therefore can create the jolting effect. Also, it is the idea the reader sees last; it sticks in the mind—as in the comedian's goal to "Always leave 'em laughing." Words like *although*, on the other hand, are attached to either the first or second idea, so the writer can make that idea either more or less noticeable.

Although I got an "A" on the exam, I failed the course.
I failed the course *although* I got an "A" on the exam.

Finally, a word like *nonetheless* lets a writer modulate the rhythm or weight of a sentence because, unlike words like *although*, it can move around and be set off from its idea by commas.

Nonetheless I failed the course.
Nonetheless, I failed the course.
I, *nonetheless,* failed the course.
I failed the course, *nonetheless.*

There is no way to know just by looking at them which transitional phrases belong to each structural group. The following chart, therefore, gives a summary of the logical and structural information, along with words that belong to each group. (The words in Group I are often called *conjunctive adverbs* or *connectors;* those in Group II are called *subordinating conjunctions* or *includers.*)

Showing Logical Connections

There are six categories of logical transition. Each is divided into two structural groups.

	Group I	**Group II**
	1. Take semicolon or period between ideas. 2. Connected idea stands second. 3. Move within their idea. 4. May be set off within idea by commas.	1. Take comma between ideas. 2. Included idea may be first or second. 3. Begin their idea. 4. May not be set off within idea by commas.
Place	in these/such places	where, anywhere, everywhere, wherever
Time	afterward, later, next, subsequently, thereafter, thereupon, then, finally, earlier, before this, formerly, now, meanwhile, still, at this/that time	after, before, while, until, since, when, whenever, as soon as, as long as, just as
Similarity	again, also, besides, further, indeed, likewise, furthermore, moreover, so too, still more, in other words, in addition, in fact, for example, for instance	as well as, just as, in the same way as/that
Contrast	conversely, however, still, nevertheless, nonetheless, rather, in contrast, on the other hand	although, (even) though, whereas, while, even if, despite the fact that, less than, more than
Condition	if so, if not, in that case	if, unless, whether, lest
Reason	accordingly, consequently, hence, therefore, thus, as a result, for this reason, it follows that, that's why	because, since, inasmuch as, insofar as, whereas, due to the fact that

EXERCISE: Using Transitional Phrases

A. Examine the sentences in the following passage. For each set of ideas, list the transitional phrase and state the relationship that it shows. Also try to explain why the author chose to unite the ideas in the way he did instead of using other structures with the same meaning.

Adapted from *Dissertations upon the English Language* by Noah Webster (1789)

1. The English tongue, though late in its progress towards perfection, has attained to a considerable degree of purity, strength and elegance.
2. It will be readily admitted that the pleasures of reading and conversing require us to be able to speak and write with ease and correctness. But there are more important reasons why the language should be reduced to fixed principles.
3. The United States were settled by emigrants from different parts of Europe; however, their descendants mostly speak the same language.
4. Because of the commerce among the various states, the differences of dialect which our ancestors brought from their native countries will gradually be destroyed.
5. This approximation of dialects is certain; nevertheless, nothing but the establishment of schools and some uniformity in the use of books can annihilate these differences.
6. A sameness of pronunciation is of considerable consequence in a political view, for provincial accents are disagreeable to strangers and sometimes have an unhappy effect upon the social affections.
7. Pride and prejudice incline men to treat the practice of their neighbors with contempt. Thus, small differences in pronunciation excite ridicule.
8. First was the habit of laughing at the singularities of strangers; thereafter was created a dissocial spirit between the inhabitants of the different states.
9. What holds true with respect to individuals as well holds true to large communities.
10. Nicknames and a vulgar tone in speaking are often discoverable in private business and public deliberations. Our political harmony is therefore concerned in a uniformity of language.

B. Use transitional phrases to connect the following pairs of ideas. Then, since you cannot assume that everyone sees the world the way you do, compare what you have written with what Henry Cabot Lodge says in "Our Blundering Foreign Policy" (p. 253), for which these sentences are adapted. Try to explain the reasons for any differences.

1. All the great constructive legislation of this country has been the work of the Republican party.
   The record of the Democratic party for constructive legislation is singularly barren.
2. The Democratic party has had one cardinal principle.
   It has been that of pushing forward the boundaries of the United States.
3. No one underrates the importance of tariffs.
   Of late years we have grown unmindful of other questions.

4. President Washington's neutrality doctrine fell with a shock upon the Americans of that day.
   They were colonists in habits of thought.

5. Americans could not realize that the struggles of Europe did not concern us.
   The establishment of the neutrality policy was one of the greatest services which Washington rendered.

6. Washington declared that it was not the business of the United States to meddle in the affairs of Europe.
   The Monroe Doctrine said that Europe must not meddle in the Western Hemisphere.

7. It has been stated that the annexation of Hawaii would be a violation of the Monroe Doctrine.
   It is not out of place to say that the Monroe Doctrine has no bearing on the extension of the United States.

8. Washington withdrew us from the affairs of Europe.
   He pointed out that our true line of advance was to the West.

9. In the United States themselves we hold the citadel of our power and greatness as a nation.
   There are outworks essential to the defence of that citadel.

10. There is a very definite policy for American statesmen to pursue in this respect.
    They wish to prove themselves worthy inheritors of the principles of Washington.

· METHODS OF DEVELOPING THE ESSAY

Ideas can be connected in more than one way. By using the signals of logical relationship, you, the writer, can impose system on individual facts and convey your own worldview to the reader. Similarly, depending on the data and your purpose, you can develop and organize your paper in various ways. Organizing strategies can be limited to a sentence, or they can shape a paragraph or an entire essay. Most essays, in fact, combine several types of organization. But in all cases, the methods you choose for developing your ideas should be seen as tools for creating the vehicle that conveys your insight or larger purpose.

Definition

Definitions are an important aspect of clear writing. The reader needs to know exactly how key words are used, so the writer must explain them through synonyms, paraphrase, or a more elaborate list of characteristics, functions, or distinguishing features. The value of definitions, however, does not require that you begin every essay with "The dictionary defines. . ." or "According to the such-and-such dictionary. . ." Your use of definitions must reflect your overall purpose and strategy.

In the following paragraph, the definition in the introduction is part of a popular strategy:

> The dictionary defines democracy as "1. Government by the people, exercised either directly or through elected representatives. 2. A social condition of equality and respect for the individual." By either of these definitions, is the German Democratic Republic a democracy?

A skilled reader will recognize this fairly common strategy and predict that it introduces a negative answer. An essay with this type of beginning almost certainly will go on to argue that the country or person or object in question does not fulfill the requirements of the definition. It is possible, of course, that the writer will surprise us and give a positive answer, but as readers who create expectations and try to predict the direction of an essay, we are doing the right thing by assuming the answer will be negative. As a writer, you must be aware of how readers interpret this type of introduction and then decide if you want to use it, and, if so, how.

A definition can also create a climactic conclusion, as in this excerpt from a speech by Susan B. Anthony, who was arguing in 1873 for the right of women to vote:

> Webster, Worcester and Bouvier all define a citizen to be a person in the United States, entitled to vote and hold office. The only question left to be settled now is: Are women persons? And I hardly believe any of our opponents will have the hardihood to say they are not.

An extended definition, moreover, can give shape to a larger segment, such as a paragraph or essay. The entire passage that follows—taken from Crève-coeur's "What Is an American"—is a definition, but never uses that word:

> What then is the American, this new man? He is either an European, or the descendant of an European, hence the strange mixture of blood, which you will find in no other country. I could point out to you a family whose grandfather was an Englishman, whose wife was Dutch, whose son married a French woman, and whose present four sons have now four wives of different nations. *He* is an American, who, leaving behind him all his ancient prejudices and manners, receives new ones from the new mode of life he has embraced, the new government he obeys, the new rank he holds. He becomes an American by being received in the broad lap of our

great *Alma Mater*. Here individuals of all nations are melted into a new race of men, whose labours and posterity will one day cause great changes in the world. Americans are the western pilgrims, who are carrying along with them that great mass of arts, sciences, vigour, and industry which began long since in the east; and they will finish the great circle. . . . The American is a new man, who acts upon new principles; he must therefore entertain new ideas, and form new opinions. From involuntary idleness, servile dependence, penury and useless labour, he has passed to toils of a very different nature, rewarded by ample subsistence.—This is an American.

Finally, a concept can be defined by inference, rather than explicitly, or by saying what it is not. That is how Ralph Waldo Emerson explained the concept "gentleman" in 1849:

It is a vulgar error to suppose that a gentleman must be ready to fight. The utmost that can be demanded of the gentleman is that he be incapable of a lie. There is a man who has good sense, is well-informed, well-read, obliging, cultivated, capable, and has an absolute devotion to truth. He always means what he says and says what he means, however courteously. You may spit upon him—nothing could induce him to spit upon you—no praises, and no possessions, no compulsion of public opinion. You may kick him—he will think it the kick of a brute—but he is not a brute.

Comparison and Contrast

Defining what something is by showing what it is not, as in the last example, often results in a comparison/contrast—also called simply a comparison in everyday speech. For instance, Emerson could have said, "This is how a gentleman behaves. . . . This is how a brute behaves. . . ."

As we saw when comparing ourselves to Mario Cuomo in Chapter 3, a comparison/contrast requires a list of traits that two or more subjects share or that distinguish them from each other. We also saw that your purpose in the essay determines which traits are important. Once you have a list of traits, there are three common ways to present them: by subjects, by traits, by similarities and differences. Using two subjects and three traits for illustration, we can schematize the three approaches.

By subjects.

A. Mario Cuomo
    trait 1 (values)
    trait 2 (ethnic group)
    trait 3 (religious commitment)

B. You (or another person)
  trait 1 (values)
  trait 2 (ethnic group)
  trait 3 (religious commitment)

By traits.

A. Values
  Mario Cuomo
  You
B. Ethnic Group
  Mario Cuomo
  You
C. Religious Commitment
  Mario Cuomo
  You

By similarities and differences.

A. Similarities
  Both subjects share these. . . .
B. Differences
  Presented either by subject or trait.

Additional subjects or traits can easily be fitted into the patterns simply by extending them.

Like definition, comparison/contrast can be limited to a sentence:

No Roman Catholic politician—including John F. Kennedy—has done more than Cuomo to make the American Catholic bishops rethink the church's relationship to political issues.

Comparison/contrast can also shape larger units. In the following paragraph John Winthrop, governor of the Massachusetts Bay Colony, first defines one subject and then defines the next. This excerpt is from a speech delivered to the General Court of the colony in 1645, when Winthrop was impeached for overstepping his authority. The words that signal the organization are in italics.

There is a *twofold* liberty, natural (I mean as our nature is now corrupt) and civil or federal. *The first* is common to man with beasts and other creatures. By this, man, as he stands in relation to man simply, hath liberty to do what he lists; it is a liberty to evil as well as to good. This liberty is incompatible and inconsistent with authority, and cannot endure the least restraint of the most just authority. The exercise and maintaining of this liberty makes men grow more evil, and in time to be worse than brute beasts. This is that great enemy of truth and peace, that wild beast, which all ordinances of God are bent against, to restrain and subdue it. *The other kind* of liberty I call civil or federal, it may also be termed moral, in reference to the covenant between God and man, in the moral law, and the politic covenants and constitutions, amongst men themselves. This liberty is the proper end and object of authority, and cannot subsist without it; and it is a liberty to that only which is good, just, and honest.

In the next paragraph, taken from *France and England in North America*, Francis Parkman first presents the similarities among the English colonies; then he presents the differences in a trait-by-trait organization, showing how specific details of the government were handled in various ways.

The thirteen English colonies were *alike*, insomuch as they all had representative governments, and the basis of English law. But the *differences* among them were great. *Some* were purely English; *others* were made up of various races. . . . *Some* had one prevailing religious creed; *others* had many creeds. *Some* had charters, and *some* had not. In *most cases* the governor was appointed by the Crown; in *Pennsylvania* and *Maryland* he was appointed by a feudal proprietor, and in *Connecticut* and *Rhode Island* he was chosen by the people.

There is a fourth, less common, approach that a writer might use in order to show that the comparison/contrast is determined by outside forces. If the outside force is historical change, for example, the organization may be chronological and the similarities and differences of the two objects will be woven into the flow of time, as in the following passage:

For much of its *first century*, the labor movement was composed mostly of *men*, because the labor force was predominantly male. Only a few occupations were opened to *women*, notably clerical work, retail sales, and garment and textile manufacturing. But this *changed during World War II*, when it became *women's* patriotic duty to replace the *men* in all occupations who had gone off to fight. *When the war ended*, however, it was *women's* duty to give the jobs back to returning *men*. This situation changed in the 1960's with the rise of feminism and the need for two wage-earners in many families. But *until recently*, *women* continued to hold low-prestige job titles, even when doing work comparable to *men's*. In 1950, 29% of the workforce were women; in 1975 40% were women. In 1960, 80% of working women were in "women's" jobs; in 1975 half a million women—an 80% *increase*—held jobs formerly regarded as for men only.

Finally, a comparison/contrast, like a definition, is sometimes implied rather than spelled out. In the following excerpt from a speech given in 1937, labor leader John L. Lewis distinguishes unionism from communism by explaining one explicitly and the other by implication:

Unionization, as opposed to communism, presupposes the relation of employment; it is based upon the wage system and it recognizes fully and unreservedly the institution of private property and the right to investment profits.

Classification

A frequent companion of comparison/contrast and definition is classification, since once a concept is defined and distinguished from other concepts, a writer can use it to classify individual facts—that is, divide them into classes or groups. If you enjoy swimming, golf, singing, and playing the guitar, you can divide a paper about your interests into two sections—one for sports and one for music—and then divide each section into two paragraphs.

1. Sports

    a. swimming

    b. golf

2. Music

    a. singing

    b. playing the guitar

Classes must be defined so that they do not overlap. If, for example, you work in a toy store and have to put trains in one aisle and wooden toys in another, you will have a problem with wooden trains because they fit both categories. Even more problematic are such categories as "toys for boys" and "toys for girls." In using classification in a paper, such problems are common; as with comparison/contrast, you will have to decide which traits are important. Imagine, for example, that you have interviewed the following people:

an Asian woman majoring in law
a white man working in the registrar's office
a black man on the football team
a black woman professor of sociology
a white woman diving coach

In order to classify their opinions, you must decide which trait matters most. Should the men be in one group and the women in another? Do all minorities constitute a single class? Is a white woman athlete more like a black male athlete, a white male office worker, or a black woman professor? In addition, you must consider the topic. If the questions concerned athletic scholarships would you classify these people the same way you would if the issue was minority recruitment or sexual harassment? These are the kinds of considerations that you, the writer, must weigh when you classify, and you must be prepared to defend your decisions.

"What Makes Mario Run?" classifies Cuomo's formative experiences into two groups: one based on his ethnic heritage, the other based on his religion. Another writer may study Cuomo's life and decide to group his experiences by how they were influenced by his being from New York City and growing up in the years right after World War II. One aspect of a reader's evaluation of a text is just this attempt to substitute alternative explanations.

A large part of "Classism, Sexism, Racism and the Situation Comedy" (p. 129) is organized by classifying. The article defines "prestige groups" and "butt groups" in *Gilligan's Island* according to the presence or absence of money, privilege, maleness, and whiteness. It then classifies each character by looking at these four traits. In the prestige group, "at the pinnacle sits Thurston Howell III . . . because of his wealth, education, and heritage," as well as maleness and whiteness. Also in this group is the Skipper, who is white, male, and "as a property owner . . . commands some respect." At the top of the butt group is Mrs. Howell; "her status and identity rely on her relationship to her husband," but "being a woman . . . she fulfills her domestic role by supervising the work of the 'girls.'" Ginger is attractive to men and therefore performs light tasks. Mary Ann, on the other hand, "lacking Ginger's beauty . . . spends much of her time cooking meals, doing laundry, and tidying the huts." The lowest of the low are the nonwhites who occasionally "invade the island, threaten to devour the men, and carry off the women."

Classification often benefits from the visual reinforcement of a chart or table.

Along with higher expectations for women has come greater disillusionment. A 1980 poll by Virginia Slims reveals that 43% of women felt that being a man was more advantageous, as compared to 31% who believed this way in 1974. The percentage saying that being a woman was better increased only slightly, from 8% to 9% (see Table 1):

Table 1: Women's Answers to the Question "Do You Believe There Are More Advantages to Being a Man or a Woman?"

	1974	1980
More advantages to being a man	31%	43%
More advantages to being a woman	8%	9%
No difference	56%	45%
No opinion	5%	3%

Visual aids are not a substitute for discussion, however. As in this illustration, the text should summarize the data in the table.

Analogy

Sometimes a writer can clarify a point by showing one or two similarities between the topic and a more widely known object. In this case, the goal is not an exhaustive list of comparisons and contrasts, nor is the purpose to classify many items. Usually this type of comparison—called *analogy*—makes an abstract idea more meaningful by presenting it in terms of something more common, everyday, or colorful.

Analogy is what John Winthrop uses in order to explain how liberty cannot exist without authority. The following excerpt follows immediately after the passage we read on page 217:

> This liberty is maintained and exercised in a way of subjection to authority; it is of the same kind of liberty wherewith Christ hath made us free. The woman's own choice makes such a man her husband; yet being so chosen, he is her lord, and she is to be subject to him, yet in a way of liberty, not of bondage, and a true wife accounts her subjection her honor and freedom, and would not think her condition safe and free, but in her subjection to her husband's authority.

An analogy is called a **simile** when the writer uses signal words such as *like, the same, similar to,* as Winthrop does in the first sentence: "the same kind of liberty wherewith Christ hath made us free." When the writer does not use a signal word, but simply equates the two ideas, as Winthrop does with the comparison to a married woman, the analogy is called a **metaphor.**

Similes and metaphors that use positive images show the writer's approval of the subject; negative images convey the opposite. Describing the fire escapes that he found on tenements in New York City, Henry James writes in *The American Scene* (1907):

> . . . [T]he appearance to which they most often conduce is that of the spaciously organized cage for the nimbler class of animals in some great zoological garden. This general analogy is irresistible—it seems to offer, in each district, a little world of bars and perches and swings for human squirrels and monkeys.

Causation

Another important method of organization is to show causation, also known as cause and effect or "the reason." In this approach, the writer tries to explain why something happened. Since merely occurring first is not the same as causing the next event, the writer must analyze the relationship between events and present sufficient evidence to prove that one caused the other.

Though himself a slaveowner, Thomas Jefferson felt that slavery caused the corruption of society, as he explains in *Notes on the State of Virginia*, written in 1782.

> There must be an unhappy influence on our people produced by the existence of slavery among us. The whole commerce between master and slave is a perpetual exercise of boisterous passions, unremitting despotism on the one part, and degrading submissions on the other. Our children see this and learn to imitate it, for man is an imitative animal: from his cradle to his grave he is learning to do what he sees others do. The parent storms; the child looks on—and thus nursed, educated and exercised in tyranny cannot but be stamped by it. The man must be a prodigy who can remain undepraved by such circumstances.

In the following passage, adapted from a lecture at the Cook County jail in Chicago in 1902, the famous lawyer Clarence Darrow gives his view of what causes crime. The organizational signals are in italics.

> . . . crime is born, not *because* people are bad; people don't kidnap other people's children *because* they want the children or *because* they are devilish, but *because* they see a chance to get some money out of it. You cannot cure this crime *by* passing a law punishing by death kidnapers of children. There is one way to cure it. There is *one way* to cure all these offenses, and that *is to* give the people a chance to live. . . .
>
> The English people once punished criminals by sending them away. They would load them on a ship and export them to Australia. . . . When these criminals got over there, and nobody else had come, they had the whole continent to run over, *and so* they could raise sheep and furnish their own meat, which is easier than stealing it. These criminals *then* became decent respectable people because they had a chance to live. . . . But finally the descendants of the English aristocracy who sent the people over to Australia found out they were getting rich, *and so* they went over to get possession of the earth as they always do, and they organized land syndicates and got control of the land and ores, and *then* they had just as many criminals in Australia as they did in England. It was not *because* the world had grown bad; it was *because* the earth had been taken away from the people.

Causation is frequently conditional. That is, the writer has a theory, or hypothesis, that a certain cause will lead to a certain result, or that if a certain action had been taken in the past it would have led to a certain result. In conditions, therefore, the form of the verbs is very important since that is what distinguishes a prediction of a future "will be" from a "could have been" of the past.

In the following passage, the great English philosopher John Stuart Mill is predicting how people will behave under certain circumstances. The transitional signals and key verbs are in italics.

> With regard to the advance of democracy, there are two different positions which it is possible for a rational person to take, according as he thinks the masses are prepared or unprepared to exercise the control which they are acquiring over their destiny, in a manner which would be an improvement over what now exists. *If he thinks* them prepared, *he will* aid the democratic movement; or, *if he deem* it to be proceeding fast enough without him, *he will* at all events refrain from resisting it. *If,* on the contrary, *he thinks* the masses unprepared for complete control over their government—seeing at the same time, that, prepared or not, they cannot long be prevented from acquiring it—*he will* exert his utmost efforts in contributing to prepare them.

In the next passage, taken from *History of the Dividing Line,* a record of the survey team sent in 1728–29 to establish the border between Virginia and North Carolina, William Byrd explains what he feels would have happened if the English settlers had treated the Indians differently than they actually did. As you read, note the importance of the verb forms.

> For my part, I must be of opinion, as I hinted before, that there is but one way of converting these poor infidels and reclaiming them from barbarity, and that is, charitably to intermarry with them, according to the modern policy of the most Christian king in Canada and Louisiana. *Had the English done* this at the first settlement of the colony, the infidelity of the Indians *had been worn* out at this day, with their dark complexions, and the country *had swarmed* with people more than it does with insects. It was certainly an unreasonable nicety that prevented their entering into so good-natured an alliance. . . . I may safely venture to say, the Indian women *would have made* altogether as honest wives for the first planters as the damsals they used to purchase from aboard the ships. It is strange, therefore, that any good Christian *should have refused* a wholesome, straight bed-fellow, when he *might have had* so fair a portion with her as the merit of saving her soul. . . .

Narration

Another way to organize ideas is narration, that is, explaining their development in relation to time. To a large degree, narration is telling a story. The
writer must therefore have a story to tell and also feel certain that the best way to
present the material is in terms of time, rather than through one of the other
methods of organization. Narration usually follows chronological order from
earliest to latest, but it can also be arranged from latest to earliest.

As with the other methods we have examined, narration must serve a purpose as one element of a larger strategy. In 1858, at the height of the debate over
slavery in the United States, Sen. William Seward of New York tried to show
that the Democratic party had repeatedly thwarted attempts at abolition. Notice
how each sentence focuses on slavery, and the chronology is announced by
dates.

> In 1824, the democracy resisted the election of John Quincy Adams—
> himself before that time an acceptable Democrat—and in 1828 it expelled
> him from the Presidency and put a slaveholder in his place, although the
> office had been filled by slaveholders thirty-two out of forty years. In 1836,
> Martin Van Buren—the first non-slaveholding citizen of a free State to
> whose election the Democratic party ever consented—signalized his inau-
> guration into the Presidency by a gratuitous announcement that under no
> circumstances would he ever approve a bill for the abolishment of slavery
> in the District of Columbia. From 1838 to 1844 the subject of abolishing
> slavery in the District of Columbia and in the national dockyards and
> arsenals, was brought before Congress by repeated popular appeals. The
> Democratic party thereupon promptly denied the right of petition.

Likewise, the following passage is organized chronologically, but the details in
the narration are included because they are relevant to racial segregation, the
topic of the piece. The passage is taken from the famous Supreme Court decision
of 1954 in *Brown v. Board of Education*, which abolished "separate but equal"
segregated schools for blacks. Citations of the cases mentioned have been
omitted.

> In the *first* cases in this Court construing the Fourteenth Amendment,
> decided *shortly after* its adoption, the Court interpreted it as proscribing all
> state-imposed discrimination against the Negro race. The doctrine of
> "separate but equal" did not make its appearance in this Court *until 1896*
> in the case of *Plessy v. Ferguson,* involving not education but transporta-
> tion. American courts have *since* labored with the doctrine for *over half a
> century.* In this Court, there *have been* six cases involving the "separate but

equal" doctrine in the field of public education. In [these] the validity of the doctrine itself *was not* challenged: inequality was found in that specific benefits enjoyed by white students were denied to Negro students of the same educational qualifications. In none of these cases was it necessary to re-examine the doctrine to grant relief to the Negro plaintiff. . . . In the *instant* cases, that question *is* directly presented.

Another example of how an author can use narration to serve a purpose is in "The Gettysburg Address." Here, instead of telling the story from beginning to end, Abraham Lincoln moves the focus back and forth in time and timeliness to connect the events of the narration to what his audience must now do.

> *Fourscore and seven years ago* our fathers *brought* forth on this continent, a new nation, *conceived* in Liberty, and dedicated to the proposition that all men *are created* equal.
>
> *Now* we *are engaged* in a great civil war; *testing* whether that nation, or any nation so conceived and so dedicated, *can long endure.* We *are met* on a great battlefield of that war. We *have come* to dedicate a portion of that field as a final resting-place for those who here *gave* their lives that that nation *might* live. It is altogether fitting and proper that we *should do* this.
>
> But, in a larger sense, we *cannot dedicate*—we cannot consecrate—we cannot hallow this ground. The brave men, *living* and *dead,* who *struggled* here *have consecrated* it, far above our poor power to add or detract. The world *will* little *note,* nor long remember, what *we say here,* but it can never forget what *they did here.* It is for us the living, rather, to be dedicated here to the unfinished work which they who *fought* here *have* thus far so nobly *advanced.* It is rather for us to be here dedicated to the great task *remaining* before us—that from these honored dead we *take* increased devotion to that cause for which they *gave* the last full measure of devotion; that we here highly *resolve* that these dead *shall* not *have died* in vain; that this nation, under God, *shall have* a new birth of freedom; and that government of the people, by the people, for the people, shall not perish from the earth.

Description

A description contains carefully selected features to prove a point or establish a sense of time and place. The fleeting reference to Matilda Cuomo as "a slender, comely woman" shows that the authors of "What Makes Mario Run?" want to place the Cuomos within a specific ethnic mold where women are seen in these terms. So again we find that the author must decide what details to include in order to serve the larger purpose.

A few telling details can support a large generalization, as in the following passage from *History of the United States*, by Henry Adams.

> Nearly every foreign traveller who visited the United States during these early years, carried away an impression sober if not sad. A thousand miles of desolate and dreary forest, broken here and there by settlements; along the seacoast a few flourishing towns devoted to commerce; no arts, a provincial literature, a cancerous disease of negro slavery, and differences of political theory fortified within geographical lines—what could be hoped for such a country except to repeat the story of violence and brutality which the world already knew by heart . . . ?

Similarly, notice how the following description of Abraham Lincoln by the novelist Nathaniel Hawthorne begins with a thesis statement and general impression that are then supported by the few chosen features:

> Unquestionably, Western man though he be, and Kentuckian by birth, President Lincoln is the essential representative of all Yankees, and the veritable speciman, physically, of what the world seems determined to regard as our characteristic qualities. . . . There is no describing his lengthy awkwardness, nor the uncouthness of his movement; and yet it seemed as if I had been in the habit of seeing him daily, and had shaken hands with him a thousand times on some village street; so true was he to the aspect of the pattern American, though with a certain extravagance which, possibly, I exaggerated still further by the delighted eagerness with which I took it in. If put to guess his calling and livelihood, I should have taken him for a country school-master as soon as anything else. He was dressed in a rusty black frock coat and pantaloons, unbrushed, and worn so faithfully that the suit had adapted itself to the curves and angularities of his figure, and had grown to be an outer skin of the man. His hair was black, still unmixed with gray, stiff, somewhat bushy, and had apparently been acquainted with neither brush nor comb that morning, after the disarrangement of the pillow; and as to a nightcap, Uncle Abe probably knows nothing of such effeminacies. His complexion is dark and sallow, betokening, I fear, an insalubrious atmosphere around the White House; he has thick black eyebrows and an impending brow; his nose is large, and the lines about his mouth are very strongly defined.

EXERCISE : Using the Methods of Development

Needless to say, the value of knowing the various methods of development lies in being able to put them together to create a fully developed essay.

Read the following excerpts from Abraham Lincoln's "Second Inaugural Address" (1865), and try to explain the method(s) of development used in each section, and what each section contributes to the overall speech.

1. At this second appearing to take the oath of the presidential office, there is less occasion for an extended address than there was at the first. Then a statement, somewhat in detail, of a course to be pursued, seemed fitting and proper. Now, at the expiration of four years, during which public declarations have been constantly called forth on every point and phase of the great contest which still absorbs the attention, and engrosses the energies of the nation, little that is new could be presented.

2. On the occasion corresponding to this four years ago, all thoughts were anxiously directed to an impending civil war. While the inaugural address was being delivered from this place, devoted altogether to *saving* the Union without war, insurgent agents were in the city seeking to *destroy* it without war—seeking to dissolve the Union, and divide effects by negotiation.

3. Both parties deprecated war; but one of them would *make* war rather than let the nation survive; and the other would *accept* war rather than let it perish. And the war came.

4. One-eighth of the whole population were colored slaves, not distributed generally over the Union, but localized in the Southern part of it. These slaves constituted a peculiar and powerful interest. All knew that this interest was, somehow, the cause of the war.

5. To strengthen, perpetuate, and extend this interest was the object for which the insurgents would rend the Union, even by war; while the government claimed no right to do more than to restrict the territorial enlargement of it.

6. Both read the same Bible, and pray to the same God; and each invokes His aid against the other. It may seem strange that any men should dare to ask a just God's assistance in wringing their bread from the sweat of other men's faces; but let us judge not that we be not judged.

7. The prayers of both could not be answered; that of neither has been answered fully. The Almighty has His own purposes. "Woe unto the world because of offenses! for it must needs be that offenses come; but woe to that man by whom the offense cometh."

8. If we shall suppose that American slavery is one of those offenses which, in the providence of God, must needs come, but which, having continued through His appointed time, He now wills to remove, and that He gives to both North and South, this terrible war, as the woe due to those by whom the offense came, shall we discern therein any departure from those divine attributes which the believers in a Living God always ascribe to Him?

9. Fondly do we hope—fervently do we pray—that this mighty scourge of war may speedily pass away. Yet, if God wills that it continue, until all the

wealth piled by the bondman's two hundred and fifty years of unrequited toil shall be sunk, and until every drop of blood drawn with the lash, shall be paid by another drawn with the sword, as was said three thousand years ago, so still it must be said, "The judgements of the Lord are true and righteous altogether."

· DEVELOPING YOUR ESSAY

In your previous essays you may already have used some of the methods of development. You may have compared someone to Mario Cuomo, or you may have shown what caused someone to make a particular decision. Let's take a look at a paper in which a student tries to create a thesis and develop it.

CHOOSING YOUR OWN WAY OF LIFE

by Maria Martinez

1   While many of us have the freedom to choose our own way of life, this is a luxury not true for people of other cultures. This was my reaction when I had the experience of meeting an Amish family in Pennsylvania. I saw that they would have to break with their family in order to succeed.

2   When you are born into an Amish family, you are obligated to be loyal to Amish customs and traditions. If you do not, the family will consider you an outcast and will treat you as if you are no longer a member of the family. For example, if an Amish boy or girl falls in love with someone who is not Amish, they are told to break off the relationship. The other person is considered too different, and maybe even sinful. The Amish stay with people of their own culture.

3   The Amish are also very religious. They go to church every Sunday. They do not listen to popular music or dance. They do not watch television. They do not eat meat except on certain days because they believe animals are sacred. In the summer they do not wear bathing suits or shorts because they believe it is sinful to expose your skin. Woman and girls wear long skirts and blouses with sleeves. The men and boys wear long trousers and shirts like you would wear with a suit, but not tank tops or tee-shirts.

4   The Amish want to remain different. They live on farms in the country. They do not drive cars, but instead use horses and buggies. They have their own schools, but children stop going to school at an early age and start doing chores or working. They want to stay isolated from the rest of society. If you are Amish and want to succeed or change your way of life, you will have to break from your family. You can not have it both ways. Your family will not support whatever you want to do.

5   In a way, this is like what Prof. Anthony Patti of Lehman College found with Italians. With help from the Italian-American Institute to Foster Higher Education, Prof. Patti formed a group to help Italian-Americans who went to college relate to their ethnic heritage. Like Prof. Patti, the members of the group

had been told to be loyal and close to their families. But when they wanted to go into the careers of their choice, they ran into trouble. The people in the group were in fields that required college degrees, but Italian culture believes practical skills are more essential than academic achievement. They had conflicts with their families when they wanted to find personal fulfillment in a different way.

6   I was luckier. When I said I wanted to go to college my family was supportive. And if I didn't want to go, that would have been all right also. My parents always said that whatever I wanted to do was my choice. They would back me a hundred percent. I did not have to choose between my family and my own life.

7   The Amish and the people in Prof. Patti's group were from cultures where tradition and loyalty are number one. They became confused and frustrated when they wanted to succeed or change their way of life. Choosing how you want to live your life is a luxury that not everyone has.

Martinez's essay has some strong features. The thesis statement is to the point, easy to notice, and sets up a promising comparison/contrast: "While many of us have the freedom to choose our own way of life, this is a luxury not true for people of other cultures." Each paragraph has a clear topic sentence, which the content of the paragraph usually clarifies with examples, especially in the form of descriptions. The third and fourth paragraphs, for example, are particularly good because the description of Amish life supplies specific details that support the generalization about the Amish's religious commitment and desire to retain their own ways. An outline of the third paragraph will illustrate its strength:

The Amish are very religious.

Example 1: They go to church every Sunday.

Example 2: They do not listen to popular music or dance.

Example 3: They do not watch television.

Example 4: They do not eat meat except on certain days.

Example 5: They believe it is sinful to expose your

skin:

    a. Women and girls wear long skirts and

       blouses.

    b. Men and boys wear long trousers and

       shirts.

The essay flows nicely, as a topic sentence outline indicates:

Many of us have freedom to choose way of life.

Not true for people of other cultures.

  I. People who do not have this luxury

    A. Amish

      1. Amish are obligated to be loyal to customs

        and traditions.

      2. Amish are very religious.

      3. Amish want to remain different.

```
    B. Italian-Americans

    This is like what Patti found.

II. People who have this luxury

    I was luckier.
```

The essay could be strengthened if the student were more precise about what she means by "succeed." A definition would have helped. She seems to imply that success must be measured by the values of non-Amish society. In this case, success by definition requires rejecting family values. If so, the feelings of the Amish are probably not so different from those of anyone else. Imagine the conflict and confusion a Catholic or black would feel if success, by definition, required breaking with family and background. As for structure, the thesis statement is good, but the first paragraph suggests that the entire essay will be about the Amish, and, perhaps, the writer. There is no hint that Italian-Americans will be included. Of course, the introduction does not have to list every point that the body of the essay will develop, but neither should it list only half the points. The introduction should be both general and specific enough to prepare the reader's expectations for what follows.

CHECKLIST FOR DEVELOPING THE ESSAY

Ideas are logically connected in terms of
  place
  time
  similarity
  contrast
  condition
  causation

Methods of developing an essay are
  definition
  comparison/contrast
  classification
  analogy
  causation
  narration
  description

· ESSAYS FOR CRITICAL READING

The Thirteenth and Fourteenth Amendments to the Constitution, which were ratified soon after the Civil War, gave the freed slaves and other blacks equal rights with whites under federal law. But with the collapse of Reconstruction and the Radical Republicans, blacks lost their newly won political power. Throughout the South, Jim Crow laws mandated separation of the races in most areas of public life. Because Homer Adolph Plessy refused to sit in the Negro car of a train, the Supreme Court ruled on a Louisiana law of 1890 requiring separate railroad cars for blacks and whites. The decision was written by Justice Henry Billings Brown.

From *PLESSY V. FERGUSON* (1896)

1   The constitutionality of this act is attacked upon the ground that it conflicts both with the Thirteenth Amendment of the Constitution, abolishing slavery, and the Fourteenth Amendment, which prohibits certain restrictive legislation on the part of the States.

2   1. That it does not conflict with the Thirteenth Amendment, which abolished slavery and involuntary servitude, except as a punishment for crime, is too clear for argument. Slavery implies involuntary servitude—a state of bondage; the ownership of mankind as a chattel, or at least the control of the labor and services of one man for the benefit of another, and the absence of a legal right to the disposal of his own person, property and services. This amendment was said in the *Slaughter House cases*, 16 Wall. 36, to have been intended primarily to abolish slavery, as it had been previously known in this country, and that it equally forbade Mexican peonage or the Chinese coolie trade, when they amounted to slavery or involuntary servitude, and that the use of the word "servitude" was intended to prohibit the use of all forms of involuntary slavery, of whatever class or name. It was intimated, however, in that case that this amendment was regarded by the statesmen of that day as insufficient to protect the colored race from certain laws which had been enacted in the Southern States, imposing upon the colored race onerous disabilities and burdens, and curtailing their rights in the pursuit of life, liberty and property to such an extent that their freedom was of little value; and that the Fourteenth Amendment was devised to meet this exigency.

3   So, too, in the *Civil Rights cases*, 109 U.S. 3, 24, it was said that the act of a mere individual, the owner of an inn, a public conveyance or place of amusement, refusing accommodations to colored people, cannot be justly regarded as imposing any badge of slavery or servitude upon the applicant, but only as involving an ordinary civil injury, properly cognizable by the laws of the State,

and presumably subject to redress by those laws until the contrary appears. "It would be running the slavery argument into the ground," said Mr. Justice Bradley, "to make it apply to every act of discrimination which a person may see fit to make as to the guests he will entertain, or as to the people he will take into his coach or cab or car, or admit to his concert or theatre, or deal with in other matters of intercourse or business."

4   A statute which implies merely a legal distinction between the white and colored races—a distinction which is founded in the color of the two races, and which must always exist so long as white men are distinguished from the other race by color—has no tendency to destroy the legal equality of the two races, or reëstablish a state of involuntary servitude. . . .

5   2. By the Fourteenth Amendment, all persons born or naturalized in the United States, and subject to the jurisdiction thereof, are made citizens of the United States and of the State wherein they reside; and the States are forbidden from making or enforcing any law which shall abridge the privileges or immunities of citizens of the United States, or shall deprive any person of life, liberty or property without due process of law, or deny to any person within their jurisdiction the equal protection of the laws. . . .

6   The object of the amendment was undoubtedly to enforce the absolute equality of the two races before the law, but in the nature of things it could not have been intended to abolish distinctions based upon color, or to enforce social, as distinguished from political equality, or a commingling of the two races upon terms unsatisfactory to either. Laws permitting, and even requiring, their separation in places where they are liable to be brought into contact do not necessarily imply the inferiority of either race to the other, and have been generally, if not universally, recognized as within the competency of the state legislatures in the exercise of their police power. The most common instance of this is connected with the establishment of separate schools for white and colored children, which has been held to be a valid exercise of the legislative power even by courts of States where the political rights of the colored race have been longest and most earnestly enforced.

7   One of the earliest of these cases is that of *Roberts* v. *City of Boston*, 5 Cush. 198, in which the Supreme Judicial Court of Massachusetts held that the general school committee of Boston had power to make provision for the instruction of colored children in separate schools established exclusively for them, and to prohibit their attendance upon the other schools. "The great principle," said Chief Justice Shaw, p. 206, "advanced by the learned and eloquent advocate for the plaintiff," (Mr. Charles Sumner), "is, that by the constitution and laws of Massachusetts, all persons without distinction of age or sex, birth or color, origin or condition, are equal before the law. . . . But, when this great principle comes to be applied to the actual and various conditions of persons in society, it will not warrant the assertion, that men and women are legally clothed with the same civil and political powers, and that children and adults are legally to have

the same functions and be subject to the same treatment; but only that the rights of all, as they are settled and regulated by law, are equally entitled to the paternal consideration and protection of the law for their maintenance and security." It was held that the powers of the committee extended to the establishment of separate schools for children of different ages, sexes and colors, and that they might also establish special schools for poor and neglected children, who have become too old to attend the primary school, and yet have not acquired the rudiments of learning, to enable them to enter the ordinary schools. Similar laws have been enacted by Congress under its general power of legislation over the District of Columbia, Rev. Stat. D.C. §§ 281, 282, 283, 310, 319, as well as by the legislatures of many of the States, and have been generally, if not uniformly, sustained by the courts. . . .

8   Laws forbidding the intermarriage of the two races may be said in a technical sense to interfere with the freedom of contract, and yet have been universally recognized as within the police power of the State. *State* v. *Gibson*, 36 Indiana, 389.

9   The distinction between laws interfering with the political equality of the negro and those requiring the separation of the two races in schools, theatres and railway carriages has been frequently drawn by this court. Thus in *Strauder* v. *West Virginia*, 100 U.S. 303, it was held that a law of West Virginia limiting to white male persons, 21 years of age and citizens of the State, the right to sit upon juries, was a discrimination which implied a legal inferiority in civil society, which lessened the security of the right of the colored race, and was a step toward reducing them to a condition of servility. Indeed, the right of a colored man that, in the selection of jurors to pass upon his life, liberty and property, there shall be no exclusion of his race, and no discrimination against them because of color, has been asserted in a number of cases. . . .

10   So far, then, as a conflict with the Fourteenth Amendment is concerned, the case reduces itself to the question whether the statute of Louisiana is a reasonable regulation, and with respect to this there must necessarily be a large discretion on the part of the legislature. In determining the question of reasonableness it is at liberty to act with reference to the established usages, customs and traditions of the people, and with a view to the promotion of their comfort, and the preservation of the public peace and good order. Gauged by this standard, we cannot say that a law which authorizes or even requires the separation of the two races in public conveyances is unreasonable, or more obnoxious to the Fourteenth Amendment than the acts of Congress requiring separate schools for colored children in the District of Columbia, the constitutionality of which does not seem to have been questioned, or the corresponding acts of state legislatures.

11   We consider the underlying fallacy of the plaintiff's argument to consist in the assumption that the enforced separation of the two races stamps the colored race with a badge of inferiority. If this be so, it is not by reason of anything found in the act, but solely because the colored race chooses to put that construction upon it.

The argument necessarily assumes that if, as has been more than once the case, and is not unlikely to be so again, the colored race should become the dominant power in the state legislature, and should enact a law in precisely similar terms, it would thereby relegate the white race to an inferior position. We imagine that the white race, at least, would not acquiesce in this assumption. The argument also assumes that social prejudices may be overcome by legislation, and that equal rights cannot be secured to the negro except by an enforced commingling of the two races. We cannot accept this proposition. If the two races are to meet upon terms of social equality, it must be the result of natural affinities, a mutual appreciation of each other's merits and a voluntary consent of individuals. As was said by the Court of Appeals of New York in *People v. Gallagher*, 93 N.Y. 438, 448, "this end can neither be accomplished nor promoted by laws which conflict with the general sentiment of the community upon whom they are designed to operate. When the government, therefore, has secured to each of its citizens equal rights before the law and equal opportunities for improvement and progress, it has accomplished the end for which it was organized and performed all of the functions respecting social advantages with which it is endowed." Legislation is powerless to eradicate racial instincts or to abolish distinctions based upon physical differences, and the attempt to do so can only result in accentuating the difficulties of the present situation. If the civil and political rights of both races be equal one cannot be inferior to the other civilly or politically. If one race be inferior to the other socially, the Constitution of the United States cannot put them upon the same plane. . . .

SIGNIFICANCE

Explain the significance of the following quotations to the point of the decision or the structure of the analysis. Where relevant, try to explain why a particular method of development is used.

"Slavery implies involuntary servitude—a state of bondage; the ownership of mankind as a chattel, or at least the control of the labor and services of one man for the benefit of another, and the absence of a legal right to the disposal of his own person, property and services."

"This amendment . . . equally forbade Mexican peonage or the Chinese coolie trade."

". . . the act of a mere individual . . . refusing accommodations to colored people, cannot be justly regarded as imposing any badge of slavery or servitude upon the applicant, but only as involving an ordinary civil injury. . . ."

"A statute which implies merely a legal distinction between the white and colored races—a distinction which is founded in the color of the two races, and which must always exist so long as white men are distinguished from the other race by color—has no tendency to destroy the legal equality of the two races. . . ."

". . . the Supreme Judicial Court of Massachusetts held that the general school committee of Boston had power to make provision for the instruction of colored children in separate schools established exclusively for them. . . ."

". . . we cannot say that a law which authorizes or even requires the separation of the two races in public conveyances is unreasonable, or more obnoxious to the Fourteenth Amendment than the acts of Congress requiring separate schools for colored children in the District of Columbia. . . ."

"The argument necessarily assumes that if . . . the colored race should become the dominant power in the state legislature, and should enact a law in precisely similar terms, it would thereby relegate the white race to an inferior position. We imagine that the white race, at least, would not acquiesce in this assumption."

"Legislation is powerless to eradicate racial instincts or to abolish distinctions based upon physical differences, and the attempt to do so can only result in accentuating the difficulties of the present situation."

FUTURE USE

Briefly summarize the decision.

What information from this decision is relevant to your essay(s)? How could you use this information?

Henry Adams was the grandson of Pres. John Quincy Adams and great-grandson of Pres. John Adams. He graduated from Harvard in 1858 and then served as secretary to his father, who was a congressman and minister to Great Britain. He then taught history at Harvard, and wrote and traveled extensively. His History of the United States of America during the Administrations of Thomas Jefferson and James Madison, published between 1889 and 1891, is still considered to be the best study of that period. It is also a model of analytical history writing. This excerpt is from Volume I, Chapter 6.

From AMERICAN IDEALS 1800
in *HISTORY OF THE UNITED STATES*
by Henry Adams

1   Nearly every foreign traveller who visited the United States during these early years, carried away an impression sober if not sad. A thousand miles of desolate and dreary forest, broken here and there by settlements; along the seacoast a few flourishing towns devoted to commerce; no arts, a provincial literature, a cancerous disease of negro slavery, and differences of political theory fortified within geographical lines—what could be hoped for such a country except to repeat the story of violence and brutality which the world already knew by heart, until repetition for thousands of years had wearied and sickened mankind? Ages must probably pass before the interior could be thoroughly settled; even Jefferson, usually a sanguine man, talked of a thousand years with acquiescence, and in his first Inaugural Address, at a time when the Mississippi River formed the Western boundary, spoke of the country as having "room enough for our descendants to the hundredth and thousandth generation." No prudent person dared to act on the certainty that when settled, one government could comprehend the whole; and when the day of separation should arrive, and America should have her Prussia, Austria, and Italy, as she already had her England, France, and Spain, what else could follow but a return to the old conditions of local jealousies, wars, and corruption which had made a slaughterhouse of Europe?

2   The mass of Americans were sanguine and self-confident, partly by temperament, but partly also by reason of ignorance; for they knew little of the difficulties which surrounded a complex society. The Due de Liancourt, like many critics, was struck by this trait. Among other instances, he met with one in the person of a Pennsylvania miller, Thomas Lea, "a sound American patriot, persuading himself that nothing good is done, and that no one has any brains, except in America; that the wit, the imagination, the genius of Europe are already in decrepitude;" and the duke added: "This error is to be found in almost all Americans,—legislators, administrators, as well as millers, and is less inno-

cent there." In the year 1796 the House of Representatives debated whether to insert in the Reply to the President's Speech a passing remark that the nation was "the freest and most enlightened in the world,"—a nation as yet in swaddling-clothes, which had neither literature, arts, sciences, nor history; nor even enough nationality to be sure that it was a nation. . . . The idea that Europe was in her decrepitude proved only ignorance and want of enlightenment, if not of freedom, on the part of Americans, who could only excuse their error by pleading that notwithstanding these objections, in matters which for the moment most concerned themselves Europe was a full century behind America. If they were right in thinking that the next necessity of human progress was to lift the average man upon an intellectual and social level with the most favored, they stood at least three generations nearer than Europe to their common goal. The destinies of the United States were certainly staked, without reserve or escape, on the soundness of this doubtful and even improbable principle, ignoring or overthrowing the institutions of church, aristocracy, family, army, and political intervention, which long experience had shown to be needed for the safety of society. Europe might be right in thinking that without such safeguards society must come to an end; but even Europeans must concede that there was a chance, if no greater than one in a thousand, that America might, at least for a time, succeed. If this stake of temporal and eternal welfare stood on the winning card; if man actually should become more virtuous and enlightened, by mere process of growth, without church or paternal authority; if the average human being could accustom himself to reason with the logical processes of Descartes and Newton!—what then?

3   Then, no one could deny that the United States would win a stake such as defied mathematics. With all the advantages of science and capital, Europe must be slower than America to reach the common goal. American society might be both sober and sad, but except for negro slavery it was sound and healthy in every part. Stripped for the hardest work, every muscle firm and elastic, every ounce of brain ready for use, and not a trace of superfluous flesh on his nervous and supple body, the American stood in the world a new order of man. From Maine to Florida, society was in this respect the same, and was so organized as to use its human forces with more economy than could be approached by any society of the world elsewhere. Not only were artificial barriers carefully removed, but every influence that could appeal to ordinary ambition was applied. No brain or appetite active enough to be conscious of stimulants could fail to answer the intense incentive. Few human beings, however sluggish, could long resist the temptation to acquire power; and the elements of power were to be had in America almost for the asking. Reversing the old-world system, the American stimulant increased in energy as it reached the lowest and most ignorant class, dragging and whirling them upward as in the blast of a furnace. The penniless and homeless Scotch or Irish immigrant was caught and consumed by it; for every stroke of the axe and the hoe made him a capitalist, and made gentlemen of his children. Wealth was the strongest agent for moving the mass of mankind;

but political power was hardly less tempting to the more intelligent and better-educated swarms of American-born citizens, and the instinct of activity, once created, seemed heritable and permanent in the race.

4   Compared with this lithe young figure, Europe was actually in decrepitude. Mere class distinctions, the *patois* or dialect of the peasantry, the fixity of residence, the local costumes and habits marking a history that lost itself in the renewal of identical generations, raised from birth barriers which paralyzed half the population. Upon this mass of inert matter rested the Church and the State, holding down activity of thought. Endless wars withdrew many hundred thousand men from production, and changed them into agents of waste; huge debts, the evidence of past wars and bad government, created interests to support the system and fix its burdens on the laboring class; courts, with habits of extravagance that shamed common-sense, helped to consume private economies. All this might have been borne; but behind this stood aristocracies, sucking their nourishment from industry, producing nothing themselves, employing little or no active capital or intelligent labor, but pressing on the energies and ambition of society with the weight of an incubus. Picturesque and entertaining as these social anomalies were, they were better fitted for the theatre or for a museum of historical costumes than for an active workshop preparing to compete with such machinery as America would soon command. . . .

5   The charge that Americans were too fond of money to win the confidence of Europeans was a curious inconsistency; yet this was a common belief. If the American deluded himself and led others to their death by baseless speculations; if he buried those he loved in a gloomy forest where they quaked and died while he persisted in seeing there a splendid, healthy, and well-built city,—no one could deny that he sacrificed wife and child to his greed for gain, that the dollar was his god, and a sordid avarice his demon. Yet had this been the whole truth, no European capitalist would have hesitated to make money out of his grave; for, avarice against avarice, no more sordid or meaner type existed in America than could be shown on every 'Change in Europe. With much more reason Americans might have suspected that in America Englishmen found everywhere a silent influence, which they found nowhere in Europe, and which had nothing to do with avarice or with the dollar, but, on the contrary, seemed likely at any moment to sacrifice the dollar in a cause and for an object so illusory that most Englishmen could not endure to hear it discussed. European travellers who passed through America noticed that everywhere, in the White House at Washington and in log-cabins beyond the Alleghanies, except for a few Federalists, every American, from Jefferson and Gallatin down to the poorest squatter, seemed to nourish an idea that he was doing what he could to overthrow the tyranny which the past had fastened on the human mind. Nothing was easier than to laugh at the ludicrous expressions of this simple-minded conviction, or to cry out against its coarseness, or grow angry with its prejudices; to see its nobler side, to feel the beatings of a heart underneath the sordid surface of a

gross humanity, was not so easy. Europeans seemed seldom or never conscious that the sentiment could possess a noble side, but found only matter for complaint in the remark that every American democrat believed himself to be working for the overthrow of tyranny, aristocracy, hereditary privilege, and priesthood, wherever they existed. Even where the American did not openly proclaim this conviction in words, he carried so dense an atmosphere of the sentiment with him in his daily life as to give respectable Europeans an uneasy sense of remoteness.

6   . . . [N]othing was more elusive than the spirit of American democracy. Jefferson, the literary representative of the class, spoke chiefly for Virginians, and dreaded so greatly his own reputation as a visionary that he seldom or never uttered his whole thought. Gallatin and Madison were still more cautious. The press in no country could give shape to a mental condition so shadowy. The people themselves, although millions in number, could not have expressed their finer instincts had they tried, and might not have recognized them if expressed by others.

7   In the early days of colonization, every new settlement represented an idea and proclaimed a mission. Virginia was founded by a great, liberal movement aiming at the spread of English liberty and empire. The Pilgrims of Plymouth, the Puritans of Boston, the Quakers of Pennsylvania, all avowed a moral purpose, and began by making institutions that consciously reflected a moral idea. No such character belonged to the colonization of 1800. From Lake Erie to Florida, in long, unbroken line, pioneers were at work, cutting into the forests with the energy of so many beavers, and with no more express moral purpose than the beavers they drove away. The civilization they carried with them was rarely illumined by an idea; they sought room for no new truth, and aimed neither at creating, like the Puritans, a government of saints, nor, like the Quakers, one of love and peace; they left such experiments behind them, and wrestled only with the hardest problems of frontier life. No wonder that foreign observers, and even the educated, well-to-do Americans of the sea-coast, could seldom see anything to admire in the ignorance and brutality of frontiersmen, and should declare that virtue and wisdom no longer guided the United States! What they saw was not encouraging. To a new society, ignorant and semibarbarous, a mass of demagogues insisted on applying every stimulant that could inflame its worst appetites, while at the same instant taking away every influence that had hitherto helped to restrain its passions. Greed for wealth, lust for power, yearning for the blank void of savage freedom such as Indians and wolves delighted in,—these were the fires that flamed under the caldron of American society, in which, as conservatives believed, the old, well-proven, conservative crust of religion, government, family, and even common respect for age, education, and experience was rapidly melting away, and was indeed already broken into fragments, swept about by the seething mass of scum ever rising in greater quantities to the surface. . . .

8   Yet even then one part of the American social system was proving itself to be rich in results. The average American was more intelligent than the average European, and was becoming every year still more active-minded as the new movement of society caught him up and swept him through a life of more varied experiences. On all sides the national mind responded to its stimulants. Deficient as the American was in the machinery of higher instruction; remote, poor; unable by any exertion to acquire the training, the capital, or even the elementary text-books he needed for a fair development of his natural powers,—his native energy and ambition already responded to the spur applied to them. Some of his triumphs were famous throughout the world; for Benjamin Franklin had raised high the reputation of American printers, and the actual President of the United States, who signed with Franklin the treaty of peace with Great Britain, was the son of a small farmer, and had himself kept a school in his youth. In both these cases social recognition followed success; but the later triumphs of the American mind were becoming more and more popular. John Fitch was not only one of the poorest, but one of the least-educated Yankees who ever made a name; he could never spell with tolerable correctness, and his life ended as it began,—in the lowest social obscurity. Eli Whitney was better educated than Fitch, but had neither wealth, social influence, nor patron to back his ingenuity. In the year 1800 Eli Terry, another Connecticut Yankee of the same class, took into his employ two young men to help him make wooden clocks, and this was the capital on which the greatest clock-manufactory in the world began its operations. In 1797 Asa Whittemore, a Massachusetts Yankee, invented a machine to make cards for carding wool, which "operated as if it had a soul," and became the foundation for a hundred subsequent patents. In 1790 Jacob Perkins, of Newburyport, invented a machine capable of cutting and turning out two hundred thousand nails a day; and then invented a process for transferring engraving from a very small steel cylinder to copper, which revolutionized cotton-printing. The British traveller Weld, passing through Wilmington, stopped, as Liancourt had done before him, to see the great flour-mills on the Brandywine. "The improvements," he said, "which have been made in the machinery of the flour-mills in America are very great. The chief of these consist in a new application of the screw, and the introduction of what are called elevators, the idea of which was evidently borrowed from the chain-pump." This was the invention of Oliver Evans, a native of Delaware, whose parents were in very humble life, but who was himself, in spite of every disadvantage, an inventive genius of the first order. Robert Fulton, who in 1800 was in Paris with Joel Barlow, sprang from the same source in Pennsylvania. John Stevens, a native of New York, belonged to a more favored class, but followed the same impulses. All these men were the outcome of typical American society, and all their inventions transmuted the democratic instinct into a practical and tangible shape. . . .

SIGNIFICANCE

Explain the significance of the following quotations to the point of the selection or structure of the analysis. Where relevant, try to explain why a particular method of development was used.

"The mass of Americans were sanguine and self-confident, partly by temperament, but partly also by reason of ignorance. . . ."

". . . in matters which for the moment most concerned themselves Europe was a full century behind America."

"Reversing the old-world system, the American stimulant increased in energy as it reached the lowest and most ignorant class, dragging and whirling them upward as in the blast of a furnace."

"Compared with this lithe young figure, Europe was actually in decrepitude."

". . . every American, from Jefferson and Gallatin down to the poorest squatter, seemed to nourish an idea that he was doing what he could to overthrow the tyranny which the past had fastened on the human mind."

"In the early days of colonization, every new settlement represented an idea and proclaimed a mission."

". . . one part of the American social system was proving itself to be rich in results. The average American was more intelligent than the average European. . . ."

FUTURE USE

Briefly summarize the selection.

What information from this selection is relevant to your essay(s)? How could you use this information?

Booker T. Washington was born into slavery in Virginia in 1856. After emancipation he struggled to receive an education and eventually became head of the Tuskegee Institute, a black college. In his address to the Atlanta Exposition in 1895 he analyzed the situation in the South and presented a plan for future relations between the races. The speech was widely hailed as the embodiment of the hopes of "moderate" blacks for racial progress through economic cooperation.

From THE ATLANTA ADDRESS
by Booker T. Washington

Mr. President and Gentlemen of the Board of Directors and Citizens:

1   One-third of the population of the South is of the Negro race. No enterprise seeking the material, civil, or moral welfare of this section can disregard this element of our population and reach the highest success. I but convey to you, Mr. President and Directors, the sentiment of the masses of my race when I say that in no way have the value and manhood of the American Negro been more fittingly and generously recognized than by the managers of this magnificent Exposition at every stage of its progress. It is a recognition that will do more to cement the friendship of the two races than any occurrence since the dawn of our freedom.

2   Not only this, but the opportunity here afforded will awaken among us a new era of industrial progress. Ignorant and inexperienced, it is not strange that in the first years of our new life we began at the top instead of at the bottom; that a seat in Congress or the state legislature was more sought than real estate or industrial skill; that the political convention of stump speaking had more attractions than starting a dairy farm or truck garden.

3   A ship lost at sea for many days suddenly sighted a friendly vessel. From the mast of the unfortunate vessel was seen a signal, "Water, water; we die of thirst!" The answer from the friendly vessel at once came back, "Cast down your bucket where you are." A second time the signal, "Water, water; send us water!" ran up from the distressed vessel, and was answered, "Cast down your bucket where you are." And a third and fourth signal for water was answered, "Cast down your bucket where you are." The captain of the distressed vessel, at last heeding the injunction, cast down his bucket, and it came up full of fresh, sparkling water from the mouth of the Amazon River. To those of my race who depend on bettering their condition in a foreign land or who underestimate the importance of cultivating friendly relations with the southern white man, who is their next-door neighbour, I would say: "Cast down your bucket where you are"—cast it down in making friends in every manly way of the people of all races by whom we are surrounded.

4   Cast it down in agriculture, mechanics, in commerce, in domestic service, and in the professions. And in this connection it is well to bear in mind that

whatever other sins the South may be called to bear, when it comes to business, pure and simple, it is in the South that the Negro is given a man's chance in the commercial world, and in nothing is this Exposition more eloquent than in emphasizing this chance. Our greatest danger is that in the great leap from slavery to freedom we may overlook the fact that the masses of us are to live by the productions of our hands, and fail to keep in mind that we shall prosper in proportion as we learn to dignify and glorify common labour and put brains and skill into the common occupations of life; shall prosper in proportion as we learn to draw the line between the superficial and the substantial, the ornamental gewgaws of life and the useful. No race can prosper till it learns that there is as much dignity in tilling a field as in writing a poem. It is at the bottom of life we must begin, and not at the top. Nor should we permit our grievances to over-shadow our opportunities.

5   To those of the white race who look to the incoming of those of foreign birth and strange tongue and habits for the prosperity of the South, were I permitted I would repeat what I say to my own race, "Cast down your bucket where you are." Cast it down among the eight millions of Negroes whose habits you know, whose fidelity and love you have tested in days when to have proved treacherous meant the ruin of your firesides. Cast down your bucket among these people who have, without strikes and labor wars, tilled your fields, cleared your forests, builded your railroads and cities, and brought forth treasures from the bowels of the earth, and helped make possible this magnificent representation of the progress of the South. Casting down your bucket among my people, helping and encouraging them as you are doing on these grounds, and to education of head, hand, and heart, you will find that they will buy your surplus land, make blossom the waste places in your fields, and run your factories.

6   While doing this, you can be sure in the future, as in the past, that you and your families will be surrounded by the most patient, faithful, law-abiding, and unresentful people that the world has seen. As we have proved our loyalty to you in the past, in nursing your children, watching by the sickbed of your mothers and fathers, and often following them with tear-dimmed eyes to their graves, so in the future, in our humble way, we shall stand by you with a devotion that no foreigner can approach, ready to lay down our lives, if need be, in defence of yours, interlacing our industrial, commercial, civil, and religious life with yours in a way that shall make the interests of both races one. In all things that are purely social we can be as separate as the fingers, yet one as the hand in all things essential to mutual progress. . . .

7   The wisest among my race understand that the agitation of questions of social equality is the extremest folly, and that progress in the enjoyment of all the privileges that will come to us must be the result of severe and constant struggle rather than of artificial forcing. No race that has anything to contribute to the markets of the world is long in any degree ostracized. It is important and right that all privileges of the law be ours, but it is vastly more important that we be

prepared for the exercises of these privileges. The opportunity to earn a dollar in a factory just now is worth infinitely more than the opportunity to spend a dollar in an opera-house.

8   In conclusion, may I repeat that nothing in thirty years has given us more hope and encouragement, and drawn us so near to you of the white race, as this opportunity offered by the Exposition; here bending, as it were, over the altar that represents the results of the struggles of your race and mine, both starting practically empty-handed three decades ago, I pledge that in your effort to work out the great and intricate problem which God has laid at the doors of the South, you shall have at all times the patient, sympathetic help of my race. Only let this be constantly in mind, that, while from representations in these buildings of the product of field, of forest, of mine, of factory, letters, and art, much good will come, yet far above and beyond material benefits will be that higher good, that, let us pray God, will come, in a blotting out of sectional differences and racial animosities and suspicions, and in a determination to administer absolute justice, even in the remotest corner; in a willing obedience among all classes to the mandates of law and a spirit that will tolerate nothing but the highest equity in the enforcement of law. This, then, coupled with our material prosperity, will bring into our beloved South a new heaven and a new earth.

SIGNIFICANCE

Explain the significance of the following quotations to the point or structure of the speech. Where relevant, try to explain why a particular method of development was used.

"One-third of the population of the South is of the Negro race. No enterprise seeking the material, civil, or moral welfare of this section can disregard this element of our population and reach the highest success."

"Ignorant and inexperienced, it is not strange that in the first years of our new life we began at the top instead of at the bottom; that a seat in Congress or the state legislature was more sought than real estate or industrial skill; that the political convention of stump speaking had more attractions than starting a dairy farm or truck garden."

"A ship lost at sea for many days suddenly sighted a friendly vessel. From the mast of the unfortunate vessel was seen a signal, 'Water, water; we die of thirst!' The answer from the friendly vessel at once came back, 'Cast down your bucket where you are.' A second time the signal, 'Water, water; send us water!' ran up from the distressed vessel, and was answered, 'Cast down your bucket where you are.' . . . The captain of the distressed vessel, at last heeding the injunction, cast down his bucket, and it came up full of fresh, sparkling water from the mouth of the Amazon River."

"To those of my race who depend on bettering their condition in a foreign land or who underestimate the importance of cultivating friendly relations with the southern white man, who is their next-door neighbour, I would say: 'Cast down your bucket where you are.'"

"Our greatest danger is that in the great leap from slavery to freedom we may overlook the fact that the masses of us are to live by the productions of our hands, and fail to keep in mind that we will prosper in proportion as we learn to dignify and glorify common labour. . . ."

"To those of the white race who look to the incoming of those of foreign birth and strange tongue and habits for the prosperity of the South, were I permitted I would repeat what I say to my own race, 'Cast down your bucket where you are.'"

"Cast down your bucket among these people who have, without strikes and labor wars, tilled your fields, cleared your forests, builded your railroads and cities, and brought forth treasures from the bowels of the earth."

"In all things that are purely social we can be as separate as the fingers, yet one as the hand in all things essential to mutual progress."

"No race that has anything to contribute to the markets of the world is long in any degree ostracized."

FUTURE USE

Briefly summarize the selection.

What information from this selection is relevant to your essay(s)? How could you use this information?

By the beginning of the twentieth century, the United States, Great Britain, and Germany seemed to have reached an unprecedented level of economic success. Max Weber, a German sociologist and political economist, sought to determine why capitalism developed only in the West and why it reached its height in these three countries. After studying the social and religious histories of China, India, the Jews, and Europe, he published his answer in The Protestant Ethic and the Spirit of Capitalism *(1904–5). The following excerpts are from the translation by Talcott Parsons.*

From *THE PROTESTANT ETHIC AND THE SPIRIT OF CAPITALISM*
by Max Weber

1   In fact, the *summum bonum* of this ethic, the earning of more and more money, combined with the strict avoidance of all spontaneous enjoyment of life, is above all completely devoid of any eudaemonistic, not to say hedonistic, admixture. It is thought of so purely as an end in itself, that from the point of view of the happiness of, or utility to, the single individual, it appears entirely transcendental and absolutely irrational. Man is dominated by making money, by acquisition as the ultimate purpose of his life. Economic acquisition is no longer subordinated to man as the means for the satisfaction of his material needs. This reversal of what we should call the natural relationship, so irrational from a naive point of view, is evidently as definitely a leading principle of capitalism as it is foreign to all peoples not under capitalistic influence. At the same time it expresses a type of feeling which is closely connected with certain religious ideas. If we thus ask, *why* should "money be made out of men," Benjamin Franklin himself, although he was a colourless deist, answers in his autobiography with a quotation from the Bible, which his strict Calvinistic father drummed into him again and again in his youth: "Seest thou a man diligent in his business? He shall stand before kings" (Prov. xxii 29). The earning of money within the modern economic order is, so long as it is done legally, the result and expression of virtue and proficiency in a calling; and this virtue and proficiency are, as it is now not difficult to see, the real Alpha and Omega of Franklin's ethic, as expressed in the passages we have quoted, as well as in all his works without exception.

2   And in truth this peculiar idea, so familiar to us to-day, but in reality so little a matter of course, of one's duty in a calling, is what is most characteristic of the social ethic of capitalistic culture, and is in a sense the fundamental basis of it. It is an obligation which the individual is supposed to feel and does feel towards the content of his professional activity, no matter in what it consists, in particu-

lar no matter whether it appears on the surface as a utilization of his personal powers, or only of his material possessions (as capital). . . .

3   . . . In the Puritan concept of the calling the emphasis is always placed on this methodical character of worldly asceticism, not, as with Luther, on the acceptance of the lot which God has irretrievably assigned to man.

4   Hence the question whether anyone may combine several callings is answered in the affirmative, if it is useful for the common good or one's own, and not injurious to anyone, and if it does not lead to unfaithfulness in one of the callings. Even a change of calling is by no means regarded as objectionable, if it is not thoughtless and is made for the purpose of pursuing a calling more pleasing to God, which means, on general principles, one more useful.

5   It is true that the usefulness of a calling, and thus its favor in the sight of God, is measured primarily in moral terms, and thus in terms of the importance of the goods produced in it for the community. But a further, and, above all, in practice the most important, criterion is found in private profitableness. For if that God, whose hand the Puritan sees in all occurrences of life, shows one of His elect a chance of profit, he must do it with a purpose. Hence the faithful Christian must follow the call by taking advantage of the opportunity. "If God show you a way in which you may lawfully get more than in another way (without wrong to your soul or to any other), if you refuse this, and choose the less gainful way, you cross one of the ends of your calling, and you refuse to be God's steward, and to accept His gifts and use them for Him when He requireth it: you may labour to be rich for God, though not for the flesh and sin" [quoting Richard Baxter, an influential Puritan minister of the seventeenth century].

6   Wealth is thus bad ethically only in so far as it is a temptation to idleness and sinful enjoyment of life, and its acquisition is bad only when it is with the purpose of later living merrily and without care. But as a performance of duty in a calling it is not only morally permissible, but actually enjoined. The parable of the servant who was rejected because he did not increase the talent which was entrusted to him seemed to say so directly. To wish to be poor was, it was often argued, the same as wishing to be unhealthy; it is objectionable as a glorification of works and derogatory to the glory of God. Especially begging, on the part of one able to work, is not only the sin of slothfulness, but a violation of the duty of brotherly love according to the Apostle's own word.

7   The emphasis on the ascetic importance of a fixed calling provided an ethical justification of the modern specialized division of labour. In a similar way the providential interpretation of profit-making justified the activities of the business man. The superior indulgence of the *seigneur* and the parvenu ostentation of the *nouveau riche* are equally detestable to asceticism. But, on the other hand, it has the highest ethical appreciation of the sober, middle-class, self-made man. "God blesseth His trade" is a stock remark about those good men who had successfully followed the divine hints. The whole power of the God of the Old

Testament, who rewards His people for their obedience in this life, necessarily exercised a similar influence on the Puritan who, following Baxter's advice, compared his own state of grace with that of the heroes of the Bible, and in the process interpreted the statements of the Scriptures as the articles of a book of statutes. . . .

8   This worldly Protestant asceticism, as we may recapitulate up to this point, acted powerfully against the spontaneous enjoyment of possessions; it restricted consumption, especially of luxuries. On the other hand, it had the psychological effect of freeing the acquisition of goods from the inhibitions of traditionalistic ethics. It broke the bonds of the impulse of acquisition in that it not only legalized it, but (in the sense discussed) looked upon it as directly willed by God. The campaign against the temptations of the flesh, and the dependence on external things, was, as besides the Puritans the great Quaker apologist Barclay expressly says, not a struggle against the rational acquisition, but against the irrational use of wealth.

9   But this irrational use was exemplified in the outward forms of luxury which their code condemned as idolatry of the flesh, however natural they had appeared to the feudal mind. On the other hand, they approved the rational and utilitarian uses of wealth which were willed by God for the needs of the individual and the community. They did not wish to impose mortification of the man of wealth, but the use of his means for necessary and practical things. The idea of comfort characteristically limits the extent of ethically permissible expenditures. . . .

10   When the limitation of consumption is combined with this release of acquisitive activity, the inevitable practical result is obvious: accumulation of capital through the ascetic compulsion to save. The restraints which were imposed upon the consumption of wealth naturally served to increase it by making possible the productive investment of capital. . . .

SIGNIFICANCE

Explain the significance of the following quotations to the point or structure of the selection. Where relevant, try to explain why a particular method of development was used.

". . . the earning of more and more money . . . is thought of so purely as an end in itself, that from the point of view of the happiness of, or utility to, the single individual, it appears entirely transcendental and absolutely irrational."

". . . Benjamin Franklin himself, although he was a colourless deist, answers in his autobiography with a quotation from the Bible, which his strict Calvinistic father drummed into him again and again in his youth: 'Seest thou a man diligent in his business? He shall stand before kings' (Prov. xxii 29)."

". . . this peculiar idea, so familiar to us to-day, but in reality so little a matter of course, of one's duty in a calling, is what is most characteristic of the social ethic of capitalistic culture, and is in a sense the fundamental basis of it."

". . . In the Puritan concept of the calling the emphasis is always placed on this methodical character of worldly asceticism, not, as with Luther, on the acceptance of the lot which God has irretrievably assigned to man."

". . . if that God, whose hand the Puritan sees in all occurrences of life, shows one of His elect a chance of profit, he must do it with a purpose. Hence the faithful Christian must follow the call by taking advantage of the opportunity."

". . . as a performance of duty in a calling it is not only morally permissible, but actually enjoined. The parable of the servant who was rejected because he did not increase the talent which was entrusted to him seemed to say so directly."

"When the limitation of consumption is combined with this release of acquisitive activity, the inevitable practical result is obvious: accumulation of capital through the ascetic compulsion to save."

FUTURE USE

Briefly summarize the selection.

What information from this selection is relevant to your essay(s)? How could you use this information?

· MAKING CONNECTIONS

1. What distinction does *Plessy v. Ferguson* (p. 233) make between civil rights and social behavior? Does Booker T. Washington (p. 244) agree or disagree with the distinction? Do you? What is the current legal status of the distinction? What evidence can you present from current social behavior that either supports or contradicts the view in *Plessy*? Which groups today, in addition to blacks, find themselves in the situation described in *Plessy*? What essay topic(s) can emerge from this discussion?

2. "Classism, Sexism, Racism and the Situation Comedy" (p. 129) suggests that situation comedies support the existing social structure. Do you agree? What evidence can you present to either support or contradict this view? What about television, or the media, in general? How is Veblen's theory of the leisure class (p. 134) relevant to the television image of the rich? How does the television image of social classes compare and contrast with the image of the rich in "Wealth" (p. 180) and of workers in "A Short History of Labor" (p. 185)? How does the image of blacks in classics like *Gone with the Wind* and *Birth of a Nation* compare and contrast with the image in "The Atlanta Address" (p. 244)? What essay topic(s) can emerge from this discussion?

3. To what extent do television and movies—or fiction in general—shape ideas and to what extent do they use the public's existing ideas? What

values underlie popular types like the mad scientist, dumb jock, absent-minded professor, sexy blonde? Which articles that you have read can shed light on this question? What essay topic(s) can emerge from this discussion?

4. How does the decision in *Plessy* reflect its time and place? Do laws and courts lead or follow public opinion? Which should they do? What light is shed on this discussion by "The Atlanta Address"? How do you think the speech was greeted by whites and blacks of the time? How do the works of scholars like Turner (p. 73), Veblen (p. 134), Weber (p. 248), and Adams (p. 238) reflect their time and place? What essay topic(s) can emerge from this discussion?

5. What does Henry Adams (p. 238) see as the greatest strength of America during the early years of the nation? Did that quality still exist by the end of the nineteenth century? How does Adams's view of American character compare and contrast with the views of Crèvecoeur, Turner, Veblen, and Weber? What essay topic(s) can emerge from this discussion?

· ADDITIONAL ESSAYS FOR DISCUSSION

From OUR BLUNDERING
FOREIGN POLICY
by Henry Cabot Lodge (1895)

1   All the great constructive legislation of this country, with hardly an exception, has been the work of the Republican party and its predecessors. The
Federalists organized the Government; the Whigs developed our industries and
set on foot our great system of internal improvements; the Republicans maintained the Union, abolished slavery, placed the last great Amendments on the
Constitution, and established our credit and our tariff. The record of the Democratic party for constructive legislation, on the other hand, despite their many
years of power, is singularly barren. But there is one direction where the Democratic party has done a great work. The Republicans under the lead of Charles
Sumner added Alaska to our domain, but with this exception all our great
acquisitions of territory have been the work of Democrats. To them we owe the
Louisiana purchase, Florida, Texas, and the Mexican cession. If the Democratic
party has had one cardinal principle beyond all others, it has been that of
pushing forward the boundaries of the United States. Under this Administration, governed as it is by free-trade influences, this great principle of the Democratic party during nearly a century of existence has been utterly abandoned.
Thomas Jefferson, admitting that he violated the Constitution while he did it,
effected the Louisiana purchase, but Mr. Cleveland has labored to overthrow
American interests and American control in Hawaii. Andrew Jackson fought for
Florida, but Mr. Cleveland is eager to abandon Samoa. The Democratic party,
in its leaders at least, has been successfully Cobdenized, and that is the underlying reason for their policy of retreat. It is the melancholy outcome of the
doctrine that there is no higher aim or purpose for men or for nations than to
buy and sell, to trade jack-knives and make everything cheap. No one underrates the importance of the tariffs or the still greater importance of a sound
currency. But of late years we have been so absorbed in these economic questions
that we have grown unmindful of others. We have had something too much of
these disciples of the Manchester school, who think the price of calico more
important than a nation's honor, the duties on pig iron of more moment than
the advance of a race.
2   It is time to recall what we have been tending to forget; that we have always
had and that we have now a foreign policy which is of great importance to our
national well-being. The foundation of that policy was Washington's doctrine of
neutrality. To him and to Hamilton we owe the principle that it was not the
business of the United States to meddle in the affairs of Europe. When this

policy was declared, it fell with a shock upon the Americans of that day, for we were still colonists in habits of thought and could not realize that the struggles of Europe did not concern us. Yet the establishment of the neutrality policy was one of the greatest services which Washington and Hamilton rendered to the cause of American nationality. The corollary of Washington's policy was the Monroe doctrine, the work of John Quincy Adams, a much greater man than the President whose name it bears. Washington declared that it was not the business of the United States to meddle in the affairs of Europe, and John Quincy Adams added that Europe must not meddle in the Western hemisphere. As I have seen it solemnly stated recently that the annexation of Hawaii would be a violation of the Monroe doctrine, it is perhaps not out of place to say that the Monroe doctrine has no bearing on the extension of the United States, but simply holds that no European power shall establish itself in the Americas or interfere with American governments.

3   The neutrality policy and the Monroe doctrine are the two great principles established at the outset by far-seeing statesmen in regard to the foreign relations of the United States. But it would be a fatal mistake to suppose that our foreign policy stopped there, or that these fundamental principles in any way fettered the march of the American people. Washington withdrew us from the affairs of Europe, but at the same time he pointed out that our true line of advance was to the West. He never for an instant thought that we were to remain stationary and cease to move forward. He saw, with prophetic vision, as did no other man of his time, the true course for the American people. He could not himself enter into the promised land, but he showed it to his people, stretching from the Blue Ridge to the Pacific Ocean. We have followed the teachings of Washington. We have taken the great valley of the Mississippi and pressed on beyond the Sierras. We have a record of conquest, colonization, and territorial expansion un-equalled by any people in the nineteenth century. We are not to be curbed now by the doctrines of the Manchester school which have never been observed in England, and which as an importation are even more absurdly out of place here than in their native land. It is not the policy of the United States to enter, as England has done, upon the general acquisition of distant possession in all parts of the world. Our government is not adapted to such a policy, and we have no need of it, for we have an ample field at home; but at the same time it must be remembered that while in the United States themselves we hold the citadel of our power and greatness as a nation, there are outworks essential to the defence of that citadel which must neither be neglected nor abandoned.

4   There is a very definite policy for American statesmen to pursue in this respect if they would prove themselves worthy inheritors of the principles of Washington and Adams. We desire no extension to the south, for neither the population nor the lands of Central or South America would be desirable addi-tions to the United States. But from the Rio Grande to the Arctic Ocean there should be but one flag and one country. Neither race nor climate forbids this

extension, and every consideration of national growth and national welfare demands it. In the interests of our commerce and of our fullest development we should build the Nicaragua canal, and for the protection of that canal and for the sake of our commercial supremacy in the Pacific we should control the Hawaiian Islands and maintain our influence in Samoa. England has studded the West Indies with strong places which are a standing menace to our Atlantic seaboard. We should have among those islands at least one strong naval station, and when the Nicaragua canal is built, the island of Cuba, still sparsely settled and of almost unbounded fertility, will become to us a necessity. Commerce follows the flag, and we should build up a navy strong enough to give protection to Americans in every quarter of the globe and sufficiently powerful to put our coasts beyond the possibility of successful attack.

5   The tendency of modern times is toward consolidation. It is apparent in capital and labor alike, and it is also true of nations. Small States are of the past and have no future. The modern movement is all toward the concentration of people and territory into great nations and large dominions. The great nations are rapidly absorbing for their future expansion and their present defence all the waste places of the earth. It is a movement which makes for civilization and the advancement of the race. As one of the great nations of the world, the United States must not fall out of the line of march.

From *PROGRESS AND POVERTY*
by Henry George (1879)

1   This association of poverty with progress is the great enigma of our times. It is the central fact from which spring industrial, social, and political difficulties that perplex the world, and with which statesmanship and philanthropy and education grapple in vain. From it come the clouds that overhang the future of the most progressive and self-reliant nations. It is the riddle which the Sphinx of Fate puts to our civilization, and which not to answer is to be destroyed. So long as all the increased wealth which modern progress brings goes but to build up great fortunes, to increase luxury and make sharper the contrast between the House of Have and the House of Want, progress is not real and cannot be permanent. The reaction must come. The tower leans from its foundations, and every new story but hastens the final catastrophe. To educate men who must be condemned to poverty, is but to make them restive; to base on a state of most glaring social inequality political institutions under which men are theoretically equal, is to stand a pyramid on its apex.

2   All-important as this question is, pressing itself from every quarter painfully upon attention, it has not yet received a solution which accounts for all the facts and points to any clear and simple remedy. This is shown by the widely varying attempts to account for the prevailing depression. They exhibit not merely a divergence between vulgar notions and scientific theories, but also show that the concurrence which should exist between those who avow the same general theories breaks up upon practical questions into an anarchy of opinion. Upon high economic authority we have been told that the prevailing depression is due to over-consumption; upon equally high authority, that it is due to over-production; while the wastes of war, the extension of railroads, the attempts of workmen to keep up wages, the demonetization of silver, the issues of paper money, the increase of labor-saving machinery, the opening of shorter avenues to trade, etc., are separately pointed out as the cause, by writers of reputation.

3   And while professors thus disagree, the ideas that there is a necessary conflict between capital and labor, that machinery is an evil, that competition must be restrained and interest abolished, that wealth may be created by the issue of money, that it is the duty of government to furnish capital or to furnish work, are rapidly making way among the great body of the people, who keenly feel a hurt and are sharply conscious of a wrong. . . .

4   What constitutes the rightful basis of property? What is it that enables a man justly to say of a thing, "It is mine"? From what springs the sentiment which acknowledges his exclusive right as against all the world? Is it not, primarily, the right of a man to himself, to the use of his own powers, to the enjoyment of the fruits of his own exertions? . . .

5   . . . There can be to the ownership of anything no rightful title which is not

derived from the title of the producer and does not rest upon the natural right of the man to himself. There can be no other rightful title, because (1st) there is no other natural right from which any other title can be derived, and (2d) because the recognition of any other title is inconsistent with and destructive of this.

6   For (1st) what other right exists from which the right to the exclusive possession of anything can be derived, save the right of a man to himself? With what other power is man by nature clothed, save the power of exerting his own faculties? How can he in any other way act upon or affect material things or other men? Paralyze the motor nerves, and your man has no more external influence or power than a log or stone. From what else, then, can the right of possessing and controlling things be derived? If it spring not from man himself, from what can it spring? Nature acknowledges no ownership or control in man save as the result of exertion. In no other way can her treasures be drawn forth, her powers directed, or her forces utilized or controlled. She makes no discriminations among men, but is to all absolutely impartial. She knows no distinction between master and slave, king and subject, saint and sinner. All men to her stand upon an equal footing and have equal rights. She recognizes no claim but that of labor, and recognizes that without respect to the claimant. If a pirate spread his sails, the wind will fill them as well as it will fill those of a peaceful merchantman or missionary bark; if a king and a common man be thrown overboard, neither can keep his head above water except by swimming; birds will not come to be shot by the proprietor of the soil any quicker than they will come to be shot by the poacher; fish will bite or will not bite at a hook in utter disregard as to whether it is offered them by a good little boy who goes to Sunday-school, or a bad little boy who plays truant; grain will grow only as the ground is prepared and the seed is sown; it is only at the call of labor that ore can be raised from the mine; the sun shines and the rain falls, alike upon just and unjust. The laws of nature are the decrees of the Creator. There is written in them no recognition of any right save that of labor; and in them is written broadly and clearly the equal right of all men to the use and enjoyment of nature; to apply to her by their exertions, and to receive and possess her reward. Hence, as nature gives only to labor, the exertion of labor in production is the only title to exclusive possession.

7   2d. This right of ownership that springs from labor excludes the possibility of any other right of ownership. If a man be rightfully entitled to the produce of his labor, then no one can be rightfully entitled to the ownership of anything which is not the produce of his labor, or the labor of some one else from whom the right has passed to him. If production give to the producer the right to exclusive possession and enjoyment, there can rightfully be no exclusive possession and enjoyment of anything not the production of labor, and the recognition of private property in land is a wrong. For the right to the produce of labor cannot be enjoyed without the right to the free use of the opportunities offered by

nature, and to admit the right of property in these is to deny the right of property in the produce of labor. When non-producers can claim as rent a portion of the wealth created by producers, the right of the producers to the fruits of their labor is to that extent denied.

8   There is no escape from this position. To affirm that a man can rightfully claim exclusive ownership in his own land when embodied in material things, is to deny that any one can rightfully claim exclusive ownership in land. To affirm the rightfulness of property in land, is to affirm a claim which has no warrant in nature, as against a claim founded in the organization of man and the laws of the material universe.

9   What most prevents the realization of the injustice of private property in land is the habit of including all the things that are made the subject of ownership in one category, as property, or, if any distinction is made, drawing the line, according to the unphilosophical distinction of the lawyers, between personal property and real estate, or things movable and things immovable. The real and natural distinction is between things which are the produce of labor and things which are the gratuitous offerings of nature; or, to adopt the terms of political economy, between wealth and land.

10   These two classes of things are in essence and relations widely different, and to class them together as property is to confuse all thought when we come to consider the justice or the injustice, the right or the wrong of property.

11   A house and the lot on which it stands are alike property, as being the subject of ownership, and are alike classed by the lawyers as real estate. Yet in nature and relations they differ widely. The one is produced by human labor, and belongs to the class in political economy styled wealth. The other is a part of nature, and belongs to the class in political economy styled land.

12   The essential character of the one class of things is that they embody labor, are brought into being by human exertion, their existence or non-existence, their increase or diminution, depending on man. The essential character of the other class of things is that they do not embody labor, and exist irrespective of human exertion and irrespective of man; they are the field or environment in which man finds himself; the storehouse from which his needs must be supplied, the raw material upon which and the forces with which alone his labor can act.

13   The moment this distinction is realized, that moment is it seen that the sanction which natural justice gives to one species of property is denied to the other; that the rightfulness which attaches to individual property in the produce of labor implies the wrongfulness of individual property in land; that, whereas the recognition of the one places all men upon equal terms, securing to each the due reward of his labor, the recognition of the other is the denial of the equal rights of men, permitting those who do not labor to take the natural reward of those who do.

14   Whatever may be said for the institution of private property in land, it is therefore plain that it cannot be defended on the score of justice.

From PLURALISM
AND MORAL FORCE
IN THE BLACK-JEWISH DIALOGUE
by William Toll

1   Above the pragmatic struggle for group security that Blacks and Jews have faced in America, each has created a myth about its moral place. As Harold Cruse and others have noted, for Blacks America meant unique enslavement, while for Jews going to America meant a unique freedom. But each of these social dramas was cloaked in the same Biblical imagery and sense of destiny. For Blacks the sin of slavery rationalized by pseudoscientific racism, embodied the cynicism and irrationality at the core of a society that prided itself on justice and the rule of law. As Leonard Sweet reminds us, from the era of Richard Allen in the 1790s through the writings of DuBois a century later, "black leaders were convinced that they had a particular role to play in American history, whether as 'testers' of America's commitment to her avowed values or as a people who, because of their history of suffering offered the infusion of a moral and spiritual dimension lacking in American history." The nation could not be morally whole until its standard of inalienable rights was applied without regard for race. Black intellectuals argued that their understanding of America provided the authentic moral cutting edge. The religious core of the Afro-American imagination, weaned on Old Testament Protestantism, rests on the archetypal parallel with the Hebrews enslaved in Egypt. For Blacks, when God brought civil war to America, His chosen people were finally freed and what was now needed was a Moses to lead them to a Promised Land. When legal freedom did not bring political or economic, much less social equality, Black leaders were further convinced that by their own treatment America was still being judged.

2   But the Jews, the original chosen people, arrived in person to challenge the authenticity of the Black man's claim as moral censor of the Republic. Blacks may have experienced their own psychic discomfiture reconciling their Biblical imagery of patriarchal Hebrews with their experience of actual Jews. As Arnold Eisen has shown, Jews did not forgo a sense of "chosenness" simply because the oppression of Europe which had heightened their indignation, became so amorphous in America. As Eisen writes, "To describe oneself as 'the Lord's special treasure' seemed absurd [in the context of American equality], and yet—and here is the essential dilemma facing American Jews—what sense could Jewishness make without that inherited self-definition? To abandon the claim to chosenness would be to discard the raison d'être that had sustained Jewish

identity and Jewish faith through the ages." While many American Jews, like Horace M. Kallen and Rabbi Mordecai Kaplan, dramatically abandoned the idea, from the 1920s through the 1950s the great majority of influential rabbis and laymen set about reconciling the Jewish sense of chosenness with the moral mission of America as exemplar of democracy and self-determination.

3   But behind the sense of chosenness which both Blacks and Jews projected, lay a peculiar cultural burden for which their moralistic imagery often acted as compensation. Indeed, if there is a psychological burden that Blacks and Jews have shared in America, it is a sense that culturally perhaps they have been less enlightened than the Anglo-Saxons, some of whose best minds developed the ideology of secular freedom. Perhaps the sociological criticism of Black primitiveness or of Jewish religious archaism had some merit. No one understood this anxiety in its full historical scope better than Richard Wright. In a talk to a Parisian audience in the late 1950s he set the issue in its proper perspective. "Your world of culture," he said, "clashed with the culture worlds of colored mankind, and the ensuing destruction of traditional beliefs . . . has set off a tide of social, cultural, political and economic revolution that grips the world today." But Wright likewise found tragedy not merit in those traditional "colored" cultures, whose inhabitants he called "men in a tragic trap." While their struggle to shore up outmoded traditions was doomed, he saw those Europeans who doted on "the primitive and pure" as "reactionary racists and psychological cripples tired of their own civilizations." Leading modernizers and nationalists of the Third World, like Carlos Romulo of the Philippines and President Sukarno of Indonesia rejected the West's racist pretensions, but could not avoid the economic and political necessity of copying Western models.

4   Jews have also been affected by this sense of deficiency. They have required revitalization because, while residing on European territory they were locked out of European society. Their separation was formalized in the imposition of ghettoes or by being forbidden to enter certain Russian cities. While some of these restrictions ended by the mid-nineteenth century, others were just being imposed. Indeed, to some degree Rabbi Milton Steinberg foreshadowed Wright's analysis of cultural inferiority when he wrote in 1933, "the tragedy of the culture of Israel lies in this, that it lost the opportunity and the ability to assimilate just at the time when the world had the most to offer." Instead, he explained, Jews, locked behind ghetto walls, had embroidered traditions that were irrelevant to humanistic and scientific thinking. When emancipation occurred further tragedy awaited. "The story of the Jew in the modern world," he concluded, "is the history of the dissolution of the ordered ghetto into chaos, and of fixed individuality into flux." The need to feel part of an enlightened world movement lay behind the rapid spread of Reform Judaism in late nineteenth-century America. Its adherents were the American-born children of German immigrants whose social habits resembled those of the Protestant upper middle class. Rabbis such as Joseph Krauskopf, Kaufmann Kohler, and Solomon Schindler were upset by

the new incidence of divorce, intermarriage and above all an apathy toward religion among this generation, and promoted Reform as a means of holding them to Judaism. They "refined" tradition into a set of ethical propositions, erected elegant temples, and established a new philanthropy to assist poor Jews so that their Judaism might embody a modern purpose.

5   How have Blacks and Jews responded to this assault by modernity on their traditional sensibilities? Despite great individual variations in perception, each group has developed a major theme on which its internal debate has focused. And each debate has expressed a compensatory desire to find within the group's traditions a moral purpose over and beyond the individualistic freedoms of the white Protestant elite. For Blacks, certainly from the 1850s, the central issue has been whether the white man's category of 'race' could have for them more than a pejorative referent. In the context of slavery, sharecropping, urban resettlement, and most recently the self-reinforcing welfare dependency of inner cities, Blacks have bitterly debated whether 'race' was simply a white man's tool to divide the poor, or whether it might provide a rallying point to countervail against a pariah caste situation. Should Blacks see themselves as a submerged caste gradually developing a middle class to lead them into the politics of competing interest groups? Or, should they strive to be the vanguard of an international "race" challenging Western power? For Jews the central issue has been whether they are an ordinary group of people with a unique religion that can be practiced in almost any political environment, or whether they constitute a nation chosen for a special destiny. Should Jews seek a safe haven within the context of religious respectability, or should they see themselves as part of the politicized world of group rivalries and even international conflicts tied to the destiny of Israel? Stated somewhat more politically, Black writers have approached ethnic pluralism as the more conservative option, while Jewish leaders see it as the more radical, because each group has come to politics from a very different social status.

6   Blacks have borne the category of "race" as a cultural burden. The concept has an ambiguous history, but by the mid-nineteenth century some European and American anthropologists even tried to demonstrate that people of European, Asian and African origins might be separate species. Stephen Jay Gould and others have traced the faulty reasoning which equated differences in phenotype to differentials in group mental capacities into the social sciences, where it continues to parade its bizarre logic through so-called intelligence tests. Blacks rejected this hereditarian theorizing, but some like Frederick Douglass went even further and rejected the view that race, even as a cultural referent, might have any meaning at all. Although taking a very different tactical stance than Douglass, Booker T. Washington really adapted his ideology of practical politics to the conditions of the post-Reconstruction world. Like Douglass, Washington argued that "race" was merely a way of referring to a situation of deprivation, and that theories which suggested that Blacks were in some basic way different from

whites were nonsense. He rejected the view that African cultures were more than "primitive," and he articulated a pragmatic economic Darwinism, which held that economic power determined all else. Only those who learned to compete most efficiently would survive.

7   Washington's great antagonist was the Harvard-trained historian, W. E. B. DuBois, who saw in the idea of "race" a means to revitalize Black self-respect. The first major Black writer to understand how cultural self-confidence underlay political mobilization, he drew on the work of prior Black writers like Alexander Crummell, Martin Delany, and George Washington Williams to reinterpret the place of Blacks in America's ethical history. Though respecting the European development of scientific method and of political liberty, he pointed to African achievements, and the struggle of Blacks for political freedom and economic autonomy to demonstrate their special capacity to test the American commitment to freedom. Despite his occasional flights of "romantic racialism," two points in his thinking should be stressed. First, he managed to develop through the Niagara Movement the basic nonpartisan strategy for modern Black pressure group agitation. Second, he gathered reams of empirical data from southern rural and northern urban Black communities to show that Blacks shared an environment and class pattern with whites, and that they had developed the social cohesion to support a group economy. What the Black masses needed, he argued, was liberation from stigma, and his program of cultural revitalization promoted moral parity, not escapist fantasies. Precisely these insights led him in the 1930s to reject the Communist Party and even the promise of industrial unions to advocate the cooperative organization of Black communities in cities which were already physically divided into ethnic enclaves. His omnivorous intellect led him not to revolutionary theory, but to therapeutic nationalism. He sought to define a basis for organization so that Blacks might become the most progressive component in the American racial equation and even the vanguard of the spiritual liberation of Africa. Here it is sufficient to note that in response to the expansion of Black social vision which DuBois made possible have come most of the innovations in Black social thought in the twentieth century. After DuBois the question became not, "How can individuals rise?," but, "How should Black consciousness revitalize itself to challenge white hegemony?". . . .

8   Jewish paradigms for America have emerged from very different considerations than the shifting structure of the economy. Though Jewish writers have documented anti-Semitic discrimination, especially in education and employment, they have largely taken economic mobility as a given. Unlike Blacks, Jews have assumed that America meant freedom. But the ambiguities of freedom itself have created for Jewish writers the crucial cultural problems. American freedom meant not only surcease from political anti-Semitism, but release from Jewish communal control, from European corporatism. The cultural component of mobility, "assimilation," is cited as the key source of Jewish structural and moral decay. Chaim Waxman, for example, has explained how sociologists like

Marshall Sklare and Charles Leibman opposed their "survivalist" imperatives to the "assimilationism" of Milton Gordon and Nathan Glazer, because ethnic Judaism seemed to be disintegrating through the secular success of so many individual Jews. Depending on the point at which a cultural "norm" is established, almost any cultural adaptation to structural change can be interpreted as moral declension.

9   The central figure to provide a moral rationale for secularization has been Horace M. Kallen, and the theory for which he is best known is "cultural pluralism." . . . The genius of Jewry, Kallen felt, had not been expressed in Biblical law, but in the story of Job. As a righteous man, Job accepted the irrationality of Nature, the power of Nature's God, but rebelled against those authorities who tried to make him see order, even a mystical purpose, where none existed. Job became Kallen's metaphor for the modern Jew, seeking his own moral authority in the traditions of his people. Cultural pluralism became the ideology for demanding individual freedom within the context of loyalty to a traditional people. It also legitimated a cultural challenge to the white Protestant elite. . . .

10   . . . The most comprehensive expansion of Kallen's theory was developed in the 1930s by his friend, Rabbi Mordecai Kaplan, founder of Reconstructionism. As a theologian, Kaplan retained faith in the unique destiny of the Jewish people, but like Kallen he was sufficiently affected by modern philosophy to doubt the need for the supernatural. In the modern world, he believed, Jewry faced a splintering as people exchanged religious faith for scientific truth, the humanistic emphasis on individual fulfillment, and the shift from concern for salvation in a "next life" to social improvement in this one. Because he believed that Jewry above all needed social cohesion, he founded a new communal institution, the community center, which sponsored a great variety of activities in addition to religious instruction. Despite the criticism of his "impious" center from traditional rabbis, Kaplan saw the center as a means for creating a new "organic community" of Jewry. Extending his vision after the creation of the state of Israel, he called for a world parliament of Jewry which might recapture the moral insights that had grown from Jewish powerlessness to offset the political opportunism of the Jewish state.

11   Kaplan's remained the preeminent vision in American Jewry until it was challenged in the 1950s by theologians like Will Herberg and Arthur A. Cohen. Herberg in particular argued that ethnicity as a social force had been superseded by a religious melting pot, with America divided between Protestant, Catholic and Jews. But while Jews and their religion were now an integral part of respectable America, the spiritual core that had sustained prior generations seemed to have dissolved. Despite considerable institutional growth, Jewry had become a rudderless enclave, clinging to empty ritual and increasingly dependent on Israel for a sense of purpose. Moved by the Holocaust and powerfully influenced by the vogue of existentialism to which philosophy gave vent after the war, Herberg

and Cohen each criticized what appeared to be an amoral optimism that seemed to characterize American life in general and which seemed to mark the further "assimilation," the death of chosenness, among American Jews. Cohen especially saw the authoritative rationale for this spiritual decay in the sociological redefinition of religion by Mordecai Kaplan. Both he and Herberg called for revitalized ritual that might, through a saving remnant, remind modern man of his limited vision and his spiritual dependence on a higher authority. . . .

From *THE AMERICAN SCENE*
by Henry James (1907)

1   New York really, I think, is all formidable foreground; or, if it be not, there is
more than enough of this pressure of the present and the immediate to cut out
the close sketcher's work for him. These things are a thick growth all round him,
and when I recall the intensity of the material picture in the dense Yiddish
quarter, for instance, I wonder at its not having forestalled, on my page, mere
musings and, as they will doubtless be called, moonings. There abides with me,
ineffaceably, the memory of a summer evening spent there by invitation of a
high public functionary domiciled on the spot—to the extreme enhancement of
the romantic interest his visitor found him foredoomed to inspire—who was to
prove one of the most liberal of hosts and most luminous of guides. . . .

2   The children swarmed above all—here was multiplication with a vengeance;
and the number of very old persons, of either sex, was almost equally remarkable; the very old persons being in equal vague occupation of the doorstep,
pavement, curbstone, gutter, roadway, and every one alike using the street for
overflow. As overflow, in the whole quarter, is the main fact of life—I was to
learn later on that, with the exception of some shy corner of Asia, no district in
the world known to the statistician has so many inhabitants to the yard—the
scene hummed with the human presence beyond any I had ever faced in quest
even of refreshment. . . .

With a reverence for intellect, one should doubtless have drunk in tribute to
an intellectual people; but I remember being at no time more conscious of that
merely portentous element, in the aspects of American growth, which reduces
to inanity any marked dismay quite as much as any high elation. The portent is
one of too many—you always come back, as I have hinted, with your easier
gasp, to *that*: it will be time enough to sigh or to shout when the relation of the
particular appearance to all the other relations shall have cleared itself up.
Phantasmagoric for me, accordingly, in a high degree, are the interesting hours I
here glance at content to remain—setting in this respect, I recognize, an excellent example to all the rest of the New York phantasmagoria. Let me speak of the
remainder only as phantasmagoric too, so that I may both the more kindly recall
it and the sooner have done with it.

3   I have not done, however, with the impression of that large evening in the
Ghetto; there was too much in the vision, and it has left too much the sense of a
rare experience. For what did it all really come to but that one had seen with
one's eyes the New Jerusalem on earth? . . .

4   . . . The scale, in this light of the New Jerusalem, seemed completely rear-
ranged; or, to put it more simply, the wants, the gratifications, the aspirations of
the "poor," as expressed in the shops (which were the shops of the "poor"),
denoted a new style of poverty; and this new style of poverty, from street to

street, stuck out of the possible purchasers, one's jostling fellow-pedestrians, and made them, to every man and woman, individual throbs in the larger harmony. One can speak only of what one has seen, and there were grosser elements of the sordid and the squalid that I doubtless never saw. That, with a good deal of observation and of curiosity, I should have failed of this, the country over, affected me as by itself something of an indication. To miss that part of the spectacle, or to know it only by its having so unfamiliar a pitch, was an indication that made up for a great many others. It is when this one in particular is forced home to you—this immense, vivid *general* lift of poverty and general appreciation of the living unit's paying property in himself—that the picture seems most to clear and the way to jubilation most to open. For it meets you there, at every turn, as the result most definitely attested. You are as constantly reminded, no doubt, that these rises in enjoyed value shrink and dwindle under the icy breath of Trusts and the weight of the new remorseless monopolies that operate as no madnesses of ancient personal power thrilling us on the historic page ever operated; the living unit's property in himself becoming more and more merely such a property as may consist with a relation to properties overwhelmingly greater and that allow the asking of no questions and the making, for co-existence with them, of no conditions. But that, in the fortunate phrase, is another story, and will be altogether, evidently, a new and different drama. There is such a thing, in the United States, it is hence to be inferred, as freedom to grow up to be blighted, and it may be the only freedom in store for the smaller fry of future generations. If it is accordingly of the smaller fry I speak, and of how large they massed on that evening of endless admonitions, this will be because I caught them thus in their comparative humility and at an early stage of their American growth. The life-thread has, I suppose, to be of a certain thickness for the great shears of Fate to feel for it. Put it, at the worst, that the Ogres were to devour them, they were but the more certainly to fatten into food for the Ogres.

5   Their dream, at all events, as I noted it, was meanwhile sweet and undisguised—nowhere sweeter than in the half-dozen picked beer-houses and cafés in which our ingenuous *enquête*, that of my fellow-pilgrims and I, wound up. These establishments had each been selected for its playing off some facet of the jewel, and they wondrously testified, by their range and their individual colour, to the spread of that lustre. It was a pious rosary of which I should like to tell each bead, but I must let the general sense of the adventure serve. Our successive stations were in no case of the "seamy" order, an inquiry into seaminess having been unanimously pronounced futile, but each had its separate social connotation, and it was for the number and variety of these connotations, and their individual plenitude and prosperity, to set one thinking. Truly the Yiddish world was a vast world, with its own deeps and complexities, and what struck one above all was that it sat there at its cups (and in no instance vulgarly the worse for them) with a sublimity of good conscience that took away the breath, a protrusion of elbow never aggressive, but absolutely proof against jostling. It was the incurable man of letters under the skin of one of the party who gasped, I

confess; for it was in the light of letters, that is in the light of our language as literature has hitherto known it, that one stared at this all-unconscious impudence of the agency of future ravage. The man of letters, in the United States, has his own difficulties to face and his own current to stem—for dealing with which his liveliest inspiration may be, I think, that they are still very much his own, even in an Americanized world, and that more than elsewhere they press him to intimate communion with his honour. For that honour, the honour that sits astride of the consecrated English tradition, to his mind, quite as old knighthood astride of its caparisoned charger, the dragon most rousing, over the land, the proper spirit of St. George, is just this immensity of the alien presence climbing higher and higher, climbing itself into the very light of publicity.

6   I scarce know why, but I saw it that evening as in some dim dawn of that promise to its consciousness, and perhaps this was precisely what made it a little exasperating. Under the impression of the mere mob the question doesn't come up, but in these haunts of comparative civility we saw the mob sifted and strained, and the exasperation was the sharper, no doubt, because what the process had left most visible was just the various possibilities of the waiting spring of intelligence. Such elements constituted the germ of a "public," and it was impossible (possessed of a sensibility worth speaking of) to be exposed to them without feeling how new a thing under the sun the resulting public would be. That was where one's "lettered" anguish came in—in the turn of one's eye from face to face for some betrayal of a prehensile hook for the linguistic tradition as one had known it. Each warm, lighted and supplied circle, each group of served tables and smoked pipes and fostered decencies and unprecedented accents, beneath the extravagant lamps, took on thus, for the brooding critic, a likeness to that terrible modernized and civilized room in the Tower of London, haunted by the shade of Guy Fawkes, which had more than once formed part of the scene of the critic's taking tea there. In this chamber of the present urbanities the wretched man had been stretched on the rack, and the critic's ear (how else should it have been a critic's?) could still always catch, in pauses of talk, the faint groan of his ghost. Just so the East Side cafés—and increasingly as their place in the scale was higher—showed to my inner sense, beneath their bedizenment, as torture-rooms of the living idiom; the piteous gasp of which at the portent of lacerations to come could reach me in any drop of the surrounding Accent of the Future. The accent of the very ultimate future, in the States, may be destined to become the most beautiful on the globe and the very music of humanity (here the "ethnic" synthesis shrouds itself thicker than ever); but whatever we shall know it for, certainly, we shall not know it for English—in any sense for which there is an existing literary measure.

WRITING ASSIGNMENTS

Write an expository essay with an introduction, development, and conclusion about one of the following topics. Use whichever method(s) of development the topic and your treatment of it require. Be sure to have a clear thesis and transitions that lead the reader from idea to idea. Feel free to summarize, paraphrase, or quote from the reading selections and to revise parts of your previous essays.

1. Compare and contrast the television images of two groups, for example men and women, Italians and blacks, or teachers and athletes.

2. Compare and contrast the image of a specific group as presented on different television shows.

3. Trace the television treatment of a particular group from some time in the past until today, for example police, Hispanics, or scientists.

4. Compare and contrast the philosophy, professionalism, or status of print news and television news.

5. Trace how a particular issue or group was treated by the news media from some time in the past to another time.

6. Discuss whether the news media are always, sometimes, or never accurate in presenting specific issues or groups.

7. Compare and contrast differing views about the origin(s) of American values.

8. Compare and contrast how two or three works of art—for example, novels, songs, plays, paintings, films—have affected the values of the United States.

9. Trace how a particular group or issue has been treated in the arts over the years.

10. Trace and analyze the evolution of the values that inform life in the United States.

11. Discuss whether there are "American" values or only values held by Americans.

12. Compare and contrast the values in the United States to those in another country.

13. Analyze a topic that emerged from the discussions for Making Connections.

14. Analyze a topic that emerged from the discussions of the selections by Lodge, George, Toll, and James.

C·H·A·P·T·E·R S·I·X

EVALUATION

You may have noticed in our discussion in Chapter 5 that even an analysis often contains elements of the writer's opinion. This is understandable because it is the writer who brings system to the individual facts that make up the world. Even in the physical sciences there is room for differences of opinion, though the influence of personality is supposed to be minimized. But, as we have been finding, in the social sciences and (perhaps) the law, when we are dealing with people's behavior, the attraction of one explanation over another often reflects the writer's emotional makeup, time, and place. Our feelings about people in general—whether we believe that they are basically good or bad, altruistic or selfish—will determine whether we are comfortable with a particular school of thought that explains behavior. Such subjectivity helps explain why respected authorities differ with each other. But an objective essay does not always have to contain opinions.

An **evaluation,** in contrast, does. The purpose of an evaluation is, as the word itself suggests, to put value on something, to make judgments about it, to give our opinion. Three scholars giving three different explanations of the origin of American values cannot all be correct, and as readers we must decide which theory we find most convincing and be able to explain why.

Of course, for our opinion to carry weight with someone else, it must be thoughtful, convincing, and well presented. In a free country we are all entitled to our opinions, but that means only that we don't go to jail for them. It does not mean that all opinions are worthy of being taken seriously; some opinions are nothing more than biases, while others are informed. When you are reduced to saying, "Well, that's just my opinion," you can be sure that you are expressing a bias with little concrete support. What we should strive for is an opinion that is grounded in knowledge and that reflects a set of values we can articulate—in other words, an informed opinion.

Armed with the knowledge that comes from careful analysis and the values we bring from our personal background, we can evaluate the record of a president or governor, the proposed solutions to a social problem, the role of television in our society, the influences on a person's behavior, the worth of a piece of music or art, and even someone else's analysis and evaluation. But in every case, the evaluation has the same requirements: an analysis of the issue, a clear set of values, and a sense of authority.

· ANALYSIS AND EVALUATION

Although an evaluation must contain an analysis, it does not stop there. The purpose of an evaluation—its main idea—is to pass judgment. To accomplish this goal, it uses the analysis as a tool. In the following editorial, for example, more space is given to the analysis than to the evaluation, but it is clear that the purpose of the editorial is to evaluate the government's policy, not simply to explain it. We see this purpose especially in the use of emotionally charged, or value-packed, words (which we have put in italics), such as the echo of Caesar's murder by Brutus in the title.

THE *UNKINDEST* CUTS

1   When freezing weather gripped much of the nation in January, hundreds of thousands of *deserving* families in *desperate need* of federal assistance to buy heating fuel were left in the cold. The Administration's budget-cutters were focusing on heating assistance, among other *vital* services, as a good place to cut back and save money.

2   Since David Stockman, the president's budget chief, believes that federal spending is the root cause of inflation, he is determined to cut the budget. However, only one-fourth of the federal budget is controllable. The other three-fourths are made up of entitlement programs, where Congress decides on eligibility and benefits. As unemployment rises, more people become entitled to jobless benefits, food stamps, welfare and Medicaid. Therefore, Mr. Stockman, along with conservatives in Congress, is determined to cut back the entitlement programs. In a memo to the president, Mr. Stockman wrote that expenditures "for food stamps, cash assistance, child nutrition, school lunches, and unemployment compensation amount to $100 billion. A carefully tailored package to reduce eligibility, overlap and abuse should be developed for these areas—with a potential savings of $10–20 billion."

3   These cutbacks single out the very people *least able to bear the burden,* the very people the government *ought to be helping.* Nobody doubts that economies must be made. But, surely, a healthy economy should not be built on the *frozen bodies of the poor,* with *lunch money* taken from *hungry school children.* We hope that those in control of the budget will exercise their mandate with more *humaneness* and *sensitivity* than that.

An analysis may also serve as a specific instance or starting point for an evaluation of a larger issue. Here, too, the main idea of the essay is the judgment, not the explanation.

IN *LIFE,* CRIME PAYS

1   Last month *Life* magazine paid $8000 to accused murderer Bernard Welch for eight snapshots of himself. Welch, who has been called "a one man crime wave" by law enforcement authorities who have linked him to a series of robberies and other crimes, came to public notice most recently as the suspect in the murder of Dr. Michael Halberstam, a prominent cardiologist in the Washington, D.C., area, who was killed when he surprised a burglar. A search of Welch's home turned up over 3000 items that had been reported stolen in the past few months.

2   It is hard not to agree with the murder victim's brother, Pulitzer Prize winning writer David Halberstam, that the *Life* transaction is "*contemptible, checkbook journalism*" which "amounts to a *tribute* to Welch *for his crimes.*" While *Life* defends its behavior as a reasonable price for news photographs, *the fact remains* that $1000 per picture is twice what the magazine usually pays to professional photographers for their work and is apparently *part of a deal* that includes an exclusive interview with Welch.

3   However *outrageous* it may be, the action by *Life* is, *unfortunately,* not unique. Similarly *sordid* cases come to mind without great effort: the millions of dollars paid to former President Nixon to appear on television talk shows; the substantial payments to the convicted Son of Sam killer in New York City for book rights to his story; the lesser sums to the lesser players in the Watergate scandal. And in a way the whole *disgusting exhibition* is almost inevitable, if *not excusable.* So long as news is seen as *just another commodity to be sold, just another product to be packaged between ads for beer and deodorants,* media businesses will compete for exclusives that will sell more of their product and thus allow them to charge higher fees for their advertising space. And unless the media *get their act together* and *behave responsibly,* it may soon pay for criminals to get caught, just so that they can sell their *titillating stories* to the highest bidder. After all, what's a few years in jail, if you can come home to a million dollars or so?

· ESTABLISHING A FRAMEWORK
OF VALUES

Writing an analysis requires knowledge of the proposed audience to the extent that the writer needs to decide how much background information to include. An explanation of a technical issue to an audience of professionals will contain fewer definitions, for example, than one aimed at a general audience. But in either case the writer does not have to worry about the political affiliation or religious convictions of the audience when the purpose is limited to explaining how something works.

But in an evaluation, the writer must often consider the politics, religion, and numerous other personal aspects of the audience because these factors are central to their values.

As we saw in the last chapter, an analysis of your friend's belief that "the new Reebok jogging shoes are fantastic" cannot be "They just are." A reasonable analysis required information to support this opinion: "They're made of a special synthetic that doesn't make your feet sweat. The innersole cushions your feet when you run. And there's a new ankle support that cuts down the chance of a bad sprain." This information, in turn, implies a set of values: sweaty feet are bad, cushioned soles are good, and spraining your ankle is bad. Your friend can assume that everybody shares these values. It would have been extremely unlikely for you to have rejected your friend's explanation by saying, "Well, that means they're not for me. I love sweaty feet. And what's the point of jogging if I can't slam my soles into the concrete and sprain my ankle?" That's why it was not necessary for your friend to state the framework, or criteria, for the opinion. Similarly, an evaluation of a new car can say that it breaks down often and requires costly repairs without having to state explicitly that frequent breakdowns and costly repairs are bad.

The question of values becomes more complicated in "The Unkindest Cuts" (p. 270). The writer of the editorial describes certain people as "deserving," considers certain services to be "vital," and says that these are "the very people the government ought to be helping." Such statements are based on values, but not necessarily values that everyone shares. If nothing else, the administration that refused to give these people money did not feel that they were deserving or that the services were vital, and obviously could not agree that it "ought to be helping" them. We must assume, though, that the writer of the editorial knew that the usual readers of the newspapers would accept these values. Likewise, when David Halberstam accuses *Life* magazine of "checkbook journalism," he must believe that checkbook journalism is bad, and since the editorial quotes him with approval, the writer clearly shares this value. But the publishers of *Life* magazine clearly disagree; they must believe either that checkbook journalism is not bad, or that it is bad but they have not indulged in it.

Sometimes a writer will assume that readers share the values underlying an evaluation. This assumption is likely, for example, when the values are considered central to the society. It is possible, of course, that a particular reader might still disagree. But a writer in the United States does not have to defend seeking authority in the Bible, the Constitution, the Founding Fathers, honesty, integrity, motherhood, and apple pie. They are simply assumed to command everyone's loyalty.

Nevertheless, a writer must know where to draw the line. At one extreme you can be sure everyone agrees with you: Everyone supports honesty, family, liberty, equality under the law. At the other extreme you must assume that most people disagree: An American quoting Stalin for support should be prepared to mount a vigorous defense. In the large middle ground, you must explain yourself: Individuality, conformity, hard work, education—all have their supporters and detractors when choices must be made among them.

It follows, therefore, that when values are not obvious or necessarily shared, the writer must explain the criteria being used. In discussing a pamphlet called "Education for Democracy," which outlines the consensus of 150 Americans in public life, Albert Shanker asks, "What ideas could possibly unite such a varied group?" And he answers:

> First, a set of convictions: ". . . that democracy is the worthiest form of human governance ever conceived . . . that we cannot take its survival or its spread—or its perfection in practice—for granted." Furthermore, "democracy's survival depends upon our transmitting to each new generation the political vision of liberty and equality that unites us as Americans."

When the writer does not explicitly state his or her values, as the reader you must be able to recognize assumptions. Notice, for instance, how former Secretary of State John Foster Dulles establishes the values that will inform the remainder of his speech:

> There are some who believe that moral considerations ought not to influence the foreign policy of a nation, that moral considerations are all right for the individual but not for the collective unity: Corporate bodies, it is argued, should be directed only by material considerations, and, thus, directors of a corporation are not free to use corporate assets for charitable purposes. To a degree, I suppose, the same principles apply to those who are trustees for a nation.

A skilled reader will realize that Mr. Dulles does not share the first two beliefs. He attributes the first to an unnamed "some who believe" and introduces the second with the distancing phrase "it is argued." This interpretation is reinforced in the next sentence by the words "to a degree" and "I suppose." Clearly, Mr. Dulles is setting up the "other guy" in order to knock him down.

An author who is convinced that the readers share the same values may ask questions that the reader is expected to answer in a particular way, as Thomas Jefferson is doing in this passage about slavery in *Notes on the State of Virginia*:

> Can a nation permit one half of its citizens to trample on the rights of the other half? Can a nation destroy the morals of one half its people and the love of country of the other? Can the liberties of a nation be secure when we remove their divine basis?

A writer who uses rhetorical questions like Jefferson does must be absolutely certain that the reader will give the desired answer. In a heterogeneous, multi-cultural, multiethnic society this is not always possible, so you should be careful when using the device.

· PROJECTING AUTHORITY

In addition to the analysis and the framework of values, an evaluation must carry an air of authority. The reader must feel confident in the writer's knowledge and integrity. The writer must convince the reader that the information is correct and that the conclusions are drawn in a reasonable way. For a writer who is already a respected public figure, this is easy; for the rest of us, still trying to win such acceptance, it is often necessary to call upon established authorities for support.

To the extent that our society is built on certain laws and values, writers can fall back on these. Is there a law that covers this? Did the Supreme Court rule on a similar case? What did George Washington say in this situation? How did Abraham Lincoln act under these circumstances?

For example, in setting the foundation for the opinion in *Brown v. Board of Education*, Chief Justice Earl Warren looks to earlier court decisions—called *precedent*—for support:

> In the first cases in this Court construing the Fourteenth Amendment, decided shortly after its adoption, the Court interpreted it as proscribing all state-imposed discriminations against the Negro race.

In the 1976 case of *Nebraska Press Association v. Stuart*, Chief Justice Warren Burger quotes Thomas Jefferson to support his own rejection of censorship:

> The unusually able lawyers who helped write the Constitution and later drafted the Bill of Rights . . . recognized that there were risks to private rights from an unfettered press. Thomas Jefferson, for example, writing in 1786 concerning press attacks on John Jay, stated: "In truth it is afflicting

that a man who has passed his life in serving the public should yet be liable to have his peace of mind disturbed by any individual who shall think proper to arraign him in a newspaper. It is however an evil for which there is no remedy. Our liberty depends on freedom of the press, and that cannot be limited without being lost."

· READING AN EVALUATION

In summary, an evaluation must have a clear analysis, a set of values, and a sense of authority. Now let's read the following evaluation and see how it accomplishes these criteria.

LEARNING TO VALUE DEMOCRACY:
STATEMENT OPENS DEBATE ON PRINCIPLES
by Albert Shanker (1987)

1   There's probably nothing as explosive to divide a community as the question of what values, if any, should be taught to the children in the local schools. Draw up a list of thou-shalt-nots or of the good and the bad and most likely you'll run into objections to "brainwashing," "propaganda" and "breaking down the line between church and state." But in order to keep a society from unraveling, a nation has to be based on a firm core set of commonly held values.

2   Does the United States have such a set of values and should our schools teach them to students? The answer is "yes" to both questions according to *Education for Democracy: A Statement of Principles*, a pamphlet just issued and produced as a joint project of the American Federation of Teachers, the Education Excellence Network and Freedom House. The *Statement* was endorsed by me and over 150 other Americans from diverse backgrounds, including Jimmy Carter, Gerald Ford, Henry Cisneros, Sidney Hook, Jeane Kirkpatrick, Lane Kirkland, George Will, Benjamin Hooks, Ann Landers and Arthur Ashe.

3   What ideas could possibly unite such a varied group?

4   First, a set of convictions: ". . . that democracy is the worthiest form of human governance ever conceived . . . that we cannot take its survival or its spread—or its perfection in practice—for granted." Furthermore, ". . . democracy's survival depends upon our transmitting to each new generation the political vision of liberty and equality that unites us as Americans."

5   Second, a set of concerns, among which:

Reprinted with permission of the author.

• There's disturbing evidence that far too many students are ignorant of the important people, ideas and events that have made our country what it is. A recent study shows that a majority of high school seniors do not know what the 1954 *Brown* vs. *Board of Education* decision was about. Nor could majorities identify Winston Churchill or Joseph Stalin. Without knowledge of the civil rights movement or of World War II or of other struggles, students can't begin to understand the kind of sacrifice and commitment needed to protect and extend our freedoms. And if a youngster has to take a wild guess that Stalin is either an olympic athlete or a Renaissance painter, he can't have much of a grasp of the terrors of a totalitarian society as a basis for comparison to his own life.

• That some curriculum materials, straining to be "fair" and present all cultures in a positive light, gloss over the unpleasant realities of non-democratic regimes. One teaching guide "talks of the high value accorded the right to strike in Eastern Europe." Another praises "the Cuban government's commitment to women's rights, noting with approval that men who refuse to share equally in household responsibilities can be penalized with 're-education or assignment to farm work.'"

6   What does the *Statement* call for?

• *More attention to world studies:* The realities of our own society, warts and all, are exposed every day in the media. But "many students remain ignorant of other, quite different worlds. How can they be expected to value or defend freedom unless they have a clear grasp of the alternatives against which to measure it?" We have to show our young people what life is like under the political systems that are in competition with our own and what dangers threaten our own institutions.

• *More attention to the history of democratic civilization:* Students must know not only the ideas that motivated our 18th Century founders, but something of the traditions that made them what they were, which means looking back at the ancient Jews and Christians, to the Greeks and Romans, to the thinkers of the Middle Ages, Renaissance and Reformation, "whose ethical beliefs gave rise to democratic thought." It also means studying democratic institutions of the past and how well or badly they stood up to challenges and for what reasons.

• *Wider reading and study in the humanities:* Young people learn values best, not through lectures, but by encountering them in the stories of how men and women faced challenges, what choices they made and for what reasons. These stories are most effectively brought to life in the best works of history, literature, philosophy, and biography.

7   *Education for Democracy* is meant to promote democratic values, but not by flag waving or blind jingoism. Those of us who endorse its principles believe that our system of government doesn't need a "bodyguard of

lies" for defense. It can survive the light of full knowledge and discussion. We want our students to think critically and not become knee-jerk patriots. Our children must learn more about the world they live in and about the past that shaped the values and institutions we live by. It's not enough just to tell them what is good in our society. They have to experience it through knowledge, reflection and discussion. "Today," the *Statement* concludes, "we ask our schools to make a greater contribution to that effort and we ask all Americans to help them do it."

8   The sponsors of *Education for Democracy* hope that it will serve as a starting point for a new national discussion about which values our schools should teach and how they should teach them. The American Federation of Teachers will encourage its members to use it as a guide for taking a good look at the curriculums in their own school districts. We hope that others will do the same.

In the last sentence of the first paragraph, Shanker states a value: "A nation has to be based on a firm core set of commonly held values." This statement establishes the importance of the issue and suggests the direction of the essay. The first question in the next paragraph asks for information, or analysis: "*Does* the United States have such a set of values?" The question that immediately follows in the same sentence is one of values: "*Should* our schools teach them to students?" The "yes" answer to both questions is then based on the authority of the 150 public figures whose points of agreement are reported in the pamphlet. The following paragraph states three interlocking values that these people share: (1) "Democracy is the worthiest form of human governance ever conceived," (2) "We cannot take its survival or its spread—or its perfection in practice—for granted," and (3) "Democracy's survival depends upon our transmitting to each new generation the political vision of liberty and equality that unites us as Americans." Shanker follows in the next two paragraphs with an analysis of facts that led to the group's belief that something had to be done. The analysis includes a survey showing that most high school seniors do not know important aspects of history and a review of curriculum materials suggesting that an attempt to be "fair" results in all ideas being presented as equally valid. Interwoven with his analysis is evaluation, in comments that indicate values or pass judgment on the findings: The evidence in the survey is "disturbing," "too many" [not just "many"] students are "ignorant" of history, the curriculum materials "gloss over the unpleasant realities" of foreign governments, without this specific information "students can't begin to understand" the sacrifices "needed" to protect freedom. The solutions that the pamphlet offers also contain analysis and evaluation; for example, since [according to the analysis] "many students remain ignorant of other, quite different worlds," "we have to" [evaluation] show them what life is like under other political systems.

· CRITICAL REVIEWS

The most widely recognized form of evaluation is probably the critical review. Every major newspaper, magazine, radio station, and television news show has a movie critic, and many also have television critics, theater critics, restaurant critics, clothing critics, book critics, and even media critics and critics-at-large. As we said earlier, the term *criticism* is often confused with fault finding, and many of the most popular critics certainly seem to relish the clever put-down. But the real value of criticism is in clarifying values and seeing how we and others live up to them.

As you read the following review by Matt Roshkow of the movie *The Onion Field* try to answer the following questions:

Does the reviewer like or dislike the movie?

What does the reviewer feel are the characteristics of a well-made movie?

How does the reviewer distinguish between a well-made movie and a worthwhile one?

Does the reviewer consider this film well made or worthwhile, or neither or both?

What does the reviewer mean by the phrase "put 'em in the chair" flick? What does he think of such films? Does he think this film is one?

1   *The Onion Field,* based on the book by Joseph Wambaugh, is the true story of what happened to two Los Angeles policemen. While conducting a routine search of a suspicious automobile, they are taken hostage by the car's occupants, and driven to a nearby farm. Believing he had already committed a capital crime, one of the criminals shoots and kills one of the officers as the other runs for safety.

2   Such is the harrowing account of what happened in the onion field. What happened in the courtroom the next seven years is the basis for the plot of the movie. The criminal who had misinterpreted the "Little Lindbergh" law and had shot the policeman, was also deceptively intelligent, a fact we see only when the two are put on trial. Through an agreement with his partner, he arranges for separate trials, and even takes over his own defense. We see the murder, and when we also view the verdict it drastically offends our sense of justice. Thus, the film manages to raise our own awareness of the corruption in our streets and in our courthouses.

3   But this is not just another "put 'em in the chair" flick, simply arousing

Reprinted by permission of Empire State Investigator.

a thirst for blood. For, since the first words of the movie are "This is a true story," our anger is not resolved within the film, and instead we are encouraged to do something about it in real life. *The Onion Field* points to today's system of criminal justice as being an area worthy of the viewer's concern. Its conclusion: our public courts have become ineffective, bogged down in their own legalities.

4   What makes the unavenged murders so appalling is that the criminals suffer less than anyone else in the film. The surviving cop is torn with guilt as his endless trial appearances force him to relive over and over the anguish of his partner's death. And he must struggle with the question of whether he should have surrendered his gun, even though refusal would have meant the immediate death of his fellow officer. We are forced to ask where the police manual ends and human intuition takes over. The film paints a sympathetic picture of the officer's dilemma and attempts to answer the question with a speech by an aging cop. "I would give my underpants if he put a gun to my head . . ." says the veteran in response to his regulation-minded superiors. Thus, the film's second conclusion: society asks much of law enforcers; it should not ask them to lay down their lives for technicalities.

5   The movie is worth seeing. It is fast-paced and extremely well acted. Apart from its questions, it also gives us a superb view of the lives of those who prowl our streets. It examines with great candor the seedy, deranged, even pathetic aspects of the urban criminal. And it gives the public a chance to enter a world that most people don't come in daily contact with. That job is left to the select few who are expected to keep it out of ordinary people's lives. As *The Onion Field* points out, unless police are aided in that process by our courts, their lives and society in general will be lost.

· EVALUATING AN EVALUATION

Of course, the very elements that go into an evaluation allow you to evaluate someone else's evaluation—or your own. We said that an evaluation must have a good analysis of the topic, a clear set of values, and an air of authority. These then become the criteria with which you can evaluate an essay. Returning to the movie review we just read, for example, we can judge its success by asking:

Does the plot outline of the movie contain enough information to support the reviewer's conclusions, but not more of the story than is needed?

Are the reviewer's values clear? Does the reader know the basis for the reviewer's recommendation?

Does the reviewer sound knowledgeable and trustworthy? Does the reader trust the reviewer's judgment?

The first paragraph objectively summarizes the plot mechanism that sets the movie in motion. The second paragraph summarizes what is apparently the bulk of the movie, namely, the courtroom drama. But the details of the story in paragraph 2 are not just laid before us; they are carefully chosen in order to support the judgment that the verdict "offends our sense of justice." Likewise, the details of the story in the fourth paragraph support the evaluation that the unavenged murders are "appalling" and "the film paints a sympathetic picture of the officer's dilemma." The answer to the first question, therefore, is that the analysis of the film presents enough information, but not too much.

As for the reviewer's values, they are clear and support the recommendation in the last paragraph. In terms of what constitutes a well-made film, the reviewer likes the pace and the acting. And in terms of what makes a film worthwhile, the reviewer approves of its social consciousness and the insights it gave him into "a world that most people don't come in daily contact with."

Finally, the review carries authority. We have a clear sense of what the reviewer values and why he likes the film. We know what the movie is about and see the validity of the reviewer's conclusions. Though we may not personally share his values about what defines a well-made or worthwhile film, the reviewer sounds reasonable within the framework that he has established.

· RESPONDING TO A TEXT

One of the most common requirements in school and business is evaluating what someone else has written. In the early grades you were probably asked to write a book report, which at first meant a few lines about whether you liked a story and later meant a summary of a story or book and whether you liked it. Eventually you were (or will be) required to evaluate what you have read—to respond to it at a mature, critical level. The text may be a poem, novel, chapter in a history book, article in a scholarly journal, financial statement of a company, or proposal to change production methods. The expectation, however, is the same: to show that you understand the author's point and to judge its value according to a set of criteria.

Now read the following review, written for a column called "People of the Book" in *Jewish People*, a New York City newspaper, and look for how the reviewer evaluates the book. In turn, you should evaluate the review by the same three criteria we used before: (1) Is there a sufficient, but not excessive, summary? (2) Are the reviewer's values clear? (3) Does the reviewer sound knowledgeable and trustworthy? In addition, note the reviewer's assumptions about the values of the audience, based on the type of publication the column appeared in.

REVIEW OF *THE IMAGE OF THE JEW IN AMERICAN LITERATURE* by Louis Harap

1   The relation of art to life is proverbially complex. Critics have long debated whether literature mirrors society or shapes it, whether an ethically reprehensible work can nonetheless be artistically commendable, whether a great writer must be morally superior to his time and place. And these are the salient issues as Louis Harap recounts the evolving perception of the Jew in American society and, therefore, literature.

2   Since it does for American literature what Montagu Frank Modder's *The Jew in the Literature of England* did for English, *The Image of the Jew in American Literature* quotes with approval Modder's beliefs "that invariably the poet, the novelist, and the dramatist reflect the attitude of contemporary society in their presentation of the Jewish character, and that the portrayal changes with the economic and social changes of each decade." But Harap adds: "While the stereotype is static . . . in that its various features have recurred in literature since the Middle Ages, the image of the Jew has nevertheless undergone a variety of alterations in accordance with the current social conditions and religious ideas."

3   And this interplay between the static and the evolving elements of the stereotype makes for continuously interesting reading. It is fascinating to learn, for instance, that during the early nineteenth century, when Jews comprised about one-tenth of one percent of the population and most writers had no personal acquaintance with Jews, hundreds of biblical novels appeared, peopled by noble Jews who followed Jesus and brutal ones who opposed him. Similarly, it is significant that this fictionalization of Jews included a concept of "Jewish" beauty: dark and exotic. As more immigrants arrived toward the end of the century, however, they represented a commercial threat, and the stereotype took on the negative features that are now associated with it. But, as Harap points out, "the anti-Semitic nature of the stereotype consists in the denial of an individual nature to Jews, whether the stereotype is positive or negative."

4   There are many pitfalls inherent in a study of this kind, but Harap is aware of them. He says, for example: "When one confronts a documented history of the ill will toward the Jews . . . there is a danger that one's perspective may be skewed. Are not the great ones thereby diminished in stature? Is not our admiration misplaced for minds that could not rise above vulgar prejudice against a persecuted people?" The questions are, of course, relevant to issues other than one's attitude toward Jews; they can be asked about the prevalence in the theater and cinema until recently of shuffling blacks, grunting Indians, inscrutable Orientals, and currently of mindless whites, pathological soldiers, racist Americans. And in this respect, Harap is instructive beyond the confines of the present study when

he correctly maintains that "at the very least, anti-Jewish prejudice hardly enhances their stature. Perhaps one is tempted to depreciate hitherto venerated literary figures, but such a response . . . would be ill-considered and lacking in perspective. . . . Traditional prejudice is implanted in the language as an index of popular attitudes. . . . [I]n resorting to the stereotype, the writer is only using a literary convention, not necessarily expressing personal views." Though ignoring injustice is not honorable, it is nonetheless distinct from committing injustice. And, in effect, Harap's book is an exhaustive, but never exhausting, study of which writers were employing conventions and which were expressing personal views.

5   It comes as no surprise that Henry Adams, who hated capitalism, socialism, progressivism and organized labor, also hated Jews. As Harap says of the man whose enduring works are appreciations of medieval architecture: "His anti-Semitism was a convenient outlet for his frustrated craving for power and for the perversity of a society that moved from the settled, patrician order of the eighteenth century to a finance capitalism in which power was held by upstarts, symbolized for Adams by the Jews." Yet it is both ironic and significant that in his autobiographical *Education,* Adams offers parallels between himself and the Jews to illustrate his alienation from society.

6   Similarly, it is not surprising that Henry James, who always seems more concerned with style than substance, "assumed the conventional social attitudes to the Jews." Thus, the stage adaptations of several short stories with bigoted allusions to Jews removed the offending parts, perhaps, Harap believes, out of deference to the many Jewish theater goers. And while James was horrified by the squalor of the Jewish ghetto in the Lower East Side, his description of it in *The American Scene* was, according to Harap, "not humane and compassionate and comprehending, but rather disgusted and dehumanized." My own reading of this work, however, suggests that Harap is too charitable. James does not simply mouth popular attitudes uncritically. He is torn, he admits, between an obligation of "tribute to an intellectual people" and his general distaste for foreigners. But because the Jews he meets are not "mere mob," because they represent a "waiting spring of intelligence," he recoils at the "betrayal of the linguistic tradition as one had known it"—and therefore chooses to dislike Jews because they threaten his world.

7   On the other hand, it is something of a jolt to learn that Hawthorne, a writer I have always respected for both his craft and humanity, confided to his *English Notebooks,* not intended for publication, that a certain ugly Jew he met in London "justified me in the repugnance I have always felt towards his race." It was also illuminating to learn that Henry Garland, a non-Jew, was so enamored of Judaism that during the closing decades of the nineteenth century he published several novels under the Jewish-

sounding pseudonym Sidney Luska, only to later adopt the anti-Semitism
of the upper class with whom his success allowed him to mingle. And it
was absolutely amazing to learn that in response to the numerous anti-
Semitic versions of the "Wandering Jew" legend, in 1891 a rabbi wrote a
relatively popular "Wandering Gentile" story, *Ben-Beor, a Story of the Anti-
Messiah.*

8   But this catalogue of surprises should not suggest that Harap's book is
limited to curiosity value. On the contrary, it is a reasoned survey of the
attitudes of the famous and obscure, documented by copious quotations
that are themselves an introduction to many lesser works. This is a welcome study of a neglected but important aspect of the relationship of
literature to life.

Drawing Conclusions

As we have seen, an evaluation must be built on an adequate analysis and
clear values, but this is only half of the foundation. What we build on this
foundation must be sound also. In other words, we must draw valid conclusions
from the evidence we present.

When examining the conclusion that we or others are drawing, there are
certain questions that we must ask about the evidence:

Is it relevant?

Is it adequate?

Is it necessary and sufficient?

Is it representative?

Is it complete?

Is it current?

Is it from a trustworthy source?

Is it in agreement with the experience of others?

Like everything else in an essay, the supporting details must be **relevant** to
the main idea. If your topic is the comfort of a jogging shoe, the price is not
relevant. But if your purpose is to list best buys, a comfort-to-price comparison of
several brands is relevant. Politics probably has no place in an evaluation of a
new car, but it may be central to a review of a book or film.

Adequacy refers both to the amount of evidence and, more importantly, to
the strength. Chocolate on your hands and a smile on your face may lead
someone to suspect you of having eaten the last fudge brownie, but they do not
add up to being caught with your hand in the cookie jar. Similarly, several
quotations from critics can support your interpretation of the theme of a novel,
but stronger support would come from an essay or preface by the author.

Relevance and adequacy sometimes combine into what is called **necessary and sufficient** evidence. Evidence is necessary if you can't prove your point without it; evidence is sufficient if it is all you need to prove your point. You can decide if you should include a quotation or anecdote or other detail by asking whether it is necessary for the conclusion you want to draw. If the conclusion can be supported without that piece of information, the detail is not necessary. Once you have collected evidence that is necessary, you want to be sure it is sufficient to support the conclusion.

Finding many examples of something is not adequate if they are all similar. The examples must be wide-ranging, that is, **representative.** To support the thesis that television portrays minorities in a bad light you cannot limit your examples to blacks or commercials or Hispanics in situation comedies. The evidence must come from a variety of television contexts and include a variety of minorities. If your examples are narrow, your thesis must be narrow: For instance, television commercials show women as frivolous.

In addition to being representative, your sample must be **complete.** You cannot hide or omit evidence that goes against your thesis. You must include it and explain it away: "It is true that blacks are portrayed sympathetically in *The Cosby Show,* but the overwhelming impression from commercials and other weekly series is stereotypical and offensive, as in. . . ."

Evidence must also be **current.** If all of your evidence comes from old television shows and articles written twenty years ago, the situation may have changed. Students rushing to write term papers at the last minute frequently use whatever sources are available the day they get to the library. But an article describing the image of women in television shows of the 1950s is out of date if your topic is today's television image. If that article is all you can find, you might want to change your topic to a comparison of the earlier image of women to the current one.

Of course, if you are writing about a topic you do not know about firsthand, you must be sure that your sources are **trustworthy.** You will have to evaluate whether they are following all the correct methods described here. In addition, you will have to determine the reputation of the author and periodical or publisher. The author may have had a grudge against the person or institution being attacked and therefore cannot be trusted to tell the whole story. Some periodicals and publishers are known for their interest in sensationalism rather than accuracy.

Finally, evidence in an essay or a source you want to use must, if possible, be in **agreement** with other information, for example what you or others know from personal experience. It would obviously be inadvisable to make generalizations about blacks based on *The Jeffersons* or *Sanford and Son.* Similarly, New Yorkers and Midwesterners have very little firsthand knowledge about each other. So it follows that a careful reader always asks whether the details in an essay reflect what he or she knows personally. If these details are accurate, the reader is likely to trust the writer's presentation of other information. If they are not accurate, the writer will lose the reader's trust.

Logical Fallacies

Each of these "thou shalts" has a companion "thou shalt not" to avoid. Thus, for example, you want to include relevant information and avoid irrelevant details. You want to create a sample that is representative and avoid one that is narrow. You want to find trustworthy sources and avoid biased ones.

In addition, there are errors in reasoning that you want to avoid in your own writing and watch for in what you read. The following are a few of the more common of these **logical fallacies.**

Ad hominem (Latin for "at the person") arguments attempt to undermine a point of view by aiming the attack at the person or people holding it. In recent politics ad hominem arguments became known as the "personality issue." A candidate's economic platform could be dismissed if the candidate smoked pot or had extramarital affairs.

Begging the question, or **circular reasoning,** results when the point to be proven is already taken for granted. "Since majority rules, there should be one-man/one-vote." This argument assumes that the majority should or does get its way. But the whole issue of one-man/one-vote is whether the majority should have absolute power over the minority.

Dominoes is the belief that the first step in a process necessarily leads to the ultimate result. The belief in the 1960s was that if the United States did not stop communism in Vietnam, all Southeast Asia would become communist. Now one often hears, "If we don't fight the communists in Central America, we'll be fighting them in Central Park." Another version is the argument that if the government bans pornography (or allows abortion) soon it will abolish all free speech (or allow the killing of the handicapped).

Everyone does it turns (supposed) majority opinion into a form of natural law. Whether applied to drugs, sex, cheating, or spying, it assumes that two wrongs make a right.

False analogy results when a similarity in one respect is used to prove a similarity in another: The Irish were once discriminated against and without help from the government gained total acceptance in American society; therefore, there is no need for special laws to help blacks today. This reasoning overlooks the possibility that there may be significant differences between the Irish situation of a hundred years and the situation of blacks today. An executive of a tobacco company told a congressional committee considering a ban on cigarette ads, "Pravda does not carry cigarette advertising. . . . Government control of information is typical of totalitarian regimes."

False authority occurs most often in the popular strategy of having famous people endorse products, policies, or politicians that are unrelated to their area of expertise. Successful football players or musicians may be the proper authorities to quote when the topic is sports or music, but they have no more authority than you do when the topic is anything else.

False dilemma sets up two choices in an either/or relationship that makes the opposing view seem absurd. "Either we ban nuclear bombs or we destroy the world" of one side of the disarmament debate is countered by the other side with "Either we match the Russians bomb for bomb or we might as well admit defeat right now." In both cases, there are other choices.

Non sequitur (Latin for "it does not follow") is a general term for an error in which the evidence is irrelevant to the conclusion. While "false authority" and "everyone does it" are non sequiturs, the possibilities may be unlimited. "My parents will cut off my allowance if you don't pass me" illustrates another kind of non sequitur.

Overgeneralization results from stretching the evidence further than it can go, as in using examples that are not representative. Applying Western values to non-Western peoples is a common "right wing" practice. Using animal behavior to support or oppose human behavior is the "left wing" variation.

Overlooked alternative ignores other possible answers: Since people who go to college earn twice as much as people who do not, a college education increases your earning power. An alternative explanation is that certain kinds of people are attracted to college in the first place.

Post hoc ergo propter hoc (Latin for "after this, therefore because of this") confuses sequence with causation. Washing your car in the morning did not make it rain in the afternoon. Similarly, banning prayer from public schools did not necessarily cause the sexual revolution.

Straw man, when done deliberately, is like a magician's sleight of hand: A diversion is set up that draws your attention away from where the action is really taking place. One form of straw man is to attack an extreme (and possibly untrue) form of the opposing view, as in the false dilemma fallacy. Students often do this unintentionally because they are not experts in the fields that they have to write about. Another version is to play on an unrelated emotional chord, as in the ad hominem attack.

Finally, we should stress that the fallacies we have described refer to the structure of the reasoning, not to your or the writer's sincerity. We are most prone to overlook these errors in essays that we agree with or in support of positions that we wish were true. As a student writer you should try to understand that a teacher who finds fault with your paper may truly agree with your opinion.

EXERCISE: Evaluating Logic

Read and evaluate the following passage. Remember, you are being asked to evaluate the reasoning, not the decency of the proposal or the speaker.

In 1873 Susan B. Anthony was convicted of illegally voting and fined $100.

At her trial she attacked the laws that denied her the right to vote. Part of her testimony follows:

1   Friends and fellow-citizens: I stand before you tonight under indictment for the alleged crime of having voted at the last Presidential election, without having a lawful right to vote. It shall be my work this evening to prove to you that in thus voting, I not only committed no crime, but, instead, simply exercised my citizen's rights, guaranteed to me and all United States citizens by the National Constitution, beyond the power of any State to deny.

2   The preamble of the Federal Constitution says: "We, the people of the United States, in order to form a more perfect union, establish justice, insure domestic tranquillity, provide for the common defense, promote the general welfare, and secure the blessings of liberty to ourselves and our posterity, do ordain and establish this Constitution for the United States of America."

3   It was we, the people; not we, the white male citizens; nor yet we, the male citizens; but we, the whole people, who formed the Union. And we formed it, not to give the blessings of liberty, but to secure them; not to the half of ourselves and the half of our posterity, but to the whole people—women as well as men. And it is a downright mockery to talk to women of their enjoyment of the blessings of liberty while they are denied the use of the only means of securing them provided by this democratic-republican government—the ballot.

4   For any State to make sex a qualification that must ever result in the disfranchisement of one entire half of the people is to pass a bill of attainder, or an *ex post facto* law, and is therefore a violation of the supreme law of the land. By it the blessings of liberty are forever withheld from women and their female posterity. To them this government has no just powers derived from the consent of the governed. To them this government is not a democracy. It is not a republic. It is an odious aristocracy; a hateful oligarchy of sex; the most hateful aristocracy ever established on the face of the globe. An oligarchy of wealth, where the rich govern the poor, an oligarchy of learning, where the educated govern the ignorant, or even an oligarchy of race, where the Saxon rules the African, might be endured; but this oligarchy of sex, which makes father, brothers, husband, sons, the oligarchs over the mother and sisters, the wife and daughters of every household—which ordains all men sovereigns, all women subjects, carries dissension, discord and rebellion into every home of the nation.

5   Webster, Worcester and Bouvier all define a citizen to be a person in the United States, entitled to vote and hold office.

6   The only question left to be settled now is: Are women persons? And I hardly believe any of our opponents will have the hardihood to say they

are not. Being persons, then, women are citizens; and no State has a right to make any law, or to enforce any old law, that shall abridge their privileges or immunities. Hence, every discrimination against women in the constitutions and laws of the several States is today null and void, precisely as is every one against Negroes.

What is Anthony's purpose in quoting from the Constitution in the second paragraph?

Given the political and social conditions of the 1780s, can we conclude, as Anthony does, that "We, the people" refers to all people in the United States and not just to white males? What additional evidence can you bring to support or contradict her interpretation?

Is the assertion in paragraph 3 correct that the ballot is the only way to achieve liberty? Is it true that without the right to vote, women did not enjoy liberty? What does *liberty* mean?

Is the preamble to the Constitution "the supreme law of the land," as Anthony calls it in paragraph 4? Is she correct in saying that denying the ballot to women violated the law? What is *law*? What additional evidence can you bring to either support or contradict her statement?

Do you agree that an oligarchy of sex is worse than one based on wealth, learning, or race? Why do you think Anthony made this comparison in paragraph 4? Does this statement prove that Anthony approved of slavery or that she was a racist or fascist?

Based on this passage, who do you think Webster, Worcester, and Bouvier were? Why is Anthony citing them in paragraph 5? What weight does their authority carry? How important is their definition of *citizen*?

Is Anthony drawing a justified conclusion in paragraph 6 when she states that since a citizen is a person who can vote, if women are persons they should be allowed to vote?

Why do you think Anthony's speech is as famous as it is? What is the source of its appeal to us?

· WRITING AN EVALUATION

Now let's see how a student created an evaluation by building on the previous discussions about television. As you read her paper, notice how she has combined observation, analysis, and authoritative sources by filtering them through values based on personal experience. Evaluate her evaluation using the criteria we have been studying.

STEREOTYPES OF WOMEN IN TELEVISION

by Nina Hines

1   Despite the agitation of the women's movement,
television continues to portray women in a stereotypical way that is inconsistent with the image of a
liberated woman. This stereotype occurs in all kinds of
shows, but especially in commercials and comedies.

2   In "Classism, Sexism, Racism and the Situation
Comedy," K. Edgington states: "The comedy of some
sitcoms relies on stereotypes. Each character represents a group and is defined largely by stereotypical
traits associated with that group. The "humor" occurs when the character, because of one or more of his
or her traits, is made to appear ridiculous. For us to
understand how heavily situation comedies apply
stereotypes requires extensive examination of individual series."

3   This article includes a study of the comedy
Gilligan's Island to demonstrate how sexism is a basic
element of the show. "Ginger, one of the "girls",
provides the series with a sex object. A Hollywood
starlet, Ginger wears evening gowns, frets over her
appearance, and carries out those tasks least likely to
result in a broken fingernail or snagged nylon." "An

offset to Ginger's spice, is Mary Ann, a wholesome farm girl from the Midwest, who is everything nice. But, lacking Ginger's beauty and possessing neither status nor valuable skill, she is seen doing the inferior domestic duties." Mrs. Howell's "title suggests that her status and identity rely on her relationship to her husband. Her main responsibility is to assure the comfort of Mr. Howell."

4   All in the Family is another comedy worth examining. Edith Bunker does what women stereotypically do. When her husband comes home, she runs to get his dinner or to get him a beer. Why should she do this? Can't he do it himself? My husband is sure not going to take me for granted like this. There is not even a suggestion that she wants to wait on him, but the show makes it clear that this is her duty. If she fails in her duty, Archie makes a big fuss. This is all part of the stereotype that women have to cater to their husband's. "Thus, sexism forms the basis of the social structure from which the comic situation draws its material. Women's positions are assigned in accordance with attachment to men."

5   Women are portrayed this same way in commercials. An article in Journal of Communication states that "Courtney and Whipple reviewed four studies on sex-role messages in television commercials con-

ducted in 1971–1973. They reported that women were most frequently used as product representatives for domestic items." This study also found that women are seen in the home more often than men. Women are shown washing laundry, doing the dishes, and cleaning the house. Women are rarely seen outdoors or at work. This reinforces the stereotype that a woman's place is in the home.

6   This article also states that another study found "women are seven times more likely to appear in ads for personal hygiene." 75% of ads for bathroom products have women. But women are rare in ads for cars, trucks and related products like gas and oil. This "supports the stereotype that a woman has no interest or ability in so masculine an area as mechanics or machines."

7   On the other hand, women dominate commercials for perfume. They are always seen trying to capture a man by smelling good. Women are supposed to run out and buy expensive perfumes just for this. The stereotype is that women are nothing without a man and pleasing a man is the ultimate aim of every woman. But what about pleasing ourselves? Perfume can also be worn for your own personal enjoyment. So why can't they drop this stereotype of the man-chasing woman?

8   Even though these stereotypes are very annoying,

they remain on television. The reason must be that the
public likes them. We cannot blame the advertisers for
using them if they sell products. The commercials would
be dropped if they were not successful. And sitcoms
would go off the air if nobody watched them. We have
nobody to blame but ourselves for the survival of these
stereotypes.

Several aspects of the preceding paper are quite good. The thesis is clear and finds support in the body of the essay; it is not overstated or overambitious, but instead is narrow enough to be treated in a short paper. Each paragraph concentrates on a single idea and supports it with details that are relevant, adequate, and representative. The specific references to what appears on television are necessary and sufficient to prove the writer's case, especially in the section about commercials. The articles cited are authoritative. The examples and articles were up to date when the paper was written (though they may be dated now). The last paragraph concludes the essay with an interesting thought about causation. The student's values—and personality—shine through.

But the student's own authority is undermined by faulty quoting and sloppy mechanics. The quotation in the second paragraph says that the stereotypical traits are the basis of the comedy. But this promises a type of example that is not delivered. If the comedy in *Gilligan's Island* is based on the fact that Mary Ann does domestic chores and in *All in the Family* on the fact that Edith gets Archie's dinner, these don't sound like shows that could run for decades. The article gives examples of how these premises create situations that provide comedy, but the student does not provide similar examples. The student had a good article to work with, but she quotes the wrong section.

In addition, she quotes too much—more than is necessary and sufficient. The second and third paragraphs are almost entirely quotations. The first two sentences in the second paragraph should have been paraphrased and edited with ellipses, and the third sentence is not worth quoting at all because it is not a clever turn of phrase or unique insight. Similarly, the third paragraph simply quotes the entire section in the article about "girls." Again, the student should have paraphrased the point and quoted only striking phrases.

Moreover, when we look at the quotations carefully, we discover that they are not accurate. "The sitcom" is quoted as "some sitcoms"; "offsetting" appears as "an offset to"; "classism and sexism form" becomes "sexism is part of"; the quotation in the second paragraph is made to look like running text when it is actually from two different places; and so on. As for mechanics, double quotation marks are used instead of single ones inside a quotation, a comma is placed outside a quotation mark instead of inside (where it stands in the sentence being quoted), and the like. These may seem like trivial quibbles, but, as we have said several times, part of a writer's credibility rests on showing a knowledge of the conventions to the skilled reader. If the reader sees that the writer is careless—or worse—with the simple things, he or she will question more than the accuracy of the mechanics. Since we have found mistakes in the writer's quotations from the article we have at hand, we are forced to wonder how accurately she represented the article we have not read, and whether she understood it. In effect, for want of a quotation mark, the credibility was lost.

CHECKLIST FOR EVALUATION

An evaluation must have
  an analysis of the issue
  a clear set of values
  a sense of authority

When examining the evidence for a conclusion, we ask
  Is it relevant?
  Is it adequate?
  Is it necessary and sufficient?
  Is it representative?
  Is it complete?
  Is it current?
  Is it from a trustworthy source?
  Is it in agreement with the experience of others?

  Among the common logical fallacies are
  Ad hominem: attacking the person instead of the point.
  Begging the question (circular reasoning): taking for granted what you are supposed to be proving.
  Dominoes: assuming the first step in a process must lead to the last.
  Everyone does it: two wrongs make a right.
  False analogy: similarity in one respect assumes similarity in others.
  False authority: quoting famous people out of their field.
  False dilemma: setting up an unreal either/or choice.
  Non sequitur: "it does not follow."
  Overgeneralization: stretching the evidence too far.
  Overlooked alternative: ignoring other possible answers.
  Post hoc ergo propter hoc: confusing sequence with causation.
  Straw man: drawing attention away from the real issue.

· ESSAYS FOR CRITICAL READING

W(illiam) E(dward) B(urghardt) Du Bois was the intellectual leader of the black revolt against the compromises of Booker T. Washington. Unlike Washington, who was born into slavery in the South, Du Bois was born in Massachusetts after the Civil War of mixed French, Dutch, and Negro ancestry. He received a Ph.D. from Harvard in 1895 and established his reputation as a gifted writer and radical thinker in 1903 with The Souls of Black Folk, *where the following selection appeared. Two years later he founded the Niagara Movement, which eventually became the NAACP, whose journal,* The Crisis, *he edited from 1910 to 1932. In 1961, at the age of 93, he joined the Communist party. He became a citizen of Ghana shortly before his death in 1963.*

From OF MR. BOOKER T. WASHINGTON AND OTHERS
by W. E. B. Du Bois

1   Easily the most striking thing in the history of the American Negro since 1876 is the ascendancy of Mr. Booker T. Washington. It began at the time when war memories and ideals were rapidly passing; a day of astonishing commercial development was dawning; a sense of doubt and hesitation overtook the freedmen's sons,—then it was that his leading began. Mr. Washington came, with a simple definite programme, at the psychological moment when the nation was a little ashamed of having bestowed so much sentiment on Negroes, and was concentrating its energies on Dollars. His programme of industrial education, conciliation of the South, and submission and silence as to civil and political rights, was not wholly original; the Free Negroes from 1830 up to wartime had striven to build industrial schools, and the American Missionary Association had from the first taught various trades; and Price and others had sought a way of honorable alliance with the best of the Southerners. But Mr. Washington first indissolubly linked these things; he put enthusiasm, unlimited energy, and perfect faith into this programme, and changed it from a by-path into a veritable Way of Life. And the tale of the methods by which he did this is a fascinating study of human life.

2   It startled the nation to hear a Negro advocating such a programme after many decades of bitter complaint; it startled and won the applause of the South, it interested and won the admiration of the North; and after a confused murmur of protest, it silenced if it did not convert the Negroes themselves.

3   To gain the sympathy and coöperation of the various elements comprising the white South was Mr. Washington's first task; and this, at the time Tuskegee was

founded, seemed, for a black man, well-nigh impossible. And yet ten years later it was done in the word spoken at Atlanta: "In all things purely social we can be as separate as the five fingers, and yet one as the hand in all things essential to mutual progress." This "Atlanta Compromise" is by all odds the most notable thing in Mr. Washington's career. The South interpreted it in different ways: the radicals received it as a complete surrender of the demand for civil and political equality; the conservatives, as a generously conceived working basis for mutual understanding. So both approved it, and to-day its author is certainly the most distinguished Southerner since Jefferson Davis, and the one with the largest personal following. . . .

4   Among his own people, however, Mr. Washington has encountered the strongest and most lasting opposition, amounting at times to bitterness, and even to-day continuing strong and insistent even though largely silenced in outward expression by the public opinion of the nation. Some of this opposition is, of course, mere envy; the disappointment of displaced demagogues and the spite of narrow minds. But aside from this, there is among educated and thoughtful colored men in all parts of the land a feeling of deep regret, sorrow, and apprehension at the wide currency and ascendancy which some of Mr. Washington's theories have gained. These same men admire his sincerity of purpose, and are willing to forgive much to honest endeavor which is doing something worth the doing. They coöperate with Mr. Washington as far as they conscientiously can; and, indeed, it is no ordinary tribute to this man's tact and power that, steering as he must between so many diverse interests and opinions, he so largely retains the respect of all. . . .

5   . . . But Booker T. Washington arose as essentially the leader not of one race but of two,—a compromiser between the South, the North, and the Negro. Naturally the Negroes resented, at first bitterly, signs of compromise which surrendered their civil and political rights, even though this was to be exchanged for larger chances of economic development. The rich and dominating North, however, was not only weary of the race problem, but was investing largely in Southern enterprises, and welcomed any method of peaceful coöperation. Thus, by national opinion, the Negroes began to recognize Mr. Washington's leadership; and the voice of criticism was hushed.

6   Mr. Washington represents in Negro thought the old attitude of adjustment and submission; but adjustment at such a peculiar time as to make his programme unique. This is an age of unusual economic development, and Mr. Washington's programme naturally takes an economic cast, becoming a gospel of Work and Money to such an extent as apparently almost completely to overshadow the higher aims of life. Moreover, this is an age when the more advanced races are coming in closer contact with the less developed races, and the race-feeling is therefore intensified; and Mr. Washington's programme practically accepts the alleged inferiority of the Negro races. Again, in our own land, the reaction from the sentiment of war time has given impetus to race-prejudice

against Negroes, and Mr. Washington withdraws many of the high demands of Negroes as men and American citizens. In other periods of intensified prejudice all the Negro's tendency to self-assertion has been called forth; at this period a policy of submission is advocated. In the history of nearly all other races and peoples the doctrine preached at such crises has been that manly self-respect is worth more than lands and houses, and that a people who voluntarily surrender such respect, or cease striving for it, are not worth civilizing.

7   In answer to this, it has been claimed that the Negro can survive only through submission. Mr. Washington distinctly asks that black people give up, at least for the present, three things,—

First, political power,

Second, insistence on civil rights,

Third, higher education of Negro youth,—

and concentrate all their energies on industrial education, the accumulation of wealth, and the conciliation of the South. This policy has been courageously and insistently advocated for over fifteen years, and has been triumphant for perhaps ten years. As a result of this tender of the palm-branch, what has been the return? In these years there have occurred:

1. The disfranchisement of the Negro.

2. The legal creation of a distinct status of civil inferiority for the Negro.

3. The steady withdrawal of aid from institutions for the higher training of the Negro.

8   These movements are not, to be sure, direct results of Mr. Washington's teachings; but his propaganda has, without a shadow of doubt, helped their speedier accomplishment. The question then comes: Is it possible, and probable, that nine millions of men can make effective progress in economic lines if they are deprived of political rights, made a servile caste, and allowed only the most meagre chance for developing their exceptional men? If history and reason give any distinct answer to these questions, it is an emphatic *No*. And Mr. Washington thus faces the triple paradox of his career:

1. He is striving nobly to make Negro artisans business men and property-owners; but it is utterly impossible, under modern competitive methods, for workingmen and property-owners to defend their rights and exist without the right of suffrage.

2. He insists on thrift and self-respect, but at the same time counsels a silent submission to civic inferiority such as is bound to sap the manhood of any race in the long run.

3. He advocates common-school and industrial training, and depreciates institutions of higher learning; but neither the Negro common-schools, nor Tuskegee itself, could remain open a day were it not for teachers trained in Negro colleges, or trained by their graduates. . . .

9   It would be unjust to Mr. Washington not to acknowledge that in several instances he has opposed movements in the South which were unjust to the Negro; he sent memorials to the Louisiana and Alabama constitutional conventions, he has spoken against lynching, and in other ways has openly or silently set his influence against sinister schemes and unfortunate happenings. Notwithstanding this, it is equally true to assert that on the whole the distinct impression left by Mr. Washington's propaganda is, first, that the South is justified in its present attitude toward the Negro because of the Negro's degradation, secondly, that the prime cause of the Negro's failure to rise more quickly is his wrong education in the past; and, thirdly, that his future rise depends primarily on his own efforts. Each of these propositions is a dangerous half-truth. The supplementary truths must never be lost sight of: first, slavery and race-prejudice are potent if not sufficient causes of the Negro's position; second, industrial and common-school training were necessarily slow in planting because they had to await the black teachers trained by higher institutions,—it being extremely doubtful if any essentially different development was possible, and certainly a Tuskegee was unthinkable before 1880; and, third, while it is a great truth to say that the Negro must strive and strive mightily to help himself, it is equally true that unless his striving be not simply seconded, but rather aroused and encouraged, by the initiative of the richer and wiser environing group, he cannot hope for great success.

10   In his failure to realize and impress this last point, Mr. Washington is especially to be criticised. His doctrine has tended to make the whites, North and South, shift the burden of the Negro problem to the Negro's shoulders and stand aside as critical and rather pessimistic spectators; when in fact the burden belongs to the nation, and the hands of none of us are clean if we bend not our energies to righting these great wrongs. . . .

SIGNIFICANCE

Explain the significance of the following quotations from the selection:

"Mr. Washington came, with a simple definite programme, at the psychological moment when the nation was a little ashamed of having bestowed so much sentiment on Negroes. . . ."

". . . it startled and won the applause of the South, it interested and won the admiration of the North; and . . . it silenced if it did not convert the Negroes themselves."

". . . Booker T. Washington arose as essentially the leader not of one race but of two,—a compromiser between the South, the North, and the Negro."

"Mr. Washington represents in Negro thought the old attitude of adjustment and submission. . . ."

"Mr. Washington distinctly asks that black people give up . . . First, political power, Second, insistence on civil rights, Third, higher education of Negro youth. . . ."

"These movements are not, to be sure, direct results of Mr. Washington's teachings; but his propaganda has . . . helped their speedier accomplishment."

"His doctrine has tended to make whites . . . shift the burden of the Negro problem to the Negro's shoulders. . . ."

FUTURE USE

Briefly summarize the selection.

Explain the basis of the evaluation. What values does Du Bois assume or present?

What aspects of Washington's program does Du Bois dislike? What is his basis for finding fault with them?

What information from this selection is relevant to your essay(s)? How could you use this information?

When Aspects of the Rise of Economic Individualism *appeared in 1933, H. M. Robertson was senior lecturer in economics at the University of Cape Town. His disapproval of Max Weber's theory of the Protestant work ethic was widely applauded, but it was also attacked by those who denied that Protestants shared the same economic ideas as Roman Catholics during and after the Reformation.*

From ASPECTS OF THE RISE OF ECONOMIC INDIVIDUALISM
by H. M. Robertson

1   Max Weber is responsible for the opinion, widely held today, that Protestantism, especially in its Puritan form, has had a very great influence in forming the "spirit of capitalism," and, therefore, in forming capitalism itself. . . .

2   According to Weber, the influence of Protestantism was not merely negative, in permitting the exercise of practices forbidden by the Catholic Church, but also positive, turning religion to capitalistic ends. The chief instrument of this he considered to be the doctrine of the "calling" which came in with Luther and introduced the ideal of an asceticism incumbent upon the laity as well as the religious; an asceticism not of the cloister, but practiced in the affairs of everyday life, by the utter sacrifice of any self-indulgence, by unremitting industry in one's "calling," which was thus promoted to the quality of a religious exercise. He asserted, moreover, that on the Calvinists taking over this doctrine they made success in one's "calling" an outward and visible sign of the acquisition of spiritual grace.

3   He employed philological arguments to bring out the importance of the doctrine of the "calling." He pointed out that there are no equivalents in the Romance (and Catholic) languages to the Protestant-German *Beruf,* the Protestant-Dutch *beroep,* the Protestant-English "calling," in the sense of "a life-task," "a definite field in which to work." He contended that Luther's reformation introduced both the word and the concept. . . .

4   Weber's case for asserting, on philological grounds, that Luther had introduced a novel conception of the "calling," bringing with it a new ideal of worldly asceticism, is not established. It seems on other grounds to have been an unnecessary innovation. The doctrine of Work has at any rate as old a history in the Christian *mores* as St. Paul's—"we commanded you, that if any would not work, neither should he eat." Mediaeval Catholicism had recognized that the deadly sin of Accidia must be combated with work as well as watchfulness. This

recognition had taken form in the Augustinian and Benedictine rules, the foundations of all monastic disciplines. The asceticism of which an essential element was a divinely ordained worldly toll was not, then, foreign to mediaeval Catholicism. And Luther had been an Augustinian monk.

5   But it is argued, this asceticism was in the Middle Ages confined to the cloister. It had no part in the lives of any of the laity. To say that is to ignore the part which the friars were sent out to play—to take religion from the cloister into everyday life. It is to ignore the motives which led to the foundation of third orders. (It is not sufficient excuse for ignoring them to say that it was not considered to be as meritorious to be a member of a third order as to be a full religious; Calvinists do not consider the butcher's "calling," even if the butcher is an elder of the Kirk, to be as honorable as the minister's.) The Franciscan Order of Penitents, as befitted an order founded in the thirteenth century, was in some ways very similar to a religious guild. But it was more than this. It called for an asceticism exercised in the world not in the cloister, and it cultivated some of the bourgeois virtues—the same virtues which Weber stressed so much when he indicated the importance of Benjamin Franklin's worldly creed, his insistence that time is money and not to be wasted, his love of detail and exact reckoning. To the members of the Franciscan third order extravagance was forbidden; also, as with the Puritans, wasting one's time at feasts or masques or dances. . . .

6   Weber has collected a number of Protestant writings which seem to favor capitalism; but he has also mentioned that there was a strong current in Puritan teaching which stressed the dangers of riches, and the Christian's duty of not striving after them. Is he right in saying that this was overshadowed by advice, pro-capitalistic in tendency, to work hard in an orderly way, especially when both elements were also prominent in Catholic teaching? He has not proved that the Puritans introduced a new economic ethic. The Protestants as well as the Catholics spoke with an ambiguous voice. But as a rule the Calvinistic contribution to the capitalist spirit was the same as that of the Jansenists or stricter school of Catholics, consisting of the encouragement of industry, thrift, order and honesty; while the Jesuits went further and favored enterprise, freedom of speculation and the expansion of trade as a social benefit. It would not be difficult to claim that the religion which favored the spirit of capitalism was Jesuitry, not Calvinism. . . .

7   It is noteworthy that the writings of the religio-sociological school on the origins of the capitalist spirit are infected with a deep hatred of capitalism. The essay on "Die Protestantische Ethik und der Geist des Kapitalismus" ushered in as heavy an attack on the capitalist position as the materialist writings of Karl Marx. This is not immediately apparent; but even a cursory second glance shows that its general tendency is to undermine the basis of a capitalist society. It attempts to show that modern capitalism is a massive and imposing superstructure on a foundation of shifting and out-of-date religious ideas, a Moloch of Calvinist selfishness. Its great preoccupation has been to show that, as a form of

social organization, capitalism was not a natural growth, but a crass construction of the Calvinist mind, and therefore as easily assailed as that which made it in its own image. It tried to demonstrate that capitalism is no mere piece of social mechanism which should be judged only on its own merits, but a creation of evil import and unreasonable origin.

8   This seems to be the natural corollary of the arguments of all who accept this line of thought. Even Professor Tawney, who, in his *Religion and the Rise of Capitalism*, has admitted that the capitalist spirit was not the offspring of Puritanism, has yet affirmed that it "found in certain aspects of later Puritanism a tonic which braced its energies and fortified its already vigorous temper." He accepted the theory that "Puritanism had its own standards of social conduct, derived partly from the obvious interests of the commercial classes, partly from its conception of the nature of God and the destiny of man," and "became a potent force in preparing the way for the commercial civilization which finally triumphed at the Revolution." He believed that two elements in Calvinism were responsible for this. One was the doctrine of the "calling." The other lay in the fact that though Calvin had given approval to the life of business enterprise whilst subjecting it to an iron discipline, the demand for discipline later dropped into the background, leaving Calvinism as a religion which demanded free play for all forms of enterprise. . . .

9   The chief factor in the triumph of bourgeois liberalism was the factor of economic development which made the bourgeoisie important. It came into its own as a secular force. The rise of bourgeois morality in England as a substitute for religion was not the product of Puritanism. In Catholic France one found preachers complaining in the eighteenth century that a "gospel of worldly probity, in which is comprised all the duties of reason and religion" had arisen "on the ruins of the gospel of Jesus Christ"; and that the bourgeois preferred to be known as *honnête homme* rather than as a good Christian. The churches in each country had been unable in the end, in spite of all their efforts, to assimilate the class of self-made men. The decline of the churches in England as witnesses to a Christian code of social ethics was not due to a Puritan belief that "the Lorde was with Joseph, and he was a luckie felowe." It was due to the unwillingness of a rising bourgeoisie to be bound by what it considered to be antiquated rules.

10   Even so, there is no reason to decry too violently the new bourgeois individualism with its profane, not Puritan, origins. It was not a mere product of greed. It inculcated a belief in honor and justice, it believed firmly in justice, thought that independently of all religion there was implanted in man a love of justice, and on this it built. It did not ask for liberty for men to indulge their antisocial greed. It asked liberty for them to look after themselves in accordance with the rules which life and business both require to be respected and the observance of which was thought to be innate to man's nature; the rules of respecting contracts and of not doing to others what one would not have done to oneself. It did not ask for economic freedom because it believed that man's spirit

of emulation raised an antithesis between the common and the private good, but because it disbelieved it. . . .

SIGNIFICANCE

Explain the significance of the following quotations from the selection:

"According to Weber, the influence of Protestantism was not merely negative, in permitting the exercise of practices forbidden by the Catholic Church, but also positive, turning religion to capitalistic ends."

"Weber's case for asserting, on philological grounds, that Luther had introduced a novel conception of the 'calling' . . . is not established."

"It would not be difficult to claim that the religion which favored the spirit of capitalism was Jesuitry, not Calvinism."

". . . the writings of the religio-sociological school on the origins of the capitalist spirit are infected with a deep hatred of capitalism."

"The chief factor in the triumph of bourgeois liberalism was the factor of economic development which made the bourgeoisie important. It came into its own as a secular force."

". . . there is no reason to decry too violently the new bourgeois individualism, with its profane, not Puritan, origins. It was not a mere product of greed. It inculcated a belief in honor and justice."

FUTURE USE

Briefly summarize the selection.

Explain the basis of the evaluation. What values does Robertson assume or present?

What aspects of Weber's theory does Robertson attack? What is his basis for disagreeing with them?

What information from this selection is relevant to your essay(s)? How could you use this information?

When, in 1896, the Supreme Court in the case of Plessy v. Ferguson *(p. 233)
upheld the legality of "separate but equal" railroad facilities, the decision noted
that the District of Columbia, which was administered directly by Congress, had
separate schools for whites and blacks. In 1954, the court analyzed the doctrine of
"separate but equal" schools for the first time. Chief Justice Earl Warren wrote
the opinion for a unanimous court.*

From *BROWN V. BOARD OF EDUCATION* (1954)

1   These cases come to us from the States of Kansas, South Carolina, Virginia,
and Delaware. They are premised on different facts and different local conditions, but a common legal question justifies their consideration together in this
consolidated opinion.

2   In each of the cases, minors of the Negro race, through their legal representatives, seek the aid of the courts in obtaining admission to the public schools of
their community on a nonsegregated basis. In each instance, they have been
denied admission to schools attended by white children under laws requiring or
permitting segregation according to race. This segregation was alleged to deprive
the plaintiffs of the equal protection of the laws under the Fourteenth Amendment. In each of the cases other than the Delaware case, a three-judge federal
district court denied relief to the plaintiffs on the so-called "separate but equal"
doctrine announced by this Court in *Plessy v. Ferguson*, 163 U.S. 537. Under
that doctrine, equality of treatment is accorded when the races are provided
substantially equal facilities, even though these facilities be separate. In the
Delaware case, the Supreme Court of Delaware adhered to that doctrine, but
ordered that the plaintiffs be admitted to the white schools because of their
superiority to the Negro schools.

3   The plaintiffs contend that segregated public schools are not "equal" and
cannot be made "equal," and that hence they are deprived of the equal protection of the laws. Because of the obvious importance of the question presented,
the Court took jurisdiction. Argument was heard in the 1952 Term, and reargument was heard this Term on certain questions propounded by the Court.

4   Reargument was largely devoted to the circumstances surrounding the adoption of the Fourteenth Amendment in 1868. It covered exhaustively consideration of the Amendment in Congress, ratification by the states, then existing
practices in racial segregation, and the views of proponents and opponents of the
Amendment. This discussion and our own investigation convince us that, although these sources cast some light, it is not enough to resolve the problem
with which we are faced. At best, they are inconclusive. The most avid proponents of the post-War Amendments undoubtedly intended them to remove all
legal distinctions among "all persons born or naturalized in the United States."

Their opponents, just as certainly, were antagonistic to both the letter and the spirit of the Amendments and wished them to have the most limited effect. What others in Congress and the state legislatures had in mind cannot be determined with any degree of certainty.

5   An additional reason for the inconclusive nature of the Amendment's history, with respect to segregated schools, is the status of public education at that time. In the South, the movement toward free common schools, supported by general taxation, had not yet taken hold. Education of white children was largely in the hands of private groups. Education of Negroes was almost nonexistent, and practically all of the race were illiterate. In fact, any education of Negroes was forbidden by law in some states. Today, in contrast, many Negroes have achieved outstanding success in the arts and sciences as well as in the business and professional world. It is true that public school education at the time of the Amendment had advanced further in the North, but the effect of the Amendment on Northern States was generally ignored in the congressional debates. Even in the North, the conditions of public education did not approximate those existing today. The curriculum was usually rudimentary; ungraded schools were common in rural areas; the school terms was but three months a year in many states; and compulsory school attendance was virtually unknown. As a consequence, it is not surprising that there should be so little in the history of the Fourteenth Amendment relating to its intended effect on public education.

6   In the first cases in this Court construing the Fourteenth Amendment, decided shortly after its adoption, the Court interpreted it as proscribing all state-imposed discriminations against the Negro race. The doctrine of "separate but equal" did not make its appearance in this Court until 1896 in the case of *Plessy* v. *Ferguson, supra,* involving not education but transportation. American courts have since labored with the doctrine for over half a century. In this Court, there have been six cases involving the "separate but equal" doctrine in the field of public education. . . . In none of these cases was it necessary to re-examine the doctrine to grant relief to the Negro plaintiff. And in *Sweatt* v. *Painter, supra,* the Court expressly reserved decision on the question whether *Plessy* v. *Ferguson* should be held inapplicable to public education.

7   In the instant cases, that question is directly presented. Here, unlike *Sweatt* v. *Painter,* there are findings below that the Negro and white schools involved have been equalized, or are being equalized, with respect to buildings, curricula, qualifications and salaries of teachers, and other "tangible" factors. Our decision, therefore, cannot turn on merely a comparison of these tangible factors in the Negro and white schools involved in each of the cases. We must look instead to the effect of segregation itself on public education.

8   In approaching this problem, we cannot turn the clock back to 1868 when the Amendment was adopted, or even to 1896 when *Plessy* v. *Ferguson* was written. We must consider public education in the light of its full development

and its present place in American life throughout the Nation. Only in this way can it be determined if segregation in public schools deprives these plaintiffs of the equal protection of the laws.

9   Today, education is perhaps the most important function of state and local governments. Compulsory school attendance laws and the great expenditures for education both demonstrate our recognition of the importance of education to our democratic society. It is required in the performance of our most basic public responsibilities, even service in the armed forces. It is the very foundation of good citizenship. Today it is a principal instrument in awakening the child to cultural values, in preparing him for later professional training, and in helping him to adjust normally to his environment. In these days, it is doubtful that any child may reasonably be expected to succeed in life if he is denied the opportunity of an education. Such an opportunity, where the state has undertaken to provide it, is a right which must be made available to all on equal terms.

10   We come then to the question presented. Does segregation of children in public schools solely on the basis of race, even though the physical facilities and other "tangible" factors may be equal, deprive the children of the minority group of equal educational opportunities? We believe that it does.

11   In *Sweatt v. Painter, supra,* in finding that a segregated law school for Negroes could not provide them equal educational opportunities, this Court relied in large part on "those qualities which are incapable of objective measurement but which make for greatness in a law school." In *McLaurin v. Oklahoma State Regents, supra,* the Court, in requiring that a Negro admitted to a white graduate school be treated like all other students, again resorted to intangible considerations: ". . . his ability to study, to engage in discussions and exchange views with other students, and, in general, to learn his profession." Such considerations apply with added force to children in grade and high schools. To separate them from others of similar age and qualifications solely because of their race generates a feeling of inferiority as to their status in the community that may affect their hearts and minds in a way unlikely ever to be undone. The effect of this separation on their educational opportunities was well stated by a finding in the Kansas case by a court which nevertheless felt compelled to rule against the Negro plaintiffs:

"Segregation of white and colored children in public schools has a detrimental effect upon the colored children. The impact is greater when it has the sanction of the law; for the policy of separating the races is usually interpreted as denoting the inferiority of the negro group. A sense of inferiority affects the motivation of a child to learn. Segregation with the sanction of law, therefore, has a tendency to [retard] the educational and mental development of negro children and to deprive them of some of the benefits they would receive in a racial[ly] integrated school system."

Whatever may have been the extent of psychological knowledge at the time of

Plessy v. *Ferguson,* this finding is amply supported by modern authority. Any language in *Plessy* v. *Ferguson* contrary to this finding is rejected.

12 We conclude that in the field of public education the doctrine of "separate but equal" has no place. Separate educational facilities are inherently unequal. Therefore, we hold that the plaintiffs and others similarly situated for whom the actions have been brought are, by reason of the segregation complained of, deprived of the equal protection of the laws guaranteed by the Fourteenth Amendment. . . .

SIGNIFICANCE

Explain the significance of the following quotations to the point of the decision or structure of the analysis:

"The plaintiffs contend that segregated public schools are not 'equal' and cannot be made 'equal,' and that hence they are deprived of the equal protection of the laws."

"An additional reason for the inconclusive nature of the Amendment's history, with respect to segregated schools, is the status of public education at that time."

"Education of Negroes was almost nonexistent, and practically all of the race was illiterate. In fact, any education of Negroes was forbidden by law in some states. Today, in contrast, many Negroes have achieved outstanding success in the arts and sciences as well as in the business and professional world."

". . . the Negro and white schools involved have been equalized, or are being equalized, with respect to . . . 'tangible' factors. Our decision, therefore, cannot turn on merely a comparison of these tangible factors in the Negro and white schools involved in each of the cases. We must look instead to the effect of segregation itself on public education."

"Today, education is perhaps the most important function of state and local governments. . . . It is required in the performance of our most basic public responsibilities, even service in the armed forces. It is the very foundation of good citizenship."

"We come then to the question presented. Does segregation of children in public schools solely on the basis of race, even though the physical facilities and other 'tangible' factors may be equal, deprive the children of the minority group of equal educational opportunity? We believe that it does."

". . . the Court, in requiring that a Negro admitted to a white graduate school be treated like all other students, again resorted to intangible considerations: '. . . his ability to study, to engage in discussions and exchange views with other students, and, in general, to learn his profession.' Such considerations apply with added force to children in grade and high schools."

"Whatever may have been the extent of psychological knowledge at the time of *Plessy* v. *Ferguson,* this finding is amply supported by modern authority."

FUTURE USE

Briefly summarize the decision.

Explain the basis of the evaluation. What values does the court assume or present?

What aspects of *Plessy* does the decision reject? What is the basis for this rejection?

What information from this selection is relevant to your essay(s)? How could you use this information?

Courts, like all of us, must often evaluate conflicting rights, rather than simply decide right and wrong. And when a decision is reviewed, the higher court must evaluate the lower court's actions.

William and Elizabeth Stern could not have children because Mrs. Stern was infertile. They contracted with Mary Beth Whitehead for $10,000 to be a "surrogate" mother—that is, to bear a child for them through artificial insemination by Mr. Stern. When the baby—named Melissa by the Sterns and Sarah by Whitehead—was born, Whitehead refused to give her up. A New Jersey State Superior Court ruled in 1987 that since the natural mother had given up her parental rights to the baby, "Baby M" should live with her natural father and could be adopted by his wife. On appeal, the New Jersey Supreme Court, by a vote of 7–0, upheld granting custody to the Sterns, but overturned the validity of the contract and the loss of the natural mother's rights.

Following are excerpts from the 95-page opinion written by Chief Justice Robert N. Wilentz.

From *IN THE MATTER OF BABY M* (1988)

1   We invalidate the surrogacy contract because it conflicts with the law and public policy of this State. While we recognize the depth of the yearning of infertile couples to have their own children, we find the payment of money to a "surrogate" mother illegal, perhaps criminal, and potentially degrading to women. Although in this case we grant custody to the natural father, the evidence having clearly proved such custody to be in the best interests of the infant, we void both the termination of the surrogate mother's parental rights and the adoption of the child by the wife/stepparent. We thus restore the "surrogate" as the mother of the child. . . .

2   We find no offense to our present laws where a woman voluntarily and without payment agrees to act as a "surrogate" mother, provided that she is not subject to a binding agreement to surrender her child. Moreover, our holding today does not preclude the Legislature from altering the current statutory scheme, within constitutional limits, so as to permit surrogacy contracts. Under current law, however, the surrogacy agreement before us is illegal and invalid. . . .

3   Mr. Stern knew he was paying for the adoption of a child; Mrs. Whitehead knew she was accepting money so that a child might be adopted; the Infertility Center knew that it was being paid for assisting in the adoption of a child. The actions of all three worked to frustrate the goals of the statute. It strains credulity to claim that these arrangements, touted by those in the surrogacy business as an attractive alternative to the usual route leading to an adoption, really amount to something other than a private placement adoption for money. . . .

4   In this case a termination of parental rights was obtained not by proving the statutory prerequisites but by claiming the benefit of contractual provisions. From all that has been stated above, it is clear that a contractual agreement to abandon one's parental rights, or not to contest a termination action, will not be enforced in our courts. The Legislature would not have so carefully, so consistently, and so substantially restricted termination of parental rights if it had intended to allow termination to be achieved by one short sentence in a contract.

5   Since the termination was invalid, it follows, as noted above, the adoption of Melissa by Mrs. Stern could not properly be granted. . . .

6   The surrogacy contract guarantees permanent separation of the child from one of its natural parents. Our policy, however, has long been that to the extent possible, children should remain with and be brought up by both of their natural parents. That was the first stated purpose of the previous adoption act . . . While not so stated in the present adoption law, this purpose remains part of the public policy of this State. . . . This is not simply some theoretical ideal that in practice has no meaning. The impact of failure to follow that policy is nowhere better shown than in the results of this surrogacy contract. A child, instead of starting off its life with as much peace and security as possible, finds itself immediately in a tug-of-war . . .

7   The surrogacy contract violates the policy of this State that the rights of natural parents are equal concerning their child, the father's right no greater than the mother's. "The parent and child relationship extends equally to every child and to every parent, regardless of the marital status of the parents." . . . The whole purpose and effect of the surrogacy contract was to give the father the exclusive right to the child by destroying the rights of the mother. . . .

8   Under the contract, the natural mother is irrevocably committed before she knows the strength of her bond with her child. She never makes a totally voluntary, informed decision, for quite clearly any decision prior to the baby's birth is, in the most important sense, uninformed, and any decision after that, compelled by a pre-existing contractual commitment, the threat of a lawsuit, and the inducement of a $10,000 payment, is less than totally voluntary. Her interests are of little concern to those who controlled this transaction.

9   Although the interest of the natural father and adoptive mother is certainly the predominant interest, realistically the *only* interest served, even they are left with less than what public policy requires. They know little about the natural mother, her genetic makeup, and her psychological and medical history. Moreover, not even a superficial attempt is made to determine their awareness of their responsibilities as parents.

10   Worst of all, however, is the contract's total disregard of the best interests of the child. There is not the slightest suggestion that any inquiry will be made at any time to determine the fitness of the Sterns as custodial parents, of Mrs. Stern as an adoptive parent, their superiority to Mrs. Whitehead, or the effect on the child of not living with her natural mother. . . .

11   This is the sale of a child, or, at the very least, the sale of a mother's right to her child, the only mitigating factor being that one of the purchasers is the father. Almost every evil that prompted the prohibition of the payment of money in connection with adoptions exists here. . . .

12   The long-term effects of surrogacy contracts are not known, but feared—the impact on the child who learns her life was bought, that she is the offspring of someone who gave birth to her only to obtain money; the impact on the natural mother as the full weight of her isolation is felt along with the full reality of the sale of her body and her child; the impact on the natural father and adoptive mother once they realize the consequences of their conduct.

13   The right asserted by the Sterns is the right of procreation; that asserted by Mary Beth Whitehead is the right to the companionship of her child. We find that the right of procreation does not extend as far as claimed by the Sterns. . . .

14   . . . The right to procreate very simply is the right to have natural children, whether through sexual intercourse or artificial insemination. It is no more than that. Mr. Stern has not been deprived of that right. Through artificial insemination of Mrs. Whitehead, Baby M is his child. The custody, care, companionship, and nurturing that follow birth are not parts of the right to procreation; they are rights that may also be constitutionally protected, but that involve many considerations other than the right of procreation. To assert that Mr. Stern's right of procreation gives him the right to the custody of Baby M would be to assert that Mrs. Whitehead's right of procreation does *not* give her the right to the custody of Baby M . . .

15   It seems to us that given her predicament, Mrs. Whitehead was rather harshly judged—both by the trial court and by some of the experts. She was guilty of a breach of contract, and indeed, she did break a very important promise, but we think it is expecting something well beyond normal human capabilities to suggest that this mother should have parted with her newly born infant without a struggle. Other than survival, what stronger force is there? We do not know of, and cannot conceive of, any other case where a perfectly fit mother was expected to surrender her newly born infant, perhaps forever, and was then told she was a bad mother because she did not. We know of no authority suggesting that the moral quality of her act in those circumstances should be judged by referring to a contract made before she became pregnant. We do not countenance, and would never countenance, violating a court order as Mrs. Whitehead did, even a court order that is wrong; but her resistance to an order that she surrender her infant, possibly forever, merits a measure of understanding. We do not find it so clear that her efforts to keep her infant, when measured against the Sterns efforts to take her away, make one, rather than the other, the wrongdoer. The Sterns suffered, but so did she. . . .

16   There has emerged a portrait of Mrs. Whitehead exposing her children to the media, engaging in negotiations to sell a book, granting interviews that seemed

helpful to her, whether hurtful to Baby M or not, that suggests a selfish, grasping woman ready to sacrifice the interests of Baby M and her other children for fame and wealth. That portrait is a half-truth, for while it may accurately reflect what ultimately occurred, its implication, that this is what Mary Beth Whitehead wanted, is totally inaccurate, at least insofar as the record before us is concerned. There is not one word in that record to support a claim that had she been allowed to continue her possession of her newly born infant, Mrs. Whitehead would have ever been heard of again; not one word in the record suggests that her change of mind and her subsequent fight for her child was motivated by anything other than love—whatever complex underlying psychological motivations may have existed. . . .

SIGNIFICANCE

Explain the significance of the following quotations from the selection:

"While we recognize the depth of the yearning of infertile couples to have their own children, we find the payment of money to a 'surrogate' mother illegal, perhaps criminal, and potentially degrading to women."

". . . to the extent possible, children should remain with and be brought up by both of their natural parents."

"Worst of all . . . is the contract's total disregard of the best interests of the child."

"This is the sale of a child. . . ."

"To assert that Mr. Stern's right of procreation gives him the right to the custody of Baby M would be to assert that Mrs. Whitehead's right of procreation does *not* give her the right to the custody of Baby M. . . ."

"It seems to us that given her predicament, Mrs. Whitehead was rather harshly judged—both by the trial court and by some of the experts."

"We know of no authority suggesting that the moral quality of her act in those circumstances should be judged by referring to a contract made before she became pregnant."

"We do not countenance . . . violating a court order as Mrs. Whitehead did . . . ; but her resistance to an order that she surrender her infant, possibly forever, merits a measure of understanding."

FUTURE USE

Briefly summarize the decision.

Explain the basis of the evaluation. What values does the court assume or present?

What objections does this decision raise concerning the decision of the lower court? What is the basis for these objections?

What information from this selection is relevant to your essay(s)? How could you use this information?

· MAKING CONNECTIONS

1. People can have different goals, or they can share the same goal but disagree about how to achieve it. In the evaluations you have just read, which disagreements arise because of different goals and which arise because of differences concerning methods? Which disagreements—whether over goals or methods—reflect differences in values? What essay topic(s) can emerge from this discussion?

2. What is the significance, if any, of the fact that Booker T. Washington (p. 244) was born into slavery in the South and W. E. B. Du Bois (p. 294) was born in the North after the Civil War? To what extent, if any, are both men's views shaped by their experiences? In what way(s) have events in this century shown one of them to be right and the other wrong? What similar clashes of programs and personalities exist today among public figures? What is the significance, if any, of the fact that many Americans today lived through the war in Vietnam but not World War II? Evaluate the answer given in *Education for Democracy* (p. 275). What essay topic(s) can emerge from this discussion?

3. How does the image of blacks in Du Bois's essay compare and contrast with the image in Washington's speech? Which image has been most common on television and in the movies? Why? Does one of these images reflect the real situation of blacks? Do the differing portrayals reflect a changing reality? How would you go about finding an answer to these questions? What about conflicting images of women, blue-collar workers, old people, or some other group? Which selections that you have read can shed light on these questions? What essay topic(s) can emerge from this discussion?

4. To what extent do the theories of Weber (p. 248) and Robertson (p. 299) about the origins of capitalism reflect differing values? How is this situation similar to or different from the theories about American values presented by Turner (p. 73), Veblen (p. 134), Carnegie (p. 180), Crèvecoeur (p. 188), and others? What effect do personal values or current opinions have on scholars? Artists and writers? Philosophers? Politicians? Do such public figures shape or reflect the values of their society? What essay topic(s) can emerge from this discussion?

5. Do the arts shape or reflect national values? What responsibility, if any, do artists, writers, musicians, or movie stars have to society? What do Cooper (p. 196), Hawthorne (p. 144), Whitman (p. 155), and James (p. 265) say about these questions? Can a work of art be great if it is immoral? What should our reaction be when we discover that a famous person we have always admired holds unsavory or amoral opinions? Should we have the same reaction if the person held racist opinions when or where they were widespread and commonly accepted? Evaluate the views in the re-

view of *The Image of the Jew in American Literature* (p. 281). What essay topic(s) can emerge from this discussion?

6. According to *Brown v. Board of Education,* what is the purpose of public education? How is this view similar to or different from the views in *Bethel School District v. Fraser* (p. 176) and "Schools Must Teach Values" (p. 126)? What do these selections say about the source of our values? Which other selections discuss the source of values? What similarities and differences do they contain? What essay topic(s) can emerge from this discussion?

7. How do the decisions in *Brown v. Board of Education* and *Plessy v. Ferguson* (p. 233) reflect their time and place? How do the values and assumptions differ in these two decisions? How did America change in the years between *Plessy* and *Brown?* Which other reading selections shed light on the changes then taking place in America? What was happening to women, workers, immigrants, the ethnic composition of the country? What essay topic(s) can emerge from this discussion?

8. What values are reflected in *In the Matter of Baby M?* Are these the prevailing values of society or is the court at odds with popular beliefs? Would all people at all times accept the view that "children should remain with and be brought up by both of their natural parents"? Are there other values in this opinion that reflect the time and place of the court? How does this compare and contrast with the decision in *Bethel* or *Brown?* What essay topic(s) can emerge from this discussion?

9. What is a *nation?* Is it simply a lot of people living in a defined space, or is it a group of people tied together in some way? What makes the United States a nation? Can there be multilingual, multiethnic, multicultural nations? Can you think of any and describe how they function? What essay topic(s) can emerge from this discussion?

· ADDITIONAL ESSAYS FOR DISCUSSION

From THE GOSPEL OF WEALTH
by William Jewett Tucker (1891)

1   In June and December of 1889 Mr. Andrew Carnegie published two articles in the *North Atlantic Review* under the titles, "Wealth," and "The Best Fields for Philanthropy," which, at the instance of Mr. Gladstone, were taken up by the *Pall Mall Gazette,* and republished under the more striking title of "The Gospel of Wealth." The term, however, originated with Mr. Carnegie, though he had not put it to so conspicuous a use. At the close of his first article he had said: "Such, in my opinion, is the true gospel concerning wealth, obedience to which is destined some day to solve the problem of the rich and the poor, and to bring 'peace on earth, among men goodwill.' "

2   The course of discussion which has followed until now the republication of these articles is quite as significant as the original articles. It is especially significant for what has not been discussed. With a single exception, the discussion has been confined to the question of the charitable disposition of private wealth, without entering at all, except in the way of illustration, upon the much more serious question of the vast concentration of wealth in private hands. And yet the argument of Mr. Carnegie had challenged attention at this very point. His "gospel" rested upon the clear and bold assumption that wealth was best placed in the hands of the few; the gospel part of his message being the duty of the few to redistribute their wealth in the interest of the many. . . .

3   Summing up Mr. Carnegie's theory, it may, I think, be fairly stated in the following terms:

The present economic system, which is established in individualism and worked through competition, is on the whole the best attainable system. The millionaire is the necessary product of that system; wealth inevitably falls under it into the hands of the few. This, too, is best, for the millionaire is the natural trustee of the poor; and he can in various ways administer wealth for the community better than the community can administer it for itself. The sole question then is, How shall the rich man fulfill his trusteeship? Not by returning his fortune, beyond a competence to his family. Not by devising his money by will. But by distributing his fortune, during his lifetime, according to his judgment of the public need. . . .

4   But this necessarian view of extreme riches is not so obvious to all as to Mr. Carnegie. For while he is asking, and answering with so much courage and assurance, this question about the disposal of the vast surplus of private wealth, society is taking hold in very serious fashion of the other end of the problem, and

asking why there should be such a vast surplus of private wealth. Mr. Carnegie's scheme of redistribution is a most interesting one, as will be seen by examining it more in detail, and, within the limits in which it is likely to be carried out, not without direct practical benefit, but it is in no sense a solution of the great social question which is stirring the mind and heart of this generation. And my present concern is that it should not be accepted as such by ethical and religious teachers. For I can conceive of no greater mistake, more disastrous in the end to religion if not to society, than that of trying to make charity do the work of justice. . . .

5   In Mr. Carnegie's third answer he states his positive principle that all private wealth above a competence should be distributed back into society during the lifetime of the owner and maker of the fortune, and according to his direction; and then proceeds to show how this can be wisely done, specifying, as the proper objects of benevolence, universities, libraries, hospitals, parks, churches of the more costly type, and in general those intermediate objects which enrich a community without pauperizing individuals. Mr. Carnegie is stoutly opposed to technical charity or almsgiving, believing that, of every thousand dollars thus spent, nine hundred and fifty are unwisely spent.

6   This is the gospel of wealth; of which it may be said, in a word, that it is an heroic remedy for the preservation of families of wealth from the corrupting power of inherited riches; that, as respects the rich man, it is a call to self-denial, not only against the hoarding of riches, but also against the gratification of a large class of ambitions common to the very rich; but that in its relation to society it is, if *accepted as the mode of social improvement*, the gospel of patronage. Society, in its institutions of relief and of culture, in its improvements and refinements, would become the object of the bounty of the few, and rightly so, as Mr. Carnegie argues, because the rich benefactor can do better for the community than it would or could do for itself. Just as formerly it was contended that political power should be in the hands of the few, because it would be better administered, so now it is contended—I quote Mr. Carnegie's words, slightly transferring them, but not changing their meaning—that "the millionaire is intrusted for the time being with a great part of the increased wealth of the community, because he can administer it for the community far better than it could or would have done for itself." This, of course, if accepted and carried out in any complete way, becomes patronage.

7   Probably, however, the first criticism which would be passed upon this scheme is, that it could not be carried out to any such degree as to produce any appreciable effect in the way of social relief. The preaching of this gospel might be expected to reach the consciences and hearts of the few, perceptibly increasing the amount of public benefactions, and very likely resulting in the organization of societies, like that which Mr. Gladstone proposes to revive, for cultivating the spirit of giving according to the increase of income. But it would manifestly fail to reach the much greater amount of irresponsible and really

dangerous wealth. It would fall upon deaf ears as it addressed itself to the ambitious, the selfish, the profligate—the really dangerous classes in modern society.

8 And it is hardly to be expected that the appeal would have the same effect upon those without as upon those within Mr. Carnegie's own class of millionaires. Mr. Carnegie represents the self-made type, the type of bold, shrewd, masterful, and withal generous and public-spirited self-made rich men. Those, on the other hand, who represent inherited wealth seldom possess precisely these personal qualities, while they are usually possessed of quite different ambitions. He might have the honorable ambition to found a house. They are under conventional bonds to perpetuate their inheritance, an obligation which fails only under the incapacity to fulfill it, or under those temptations to vice which betray it.

9 But, allowing that the scheme is more practicable than it seems, then the criticism follows, to which I have referred, that to the degree in which it becomes successful it amounts to patronage; and, in the long run, society cannot afford to be patronized. It is better for any community to advance more slowly than to gain altogether by gifts rather than, in large part, by earnings. Within proper limits, the public is advantaged by the gifts of the rich, but if the method becomes the accepted method, to be expected and relied upon, the decline of public self-respect has begun. There is a public public spirit to be cherished as well as a private public spirit.

10 But these criticisms do not reach the heart of the matter. They do not run as deep as the current thought. That, as I have intimated, is growing more and more intent upon one inquiry, Why should there be this vast amount of wealth in the hands of the few? The question is not, How shall private wealth be returned to the public? but, Why should it exist in such bewildering amounts? Mr. Carnegie's gospel is really a belated gospel. It comes too late for a social remedy. What it does accomplish is to call attention to the fact of the enormous surplus of private wealth. The honest and courageous endeavor of a millionaire to return his fortune to society, and his call to his fellow-millionaires to do likewise, brings them, as a class, before the public, and puts the public upon a reckoning of the volume of wealth in their hands. Consciously or unconsciously, Mr. Carnegie has hit upon the great object-lesson in our economic civilization. It is not pauperism, conspicuous and grievous as that is, but the concentration of wealth. The most striking, and in many ways the most startling, feature of the economic situation is, not that the poor are growing poorer—that I doubt, except with those too low for computation—but that the rich are becoming so very rich. The question before us, be it remembered, is not that of capital, or of corporate wealth, or of ordinary private wealth, but of extreme riches in the hands of the few—the enormous concentration of wealth.

11 Let me call up one or two facts as a reminder of the proportion in which

wealth is held in private fortunes. The concentration of landed wealth in England has been for a long time a conspicuous fact. But it is fast losing its prominence through the increase of wealth in other interests. The income from landed property in 1862 was 60¼ millions; in 1889, was 58¼ millions. The income from trade, in 1862, was 182 millions; in 1889, was 336 millions. Yet, under this change in the sources of wealth, the proportion of wealth in the hands of the few remained practically unchanged. It is estimated that two-thirds of the property of England is still owned by one-thirtieth of the population.

12   Applying the same methods of computation as are in use in England to this country, with such modifications as may be gained from ascertained facts, it is estimated that two-thirds of the property of the United States is in the hands of one-seventieth of the population. It also seems safe to assume that more than one-half of the wealth of the country is in possession of less than fifty thousand families. Calculations with reference to particular families, like those made by Mr. Thomas G. Shearman, in *The Forum*, may be in some instances inaccurate, without affecting the general aggregate.

13   The force of this reminder of the present and increasing concentration of wealth in England and America is intensified by one or two other facts bearing upon the character and use of a portion of this immense surplus. One fact is that of the growing amount of wealth in the form of demoralizing capital. The amount invested in the liquor traffic is the most evident example, of which it may be said that the whole sum is practically a corruption fund, to be used as the exigencies of the business may demand. A second fact is that of the growing amount of irresponsible wealth, wealth that is in the hands of those who are incapable of its management as capital, but who may control it to private ends. I refer now especially to property left in large estates to women, a large percentage of which becomes the object of cupidity to adventurers and fortune-hunters. Some two years ago my attention was called, by an eminent lawyer who had a large knowledge of estates, to the fact that one of the chief signs which marked the corruption of the Roman Commonwealth, namely, the transfer of great fortunes to women, who became for this reason the prey of designing men, was repeating itself in a very noticeable way in this country. I attempt no comparison of the amount of inherited wealth which is passing through this medium into the hands of foreign profligates, measured by the sums devised for charitable purposes, but evidently the amount is large and increasing. . . .

14   The growing disposition to apply the principle of taxation very vigorously to estates represents in a pronounced way the tendency to restrain the further concentration of wealth. This principle meets with Mr. Carnegie's unqualified approval. He refers to it as a "cheering indication of the growth of a salutary change in public opinion. . . . Of all forms of taxation this seems the wisest. Men who continue hoarding great sums all their lives, the proper use of which for public ends would work good to the community, from which it chiefly came,

should be made to feel that the community, in the form of the state, cannot thus be deprived of its proper share. By taxing estates heavily at death, the state shows its condemnation of the selfish millionaire's unworthy life."

15   This principle has now become well established in legislation. It is recognized in England under the term "death duties." Estates above $50,000 are taxed, and Mr. Goschen recommends that the tax be a graduated or progressive one. The same principle, under the form of a "collateral inheritance tax," is in operation in one or more of the States of the Union, and bills for its adoption are pending before several legislatures.

16   But the theory of a progressive tax on inheritance carries with it logically the theory of a progressive income tax. There are minor differences; but there is no valid reason why a great fortune should not come under the same principle with a great estate. . . .

17   It has been my object in this article to call attention to the moral significance of great fortunes, to show the ethical bearing of the amassing of private wealth. I have not cared to enter the field of the methods of social relief and reform. Methods belong to economists and legislators. The concern of moral and religious teachers is with principles. They have to do legitimately with the ethical factor which is put into, or which is left out of, all proposed reforms. They are bound to test all theories which are offered in aid of society, and to test them all the more if they are offered with moral earnestness and under religious names. They have the right to ask of any new scheme whether it will leave society better or worse in the end for its adoption. My criticism of Mr. Carnegie's scheme has been that, to the degree in which it is organized and made the ruling method of adjusting wealth to society, it becomes a vast system of patronage, than which nothing can in the final issue create a more hopeless social condition. And further, that the assumption upon which it rests, that wealth is the inevitable possession of the few, and is best administered by them for the many, begs the whole question of economic justice now before society, and relegates it to the field of charity. But charity, as I have claimed, cannot solve the problems of the modern world. And the point is reached at which this claim is seen to be valid, whenever any scheme is proposed for the redistribution of wealth through charity, leaving the question of the original distribution of wealth unsettled, or settled only to the satisfaction of the few. What the ethical question of to-morrow in the economic world may be I know not. But the ethical question of to-day centres, I am sure, in the distribution rather than in the redistribution of wealth. I would hinder no man's gifts in the largest charity; I would withhold no honor from the giver; but I would accept no amount in charity as a measure of the present social need, or in settlement of the present economic demand.

From CONTENT COUNTS
by Paul Gagnon (1987)

1   What are the chances for improving education in America? After so many failed, or misguided, attempts at reform in the past, is it reasonable to expect very much good to come out of the latest? One source of hope is the duration of our current attempt. Four years have passed since A Nation at Risk opened the debate, which shows no signs of letting up. Contrary to expectations, public interest seems to be higher than ever. But the better, deeper reasons for optimism are to be found in the substance of the educational debate of the 1980s, which has reached a higher level of common sense and pedagogical sophistication than any other in this century. The debate over what to teach, to whom, and how to teach it has finally been sprung free from the dreary old quarrels between "traditionalists" and "innovators," between "content people" and "methods people," between substance and skills.

2   Every major reform report since 1983 has said what good teachers have known all along: that these are silly dichotomies and that one has to take something from all sides to succeed in the classroom. Cultural Literacy* and What Do Our 17-Year-Olds Know?** typify the best of the reports in their insistence that all children in a democracy, regardless of their backgrounds or social prospects, should be brought together in a common, academic core curriculum. And because our students are vastly diverse, they should be taught by the most varied, flexible, and innovative methods. Not either/or, but both: tradition and innovation, content and methods, substance and skills.

3   We are free of the old clichés, the simple, single answers. Keeping several imperatives in our heads at once, we are ready to debate what is most worth learning and how to teach it, at different levels, to different kinds of students, in different sorts of schools. But are we? The news is not all good, if one judges by the knee-jerk hostility of certain academicians to the works of Hirsch, Finn, and Ravitch. Whereas the general run of reviews in newspapers and weeklies has been favorable, with reviewers willing to deal seriously with the authors' main ideas and recommendations, the commentaries by academicians have ranged from evasive to vitriolic. In letters to the editor, in campus forums, at professional meetings, and in prestigious journals—many have savaged both books, seeing little use or virtue in them. . . .

*E. D. Hirsch, Jr.: Cultural Literacy: What Every American Needs to Know. Boston, Houghton-Mifflin, 1987.

**Diane Ravitch and Chester Finn: What Do Our 17-Year-Olds Know? New York, Harper & Row, 1987.

4   For writing the best-selling *Cultural Literacy: What Every American Needs to Know,* E. D. Hirsch, Jr. suffers a like fate at the hands of his academic reviewer in *The Chronicle of Higher Education* (September 16, 1987). Straw men—what Hirsch does not say—are zestfully demolished. His central ideas and recommendations are either caricatured or ignored. This critic, too, takes the author-as-simpleton approach, suggesting throughout that Hirsch offers his five thousand terms, names, places, and literary allusions as everything anybody would ever have to know to win success, happiness, and adulthood:

> Perhaps the greatest flaw in Mr. Hirsch's thesis is the idea that learning a body of culturally approved information will enable students to live successfully as adults. The presumption that digesting bits of sanctioned knowledge will prepare them to deal with the ambiguity, contradiction, and complexity of adult life is astoundingly ill conceived. What one needs as an adult is a critically adept cast of mind, not a list of names and phrases. . . . How will learning Mr. Hirsch's list enable women to decide whether or not to have an abortion, or help two people build trust into their relationship, or tell us how to make sense out of death?

5   Nor will it help one hit a golfball or mix an acceptable martini. Hirsch is not, of course, talking about either education or maturation, but about the background information, best acquired in the early grades, that everyone needs in order to take the next steps, to secondary and higher education and to whatever professional, public, or personal life may be possible. . . .

6   Like Chester Finn and Diane Ravitch, Hirsch declares that a common and substantial curriculum is a prerequisite to equal educational opportunity and to a healthy democratic system of self-government. The aim of universal literacy, he says, has never been socially neutral. In his "I Have a Dream" speech, Martin Luther King, Jr. saw a country

> where the children of former slaves sit down at the table of equality with the children of former slave owners, where men and women deal with each other as equals and judge each other on their characters and achievements rather than their origins.

7   In the present day, Hirsch continues, that dream depends upon mature literacy:

> No modern society can hope to become a just society without a high level of universal literacy. Putting aside for the moment the practical arguments about the economic uses of literacy, we can contemplate the even more basic principle that underlies our national system of education in the first place—that people in a democracy can be entrusted to decide all important matters for themselves because they can deliberate and communicate with one another. Universal literacy is inseparable from democracy and is

the canvas for Martin Luther King's picture as well as for Thomas Jefferson's.

8   The civic importance of cultural literacy, Hirsch concludes, is clear: "True enfranchisement depends upon knowledge, knowledge upon literacy, and literacy upon cultural literacy."

9   The *Chronicle's* critic says nothing of the book's concern for democracy, either in schooling or in the larger society. Instead, he charges elitism. *Cultural Literacy's* now-famous list of what Americans need to know, he says, "reflects only the values, beliefs, and knowledge of the dominant cultural group in our society." Reading the list gives a sharply different impression. Beginning with A, we find acid rain, AFL-CIO, affirmative action, agribusiness, air pollution, alienation, anti-Semitism, anarchy, aphrodisiac, apartheid, atheism, Aristophanes, Allah, and anal personality—to pick only a few of our safe, elitist subjects. Under K, we meet Kafka, *Das Kapital*, Kent State, Keynesian economics, Dr. King, the Koran, and the KKK, and we run on to Rousseau, Steinem, Taoism, UNESCO, Vietnam, and the WPA.

10   That any set body of subject matter is elitist and oppressive is a familiar refrain from the self-appointed defenders of the powerless. The powerless do not necessarily see it the same way. Hirsch cites the revolutionary newspaper *The Black Panther* as "highly conservative" in its language and cultural assumptions, "as it had to be in order to communicate effectively." The Black Panther party platform of 1972 quoted several "traditional" sources, indicating, said Hirsch, that

> The writers for *The Black Panther* had clearly received a rigorous traditional education in American history, in the Declaration of Independence, the Pledge of Allegiance to the Flag, the Gettysburg Address, and the Bible, to mention only some of the direct quotations and allusions in these passages. They also received rigorous traditional instruction in reading, writing, and spelling. . . . Radicalism in politics, but conservatism in literate knowledge and spelling: to be a conservative in the *means* of communication is the road to effectiveness in modern life, in whatever direction one wishes to be effective. To withhold traditional culture from the school curriculum, and therefore from students, in the name of the school curriculum, and therefore from students, in the name of progressive ideas is in fact an unprogressive action that helps preserve the political and economic status quo.

11   The *Chronicle's* reviewer finds Hirsch's approach to schooling narrow and bureaucratic, assuming that students can be turned into good workers and citizens "by drilling certain facts into them":

> Teachers would be relieved of the need to emphasize context, to develop programs that relate to their students' experiences, and to involve students

in the exploration of their culture. Instead, they would simply be guardians of the sacred 5,000 pieces of knowledge without which one cannot hope to "get ahead."

12   Hirsch, of course, believes nothing of the kind. Schools across the nation, he says, should have common goals, but their ways of achieving them should be varied and adaptive. . . .

13   Hirsch's proffered list is neither static nor "sacred." We need to teach current mainstream culture, and that is always changing. Today the "*Brown* decision" is cultural literacy; in 1945 it did not exist. Nor is the list sacred in the sense of superiority to other people's cultures. . . .

14   Will Academicians and university educationists find the good will to honestly seek that middle ground upon which Hirsch's hoped-for discussion and compromise can take place? The signs are not good when reviewers in influential places are unwilling to consider, even to mention, the central ideas and major recommendations of Finn, Ravitch and Hirsch. Nor was it hopeful to read in *The Chronicle of Higher Education* (August 5th, 1987) that eminent professors at a conference of English teachers derided *Cultural Literacy* as "out of touch with the multicultural American classroom" that called for "student-centered learning"—comments revealing that they had not bothered to read what Hirsch has to say.

15   We must hope that this first round of academic commentary will not prove typical of what is to follow, because the willingness of university people to join openly in debate over the problems and opportunities of improving our schools will be crucial to our chances for success.

From a Review
of *LEAVES OF GRASS*
by George Saintsbury (1874)

1   Several years have now passed since Walt Whitman's poetical works and claims were first brought before the notice of Englishmen of letters, yet it is more than doubtful whether, even among this class, there is any clear and decided view of his merits to be found prevailing. His poems have suffered the usual fate of such abnormal productions; it has been considered that admiration of them must be a kind of voluntary eccentricity, a gratuitous flourish in the face of respectability and orthodoxy. And it cannot be denied that he has not altogether escaped that worst of all calamities to a literary man, the admiration of the incompetent. It is true that he has been praised, with discrimination as well as with emphasis, by Mr. Swinburne; but unfortunately Mr. Swinburne's praise is mainly a passport to the favour of those who would be likely to appreciate Whitman without any passport at all. The testimony of his other panegyrists has been not a little weakened: in some by supposed national or political prejudices; in others, as already mentioned, by notorious literary incompetence.

2   It is very much to be hoped that the publication of this new edition of the 'Leaves of Grass' may be the occasion of a deeper and wider study of the American poet, a study which may be carried on purely as a matter of literature, and not with any lurking intention to illustrate preconceived ideas as to the merits or demerits of ·Walt Whitman's principles, practice, or mode of expression. . . .

3   It is not difficult to point out the central thesis of Walt Whitman's poetical gospel. It is briefly this: the necessity of the establishment of a universal republic, or rather brotherhood of men. And to this is closely joined another, or rather a series of others, indicating the type of man of which this universal republic is to consist, or perhaps which it is to produce. The poet's language in treating the former of these two positions is not entirely uniform; sometimes he speaks as of a federation of nations, sometimes as if mankind at large were to gravitate towards the United States, and to find in them the desired Utopia. But the constitution of the United States, at least that constitution as it ought to be, is always and uniformly represented as a sufficient and the only sufficient political means of attaining this Utopia, nay, as having to some extent already presented Utopia as a fact. Moreover, passing to the second point, the ideal man is imaged as the ideal Yankee, understanding that word of course as it is understood in America, not in Europe. He is to be a rather magnificent animal, almost entirely uncultured (this is not an unfair representation, although there are to be found certain vague panegyrics on art, and especially on music), possessing a perfect *physique*, well nourished and clothed, affectionate towards his kind, and above all things firmly resolved to admit no superior. As is the

ideal man, so is the ideal woman to be. Now it may be admitted frankly and at once, that this is neither the creed nor the man likely to prove attractive to many persons east of the Atlantic. If it be said that the creed is a vague creed, and the man a detestable man, there will be very little answer attempted. Many wonderful things will doubtless happen "when," as the poet says, "through these States walk a hundred millions of superb persons;" but it must be allowed that there is small prospect of any such procession. One is inclined for very many sound reasons, and after discarding all prejudices, to opine that whatever salvation may await the world may possibly come from quarters other than from America. Fortunately, however, admiration for a creed is easily separable from admiration for the utterance and expression of that creed, and Walt Whitman as a poet is not difficult to disengage from Walt Whitman as an evangelist and politician. The keyword of all his ideas and of all his writings is universality. His Utopia is one which shall be open to everybody; his ideal of man and woman one which shall be attainable by everybody; his favourite scenes, ideas, subjects, those which everybody, at least to some extent, can enjoy and appreciate. He cares not that by this limitation he may exclude thoughts and feelings, at any rate phases of thought and feeling, infinitely choicer and higher than any which he admits. To express this striving after universality he has recourse to methods both unusual and (to most readers) unwelcome. The extraordinary jumbles and strings of names, places, employments, which deface his pages, and which have encouraged the profane to liken them to auctioneers' catalogues or indexes of encyclopædias, have no other object than to express this universal sympathy, reaching to the highest and penetrating to the lowest forms of life. The exclusion of culture, philosophy, manners, is owing also to this desire to admit nothing but what is open to every human being of ordinary faculty and opportunities. Moreover it is to this that we may fairly trace the prominence in Whitman's writings of the sexual passion, a prominence which has given rise, and probably will yet give rise, to much unphilosophical hubbub. This passion, as the poet has no doubt observed, is almost the only one which is peculiar to man as man, the presence of which denotes virility if not humanity, the absence of which is a sign of abnormal temperament. Hence he elevates it to almost the principal place, and treats of it in a manner somewhat shocking to those who are accustomed to speak of such subjects (we owe the word to Southey) *enfarinhadamente*. As a matter of fact, however, the treatment, though outspoken, is eminently "clean," to use the poet's own word; there is not a vestige of prurient thought, not a syllable of prurient language. Yet it would be a great mistake to suppose that sexual passion occupies the chief place in Whitman's estimation. There is according to him something above it, something which in any ecstasies he fails not to realize, something which seems more intimately connected in his mind with the welfare of mankind, and the promotion of his ideal republic. This is what he calls "robust American love." He is never tired of repeating "I am the poet of comrades"—Socrates himself seems renascent in this apostle of friendship. In the ears of a world (at least on this side the Atlantic) incredulous of such things, he reiterates the expressions of Plato to Aster, of Socrates respecting Charmides, and in this respect fully justifies (making allowance for altered manners) Mr. Symonds' assertion of his essentially Greek character, an assertion which most students of Whitman will heartily endorse. But we must again repeat that it is not so much in the matter as in the manner of his Evangel that the strength of Whitman lies. It is impossible not to notice his exquisite descriptive faculty, and his singular felicity in its use. Forced as he is, both by natural inclination and in the carrying out of his main idea, to take note of "the actual earth's equalities," he has literally filled his pages with the song of birds, the hushed murmur of waves, the quiet and multiform life of the forest and the meadow. And in these descriptions he succeeds in doing what is most difficult, in giving us the actual scene or circumstance as it impressed him, and not merely the impression itself. This is what none but the greatest poets have ever save by accident done, and what Whitman does constantly and with a sure hand. . . .

4   Such in matter and in manner are Walt Whitman's 'Leaves of Grass,' and there only remains to be added one recommendation to their study. The book, aggressive and vainglorious as it seems, is in reality remarkably free from vituperativeness of tone. Hardly to some "eunuchs, consumptive and genteel persons" is strong language used, and after all it rests with every reader whether he chooses to class himself with these. Amid all the ecstatic praise of America there is no abuse of England; amid all the excitement of the poems on the War there is little personal abuse of the Secessionists. No Englishman, no one indeed, whether American or Englishman, need be deterred from reading this book, a book the most unquestionable in originality, if not the most unquestioned in excellence, that the United States have yet sent us.

From TWICE-TOLD TALES
BY NATHANIEL HAWTHORNE:
A REVIEW
by Edgar Allan Poe (1842)

1   We said a few hurried words about Mr. Hawthorne in our last number, with the design of speaking more fully in the present. We are still, however, pressed for room, and must necessarily discuss his volumes more briefly and more at random than their high merits deserve.

2   The book professes to be a collection of *tales*, yet is, in two respects, mis-named. These pieces are now in their third republication, and, of course, are thrice-told. Moreover, they are by no means *all* tales, either in the ordinary or in the legitimate understanding of the term. Many of them are pure essays. . . .

3   But it is of his tales that we desire principally to speak. The tale proper, in our opinion, affords unquestionably the fairest field for the exercise of the loftiest talent, which can be afforded by the wide domains of mere prose. Were we bidden to say how the highest genius could be more advantageously employed for the best display of its own powers, we should answer, without hesitation—in the composition of a rhymed poem, not to exceed in length what might be perused in an hour. Within this limit alone can the highest order of true poetry exist. We need only here say, upon this topic, that, in almost all classes of composition, the unity of effect or impression is a point of the greatest impor-tance. It is clear, moreover, that this unity cannot be thoroughly preserved in productions whose perusal cannot be completed at one sitting. We may continue the reading of a prose composition, from the very nature of prose itself, much longer than we can persevere, to any good purpose; in the perusal of a poem. This latter, if truly fulfilling the demands of the poetic sentiment, induces an exaltation of the soul which cannot be long sustained. All high excitements are necessarily transient. Thus a long poem is a paradox. And, without unity of impression, the deepest effects cannot be brought about. Epics were the offspring of an imperfect sense of Art, and their reign is no more. A poem *too* brief may produce a vivid, but never an intense or enduring impression. Without a certain continuity of effort—without a certain duration or repetition of purpose—the soul is never deeply moved. There must be the dropping of the water upon the rock. De Béranger has wrought brilliant things—pungent and spirit-stirring—but, like all immasive bodies, they lack *momentum*, and thus fail to satisfy the Poetic Sentiment. They sparkle and excite, but, from want of continuity, fail deeply to impress. Extreme brevity will degenerate into epigrammatism; but the sin of extreme length is even more unpardonable. *In medio tutissimus ibis.*

4   Were we called upon, however, to designate that class of composition which, next to such a poem as we have suggested, should best fulfil the demands of high

genius—should offer it the most advantageous field of exertion—we should unhesitatingly speak of the prose tale, as Mr. Hawthorne has here exemplified it. We allude to the short prose narrative, requiring from a half-hour to one or two hours in its perusal. The ordinary novel is objectionable, from its length, for reasons already stated in substance. As it cannot be read at one sitting, it deprives itself, of course, of the immense force derivable from *totality*. Worldly interests intervening during the pauses of perusal, modify, annul, or counteract, in a greater or less degree, the impressions of the book. But simple cessation in reading would, of itself, be sufficient to destroy the true unity. In the brief tale, however, the author is enabled to carry out the fulness of his intention, be it what it may. During the hour of perusal the soul of the reader is at the writer's control. There are no external or extrinsic influences—resulting from weariness or interruption.

5   A skilful literary artist has constructed a tale. If wise, he has not fashioned his thoughts to accommodate his incidents; but having conceived, with deliberate care, a certain unique or single *effect* to be wrought out, he then invents such incidents—he then combines such events as may best aid him in establishing this preconceived effect. If his very initial sentence tend not to the outbringing of this effect, then he has failed in his first step. In the whole composition there should be no word written, of which the tendency, direct or indirect, is not to the one pre-established design. And by such means, with such care and skill, a picture is at length painted which leaves in the mind of him who contemplates it with a kindred art, a sense of the fullest satisfaction. The idea of the tale has been presented unblemished, because undisturbed; and this is an end unattainable by the novel. Undue brevity is just as exceptionable here as in the poem; but undue length is yet more to be avoided.

6   We have said that the tale has a point of superiority even over the poem. In fact, while the *rhythm* of this latter is an essential aid in the development of the poem's highest idea—the idea of the Beautiful—the artificialities of this rhythm are an inseparable bar to the development of all points of thought or expression which have their basis in *Truth*. But Truth is often, and in very great degree, the aim of the tale. Some of the finest tales are tales of ratiocination. Thus the field of this species of composition, if not in so elevated a region on the mountain of Mind, is a table-land of far vaster extent than the domain of the mere poem. Its products are never so rich, but infinitely more numerous, and more appreciable by the mass of mankind. The writer of the prose tale, in short, may bring to his theme a vast variety of modes or inflections of thought and expression—(the ratiocinative, for example, the sarcastic, or the humorous) which are not only antagonistical to the nature of the poem, but absolutely forbidden by one of its most peculiar and indispensable adjuncts; we allude, of course, to rhythm. It may be added here, *par parenthèse*, that the author who aims at the purely beautiful in a prose tale is laboring at a great disadvantage. For Beauty can be better treated in the poem. Not so with terror, or passion, or horror, or a

multitude of such other points. And here it will be seen how full of prejudice are the usual animadversions against those *tales of effect,* many fine examples of which were found in the earlier numbers of *Blackwood.* The impressions produced were wrought in a legitimate sphere of action, and constituted a legitimate although sometimes an exaggerated interest. They were relished by every man of genius: although there were found many men of genius who condemned them without just ground. The true critic will but demand that the design intended be accomplished, to the fullest extent, by the means most advantageously applicable.

7   We have very few American tales of real merit—we may say, indeed, none, with the exception of *The Tales of a Traveller* of Washington Irving, and these *Twice-Told Tales* of Mr. Hawthorne. Some of the pieces of Mr. John Neal abound in vigor and originality; but, in general, his compositions of this class are excessively diffuse, extravagant, and indicative of an imperfect sentiment of Art. Articles at random are, now and then, met with in our periodicals which might be advantageously compared with the best effusions of the British Magazines; but, upon the whole, we are far behind our progenitors in this department of literature.

Of Mr. Hawthorne's tales we should say, emphatically, that they belong to the highest region of Art—an Art subservient to genius of a very lofty order. We had supposed, with good reason for so supposing, that he had been thrust into his present position by one of the impudent *cliques* which beset our literature, and whose pretensions it is our full purpose to expose at the earliest opportunity; but we have been most agreeably mistaken. We know of few compositions which the critic can more honestly commend than these *Twice-Told Tales.* As Americans, we feel proud of the book. . . .

WRITING ASSIGNMENTS

Write an essay on one of the following topics. Be sure that the basis of your evaluation is clear and that your reasoning is solid. Feel free to draw on the readings, your previous essays, and class discussions.

1. Analyze and evaluate the values in one of the selections in this chapter.
2. Evaluate one of the selections in the previous chapters.
3. Evaluate one of your previous essays.
4. Evaluate the responsibility of the media.
5. Evaluate the accuracy of news reporting.
6. Evaluate the treatment of one or more groups on television.
7. Evaluate the role of school in this country.
8. Evaluate the purpose of education.
9. Evaluate American values.
10. Evaluate the idea of America as a melting pot.

11. Evaluate an issue that emerged from the discussions for Making Connections or one of the additional essays.

12. In 1982 President Ronald Reagan said: "I have always believed . . . that a divine plan placed this great continent here between the oceans to be found by people from every corner of the Earth who had a special love of faith and freedom." Evaluate his statement.

13. In 1986 voters in California approved an amendment to the state constitution which said in part:

    English is the official language of the State of California. . . . The Legislature and officials of the State of California shall take all steps necessary to insure that the role of English as the common language of the State of California is preserved and enhanced. The Legislature shall make no law which diminishes or ignores the role of English as the common language. . . .

    Evaluate this amendment.

14. A study by the Foundation for Traffic Safety of the American Automobile Association entitled "Myths, Men and Beer: An Analysis of Beer Commercials on Broadcast Television, 1987" found that "beer commercials link drinking and driving explicitly through images of and references to beer with images of moving cars" and called for the prohibition of such advertisements. Evaluate the findings and the recommendation.

15. An article in *Newsweek* (December 27, 1982) entitled "How the Bible Made America" says:

    . . . historians are discovering that the Bible, perhaps even more than the Constitution, is our founding document: the source of the powerful myth of the United States as a special, sacred nation, a people called by God to establish a model society, a beacon to the world.

    Evaluate the statement.

16. In 1987 Americans spent more than $250 million on "designer fragrances"—distinct from and in addition to room deodorants—for their homes. According to Annette Green, executive director of the Fragrance Foundation of New York, the purpose is "not to mask odors, necessarily, but to add a whole other sensory dimension to their homes." Evaluate this trend.

C·H·A·P·T·E·R S·E·V·E·N

PERSUASION

Although we want the reader to accept our analysis or evaluation, the actual purpose of these essays is to analyze or evaluate, not to persuade. It is possible, however, to write an essay where the purpose, the main point, is to persuade the reader to accept our ideas. This is the case in friendly arguments, many newspaper editorials, and almost all business proposals. For example, you may want to convince a friend that the Patriots are a better team than the Dolphins, or that Eddie Murphy is funnier than Jay Leno. A newspaper columnist may want to prove that the government's motivation for our policy in Central America is not what the president says it is; a manager may want to urge his or her superiors to adopt a suggestion that will improve employee morale. The purpose may be to urge the audience to answer a call to action, vote for a particular candidate, or institute a particular policy.

One thing that all these topics have in common is that there are at least two valid positions that a reasonable person can take. It is common for politicians to regale cheering supporters with what they want to hear, and religious leaders frequently find themselves preaching to the already converted, since these are, after all, the people who come to rallies and services. But this is not what we mean by persuasion. In theory at least, no one is in favor of war or sin, so it is not necessary to persuade people to be against them. However, when two or more positions have reasonable supporters, reasonable people can try to persuade each other to adopt a particular position. Thus, in an essay whose main purpose is to persuade, the writer must address an issue that is arguable. Such issues are numerous, but they must be carefully defined and limited. No one is in favor of poverty, but reasonable people can disagree about specific ways of fighting it.

Although no one is in favor of crime, reasonable people can disagree about whether a specific act should be considered criminal.

In addition, all attempts to persuade share the same elements—an analysis of a situation or problem, an evaluation of alternative explanations or solutions, and convincing reasons for accepting one choice and rejecting the others. As you know already, analysis is the core of much good writing. Your topic has to be clear to the reader and has to be presented in a way that shows your knowledge and thoughtfulness. To be persuasive, you must also make the basis of your evaluation clear to the audience, and you must show that you know the alternatives to your position and that you have considered them carefully.

· WEIGHING ALTERNATIVE SOLUTIONS

Sometimes a writer will list alternatives to a position and then disprove them point by point. In the following excerpt from his famous "Give me liberty or give me death" speech, Patrick Henry is trying to convince the provincial assembly of Virginia that the only course left to them is armed struggle against the British. He therefore lists possible alternative ways of dealing with the British government and then rejects them.

I ask gentlemen, sir, what means this martial array, if its purpose be not to force us to submission? Can gentlemen assign any other possible motives for it? Has Great Britain any enemy, in this quarter of the world, to call for all this accumulation of navies and armies? No, sir, she has none. They are meant for us; they can be meant for no other. They are sent over to bind and rivet upon us those chains which the British ministry have been so long forging. And what have we to oppose to them? Shall we try argument? Sir, we have been trying that for the last ten years. Have we anything new to offer on the subject? Nothing. We have held the subject up in every light of which it is capable; but it has been all in vain. Shall we resort to entreaty and humble supplication? What terms shall we find which have not been already exhausted? Let us not, I beseech you, sir, deceive ourselves longer. Sir, we have done everything that could be done, to avert the storm which is now coming on. We have petitioned; we have remonstrated; we have supplicated; we have prostrated ourselves before the throne, and have implored its interposition to arrest the tyrannical hands of the ministry and Parliament. Our petitions have been slighted; our remonstrances have produced additional violence and insult; our supplications have been disregarded; and we have been spurned, with contempt, from the foot of the throne. In vain, after these things, may we indulge the fond hope of peace and reconciliation. There is no longer any room for hope. If we wish to be free—if we mean to preserve inviolate

those inestimable privileges for which we have been so long contending—
if we mean not basely to abandon the noble struggle in which we have
been so long engaged, and which we have pledged ourselves never to
abandon until the glorious object of our contest shall be obtained, we must
fight! I repeat it, sir, we must fight! An appeal to arms and to the God of
Hosts is all that is left us!

Calling for Change

One possible alternative to a problematic situation may be to do nothing, or
to continue doing what is being done. In this case, just showing that a problem
exists proves that continuing business as usual is not wise. However, that does
not automatically mean your solution is any better. Proving that a problem exists
is not the same as proving that your proposal will solve the problem: Many
remedies have proven to be worse than the original illness. You must convince
the reader that your proposal is worth trying.

When you read the following editorial, look for the elements we have just
outlined:

What is the situation or problem? Is it carefully defined or limited? Is it
arguable? Is it analyzed adequately?

What is the proposed solution? Is it reasonable? Is it supported convincingly?

Are alternative solutions offered? Do people actually hold them or are they
straw men? Are they fairly evaluated? Are they convincingly disproved?

SILENCE TERROR WITH SILENCE

1   As a police newspaper we are painfully and constantly aware of the
conflicting needs of those who seek to inform and those who seek to
protect. Numerous cases have gone to the courts because information was
seen as an obstacle to protection or protection was viewed as a threat to
information. The problem is not a simple one to solve, and it would be
both false and foolish to suggest that it is. But one increasingly popular
trend annoys us in our role as a news service as well as our role as a law
enforcement agency. And that is the ease with which terrorist groups can
manipulate the media by staging "events."

2   The papers and broadcast media are filled with stories about this or that
"previously unknown group" that has just grabbed the public's attention
by exploding a bomb and calling the news service to "claim responsibility."
It is almost as if they are on the phone before they have completed their
escape. And the logic is obvious. If your organization contains only two or

Reprinted by permission.

three members, you can hardly put together a peaceful demonstration that will attract media attention. But if you explode a bomb, everyone will come running to publicize your communiques and propaganda. And what better way to advertise and attract another two or three fanatics? It is certainly cheaper than running a full page ad in a newspaper.

3   These bombings are particularly cowardly. Like the recent one in New York City that almost killed a passing policeman, they involve no danger to the terrorists, have little effect on the target, and pose a mortal danger to only one group—innocent passersby. This is not to say that some of these bombs are not intended to kill innocents. They are. But they are the minority. Most seem to be more for the purpose of attracting media attention. And this they do only too well.

4   But since these cowardly bombings are orchestrated as media events, the media has a responsibility not to become an accomplice to terrorism and possible injury and murder. If the news media made it clear that there would be no free publicity for every fanatical group that commits an act of violence, many of these acts would not occur. And this attitude on the part of the media need not reduce the commitment to reporting the news. It would still be possible to report that a bomb exploded at such and such a place; but it does not seem necessary to add by whom and why. And it certainly is not necessary to publish political tracts distributed by the perpetrators. In effect this will reduce the amount of information passed on to the public, but it will also reduce the motivation of many groups for committing acts of violence in the first place.

5   A balance must be sought between the unlimited right to report the news and the undesirable consequence of becoming an accomplice to more and more violence. Making clear that the media are not at the beck and call of terrorists may be a small first step in the right direction.

As you probably realized when you read the preceding editorial, the first paragraph takes the large issue of "the conflicting needs of those who seek to inform and those who seek to protect"—an issue much too large for a brief essay—and narrows it down to the problem of "the ease with which terrorist groups can manipulate the media by staging 'events.'" The second paragraph explains what the writer means by this charge: Terrorist groups commit crimes in order to get media coverage of themselves and their philosophies. The paragraph also makes clear that, at least in 1980 when the essay was written, the groups involved were small and probably local. This point is supported also in the third paragraph where we are told that the primary goal of these crimes is to gain attention, not necessarily to hurt anyone—a situation that was certainly not true by the late 1980s. The problem, then, is how the media should handle such cases—an arguable issue since it pits "those who seek to inform" against "those who seek to protect."

The proposed solution is in the fourth paragraph: The news media must make it clear that there will be "no free publicity for every fanatical group that commits an act of violence." The causation presented in support of this solution seems reasonable. The writer argues that since the purpose of the violence is the subsequent publicity, if the publicity—the "reward"—were removed, the violence would not occur. The writer bolsters this logic with an appeal to the moral responsibility of the media: Since the violence itself is intended to motivate a specific reaction from the media, there is a "responsibility not to become an accomplice to terrorism." The solution may not convince every reader—a fact that is not surprising—but it is presented in a reasoned way.

The reasonable tone of the writer is also seen in the way the alternative is presented. Although not stated explicitly, the alternative is clearly to report everything. The writer grants that there is no easy answer to a complex problem; those who seek to inform are honest, decent people, and so are those who seek to protect. The first sentence of the editorial sets the tone by pointing out that as editor of a law enforcement newspaper, the writer personally feels both sides in the conflict. That, presumably, accounts for the attempt to distinguish news from manipulation. Where and when a bomb went off is news; reading a manifesto is allowing oneself to be used. Reporting who did it and why is a gray area: It is news, but it is also free publicity. The alternative of reporting everything a terrorist asks is as unacceptable as reporting nothing. The writer's suggestion is that "a balance must be sought" between unlimited reporting and becoming an accomplice.

We can say, then, that the problem is clear, the solution is reasonable, and the alternatives—reporting everything or nothing—have been made to look extreme. The solution is attractive because it takes a middle ground.

The middle ground is not always available, however. Sometimes there must be a winner and loser, and then opposition to the proposed solution is sure to come from one side or the other. In our form of democratic government, the clash of rights and responsibilities produces dozens of examples: Should the guarantee of free speech protect pornography or racist literature? Should the right of free association include the right to bar women or blacks from private clubs? Should the mentally unstable be hospitalized against their will? Should sane, consenting adults have the right to injure themselves by taking drugs or not wearing seat belts? Should protecting the environment or an endangered species of bird be allowed to interfere with the creation of electricity or jobs? In the United States, where the government cannot simply impose its will, all such issues are arguable.

· APPEALS TO AUTHORITY

You as a writer do not always have the personal experience or knowledge that the editorial writer claims. When you are personally connected, you should say so: "As an editor and police officer, I understand the conflict" or "After ten years of competing in gymnastics tournaments, I can speak from experience about sports medicine." When you cannot make personal claims, you must muster and identify other sources of support.

The following essay, written by a nurse who is a part-time student, represents such a case. As you read it, look for the required elements of a proposal: the problem, the solution, and the rejection of the alternatives. In addition, evaluate whether the student creates a sense of authority and presents evidence strong enough to overcome the inevitable objections of the losing side.

HOSPITALS SHOULD BAN SMOKING IN LOUNGES
by Edlyne Charles

1   When someone objects to another person's smoking in a room, he or she is not just being a crank or over-reacting. More and more evidence is accumulating that smokers' smoke can harm the nonsmoker's health.

2   There has been a great deal of publicity about the adverse effects of cigarettes. Any smoker can feel and see some of these effects without outside help: morning cough, raspy throat, sour taste in the mouth, yellow-stained teeth and fingers, bad breath, and stinking hair and clothes. More important are the hidden effects: cigarette smoke has been proven to cause several disabling or fatal diseases. And today there are also legal consequences of lighting up near a nonsmoker. Therefore, I believe that hospitals, of all places, should not allow smoking in their lounges.

3   If you have ever sat in a restaurant and had a meal ruined because someone nearby was having an after-

dinner smoke, or if you have ever stood in a crowded
elevator suffering silently while one person puffed
away on a cigarette, then you know what it is like to be
subjected to a smoker's so-called "right to smoke."

4   Admittedly, there are some seemingly valid arguments for allowing smoking in public places. Many
smokers insist that smoking is a legal, pleasurable
pastime they should not be denied. Others say they cannot enjoy a meal, ride comfortably in a plane or bus, or
take a test without smoking. And since nicotine is
addictive, many smokers are indeed uncomfortable if
forced to refrain from smoking. And smokers claim that
if smoking is hurting their health, that is their
right. But these arguments are baseless. A smoker's
discomfort at refraining from smoking is comparable to
a nonsmoker's discomfort at being forced to inhale cigarette smoke; and while the smoker will benefit from
putting out a cigarette, the nonsmoker's health may be
endangered when a smoker lights up. Even if smokers may
take chances with their own bodies, they have no license to do so with the lives of others.

5   The arguments nonsmokers make, often considered
merely petty, are actually stronger than those of
smokers.

6   In the last decade or so, people have finally
begun to consider the rights of nonsmokers. In January

1984, the National Interagency Council on Smoking and Health composed a Nonsmokers' Bill of Rights asserting a nonsmoker's right to breathe clean air, speak out against tobacco smoke, act to prevent or discourage smoking, and seek the restriction of smoking in public places.

7   The data nonsmokers need to make their case are collected in The Scientific Case against Smoking, by Ruth Winter, and The Smoking Digest, produced by the Office of Cancer Communications of the National Cancer Institute.

8   A study conducted to measure tobacco smoke exposure of nonsmokers in a variety of public places found that smoke concentrations often are higher than permitted by the annual average air quality standard for clean air. Even with increased ventilation and the use of filters and air cleaning devices, studies have shown that on airplane flights there still remain a significant number of cabin occupants who are annoyed by cigarette smoke.

9   Dr. F. Schmidt, in his article "Health Risks of Passive Smoking," writes that a single smoked cigarette releases thirty milligrams or more of tar. If the cigarette is smoked in a closed room, it can render the air unhealthy according to the air quality index of the U.S. Environmental Protection Agency. Further,

the concentration of nitrosomine, a cancer causing agent, in side stream smoke (which comes from the lighted tip of a cigarette between puffs) exceeds that found in mainstream smoke (the smoke inhaled by the smoker) by up to fifty times. Also, benzopyrene, a known cancer causing agent, has been measured at levels ten to thirty times higher in smoky rooms than in outside air.

10   Health researchers report that the effects of passive smoke on nonsmokers range from eye and throat irritation, to a worsening of respiratory and circulatory symptoms, to increased risk of throat cancer, which is 10% to 20% higher than when they are not exposed. After ten minutes of exposure to cigarette smoke, nonsmokers had a 35% reduction in three constituents of the tear film in their eyes. Deterioration of the naturally antiseptic and protective tear film may promote eye infection. This is what causes the eyes to water when a person enters a smoke-filled room. The tar, nicotine, and carbon monoxide in side stream smoke can aggravate symptoms of heart and lung disease, worsen allergies and colds, and even reduce the ability of the circulatory system to carry oxygen through the body. Studies have shown blood nicotine levels in nonsmokers exposed to cigarette smoke to be 20% of the levels found in smokers.

11   A less noticeable but perhaps more dangerous effect of cigarette smoke in enclosed spaces, even when ventilation is adequate, is the production of carbon monoxide levels well above the air quality standard of 9 ppm (parts per million). This amount of carbon monoxide in a smoke-filled room has been shown to decrease the amount of exercise that induces angina pectoris (chest pain) in patients with coronary artery disease and to reduce exercise time before shortness of breath occurs in patients with chronic lung disease.

12   And cigarette smoke may also cause health problems in children by adversely affecting immunity to infections. Children of parents who smoke have been reported in many studies to have more bronchitis and pneumonia during the first year of life, and, in the long run, possibly greater susceptibility to respiratory tract cancer due to the presence of carcinogenic tars. Therefore, children should not be exposed to smoke-filled rooms, as is the case when parents with children visit a hospital.

13   Given this medical evidence, a hospital, of all places, should not allow smoking in its lounges.

14   But there are more reasons. When we consider the two major national problems of health policy, we find cigarette smoking intensifies and complicates each

one. The first one is the spiraling cost of health
care. Health care officials report that smoking accounts for an estimated $10–$15 billion in health
care expenses, not to mention the cost of lost productivity, through accident and illness. The second major
policy problem is the over-emphasis on expensive medical technology and institutional care. Certainly, if
the U.S. government is to shift its health strategy
toward prevention rather than merely curative medicine, it cannot ignore smoking, since smoking is the
largest preventable cause of death in America. Demog-
raphers identify 80,000 deaths each year from lung cancer, up to 225,000 deaths from cardiovascular disease,
and more than 19,000 from chronic pulmonary disease.
That is why smoking is Public Enemy Number One in
America.

15   In addition, smoking is the leading cause of
death in home fires: 2,000 Americans are burnt to death
every year in fires started by smokers. Insurance companies estimate that one out of four fires is caused by
smoking. Hundreds of millions of dollars are lost this
way in destroyed homes and factories.

16   No person, given these staggering costs, can reasonably conclude that smoking is simply a private concern. It is demonstrably a public health problem also.
A hospital should not be a party to supporting a habit

```
that is so costly in terms of life and money. Hospitals
should be leading the right to change the irritating
ways of smokers. In the meantime, hospitals should ban
smoking in their own lounges.
```

As in the editorial about terrorism, the problem and solution in the preceding essay are clear. Given the known health risks of smoking, the writer proposes that it be banned in hospital lounges.

A reader might object, however, that the writer is setting up a false either/or choice; there seems to be a middle ground between total permission and total ban, and that is establishment of special smoking lounges. The writer does not even consider this alternative. Omitting a viable alternative is a logical fallacy that can be a fatal flaw, but it is actually a strength here because of the authority and evidence in the essay. The writer is a nurse who has obvious competence in understanding and presenting an issue of health policy. Her summaries of research have the ring of truth to them; she gives clean air specifications, death rates, medical costs, and she explains them in a way that a nonspecialist can understand. Then she asks for adoption of a limited proposal. Though she musters evidence to show that smoking definitely causes illness, she does not make the extreme claim that people do not have the right to injure themselves; nor does she demand that smoking be banned in public places. Her proposal is limited to hospital lounges and therefore has an added moral strength. Of all places, she says, hospitals should set a proper example. Hospitals, which are dedicated to public health, cannot ignore the overwhelming evidence. They have a moral obligation to ban smoking from their own lounges. It now becomes clear that the middle ground would lack this moral power. Given the fact that she is a nurse and her proposal is addressed to hospital administrators, it would have been almost immoral for the writer to present all this evidence and then say that hospitals should allow smoking in some places. The either/or approach highlights the moral imperative of her suggestion.

· APPEALS TO EMOTION

If the essay about smoking and the preceding editorial have a weakness, it may be that they are too reasonable, too objective. Calling objectivity a weakness may seem like a contradiction, since we have been telling you all along to move away from personal opinion and try to see the larger picture. But the goal of persuasion is to convince the reader that your opinion is worth adopting, that your opinion is better than the reader's own. As we have just seen, creating a strong case requires a convincing analysis, a reasoned evaluation, and a rational solution.

It can also require an appeal to the reader's emotions, an approach which can be very tricky. On the one hand, even if your logic is convincing, the reader has to want to be logical. On the other, appeals to emotion very commonly are attempts to make people act illogically. Therefore, you have to find a middle ground—an appeal that is reasonable and honorable.

For example, nobody doubts that hunger is a problem in many places, yet almost no one devotes his or her life to relieving hunger. In fact, most people don't even send a few dollars when they get letters from CARE or UNICEF or the Red Cross or the Catholic Charities or the Salvation Army. Is it that we don't approve of what they are doing? On the contrary, everyone respects—even stands in awe of—the selfless devotion of nuns and doctors who give up comfortable lives to work in inner city slums or the Third World. The reason we don't respond is that we can accept the logic of what has to be done and still not be emotionally moved to do it. To be persuaded to act, the reader has to be personally touched.

Ironically, one of the consequences of the so-called information explosion—the speed with which news, for instance, travels across the globe—is that we can easily become dulled. In a small town, and even in fair-sized cities until recently, where everyday life goes along unexceptionally, a major fire is rare and therefore "news," and the serious illness of a neighbor has immediate impact on everyone's life. In the "global village," though, there is always a fire somewhere, always someone getting sick, whether in Brazil or Ethiopia or India. For the United States alone, the FBI reports an annual average since 1980 of 35 million crimes, including 20,000 homicides and 90,000 forcible rapes. These 50 murders and 250 rapes a day guarantee enough material for any tabloid. And, in fact, some news shows seem to have a nightly menu: a political photo opportunity, a civil war, a murder, a plane crash, a fire, and a sick child—regardless of where in the world the event takes place. Viewers therefore become callous, since they cannot remain emotionally charged forever. Thus, not every appeal to emotions can be accepted.

Nor should it be. Advertisements, for example, regularly appeal to our emotions for the basest and most foolish things. Is your life not as exciting as you want it to be? Does your boss not treat you the way you feel you ought to be treated? Do you want to party all the time like these beautiful people do? Then buy this (1) toothpaste, (2) deodorant, (3) vacation, (4) car, or (5) all of the above. An appeal to emotion should not prey on insecurities, and it should certainly not play to the audience's prejudices.

To be valid, an appeal to emotion must be reasonable and honorable: "Protect your children's lives by teaching them to use their seat belts." This is reasonable because parents naturally worry about their children's safety. And it is honorable because using seat belts can be shown to save children's lives in accidents. On the other hand, consider this appeal: "The best colleges get more selective every year. Guarantee your children's future. Buy the XYZ Learning System today." This ad promises more than it can deliver. No "learning system" guarantees anything. Although it may be true that good colleges have been getting more selective, it is not necessarily true that this trend will continue, since the number of applicants may shrink as tuition rises. Moreover, graduating from Harvard or Yale does not necessarily guarantee one's future. And even if it did, buying a particular product will not necessarily get your child into Harvard or Yale. This appeal to the parents' insecurities is not reasonable. And finally, consider this: "Keep out Asian refugees. They take jobs away from Americans." It appeals to the basest emotions: selfishness and (latent) racism. To the extent that the United States has a history that evokes pride, it is not in manifestations of selfishness and racism but in being a haven from persecution. Very few "Americans" are descended from Americans; they are descended from immigrants of one kind or another. Moreover, Asians do not "take jobs away" from anyone. Like all other immigrants over the centuries, they compete for the worst jobs until they or their children work their way up economically and socially. The appeal is therefore both unreasonable and dishonorable.

Valid appeals to emotion, then, can ask people to act out of fear, pride, patriotism, or any other motivating force. But the appeal should address honorable instincts.

For example, when John F. Kennedy was nominated to be the presidential candidate of the Democratic party in 1960, his acceptance speech had to deal with the fact that he was Catholic and the only Catholic before him to run for president, Al Smith, had been soundly defeated in 1928. Here is how Kennedy asked for votes by appealing to the public to reject religious prejudice:

> I am fully aware of the fact that the Democratic party, by nominating someone of my faith, has taken on what many regard as a new and hazardous risk—new, at least, since 1928. But I look at it this way: the Democratic party has once again placed its confidence in the American people, and in their ability to render a free, fair judgment. And you have, at the same time, placed your confidence in me, and in my ability to render a free, fair judgment—to uphold the Constitution and my oath of office—and to reject any kind of religious pressure or obligation that might directly or indirectly interfere with my conduct of the presidency in the national interest. My record of fourteen years supporting public education—supporting complete separation of church and state—and resisting pressure from any source on any issue should be clear by now to everyone.
>
> I hope that no American, considering the really critical issues facing this country, will waste his franchise by voting either for me or against me solely on account of my religious affiliation. It is not relevant, I want to

stress, what some other political or religious leader may have said on this subject. It is not relevant what abuses may have existed in other countries or in other times. It is not relevant what pressures, if any, might conceivably be brought to bear on me. I am telling you now what you are entitled to know: that my decisions on every public policy will be my own—as an American, a Democrat and a free man. . . .

In a sense Kennedy is trying to convince the voters that honorable people do not mix religion with politics: He is asking them to ignore his religion and promising to ignore it himself when making policy. It is interesting to note that in 1986 Mario Cuomo no longer felt the need to deny his religious motivation, but actually gloried in it, just as other public figures have made pride in their race or ethnic background central to their campaigns.

Pride in what we consider proper behavior is central to morality. In the same speech in which Kennedy spoke about religious prejudice, he again and again appealed to the public's pride in doing the right thing. The unveiling of his famous New Frontier is an example:

1   . . . I stand tonight facing West on what was once the last frontier. From the lands that stretch three thousand miles behind me, the pioneers of old gave up their safety, their comfort and sometimes their lives to build a new world here in the West. They were not the captives of their own doubts, the prisoners of their own price tags. Their motto was not "every man for himself"—but "all for the common cause." They were determined to make that new world strong and free, to overcome its hazards and its hardships, to conquer the enemies that threatened from without and within.

2   Today some would say that those struggles are all over—that all the horizons have been explored—that all the battles have been won—that there is no longer an American frontier.

3   But I trust that no one in this vast assemblage will agree with those sentiments. For the problems are not all solved and the battles are not all won—and we stand today on the edge of a New Frontier—the frontier of the 1960's—a frontier of unknown opportunities and perils—a frontier of unfulfilled hopes and threats.

4   Woodrow Wilson's New Freedom promised our nation a new political and economic framework. Franklin Roosevelt's New Deal promised security and succor to those in need. But the New Frontier of which I speak is not a set of promises—it is a set of challenges. It sums up not what I intend to *offer* the American people, but what I intend to *ask* of them. It appeals to their pride, not their pocketbook—it hold out the promise of more sacrifice instead of more security.

5   But I tell you the New Frontier is here, whether we seek it or not. Beyond that frontier are uncharted areas of science and space, unsolved problems of peace and war, unconquered pockets of ignorance and prejudice, unanswered questions of poverty and surplus. It would be easier to shrink back from that frontier, to look to the safe mediocrity of the past, to be lulled by good intentions and high rhetoric—and those who prefer that course should not cast their votes for me, regardless of party.

6   But I believe the times demand invention, innovation, imagination, decision. I am asking each of you to be new pioneers on that New Frontier. My call is to the young in heart, regardless of age—to the stout in spirit, regardless of party—to all who respond to the Scriptural call: "Be strong and of good courage; be not afraid, neither be thou dismayed."

As you no doubt understood, Kennedy draws a parallel between the courage and accomplishments of the pioneers and the courage needed by his audience to do the right thing. He recalls the popular American belief that the pioneers disregarded safety and comfort because they had a mission—"to make that new world strong and free." He assures the audience that, even though some people would say "those struggles are all over" and no exciting challenges remain, he knows that "no one in this vast assemblage will agree" with that mistaken view. He thus unites his listeners' personal pride and their patriotism in his appeal. Finally, he solidifies it with a quotation from the Bible, another source of emotional attachment: "Be strong and of good courage."

This biblical encouragement of patriotic commitment continues in the next section of the speech, which includes such echoes of the Gettysburg Address as "any nation so conceived—can long endure." In addition, Kennedy portrays his program as a sacred mission and trust that cannot be ignored.

7   For courage—not complacency, is our need today—leadership—not salesmanship. And the only valid test of leadership is the ability to lead, and lead vigorously. A tired nation, said David Lloyd George, is a Tory nation—and the United States today cannot afford to be either tired or Tory.

8   There may be those who wish to hear more—more promises to this group or that—more harsh rhetoric about the men in the Kremlin—more assurances of a golden future, where taxes are always low and subsidies ever high. But my promises are in the platform you have adopted—our ends will not be won by rhetoric and we can have faith in the future only if we have faith in ourselves.

9   For the harsh facts of the matter are that we stand on this frontier at a turning-point in history. We must prove all over again whether this nation—or any nation so conceived—can long endure—whether our soci-

ety—with its freedom of choice, its breadth of opportunity, its range of
alternatives—can compete with the single-minded advance of the Communist system.

10   Can a nation organized and governed such as ours endure? That is the
real question. Have we the nerve and the will? Can we carry through in an
age where we will witness not only new breakthroughs in weapons of
destruction—but also a race for mastery of the sky and the rain, the ocean
and the tides, the far side of space and the inside of men's minds?

11   Are we up to the task—are we equal to the challenge? Are we willing
to match the Russian sacrifice of the present for the future—or must we
sacrifice our future in order to enjoy the present?

12   That is the question of the New Frontier. That is the choice our nation
must make—a choice that lies not merely between two men or two parties, but between the public interest and private comfort—between national greatness and national decline—between the fresh air of progress
and the stale, dank atmosphere of "normalcy"—between determined dedication and creeping mediocrity.

13   All mankind waits upon our decision. A whole world looks to see what
we will do. We cannot fail their trust, we cannot fail to try.

Kennedy's appeal to missionary zeal is immediately followed by a brief reference to the distance already traveled and the road still ahead. The speech then
concludes with another encouraging quotation from the Bible, which Kennedy
uses to equate "they that wait upon the Lord" with those who accept his
challenge.

14   It has been a long road from that first day in New Hampshire to this
crowded convention city. Now begins another long journey, taking me
into your cities and homes all over America. Give me your help, your
hand, your voice, your vote. Recall with me the words of Isaiah: "They
that wait upon the Lord shall renew their strength; they shall mount up
with wings as eagles; they shall run, and not be weary."

15   As we face the coming challenge, we too, shall wait upon the Lord, and
ask that He renew our strength. Then shall we be equal to the test. Then
we shall not be weary. And then we shall prevail.

Using Humor to Persuade

Although persuasion is a serious purpose, it can be aided by the tool of
humor. As with appeals to emotion, humor is tricky, since the line between good
taste and grossness differs from person to person and shifts from time to time.
Nonetheless, good writers have always employed humor, and you can also—if
you are careful.

An especially effective use of humor in persuasion is to make the audience laugh at the opposing view by showing that if it is adopted it will lead to absurd results. Such a *reductio ad absurdum*, or "reduction to absurdity," is illustrated in the following passage, in which Patrick Henry attacks those who believed that the American colonists should not fight the British until they were strong enough.

> They tell us that we are weak; unable to cope with so formidable an adversary. But when shall we be stronger? Will it be the next week, or the next year? Will it be when we are totally disarmed, and when a British guard shall be stationed in every house? Shall we gather strength by irresolution and inaction? Shall we acquire the means of effectual resistance, by lying supinely on our backs, hugging the delusive phantom of hope, until our enemies shall have bound us hand and foot?

Reduction to absurdity can also be accomplished by exaggeration, as in the collection of details in the second and third paragraphs of the following essay. Here the riddle and humor in the first three paragraphs draw the reader into the serious discussion that begins in the fourth paragraph.

ENGLISH IS A WOMEN'S PROBLEM
by Evelyn B. Melamed (1982)

1   I take for my text a riddle currently making the rounds: A man and his son were injured in a car accident and rushed to the hospital. As the boy was brought into the emergency room, the doctor on duty gasped, "My God, that's my son!" How could that be?

2   Though the usual attempts at an answer focus on mistaken identity, adoption and similar contrivances, the key to this little puzzle lies in the relation of language to perception. But before we get to that, consider this popular scenario: At long last, through feminine wiles, Jane Doe has finally hooked Mr. Right. The preacher pronounces them man and wife and she is now Mrs. John Smith, ready to live happily ever after as a housewife. The plot of countless Hollywood movies. The dream of every coed who spends four years in college pursuing the Mrs. degree. But look at the words: *feminine wiles, hooked Mr. Right, man and wife, housewife.* What do they say about the American attitude toward women? Mr. Right is still a man; but the woman is now a wife. A husband can still be John Smith; but Jane Doe is now Mrs. Somebody-else. Is this the way more than half of our population should be treated?

3   Or consider this: women have women's problems and go to a woman's doctor, but men have jock itch and go to a urologist. Women go to the powder room, worry about feminine hygiene, suffer from the blues, need

extra protection; start out as chicks, lookers, vamps, dolls, cuties, dumb blondes; try to avoid becoming fallen women, scarlet women, molls, whores, bitches, temptresses, jezebels, bawds; and end up as hags, crones, witches, old maids, dried up old bitties.

4   Even if we don't fully subscribe to the so-called Sapir-Whorf Hypothesis that language shapes thought, nonetheless we have to admit that language colors the way we see the world. As a mother, I worry that my son will be insensitive to half the world and my daughter will be misled by words like *businessman, mankind, man's achievements,* into assuming that all important jobs are held by men or, even, that everything worthwhile is masculine. And as a career woman I fear that adults too are at least subconsciously influenced when they say "I'll have my *girl* type that" or "That's just an old *wives'* tale." And, given the number of women working in factories, why are synthetics considered *man*-made?

5   Of course, it's foolish to blame the language for the biases and preju-dices which it reflects; language is inanimate and is merely the product of a people's history and culture. But there is a vicious circle here. Language is man-made—that's right, made by *men*—and therefore reflects men's view of women; but by using these words, we reinforce the prejudices and perpetuate them. There was a time not so long ago when decent people didn't hesitate to say *nigger, chink, spick, greaser,* "He *japped* us" or "I *jewed* them down." Now these expressions are avoided by sensitive speakers. Why is it, then, that people who would never dream of addressing a Black as *boy,* still feel it is socially acceptable to denigrate grown women as *girls?*

6   Obviously, the language contains offensive references to women be-cause women, like other powerless groups, have historically been in a demeaning situation. And this being the case, some well-meaning people argue that a word like *businessman* implies *man* only because that is the reality: when women constitute a significant portion of executives, they argue, the suffixed *man* will cease to mean "male" and will be either neuter or androgynous, as in *mankind, the common man* and *man's best friend.* But this misses the point. So long as *man* contrasts with *woman* it cannot be neutral, even if there are a lot of women *businessmen* or *firemen* or *policemen.* And, far from being neutral, *mankind* means "humanity" pre-cisely because women were excluded as insignificant—in exactly the same way that an owner of Black slaves could write in the Declaration of Independence that all men are created equal and endowed with the un-alienable right of liberty.

7   Since the problem is one of power, women cannot hope to command fair treatment until they amass and use their power. When women sit at the head of the corporate table, they will have their *secretaries*—whether male or female—take notes; when women editors review manuscripts for publication, they will commission works on *folklore,* not old wives' tales;

and when women are truly equal with their male co-workers, perhaps they will also be able to *go to the john*, if they want, instead of powdering their noses.

8   But until that day comes, there is no reason to put up with the daily irritation of sexist language. And maybe, just maybe, when fair-minded people start avoiding offensive language, they will also become less comfortable with the injustices that underlie it—the injustices that make us assume that a secretary or prostitute is a woman, but, to return to the opening riddle, a doctor is not.

In addition to the use of humor for a serious purpose, the essay also shows how an author can modify the expository conventions. For example, instead of having a straightforward thesis statement, the introduction presents a riddle. The second paragraph promises a solution—after we consider the relationship of language and perception in the next two paragraphs. By the fourth paragraph, the reader has been hooked and follows the essay to the solution of the riddle in the conclusion.

Using Irony, Sarcasm, Satire

Two other powerful tools of persuasion are **irony**—saying the opposite of what you mean—and the biting irony known as **sarcasm,** as in the following:

In response to the public outcry over waste in government, our brave leaders took quick and decisive action and—appointed a committee to study the problem. That's just what we need!

Irony and sarcasm are especially difficult to use because you must be absolutely certain that your audience shares your values and knowledge; if not, there is the real possibility that your words will be taken at face value. If, for example, someone felt that a committee to study waste in government is a decisive solution, the author's irony would be missed. A similar situation occurs when a friend asks how the chemistry exam went and you say, "Piece of cake. I aced it." Unless your tone of voice or facial expression clearly signal irony, only someone who knows how you have been doing in the course can know whether the answer is literally true or ironic.

Extended irony for the purpose of ridiculing evil or foolishness is known as **satire.** For example, during the bitter debate in the years before the Civil War, Sen. Charles Sumner of Massachusetts satirized Sen. Andrew Pickens Butler of South Carolina and Sen. Stephen Douglas of Illinois for defending slavery. His method includes an extended analogy to the characters and events of *Don Quixote,* itself a satire of Spanish history.

1   . . . I must say something of a general character, particularly in response to what has fallen from Senators who have raised themselves to
eminence on this floor in championship of human wrongs. I mean the
Senator from South Carolina [Mr. Butler], and the Senator from Illinois
[Mr. Douglas], who, though unlike as Don Quixote and Sancho Panza,
yet, like this couple, sally forth together in the same adventure. I regret
much to miss the elder Senator from his seat; but the cause, against which
he has run a tilt, with such activity of animosity, demands that the opportunity of exposing him should not be lost; and it is for the cause that I
speak. The Senator from South Carolina has read many books of chivalry,
and believes himself a chivalrous knight, with sentiments of honor and
courage.

2   Of course he has chosen a mistress to whom he has made his vows, and
who, though ugly to others, is always lovely to him; though polluted in the
sight of the world, is chaste in his sight—I mean the harlot, Slavery. For
her, his tongue is always profuse in words. Let her be impeached in
character, or any proposition made to shut her out from the extension of
her wantonness, and no extravagance of manner or hardihood of assertion
is then too great for this Senator. The frenzy of Don Quixote, in behalf of
his wench, Dulcinea del Toboso, is all surpassed. The asserted rights of
slavery, which shock equality of all kinds, are cloaked by a fantastic claim
of equality. If the slave States cannot enjoy what, in mockery of the great
fathers of the Republic, he misnames equality under the Constitution—in
other words, the full power in the national territories to compel fellow-
men to unpaid toil, to separate husband and wife, and to sell little children
at the auction block—then, sir, the chivalric Senator will conduct the
State of South Carolina out of the Union! Heroic knight! Exalted Senator! A second Moses come for a second Exodus! . . . .

3   As the Senator from South Carolina is the Don Quixote, the Senator
from Illinois [Mr. Douglas] is the squire of slavery, its very Sancho Panza,
ready to do all is humiliating offices. . . .

Perhaps the most famous satire in the English language is Jonathan Swift's *A
Modest Proposal*, which addresses the still unsolved question of how to eliminate
poverty. Because the Catholics of Ireland had supported James in 1689–91 in his
unsuccessful war for the English throne, the victorious William confiscated their
lands, and took away their right to vote, run schools, bear arms, and own such
luxuries as an expensive horse. In addition, the Irish in general were prohibited
from exporting wool and found themselves paying rent to William's supporters
who owned their land but lived in England. Grinding poverty led to emigration
when possible, especially to America. Swift's *Proposal*, written in 1729, ridicules
the selfishness of the wealthy by reasonably—and ironically—proposing that
they follow their behavior to its logical conclusion. As you read the following

excerpt (which, of course, in its brevity cannot do justice to a carefully wrought work of art), pay careful attention to how and when you realize that his proposal is not to be taken seriously. This point is important, for in our own day similar and worse suggestions have been implemented, and this fact reminds us that satire works only when you can be sure of the moral footing of your audience.

1   The number of souls in this kingdom being usually reckoned one million and a half, of these I calculate there may be about two hundred thousand couples whose wives are breeders; from which number I subtract thirty thousand couples who are able to maintain their own children, although I apprehend there cannot be so many under the present distress of the kingdom; but this being granted, there will remain an hundred and seventy thousand breeders. I again subtract fifty thousand for those women who miscarry, or whose children die by accident or disease within the year. There only remain an hundred and twenty thousand children of poor parents annually born. The question therefore is, how this number shall be reared and provided for, which, as I have already said, under the present situation of affairs, is utterly impossible by all the methods hitherto proposed. For we can neither employ them in handicraft or agriculture; we neither build houses (I mean in the country) nor cultivate land. They can very seldom pick up a livelihood by stealing till they arrive at six years old. . . .

2   I am assured by our merchants that a boy or girl before twelve years old is no salable commodity; and even when they come to this age they will not yield above three pounds, or three pounds and half a crown at most on the Exchange; which cannot turn to account either to the parents or the kingdom, the charge of nutriment and rags having been at least four times that value.

3   I shall now therefore humbly propose my own thoughts, which I hope will not be liable to the least objection.

4   I have been assured by a very knowing American of my acquaintance in London, that a young healthy child well nursed is at a year old a most delicious, nourishing, and wholesome food, whether stewed, roasted, baked, or boiled; and I make no doubt that it will equally serve in a fricassee or a ragout.

5   I do therefore humbly offer it to public consideration that of the hundred and twenty thousand children, already computed, twenty thousand may be reserved for breed, whereof only one fourth part to be males, which is more than we allow to sheep, black cattle, or swine; and my reason is that these children are seldom the fruits of marriage, a circumstance not much regarded by our savages, therefore one male will be sufficient to serve four females. That the remaining hundred thousand may at a year old be offered in sale to the persons of quality and fortune through the kingdom, always advising the mother to let them suck plentifully in the

last month, so as to render them plump and fat for a good table. A child will make two dishes at an entertainment for friends; and when the family dines alone, the fore or hind quarter will make a reasonable dish, and seasoned with a little pepper or salt will be very good boiled on the fourth day, especially in winter.

6   I have reckoned upon a medium that a child just born will weigh twelve pounds, and in a solar year if tolerably nursed increaseth to twenty-eight pounds.

7   I grant this food will be somewhat dear, and therefore very proper for landlords, who, as they have already devoured most of the parents, seem to have the best title to the children. . . .

Swift goes on to list several monstrous reasons for accepting his proposal and then near the end presents his actual recommendations—by ironically rejecting them out of hand.

8   I can think of no one objection that will possibly be raised against this proposal, unless it should be urged that the number of people will be thereby much lessened in the kingdom. This I freely own, and it was indeed one principal design in offering it to the world. I desire the reader will observe, that I calculate my remedy for this one individual kingdom of Ireland and for no other that ever was, is, or I think ever can be upon earth. Therefore let no man talk to me of other expedients: of taxing our absentees at five shillings a pound: of using neither clothes nor household furniture except what is of our own growth and manufacture: of utterly rejecting the materials and instruments that promote foreign luxury: of curing the expensiveness of pride, vanity, idleness, and gaming in our women: of introducing a vein of parsimony, prudence, and temperance: of learning to love our country, in the want of which we differ even from Laplanders and the inhabitants of Topinamboo: of quitting our animosities and factions, nor acting any longer like the Jews, who were murdering one another at the very moment their city was taken: of being a little cautious not to sell our country and conscience for nothing: of teaching landlords to have at least one degree of mercy toward their tenants: lastly, of putting a spirit of honesty, industry, and skill into our shopkeepers; who, if a resolution could now be taken to buy only our native goods, would immediately unite to cheat and exact upon us in the price, the measure, and the goodness, nor could ever yet be brought to make one fair proposal of just dealing, though often and earnestly invited to it.

9   Therefore I repeat, let no man talk to me of these and the like expedients, till he hath at least some glimpse of hope that there will ever be some hearty and sincere attempt to put them in practice.

Though Swift introduces his recommendations with a rejection—"let no man talk to me of other expedients"—it is ironic; he actually prefers these alternatives to his supposed solution. We know this because the proposal to sell babies as food is too monstrous for decent people to entertain, and Swift was a decent man. On the other hand, in other times and other places worse atrocities have occurred. Thus, irony and satire, which depend on author and reader sharing moral values, are difficult to write and must be approached carefully.

· WRITING A PERSUASIVE ESSAY

As the previous examples have shown, there are many occasions for persuasion. The next essay is in the form of a proposal addressing a problem in business. As you read it, examine how the student presents the problem and supports her solution. Pay special attention to whether the problem is carefully defined and limited, whether the solution is clear, whether it is supported convincingly, and whether alternative solutions are rejected for good reasons.

QUALITY CIRCLE: THE CURE FOR WORKER APATHY

by Priscilla Scott

1   A problem many American companies share today is
the feeling of apathy among their employees. "Sense of
apathy" is perhaps a better phrase, since apathy is a
lack of feeling: indifference. Employees arrive at work
precisely on time in the morning, fulfill their expected duties (no more, no less), and leave precisely
on time in the evening. They do their work, but with
indifference.

2   A cure for this apathy is Quality Circle, a technique for bringing workers into the decision-making
loop and thus making them care about their jobs. My

purpose in this essay will be to define, analyze, and
evaluate Quality Circle in order to show how it elimi-
nates indifference and promotes motivation and productivity.

3   A Quality Circle is a small group of people who
meet for a suggested time of one hour per week to identify, analyze, and solve problems in their own department. The concept is that people who work in a particular area are the experts in that area and when they are
given training in how to analyze, evaluate, and solve
problems, they become an effective and powerful force
that benefits both them and their organization.

4   Generally Quality Circle focuses on the group
process and not on the individuals within the groups.
However, while gathering to accomplish their goal, another equally important aspect of the process is taking
place. Quality Circle contributes a great deal to the
development of individual members. Very often individuals perform far below their potential because the
work situation has a negative impact on their self-
esteem. However, in organizations with Quality Circle
the members have a means to develop a sense of accomplishment which increases their self-esteem; and employees who have a high sense of self-esteem are more
motivated, produce higher quality work, increase volume, and have a greater sense of commitment to their
organization. They develop a better relationship with

themselves, their jobs, their co-workers, management, and the company as a whole.

5   Before the circle can approach a problem, several months are spent learning the procedure which will make the circle an effective problem-solving unit. Through the use of video, charts, discussions, and quizzes, problem-solving techniques are explored, analyzed, and evaluated.

6   The first step is problem identification where members brainstorm for possible problems in their area. Through brainstorming, each member spontaneously contributes his or her ideas, one at a time, in turn, with each idea recorded on chart paper by one appointed member. No criticism is exchanged nor are ideas judged or evaluated at this time. Circle guidelines instruct members to listen to each other and to separate ideas from personalities so that judgments and criticism are withheld. All ideas are accepted and listed, which creates an atmosphere for creativity to emerge.

7   After brainstorming, potential projects are discussed thoroughly among the circle. Management and personnel from other departments may be invited to any meeting for additional information before selecting a project. After all problems are discussed, a voting process is used to narrow down the choices. After the first vote is taken, the four top choices are circled on

the chart paper and discussed, with each person having
a chance to express why he or she liked their particular
choice. The second and final vote is then taken with the
problem to be solved selected by majority vote.

8　　　　In the next step, information gathering, all
available information is collected. This may include
statistical data, interviews with co-workers, observations by circle members, and the additional collection of whatever data is appropriate for the problem
being researched. Sampling techniques are often used
to speed the process and the information is convenient-
ly collected using check sheets, checklists, drawings,
etc. Decisions often must be made on the data
collected.

9　　　　After the information is collected, it is examined during the information analysis step. Now the
group is taught how to record the information on various charts and graphs, including histograms, and control charts.

10　　　After the main problem has been clearly identified, it is now time to look for the most significant
causes. Possible causes of the problem are listed and
discussed along with their effects. This is because it
is important to verify the cause before a logical and
workable solution can be determined in order to protect
the validity of the solution. Cause and effect problem

analysis does this in a most effective and enjoyable manner in that all members are very much involved.

11   Brainstorming is again used to generate ideas and solutions and is combined with the reinforcement of the specific data which has been collected and documented on charts and graphs. Through cause verification the solution can be clearly identified and selected.

12   The final step is to verify the solution. The solution is often verified through the results of the information and data which were collected and recorded on the various charts, graphs, and checksheets. However, it may be necessary to seek the further advice of experts in specific areas if the solution is dependent upon the help of another department, e.g., programming, marketing, etc.

13   In summary, Quality Circle works by identifying problems, then selecting a specific problem, analyzing it, and recommending a solution to management. The employees have a positive attitude such as "We can do it" as opposed to "Management won't listen anyway."

14   The concept of Quality Circle as used today was originated in Japan in 1961 by Dr. Kaoru Ishikawa, an engineering professor at Tokyo University. Quality Circle first came to the United States in 1974, brought by two companies, Lockheed and Honeywell.

However, Quality Circle did not receive major attention as a practical concept in American management
until 1979.

15   In the years since then, it has had notable success. United Family Life Insurance Company of Atlanta,
Georgia, implemented a pilot program for Quality
Circle. Within a year the circle had completed two
projects, and both had resulted in dollar savings.
Quality Circle was introduced to Mohawk Data Sciences
Corporation in Herkimer, New York. MDS is a major sup-
plier of computer and communications services with
5,400 employees worldwide. MDS management approved a
proposal submitted by the Quality Circle for the Assembly Area that resulted in annual savings of over
$31,000. According to Quality Circle studies, 80% of
all Circle recommendations are approved by management.

16   Guideposts Associates in Carmel, New York, currently has a total of twelve Quality Circles operating
one hour each, weekly. With an average of ten members in
each circle, earning $6. per hour, these circles cost
Guideposts approximately $60. each per week. Multiply
this times the number of circles meeting each week and
the figure shows that Guideposts is paying approximately $37,440 a year to allow their employees to par-
ticipate in Quality Circle. This further amounts to

6,240 work hours per year being expended in Quality
Circle.

17   What does Guideposts, along with other companies
funding Quality Circle, stand to gain from their
investment?

18   "The Shadow Knows," Guideposts' Customer Services Quality Circle, recently completed their first
management presentation. The circle elected to convince management that a more efficient system for responding to the hundreds of customer problems and com-
plaints each day was to generate the letter responses
directly from the computer. The current procedure was to
manually write each response and then forward it to the
word processing department for typing.

19   Specific data was collected to determine exactly
how much time was being wasted through a duplicated
effort of allowing two departments to do basically the
same thing. After data was collected from the word
processing and customer services departments, the programming department was then asked if a program would be
feasible to develop. The circle followed the standard
format for resolving a problem; the information was
gathered, analyzed, and verified, a solution was identified, selected, and verified. During the presentation each circle member took a turn speaking, individually presenting specific information. The cir-

cle inspired effective teamwork, increased employee
motivation, and promoted job involvement while bringing out the problem-solving capabilities of each
member.

20   Not only did this presentation succeed in imple-
menting a new and improved procedure, but each member
was able to contribute to the betterment of the organization. Management was impressed at how well the individual members did their part of the presentation,
making use of logical and sophisticated problem analysis techniques.

21   Through working in Circles, members learn not
only more effective ways of dealing with each other,
they also develop skills in working with management.
They develop confidence as they see that they are recognized as experts at what they do, and management begins to see their employees in a new light. Leadership
skills, public speaking ability, knowledge of the
job, and knowledge of the company are evident. As circle members develop more positive attitudes toward
management, they also begin to feel more positive toward the company. They become more involved in making
improvements through circle projects, and as the company recognizes and acknowledges these contributions, an atmosphere of mutual respect and acceptance
emerges.

22   A participative form of coexistence between em-

ployees and management is absolutely essential to the progress and welfare of any organization. All organizations must involve employees to help ensure continued success and existence. "To circle or not to circle" is the question and it must be answered YES.

Bibliography

Dewar, Donald. <u>Quality Circle Answers to 100 Frequently Asked Questions</u>. Red Bluff, CA.: Quality Circle Institute, 1979.

_____. "What Techniques to Use." <u>Quality Circle Digest</u> (Nov. 1983): 58–59.

Dreyfus, Christine. "When Benefits Spill Over." <u>Training News</u> (Nov. 1984): 14.

Elwood, Robert W. "Motivation, Participation and the Knowledge Worker." <u>Quality Circle Digest</u> (Nov. 1982): 38.

Nelson, Ron W. "To Circle or Not to Circle." <u>Quality Circle Digest</u> (Jan. 1983): 74–75.

Pattarini, Nancy. "United Family Circles: A Life Insurance Company's Approach to Quality." <u>Resources</u>. Atlanta: Life Office Management Assoc., 1982.

The strengths of the paper are the description of Quality Circle and the use of authoritative sources. The reader has no doubts about the goals and methods of Quality Circle, and the benefits it has brought to several companies are clearly and convincingly illustrated. The student does not spend much time proving that a problem exists. But almost everyone knows the charge—whether true or not—that American workers are indifferent to quality. And the fact that the solution originated in Japan makes it immediately interesting to readers familiar with America's trade deficit and concepts like the Protestant work ethic. If the paper has a weakness, it is in being too one-sided: All the sources seem to be selling Quality Circle and no alternative solutions are considered. Even if we grant that workers are apathetic and more involvement in decision making is needed, there may be other ways to achieve acceptable results. But, in sum, the paper addressed a problem and offers good support for a particular solution.

CHECKLIST FOR PERSUASION

An essay to persuade must
    address an arguable issue
    analyze the problem
    evaluate alternative solutions
    prove one choice
    reject the other choices

When evaluating a persuasive essay, ask
    Is the problem clearly defined?
    Is it arguable?
    Is it analyzed adequately?
    Is the proposed solution clear?
    Is it reasonable?
    Is it supported convincingly?
    Are alternative solutions offered?
    Are they presented fairly?
    Are they convincingly disproved?

· ESSAYS FOR CRITICAL READING

The following selection appeared in FBI Law Enforcement Bulletin in 1985. In it, Lt. Col. Harold B. Wilber, who was Provost Marshal of the U.S. Marine Corps at the time, first evaluates the behavior of the media, then explains what makes terrorism "news," and concludes with recommendations for proper media behavior. The evaluation and conclusion are reprinted here.

From THE ROLE OF THE MEDIA DURING A TERRORIST INCIDENT by Lt. Col. Harold B. Wilber

1   Terrorism has proliferated in recent years. However, where there used to be a problem in defining terrorists acts, there now seems to be a consensus that this epidemic of violence is simply another means of war. In this war, the bombs have become bigger, the kidnapings more daring, and the threats of mass-scale, high technology extortion more real as terrorists become more willing to kill. In spite of this, terrorists have been unable to translate the consequences of terrorism into concrete political gains. Nor have they yet to reveal a convincingly workable strategy that relates terrorist violence to positive political power. In that sense, terrorism has failed.[1]

2   Yet, terrorism remains on the rise, and U.S.-related targets are expected to surpass the number which saw them as targets during 1983's terrorist incidents. The terrorists, in their failure, are not slow learners; they suffer from self-delusion in that they wage fantasy wars, thus allowing themselves to commit acts of violence that would otherwise be immoral. And, our characterization of all terrorist acts as a form of warfare either officially or through the media could be playing into the terrorists' hands by elevating them to warrior status.

3   According to Kupperman, "the media provide enormous political leverage to an act which, on its own, would simply be an act of criminal barbarism."[2] Because of technological strides within the last 10 years, the world is now the terrorists' captive audience. Coverage of hostage situations is broadcast live; events patronizingly unfold to the authorities and the general public simul-

---

[1]"Chances of Success Are Small, But No More Dying in Terrorist Attacks," *The Daytona Beach Sunday News Journal*, November 13, 1983, p. 5B

[2]Marvin E. Wolfgang, special ed., "International Terrorism," *The Annals of the American Academy of Political and Social Science* (Beverly Hills: SAGE Publications, Inc., 1962).

Reprinted from FBI Law Enforcement Bulletin.

taneously. We didn't learn of U.S. Army Brigadier General James L. Dozier's captivity, we lived it. When General Dozier was kidnaped by Italy's Red Brigade on December 17, 1981, and until his release on January 28, 1982, we vicariously shared his ordeal through media coverage of that terrorist act. It appears to be a legitimate concern that terrorists will seek out more spectacular methods of attracting publicity as the media lose interest in covering now mundane hijackings and kidnappings. The fanatical attack on the U.S. Marine Headquarters in Beirut, Lebanon, on October 23, 1983, bears this out. Likewise, something more than peacenik campouts around our European missile installations ought to be considered in our counterterrorist planning. Attacks against such installations or the kidnapping of American officials loom. And the inclusion of the media in our counterterrorist planning is a necessity that cannot be overlooked.

4   Throughout the previous decade, media and terrorism were engaged in an incestuous relationship. Bluntly stated, terrorism is a creature of the media. Thus, terrorism is an act of theater designed to have a strong psychological impact upon a vast audience. The image becomes as important as the reality, for the terrorist victim is rarely the ultimate target.[3] It can no longer be said, too, that the media are unaware of their operative role in the terror syndrome; they must acknowledge their effect.

5   In the context of the Iranian hostage crisis, the question then becomes whether event-oriented sensationalism is inextricably linked with mundane commercialism, with respect to television and the press. Iran proved once again, beyond any doubt, that terrorism is quintessentially the propaganda that also sells newspapers and increases TV ratings. In April 1977, a major television network issued a series of internal guidelines for the coverage of terrorist incidents. Yet, throughout the Iranian captivity, these guidelines were ignored to a far greater extent than they were observed. All three television networks, taking advantage of the Iranian drama, developed a blind eye to professional, ethical considerations in a fervent competitive quest for audiences. For example, despite policies prohibiting nonspontaneous interviews, all three networks jumped at the chance to broadcast their correspondents' controlled conversations with the Ayatollah on Sunday evening, November 18, 1979.[4]

6   There is no doubt that during this period, the embassy militants proved themselves masters of manipulation vis-a-vis American television by scheduling "events" to meet satellite and nightly news broadcast deadlines in the United States. Well might *Newsweek* magazine, during the last week of December 1979, raise the question of just who is actually the hostage of whom.[5]

7   The role of the U.S. media with respect to the global terrorist challenge is

[3]Abraham H. Miller, *Terrorism, The Media and the Law* (Dobbs Ferry, NY: Transnational Publishers, Inc., 1982), p. 58.
[4]Ibid. p. 59.
[5]Ibid. p. 60.

still fuzzy. If television and the press are unable or unwilling to adopt meaningful professional standards and to adhere to reasonable voluntary guidelines relative to the coverage of terrorist violence and its perpetrators, then it is conceivable that at some future date, assertions of national interest may ultimately take priority over the public's historic rights to be informed.[6] It is far better to come to grips with the issue now than to place trust in luck or crisis management. We, in the law enforcement business, must work with the media with the view of establishing mutually acceptable, realistic, and workable standards to be applied by both sides during terrorist incidents. An early goal is to establish a relationship with the media that does not foster the idea of "sides."

8   Today, the problem confronting officials and the news industry is to balance the right of access to newsworthy events, the right to gather news freely, the right to publish freely, and the right to disseminate information that becomes news against potential injury to hostages and loss of life. We, in our balancing act of dealing with the media, need to be mindful not to go overboard to the extent that the terrorist incident may be further jeopardized by any excessive cooperation. First amendment rights are not absolute, and specifically, "the right to speak and publish does not carry with it the unrestrained right to gather information."[7]

9   No hard rules can be prescribed to govern media performance during incidents of terror and extraordinary violence. However, whatever principles are adopted must be generated by the media themselves, out of a recognition of special public responsibility. In general, the essence of an appropriate approach to newsgathering is summarized in the principle of minimum intrusiveness. Representatives of the media should avoid creating any obvious media presence at an incident scene that is greater than that required to collect full, accurate, and balanced information on the actions of participants and the official response to them. Similarly, the essence of an appropriate approach to contemporaneous reporting of extraordinary violence lies in the principle of complete, noninflammatory coverage. The public is best served by reporting that omits no important detail and that attempts to place all details in context.

10   News media organizations and representatives wishing to adopt the principle of minimum intrusiveness in their gathering of news related to incidents of extraordinary violence should consider the following devices, among others:

1. Use of pool reporters to cover activities at incident scenes or within police lines;
2. Self-imposed limitations on the use of high-intensity television lighting, obtrusive camera equipment, and other special newsgathering techniques at incident scenes;

[6]Ibid. p. 61.
[7]Zemel v. Rusk, 381 US 1, 16–17 (1965).

3. Limitations on media solicitation of interviews with barricaded or hostage-holding suspects and other incident participants;

4. Primary reliance on officially designated spokesmen as sources of information concerning law enforcement operations and plans; and

5. Avoidance of inquiries designed to yield tactical information that would prejudice law enforcement operations if subsequently disclosed.

11   Also, news media organizations and representatives wishing to follow the principle of complete, noninflammatory coverage in contemporaneous reporting of incidents of extraordinary violence should consider the following:

1. Delayed reporting of details believed to have a potential for inflammation or aggravation of an incident that significantly outweighs their interest to the general public;

2. Delayed disclosure of information relating to incident location, when that information is not likely to become public knowledge otherwise and when the potential for incident growth or spread is obviously high;

3. Delayed disclosure of information concerning official tactical planning that, if known to incident participants, would seriously compromise law enforcement efforts;

4. Balancing of reports incorporating self-serving statements by incident participants with contrasting information from official sources and with data reflecting the risks that the incident has created to noninvolved persons;

5. Systematic predisclosure verification of all information concerning incident-related injuries, deaths, and property destruction; and

6. Avoidance, to the extent possible, of coverage that tends to emphasize the spectacular qualities of an incident or the presence of spectators at an incident scene.

12   The foregoing lists are really basic, commonsense, but more importantly, workable and palatable guidelines that the media and officials can use together on this issue.

13   It may well be unrealistic to expect competing elements of the news business to subscribe to detailed codes of responsibility or to adopt precisely formulated common guidelines for coverage. It is not unrealistic, however, to expect that a full exchange of views will demonstrate to the executive and staff of every news organization that their problems in the coverage of extraordinary violence are not unique ones and that solutions of general applicability do exist. From such a demonstration may grow the kind of informally cooperative scheme of self-regulation in which each news organization posits its own guidelines for coverage on the general expectation that their competitors are doing likewise.

14   These are not new concepts to the press. The admonition to exercise self-restraint was heard throughout the Vietnam war and during Watergate. If the

press had acquiesced to such appeals, the truth would have taken even longer to emerge, if at all. We do not want government intrusion into freedom of the press because that right is too important. At the same time, the right of a hostage to survive and the right of a society to self-preservation are also important rights, too important to be left to the media. That is the conflict that has brought the press, law enforcement, and the academic communities together in mutual distrust, admittedly, but in mutual concern that will help pave the road to reasonable accommodation, if not to resolution. We in military and civilian law enforcement can harness this concern and apply the basic techniques of cooperating with the media, with the end result that our agencies and communities would be served well.

FUTURE USE

Briefly summarize the essay.

What is the problem that Wilber wants to solve? What is the solution that he proposes? What are the alternatives?

How do you think his intended audience responded to his solution? What is your response to his solution?

Explain five significant passages from the selection.

Show how two passages from the selection are relevant to your essay(s).

Dianne Feinstein was the first woman mayor of San Francisco and was frequently mentioned as a vice presidential candidate for the Democrats in 1984. The following selection is from a speech she delivered in 1983 to the Leadership Conference for Democratic Women, which was sponsored by the Women's National Democratic Club.

From WOMEN IN POLITICS: TIME FOR A CHANGE
by Dianne Feinstein

1   . . . There is an incredulity and improbability that has surrounded women's rise to the top of the political ladder. I suggest to you that times and traditions have changed, and that women have changed, too.

2   I am delighted to be here today addressing women who have jumped into political life with both feet. Your program tells me you are setting new goals and articulating women's priorities for the next election year.

3   But what are women's issues? Many people consider women's issues to be those areas intrinsically related to women, their bodies, and their families—like abortion and school issues. The E.R.A. has been an interesting departure. The campaign for ratification and its subsequent setbacks presented women with the opportunity to become a major political force in the country.

4   In my view, the time has come for us to draw a broader agenda. The time has come for women to reach out and grapple with the major issues of our day.

5   I submit to you that it is time women realize they are not a minority. We are a majority—in virtually every state, every city in this country, and in this world. We are a majority of voters, too, Let us not forget that.

6   War and peace, the economy, the national defense, housing, and jobs are all our issues, issues we should join today—right now. Let us stop building fences around ourselves and the questions facing our society: the issues belong to all of us. Issues like mortgage revenue bonds, programs for the homeless, urban reconstruction banks, tax reform and indexing, health care, and other such programs should be as familiar to us as that simple twenty-four-word amendment to the Constitution.

7   There is good reason for our concern right now. Never in history have more people been made richer—or poorer—than during the current administration. Never since the Great Depression have we seen more people out of work. Even today, in the midst of a recovery, we have almost 10 million Americans without jobs. Even on Jimmy Carter's old "misery index," the American people are no better off than they were four years ago. As a matter of fact, many millions are far worse off.

Reprinted with permission of the author.

8   It is time for women to speak out on the economy—because it is our pocket-books that are vitally affected every day. Half this nation's work force is women, and we are also half the unemployed.

9   It is time we women took up the issue of a balanced budget, social security reform, and the question of "defense versus the cities," which this administration has "lurched" us into.

10   It is time for women to take a strong stand on the nuclear question—to support a bilateral nuclear freeze–just as we stood strong against Vietnam. Who loses more in war than we women? Whose children, husbands, and sweethearts die? Who are condemned to the agony of uncertainty by that three-letter label, MIA, so familiar now to us all?

11   It is time for women to speak out for our cities. Seventy percent of Americans live and work in cities, and the cities and their people are hurting—oh, how they are hurting: soup kitchens blossoming, health centers closing, and hopes fading.

12   It is time for women to join the environmental movement in a major way, to see to it, once and for all, that toxic wastes do not inundate our neighborhoods, that our children and their children can breathe clean air and drink unpolluted water. This country's battle to protect the environment has suffered mightily in the last three years.

13   It is time for women to demand social justice for all minorities—for blacks, Hispanics, Asian-Americans, and all Americans. We have fought for our own rights. We know the problem.

14   In short, women of America must proclaim an agenda of conscience. It is our time to act, and we should do so boldly and with confidence. . . .

FUTURE USE

Briefly summarize the selection.

What is the problem that Mayor Feinstein wants to solve? What is the solution that she proposes? What are the alternatives?

How do you think her audience responded to her solution? What is your response to her solution?

Explain five significant passages from the selection.

Show how two passages from the selection are relevant to your essay(s).

In 1896 Emilio Aguinaldo led a revolt against Spanish control of the Philippines. After the battleship Maine was blown up in Manila harbor in February 1898, the United States went to war against Spain and took possession of the islands under a treaty in 1899. But Aguinaldo and his followers declared the Philippines independent and continued their insurrection, now against the United States. The war was bitterly debated in Congress and the American press. In 1900, Sen. Albert J. Beveridge introduced this resolution:

> Be it resolved by the Senate and House of Representatives of America in Congress assembled, That the Philippine Islands are territory belonging to the United States; that it is the intention of the United States to retain them as such and to establish and maintain such governmental control throughout the archipelago as the situation may demand.

After the president pro tempore had the resolution read, Senator Beveridge spoke at length in support of it.

IN SUPPORT OF THE RESOLUTION ON THE PHILIPPINES
by Albert J. Beveridge

1   . . . Mr. President, the times call for candor. The Philippines are ours forever, "territory belonging to the United States," as the Constitution calls them. And just beyond the Philippines are China's illimitable markets. We will not retreat from either. We will not repudiate our duty in the archipelago. We will not abandon our opportunity in the Orient. We will not renounce our part in the mission of our race, trustee, under God, of the civilization of the world. And we will move forward to our work, not howling out regrets like slaves whipped to their burdens, but with gratitude for a task worthy of our strength, and thanksgiving to Almighty God that He has marked us as His chosen people, henceforth to lead in the regeneration of the world.

2   This island empire is the last land left in all the oceans. If it should prove a mistake to abandon it, the blunder once made would be irretrievable. If it proves a mistake to hold it, the error can be corrected when we will. Every other progressive nation stands ready to relieve us.

3   But to hold it will be no mistake. Our largest trade henceforth must be with Asia. The Pacific is our ocean. More and more Europe will manufacture the most it needs, secure from its colonies the most it consumes. Where shall we turn for consumers of our surplus? Geography answers the question. China is our natural customer. She is nearer to us than to England, Germany, or Russia, the commercial powers of the present and the future. They have moved nearer to China by securing permanent bases at her borders. The Philippines give us a base at the door of all the East.

4   Lines of navigation from our ports to the Orient and Australia; from the Isthmian Canal to Asia; from all Oriental ports to Australia, converge at and separate from the Philippines. They are a self-supporting, dividend-paying fleet, permanently anchored at a spot selected by the strategy of Providence, commanding the Pacific. And the Pacific is the ocean of the commerce of the future. Most future wars will be conflicts for commerce. The power that rules the Pacific, therefore, is the power that rules the world. And, with the Philippines, that power is and will forever be the American Republic. . . .

5   . . . Mr. President, reluctantly and only from a sense of duty am I forced to say that American opposition to the war has been the chief factor in prolonging it. Had Aguinaldo not understood that in America, even in the American Congress, even here in the Senate, he and his cause were supported; had he not known that it was proclaimed on the stump and in the press of a faction in the United States that every shot his misguided followers fired into the breasts of American soldiers was like the volleys fired by Washington's men against the soldiers of King George, his insurrection would have dissolved before it entirely crystallized.

6   The utterances of American opponents of the war are read to the ignorant soldiers of Aguinaldo and repeated in exaggerated form among the common people. Attempts have been made by wretches claiming American citizenship to ship arms and ammunition from Asiatic ports to the Filipinos, and these acts of infamy were coupled by the Malays with American assaults on our Government at home. The Filipinos do not understand free speech, and therefore our tolerance of American assaults on the American President and the American Government means to them that our President is in the minority or he would not permit what appears to them such treasonable criticism. It is believed and stated in Luzon, Panay, and Cebu that the Filipinos have only to fight, harass, retreat, break up into small parties, if necessary, as they are doing now, but by any means hold out until the next Presidential election, and our forces will be withdrawn.

7   All this has aided the enemy more than climate, arms, and battle. Senators, I have heard these reports myself; I have talked with the people; I have seen our mangled boys in the hospital and field; I have stood on the firing line and beheld our dead soldiers, their faces turned to the pitiless southern sky, and in sorrow rather than anger I say to those whose voices in America have cheered those misguided natives on to shoot our soldiers down, that the blood of those dead and wounded boys of ours is on their hands, and the flood of all the years can never wash that stain away. In sorrow rather than anger I say these words, for I earnestly believe that our brothers knew not what they did.

8   But, Senators, it would be better to abandon this combined garden and Gibraltar of the Pacific, and count our blood and treasure already spent a profitable loss, than to apply any academic arrangement of self-government to these children. They are not capable of self-government. How could they be? They are not of a self-governing race. They are Orientals, Malays, instructed by Spaniards in the latter's worst estate.

9   They know nothing of practical government except as they have witnessed the weak, corrupt, cruel, and capricious rule of Spain. What magic will anyone employ to dissolve in their minds and characters those impressions of governors and governed which three centuries of misrule has created? What alchemy will change the oriental quality of their blood and set the self-governing currents of the American pouring through the Malay veins? How shall they, in the twinkling of an eye, be exalted to the heights of self-governing peoples which required a thousand years for us to reach, Anglo-Saxon though we are?

10   Let men beware how they employ the term "self-government." It is a sacred term. It is the watchword at the door of the inner temple of liberty, for liberty does not always mean self-government. Self-government is a method of liberty—the highest, simplest, best—and it is acquired only after centuries of study and struggle and experiment and instruction and all the elements of the progress of man. Self-government is no base and common thing, to be bestowed on the merely audacious. It is the degree which crowns the graduate of liberty, not the name of liberty's infant class, who have not yet mastered the alphabet of freedom. Savage blood, oriental blood, Malay blood, Spanish example—are these the elements of self-government?

11   We must act on the situation as it exists, not as we would wish it. . . .

FUTURE USE

Briefly summarize the selection.

What is the problem that Senator Beveridge wants to solve? What is the solution that he proposes? What are the alternatives?

How do you think his audience responded to his solution? What is your response to his solution?

Explain five significant passages from the selection.

Show how two passages from the selection are relevant to your essay(s).

Pres. Jimmy Carter tried to make human rights a central element of American foreign policy. In the course of a speech commemorating the thirtieth anniversary of the Universal Declaration of Human Rights, in 1978, he called upon Congress to live up to America's historic ideals.

From UNIVERSAL DECLARATION OF HUMAN RIGHTS
by Jimmy Carter

1 . . . In the coming year, I hope that Congress will take a step that has been long overdue for a generation, the ratification of the Convention on the Prevention and Punishment of the Crime of Genocide. As you know, the genocide convention was also adopted by the United Nations General Assembly 30 years ago this week, one day before the adoption of the Universal Declaration. It was the world's affirmation that the lesson of the Holocaust would never be forgotten, but unhappily, genocide is not peculiar to any one historical era.

2 Eighty-three other nations have ratified the genocide convention. The United States, despite the support of every President since 1948, has not. In international meetings at the United Nations and elsewhere, when I meet with foreign leaders, we are often asked why. We do not have an acceptable answer.

3 I urge the United States Senate to observe this anniversary in the only appropriate way, by ratifying the genocide convention at the earliest possible date.

4 This action must be the first step toward the ratification of other human rights instruments, including those I signed a year ago. Many of the religious and human rights groups represented here have undertaken a campaign of public education on behalf of these covenants. I commend and appreciate your efforts.

5 Refugees are the living, homeless casualties of one very important failure on the part of the world to live by the principles of peace and human rights. To help these refugees is a simple human duty. As Americans, as a people made up largely of the descendants of refugees, we feel that duty with special keenness.

6 Our country will do its utmost to ease the plight of stranded refugees from Indochina and from Lebanon and of released political prisoners from Cuba and from elsewhere. I hope that we will always stand ready to welcome more than our fair share of those who flee their homelands because of racial, religious, or political oppression.

7 The effectiveness of our human rights policy is now an established fact. It has contributed to an atmosphere of change—sometimes disturbing—but which has encouraged progress in many ways and in many places. In some countries, political prisoners have been released by the hundreds, even thousands. In others, the brutality of repression has been lessened. In still others there's a

movement toward democratic institutions or the rule of law when these movements were not previously detectable.

8   To those who doubt the wisdom of our dedication, I say this: Ask the victims. Ask the exiles. Ask the governments which continue to practice repression. Whether in Cambodia or Chile, in Uganda or South Africa, in Nicaragua or Ethiopia or the Soviet Union, governments know that we in the United States care. And not a single one of those who is actually taking risks or suffering for human rights has ever asked me to desist in our support of basic human rights. From the prisons, from the camps, from the enforced exiles, we receive one message: Speak up, persevere, let the voice of freedom be heard.

9   I'm very proud that our nation stands for more than military might or political might. It stands for ideals that have their reflection in the aspirations of peasants in Latin America, workers in Eastern Europe, students in Africa, and farmers in Asia.

10   We do live in a difficult and complicated world, a world in which peace is literally a matter of survival. Our foreign policy must take this into account. Often, a choice that moves us toward one goal tends to move us further away from another goal. Seldom do circumstances permit me or you to take actions that are wholly satisfactory to everyone.

11   But I want to stress again that human rights are not peripheral to the foreign policy of the United States. Our human rights policy is not a decoration. It is not something we've adopted to polish up our image abroad or to put a fresh coat of moral paint on the discredited policies of the past. Our pursuit of human rights is part of a broad effort to use our great power and our tremendous influence in the service of creating a better world, a world in which human beings can live in peace, in freedom, and with their basic needs adequately met.

12   Human rights is the soul of our foreign policy. And I say this with assurance, because human rights is the soul of our sense of nationhood.

13   For the most part, other nations are held together by common racial or ethnic ancestry, or by a common creed or religion, or by ancient attachments to the land that go back for centuries of time. Some nations are held together by the forces, implied forces of a tyrannical government. We are different from all of those, and I believe that we in our country are more fortunate.

14   As a people we come from every country and every corner of the earth. We are of many religions and many creeds. We are of every race, every color, every ethnic and cultural background. We are right to be proud of these things and of the richness that lend to the texture of our national life. But they are not the things which unite us as a single people.

15   What unites us—what makes us Americans—is a common belief in peace, in a free society, and a common devotion to the liberties enshrined in our Constitution. That belief and that devotion are the sources of our sense of national community. Uniquely, ours is a nation founded on an idea of human rights. From our own history we know how powerful that idea can be. . . .

FUTURE USE

Briefly summarize the selection.

What is the problem that President Carter wants to solve?

What is the solution that he proposes? What are the alternatives?

How do you think his audience responded to his suggestion? What is your response to his suggestion?

Explain five significant passages from the selection.

Show how two passages from the selection are relevant to your essay(s).

· MAKING CONNECTIONS

1. How does Lt. Col. Harold Wilber (p. 363) think the media should behave in a crisis? Who determines what a crisis is and when one exists? What is the significance of his reference to Vietnam and Watergate in the last paragraph? Do these examples support or weaken his case? What does he think results from competition among news organizations? Do you agree? Is the result of this competition good or bad? What essay topic(s) can emerge from this discussion?

2. Why does Wilber think he has the right to tell the media how to behave? What would a media executive say about the behavior of the military (or FBI) during a crisis? What is the role of the military in a democracy? What do you think Senator Beveridge (p. 253) would have said? What do you think former-President Carter (p. 373) would say? What, if anything, are purely military matters? What is the role of the media in relation to the military? What essay topic(s) can emerge from this discussion?

3. What assumptions does Wilber make about the values and opinions of his audience? How can you determine whether he believes that the audience shares his feelings about the privileges and abuses of the media? Compare and contrast his relationship to the audience to the relationship established by Edgington in "Classism, Sexism, Racism . . ." (p. 129), or by the author of "A Short History of American Labor" (p. 185). What essay topic(s) can emerge from this discussion?

4. Why does Mayor Dianne Feinstein (p. 368) believe that women should care about such issues as the economy, nuclear arms, and the environment? What does her reasoning imply about the concerns of women? How are these concerns reflected in stereotypes of women? Does she accept these stereotypes or reject them? Do you think she would accept or deny the reality of women like those described in "Classism, Sexism, Racism . . ." (p. 129)? What is the relationship, if any, of stereotypes to reality? What essay topic(s) can emerge from this discussion?

5. How does Feinstein get from women's issues to her proposal at the end that

women should champion the cause of all minorities? What do you think about the logic of her case? What values does she assume her audience shares with her? Do you share these values? How are these values related to the prevailing values of society? How, if at all, are these values presented on television, in the movies, and in popular music? What essay topic(s) can emerge from this discussion?

6. What values does Senator Beveridge rely on to support his resolution (p. 253)? Where do you think these values came from? Were they the prevailing values of his day? What is the status of these values today? How are these values similar to or different from those of President Carter (p. 373)? Turner (p. 73)? Carnegie (p. 180)? Crèvecoeur (p. 188)? President Reagan (p. 329, number 12)? What essay topic(s) can emerge from this discussion?

7. If a character in a movie today gave Beveridge's speech (p. 253), how would you know whether to take it at face value or as satire? Which movies (or television shows) and which actors would portray these sentiments sympathetically? Which movies (or television shows) and which actors would make fun of these sentiments? What does this tell you about irony and satire? What does it tell you about the entertainment media? What essay topic(s) can emerge from this discussion?

8. What does President Carter (p. 373) believe unites Americans into a nation? Do you agree? Is a commitment to human rights really the "soul of our foreign policy," as he says, or is it merely "something we've adopted to polish up our image"? Why do refugees want to enter the United States and not, for example, the Soviet Union? Should we "stand ready to welcome . . . those who flee their homelands because of . . . oppression"? What essay topic(s) can emerge from this discussion?

9. Why does Jonathan Swift (p. 351) say that an American recommended eating babies? What did America represent to Swift's audience? What does America represent to Europe today? What do you think of the alternative solutions that Swift rejects? What relevance does this essay have today? What essay topic(s) can emerge from this discussion?

· ADDITIONAL ESSAYS FOR DISCUSSION

From *UNCLE TOM'S CABIN*
by Harriet Beecher Stowe (1851–52)

1   The author hopes she has done justice to that nobility, generosity, and humanity, which in many cases characterize individuals at the south. Such instances save us from utter despair of our kind. But, she asks any person who knows the world, are such characters *common*, anywhere?

2   For many years of her life, the author avoided all reading upon or allusion to the subject of slavery, considering it as too painful to be inquired into, and one which advancing light and civilization would certainly live down. But, since the legislative act of 1850, when she heard, with perfect surprise and consternation, Christian and humane people actually recommending the remanding escaped fugitives into slavery, as a duty binding on good citizens,—when she heard, on all hands, from kind, compassionate, and estimable people, in the free states of the north, deliberations and discussions as to what Christian duty could be on this head,—she could only think, These men and Christians cannot know what slavery is; if they did, such a question could never be open for discussion. And from this arose a desire to exhibit it in a *living dramatic reality*. She has endeavored to show it fairly, in its best and its worst phases. In its *best* aspect, she has, perhaps, been successful; but, oh! who shall say what yet remains untold in that valley and shadow of death that lies the other side?

3   To you, generous, noble-minded men and women, of the south,—you, whose virtue, and magnanimity, and purity of character, are the greater for the severer trial it has encountered,—to you is her appeal. Have you not, in your own secret souls, in your own private conversings, felt that there are woes and evils, in this accursed system, far beyond what are here shadowed, or can be shadowed? Can it be otherwise? Is *man* ever a creature to be trusted with wholly irresponsible power? And does not the slave system, by denying the slave all legal right of testimony, make every individual owner an irresponsible despot? Can anybody fail to make the inference what the practical result will be? If there is, as we admit, a public sentiment among you, men of honor, justice, and humanity, is there not also another kind of public sentiment among the ruffian, the brutal, and debased? And cannot the ruffian, the brutal, the debased, by slave law, own just as many slaves as the best and purest? Are the honorable, the just, the high-minded and compassionate, the majority anywhere in this world?

4   The slave-trade is now, by American law, considered as piracy. But a slave-trade, as systematic as ever was carried on on the coast of Africa, is an inevitable attendant and result of American slavery. And its heart-break and its horrors, *can* they be told?

5   The writer has given only a faint shadow, a dim picture, of the anguish and despair that are, at this very moment, riving thousands of hearts, shattering thousands of families, and driving a helpless and sensitive race to frenzy and despair. There are those living who know the mothers whom this accursed traffic has driven to the murder of their children; and themselves seeking in death a shelter from woes more dreaded than death. Nothing of tragedy can be written, can be spoken, can be conceived, that equals the frightful reality of scenes daily and hourly on our shores, beneath the shadow of American law, and the shadow of the cross of Christ.

6   And now, men and women of America, is this a thing to be trifled with, apologized for, and passed over in silence? Farmers of Massachusetts, of New Hampshire, of Vermont, of Connecticut, who read this book by the blaze of your winter-evening fire,—strong-hearted, generous sailors and ship-owners of Maine,—is this a thing for you to countenance and encourage? Brave and generous men of New York, farmers of rich and joyous Ohio, and ye of the wide prairie states,—answer, is this a thing for you to protect and countenance? And you, mothers of America,—you, who have learned, by the cradles of your own children, to love and feel for all mankind,—by the sacred love you bear your child; by your joy in his beautiful, spotless infancy; by the motherly pity and tenderness with which you guide his growing years; by the anxieties of his education; by the prayers you breathe for his soul's eternal good;—I beseech you, pity the mother who has all your affections, and not one legal right to protect, guide, or educate the child of her bosom! By the sick hour of your child; by those dying eyes, which you can never forget; by those last cries, that wrung your heart when you could neither help nor save; by the desolation of that empty cradle, that silent nursery,—I beseech you, pity those mothers that are constantly made childless by the American slave-trade! And say, mothers of America, is this a thing to be defended, sympathized with, passed over in silence?

7   Do you say that the people of the free states have nothing to do with it, and can do nothing? Would to God this were true! But it is not true. The people of the free states have defended, encouraged, and participated; and are more guilty for it, before God, than the south, in that they have *not* the apology or education of custom.

8   If the mothers of the free states had all felt as they should, in times past, the sons of the free states would not have been the holders, and, proverbially, the hardest masters of slaves; the sons of the free states would not have connived at the extension of slavery, in our national body; the sons of the free states would not, as they do, trade the souls and bodies of men as an equivalent to money, in their mercantile dealings. There are multitudes of slaves temporarily owned, and sold again, by merchants in northern cities; and shall the whole guilt or obloquy of slavery fall only on the south?

9   Northern men, northern mothers, northern Christians, have something more to do than denounce their brethren at the south; they have to look to the evil among themselves.

10   But, what can any individual do? Of that, every individual can judge. There is one thing that every individual can do,—they can see to it that *they feel right.* An atmosphere of sympathetic influence encircles every human being; and the man or woman who *feels* strongly, healthily, and justly on the great interests of humanity, is a constant benefactor to the human race. See, then, to your sympathies in this matter! Are they in harmony with the sympathies of Christ? or are they swayed and perverted by the sophistries of worldly policy?

11   Christian men and women of the north! still further,—you have another power; you can *pray!* Do you believe in prayer? or has it become an indistinct apostolic tradition? You pray for the heathen abroad; pray also for the heathen at home. And pray for those distressed Christians whose whole chance of religious improvement is an accident of trade and sale; from whom any adherence to the morals of Christianity is, in many cases, an impossibility, unless they have given them, from above, the courage and grace of martyrdom.

12   But, still more. On the shores of our free states are emerging the poor, shattered, broken remnants of families,—men and women, escaped, by miraculous providences, from the surges of slavery,—feeble in knowledge, and, in many cases, infirm in moral constitution, from a system which confounds and confuses every principle of Christianity and morality. They come to seek a refuge among you; they come to seek education, knowledge, Christianity.

13   What do you owe to these poor unfortunates, O Christians? Does not every American Christian owe to the African race some effort at reparation for the wrongs that the American nation has brought upon them? Shall the doors of churches and school-houses be shut upon them? Shall states arise and shake them out? Shall the Church of Christ hear in silence the taunt that is thrown at them, and shrink away from the helpless hand that they stretch out; and, by her silence, encourage the cruelty that would chase them from our borders? If it must be so, it will be a mournful spectacle. If it must be so, the country will have reason to tremble, when it remembers that the fate of nations is in the hands of One who is very pitiful, and of tender compassion.

14   Do you say, "We don't want them here; let them go to Africa?"

15   That the providence of God has provided a refuge in Africa, is, indeed, a great and noticeable fact; but that is no reason why the Church of Christ should throw off that responsibility to this outcast race which her profession demands of her.

16   To fill up Liberia with an ignorant, inexperienced, half-barbarized race, just escaped from the chains of slavery, would be only to prolong, for ages, the period of struggle and conflict which attends the inception of new enterprises. Let the Church of the north receive these poor sufferers in the spirit of Christ; receive them to the educating advantages of Christian republican society and schools, until they have attained to somewhat of a moral and intellectual maturity, and then assist them in their passage to those shores, where they may put in practice the lessons they have learned in America.

17   There is a body of men at the north, comparatively small, who have been doing this; and, as the result, this country has already seen examples of men,

formerly slaves, who have rapidly acquired property, reputation, and education. Talent has been developed, which, considering the circumstances, is certainly remarkable; and, for moral traits of honesty, kindness, tenderness of feeling,— for heroic efforts and self-denials, endured for the ransom of brethren and friends yet in slavery,—they have been remarkable to a degree that, considering the influence under which they were born, is surprising.

18   The writer has lived, for many years, on the frontier-line of slave states, and has had great opportunities of observation among those who formerly were slaves. They have been in her family as servants; and, in default of any other school to receive them, she has, in many cases, had them instructed in a family school, with her own children. She has also the testimony of missionaries, among the fugitives in Canada, in coincidence with her own experience; and her deductions, with regard to the capabilities of the race, are encouraging in the highest degree. . . .

19   This is an age of the world when nations are trembling and convulsed. A mighty influence is abroad, surging and heaving the world, as with an earthquake. And is America safe? Every nation that carries in its bosom great and unredressed injustice has in it the elements of this last convulsion.

20   For what is this mighty influence thus rousing in all nations and languages those groanings that cannot be uttered, for man's freedom and equality?

21   O Church of Christ, read the signs of the times! Is not this power the spirit of HIM whose kingdom is yet to come, and whose will to be done on earth as it is in heaven?

22   But who may abide the day of his appearing? "For that day shall burn as an oven: and he shall appear as a swift witness against those that oppress the hireling in his wages, the widow and the fatherless, and that *turn aside the stranger in his right:* and he shall break in pieces the oppressor."

23   Are not these dread words for a nation bearing in her bosom so mighty an injustice? Christians! every time that you pray that the kingdom of Christ may come, can you forget that prophecy associates in dread fellowship, the *day of vengeance* with the year of his redeemed?

24   A day of grace is yet held out to us. Both North and South have been guilty before God; and the *Christian Church* has a heavy account to answer. Not by combining together, to protect injustice and cruelty, and making a common capital of sin, is this Union to be saved,—but by repentance, justice and mercy; for, not surer is the eternal law by which the millstone sinks in the ocean, than that stronger law by which injustice and cruelty shall bring on nations the wrath of Almighty God!

From CIVIL DISOBEDIENCE
by Henry David Thoreau (1849)

1   I heartily accept the motto,—"That government is best which governs least;" and I should like to see it acted up to more rapidly and systematically. Carried out, it finally amounts to this, which also I believe,—"That government is best which governs not at all;" and when men are prepared for it, that will be the kind of government which they will have. Government is at best but an expedient; but most governments are usually, and all governments are sometimes, inexpedient. The objections which have been brought against a standing army, and they are many and weighty, and deserve to prevail, may also at last be brought against a standing government. The standing army is only an arm of the standing government. The government itself, which is only the mode which the people have chosen to execute their will, is equally liable to be abused and perverted before the people can act through it. Witness the present Mexican war, the work of comparatively a few individuals using the standing government as their tool; for, in the outset, the people would not have consented to this measure.

2   This American government,—what is it but a tradition, though a recent one, endeavoring to transmit itself unimpaired to posterity, but each instant losing some of its integrity? It has not the vitality and force of a single living man; for a single man can bend it to his will. It is a sort of wooden gun to the people themselves. But it is not the less necessary for this; for the people must have some complicated machinery or other, and hear its din, to satisfy that idea of government which they have. Governments show thus how successfully men can be imposed on, even impose on themselves, for their own advantage. It is excellent, we must all allow. Yet this government never of itself furthered any enterprise, but by the alacrity with which it got out of its way. *It* does not keep the country free. *It* does not settle the West. *It* does not educate. The character inherent in the American people has done all that has been accomplished; and it would have done somewhat more, if the government had not sometimes got in its way. For government is an expedient by which men would fain succeed in letting one another alone; and, as has been said, when it is most expedient, the governed are most let alone by it. Trade and commerce, if they were not made of India-rubber, would never manage to bounce over the obstacles which legislators are continually putting in their way; and, if one were to judge these men wholly by the effects of their actions and not partly by their intentions, they would deserve to be classed and punished with those mischievous persons who put obstructions on the railroads.

3   But, to speak practically and as a citizen, unlike those who call themselves no-government men, I ask for, not at once no government, but *at once* a better government. Let every man make known what kind of government would command his respect, and that will be one step toward obtaining it.

4   After all, the practical reason why, when the power is once in the hands of the people, a majority are permitted, and for a long period continue, to rule is not because they are most likely to be in the right, nor because this seems fairest to the minority, but because they are physically the strongest. But a government in which the majority rule in all cases cannot be based on justice, even as far as men understand it. Can there not be a government in which majorities do not virtually decide right and wrong, but conscience?—in which majorities decide only those questions to which the rule of expediency is applicable? Must the citizen ever for a moment, or in the least degree, resign his conscience to the legislator? Why has every man a conscience, then? I think that we should be men first, and subjects afterward. It is not desirable to cultivate a respect for the law, so much as for the right. The only obligation which I have a right to assume is to do at any time what I think right. . . .

5   How does it become a man to behave toward this American government to-day? I answer, that he cannot without disgrace be associated with it. I cannot for an instant recognize that political organization as *my* government which is the *slave's* government also.

6   All men recognize the right of revolution; that is, the right to refuse allegiance to, and to resist, the government, when its tyranny or its inefficiency are great and unendurable. But almost all say that such is not the case now. But such was the case, they think, in the Revolution of '75. If one were to tell me that this was a bad government because it taxed certain foreign commodities brought to its ports, it is most probable that I should not make an ado about it, for I can do without them. All machines have their friction; and possibly this does enough good to counterbalance the evil. At any rate, it is a great evil to make a stir about it. But when the friction comes to have its machine, and oppression and robbery are organized, I say, let us not have such a machine any longer. In other words, when a sixth of the population of a nation which has undertaken to be the refuge of liberty are slaves, and a whole country is unjustly overrun and conquered by a foreign army, and subjected to military law, I think that it is not too soon for honest men to rebel and revolutionize. What makes this duty the more urgent is that fact that the country so overrun is not our own, but ours is the invading army. . . .

7   Practically speaking, the opponents to a reform in Massachusetts are not a hundred thousand politicians at the South, but a hundred thousand merchants and farmers here, who are more interested in commerce and agriculture than they are in humanity, and are not prepared to do justice to the slave and to Mexico, *cost what it may.* I quarrel not with far-off foes, but with those who, near at home, coöperate with, and do the bidding of, those far away, and without whom the latter would be harmless. We are accustomed to say, that the mass of men are unprepared; but improvement is slow, because the few are not materially wiser or better than the many. It is not so important that many should be as good as you, as that there be some absolute goodness somewhere; for that will leaven

the whole lump. There are thousands who are *in opinion* opposed to slavery and to the war, who yet in effect do nothing to put an end to them; who, esteeming themselves children of Washington and Franklin, sit down with their hands in their pockets, and say that they know not what to do, and do nothing; who even postpone the question of freedom to the question of free-trade, and quietly read the prices-current along with the latest advices from Mexico, after dinner, and, it may be, fall asleep over them both. What is the price-current of an honest man and patriot to-day? They hesitate, and they regret, and sometimes they petition; but they do nothing in earnest and with effect. They will wait, well disposed, for others to remedy the evil, that they may no longer have it to regret. At most, they give only a cheap vote, and a feeble countenance and God-speed, to the right, as it goes by them. There are nine hundred and ninety-nine patrons of virtue to one virtuous man. But it is easier to deal with the real possessor of a thing than with the temporary guardian of it.

8   All voting is a sort of gaming, like checkers or backgammon, with a slight moral tinge to it, a playing with right and wrong, with moral questions; and betting naturally accompanies it. The character of the voters is not staked. I cast my vote, perchance, as I think right; but I am not vitally concerned that that right should prevail. I am willing to leave it to the majority. Its obligation, therefore, never exceeds that of expediency. Even voting *for the right* is *doing* nothing for it. It is only expressing to men feebly your desire that it should prevail. A wise man will not leave the right to the mercy of chance, nor wish it to prevail through the power of the majority. There is but little virtue in the action of masses of men. When the majority shall at length vote for the abolition of slavery, it will be because they are indifferent to slavery, or because there is but little slavery left to be abolished by their vote. *They* will then be the only slaves. Only *his* vote can hasten the abolition of slavery who asserts his own freedom by his vote. . . .

9   I do not hesitate to say, that those who call themselves Abolitionists should at once effectually withdraw their support, both in person and property, from the government of Massachusetts and not wait till they constitute a majority of one, before they suffer the right to prevail through them. I think that it is enough if they have God on their side, without waiting for that other one. Moreover, any man more right than his neighbors constitutes a majority of one already.

10   I meet this American government, or its representative, the state government, directly, and face to face, once a year—no more—in the person of its tax-gatherer; this is the only mode in which a man situated as I am necessarily meets it; and it then says distinctly, Recognize me; and the simplest, most effectual, and, in the present posture of affairs, the indispensablest mode of treating with it on this head, of expressing your little satisfaction with and love for it, is to deny it then. My civil neighbor, the tax-gatherer, is the very man I have to deal with,—for it is, after all, with men and not with parchment that I quarrel,—and he has voluntarily chosen to be an agent of the government. How shall he

ever know well what he is and does as an officer of the government, or as a man, until he is obliged to consider whether he shall treat me, his neighbor, for whom he has respect, as a neighbor and well-disposed man, or as a maniac and disturber of the peace, and see if he can get over this obstruction to his neighborliness without a ruder and more impetuous thought or speech corresponding with his action. I know this well, that if one thousand, if one hundred, if ten men whom I could name,—if ten *honest* men only,—ay, if *one* HONEST man, in this State of Massachusetts, *ceasing to hold slaves*, were actually to withdraw from this copartnership, and be locked up in the county jail therefor, it would be the abolition of slavery in America. For it matters not how small the beginning may seem to be: what is once well done is done forever. But we love better to talk about it: that we say is our mission. Reform keeps many scores of newspapers in its service, but not one man. If my esteemed neighbor, the State's ambassador, who will devote his days to the settlement of the question of human rights in the Council Chamber, instead of being threatened with the prisons of Carolina, were to sit down the prisoner of Massachusetts, that State which is so anxious to foist the sin of slavery upon her sister,—though at present she can discover only an act of inhospitality to be the ground of a quarrel with her,—the Legislature would not wholly waive the subject the following winter.

11   Under a government which imprisons any unjustly, the true place for a just man is also a prison. The proper place to-day, the only place which Massachusetts has provided for her freer and less desponding spirits, is in her prisons, to be put out and locked out of the State by her own act, as they have already put themselves out by their principles. It is there that the fugitive slave, and the Mexican prisoner on parole, and the Indian come to plead the wrongs of his race should find them; on that separate, but more free and honorable ground, where the State places those who are not *with* her, but *against* her,—the only house in a slave State in which a free man can abide with honor. If any think that their influence would be lost there, and their voices no longer afflict the ear of the State, that they would not be as an enemy within its walls, they do not know by how much truth is stronger than error, nor how much more eloquently and effectively he can combat injustice who has experienced a little in his own person. Cast your whole vote, not a strip of paper merely, but your whole influence. A minority is powerless while it conforms to the majority; it is not even a minority then; but it is irresistible when it clogs by its whole weight. If the alternative is to keep all just men in prison, or give up war and slavery, the State will not hesitate which to choose. If a thousand men were not to pay their tax-bills this year, that would not be a violent and bloody measure, as it would be to pay them, and enable the State to commit violence and shed innocent blood. This is, in fact, the definition of a peaceable revolution, if any such is possible. . . .

From *THE SHAME OF THE CITIES*
By Lincoln Steffens (1904)

1   This is not a book. It is a collection of articles reprinted from *McClure's Magazine*. . . . They were written with a purpose, they were published serially with a purpose, and they are reprinted now together to further that same purpose, which was and is—to sound for the civic pride of an apparently shameless citizenship. . . .

2   When I set out on my travels, an honest New Yorker told me honestly that I would find that the Irish, the Catholic Irish, were at the bottom of it all everywhere. The first city I went to was St. Louis, a German city. The next was Minneapolis, a Scandinavian city, with a leadership of New Englanders. Then came Pittsburg, Scotch Presbyterian, and that was what my New York friend was. "Ah, but they are all foreign populations," I heard. The next city was Philadelphia, the purest American community of all, and the most hopeless. And after that came Chicago and New York, both mongrel-bred, but the one a triumph of reform, the other the best example of good government that I had seen. The "foreign element" excuse is one of the hypocritical lies that save us from the clear sight of ourselves.

3   Another such conceit of our egotism is that which deplores our politics and lauds our business. This is the wail of the typical American citizen. Now, the typical American citizen is the business man. The typical business man is a bad citizen; he is busy. If he is a "big business man" and very busy, he does not neglect, he is busy with politics, oh, very busy and very businesslike. I found him buying boodlers in St. Louis, defending grafters in Minneapolis, originating corruption in Pittsburg, sharing with bosses in Philadelphia, deploring reform in Chicago, and beating good government with corruption funds in New York. He is a self-righteous fraud, this big business man. He is the chief source of corruption, and it were a boon if he would neglect politics. But he is not the business man that neglects politics; that worthy is the good citizen, the typical business man. He too is busy, he is the one that has no use and therefore no time for politics. When his neglect has permitted bad government to go so far that he can be stirred to action, he is unhappy, and he looks around for a cure that shall be quick, so that he may hurry back to the shop. Naturally, too, when he talks politics, he talks shop. His patent remedy is quack; it is business.

4   "Give us a business man," he says ("like me," he means). "Let him introduce business methods into politics and government; then I shall be left alone to attend to my business."

5   There is hardly an office from United States Senator down to Alderman in any part of the country to which the business man has not been elected; yet politics remains corrupt, government pretty bad, and the selfish citizen has to hold himself in readiness like the old volunteer firemen to rush forth at any

hour, in any weather, to prevent the fire; and he goes out sometimes and he puts out the fire (after the damage is done) and he goes back to the shop sighing for the business man in politics. The business man has failed in politics as he has in citizenship. Why?

6   Because politics is business. That's what's the matter with it. That's what's the matter with everything,—art, literature, religion, journalism, law, medicine,—they're all business, and all—as you see them. Make politics a sport, as they do in England, or a profession, as they do in Germany, and we'll have—well, something else than we have now,—if we want it, which is another question. But don't try to reform politics with the banker, the lawyer, and the dry-goods merchant, for these are business men and there are two great hindrances to their achievement of reform: one is that they are different from, but no better than, the politicians; the other is that politics is not "their line." There are exceptions both ways. Many politicians have gone out into business and done well (Tammany ex-mayors, and nearly all the old bosses of Philadelphia are prominent financiers in their cities), and business men have gone into politics and done well (Mark Hanna, for example). They haven't reformed their adopted trades, however, though they have sometimes sharpened them most pointedly. The politician is a business man with a specialty. When a business man of some other line learns the business of politics, he is a politician, and there is not much reform left in him. Consider the United States Senate, and believe me.

7   The commercial spirit is the spirit of profit, not patriotism; of credit, not honor; of individual gain, not national prosperity; of trade and dickering, not principle. "My business is sacred," says the business man in his heart. "Whatever hinders it, is wrong; it must be. A bribe is bad, that is, it is a bad thing to take; but it is not so bad to give one, not if it is necessary to my business." "Business is business" is not a political sentiment, but our politician has caught it. He takes essentially the same view of the bribe, only he saves his self-respect by piling all his contempt upon the bribe-giver, and he has the great advantage of candor. "It is wrong, maybe," he says, "but if a rich merchant can afford to do business with me for the sake of a convenience or to increase his already great wealth, I can afford, for the sake of a living, to meet him half way. I make no pretensions to virtue, not even on Sunday." And as for giving bad government or good, how about the merchant who gives bad goods or good goods, according to the demand?

8   But there is hope, not alone despair, in the commercialism of our politics. If our political leaders are to be always a lot of political merchants, they will supply any demand we may create. All we have to do is to establish a steady demand for good government. . . .

9   But do the people want good government? Tammany says they don't. Are the people honest? Are the people better than Tammany? Are they better than the merchant and the politician? Isn't our corrupt government, after all, representative?

10   President Roosevelt has been sneered at for going about the country preaching as a cure for our American evils, good conduct in the individual, simple honesty, courage, and efficiency. "Platitudes!" the sophisticated say. Platitudes? If my observations have been true, the literal adoption of Mr. Roosevelt's reform scheme would result in a revolution, more radical and terrible to existing institutions from the Congress to the Church, from the bank to the ward organization, than socialism or even than anarchy. Why, that would change all of us—not alone our neighbors, not alone the grafters, but you and me.

11   No, the contemned methods of our despised politics are the master methods of our braggart business, and the corruption that shocks us in public affairs we practice ourselves in our private concerns. There is no essential difference between the pull that gets your wife into society or for your book a favorable review, and that which gets a heeler into office, a thief out of jail, and a rich man's son on the board of directors of a corporation; none between the corruption of a labor union, a bank, and a political machine; none between a dummy director of a trust and the caucus-bound member of a legislature; none between a labor boss like Sam Parks, a boss of banks like John D. Rockefeller, a boss of railroads like J. P. Morgan, and a political boss like Matthew S. Quay. The boss is not a political, he is an American institution, the product of a freed people that have not the spirit to be free.

12   And it's all a moral weakness; a weakness right where we think we are strongest. Oh, we are good—on Sunday, and we are "fearfully patriotic" on the Fourth of July. But the bribe we pay to the janitor to prefer our interests to the landlord's, is the little brother of the bribe passed to the alderman to sell a city street, and the father of the air-brake stock assigned to the president of a railroad to have this life-saving invention adopted on his road. And as for graft, railroad passes, saloon and bawdy-house blackmail, and watered stock, all these belong to the same family. We are pathetically proud of our democratic institutions and our republican form of government, of our grand Constitution and our just laws. We are a free and sovereign people, we govern ourselves and the government is ours. But that is the point. We are responsible, not our leaders, since we follow them. We *let* them divert our loyalty from the United States to some "party"; we *let* them boss the party and turn our municipal democracies into autocracies and our republican nation into a plutocracy. We cheat our government and we let our leaders loot it, and we let them wheedle and bribe our sovereignty from us. True, they pass for us strict laws, but we are content to let them pass also bad laws, giving away public property in exchange; and our good, and often impossible, laws we allow to be used for oppression and blackmail. And what can we say? We break our own laws and rob our own government, the lady at the customhouse, the lyncher with his rope, and the captain of industry with his bribe and his rebate. The spirit of graft and of lawlessness is the American spirit.

13   And this shall not be said? Not plainly? William Travers Jerome, the fearless District Attorney of New York says, "You can say anything you think to the

American people. If you are honest with yourself you may be honest with them, and they will forgive not only your candor, but your mistakes." This is the opinion, and the experience too, of an honest man and a hopeful democrat. Who says the other things? Who says "Hush," and "What's the use?" and "ALL'S well," when all is rotten? It is the grafter; the coward, too, but the grafter inspires the coward. The doctrine of "addition, division, and silence" is the doctrine of graft. "Don't hurt the party," "Spare the fair fame of the city," are boodle yells. The Fourth of July oration is the "front" of graft. There is no patriotism in it, but treason. It is part of the game. The grafters call for cheers for the flag, "prosperity," and "the party," just as a highway man commands "hands up," and while we are waving and shouting, they float the flag from the nation to the party, turn both into graft factories, and prosperity into a speculative boom to make "weak hands," as the Wall Street phrase has it, hold the watered stock while the strong hands keep the property. "Blame us, blame anybody, but praise the people," this, the politician's advice, is not the counsel of respect for the people, but of contempt. By just such palavering as courtiers play upon the degenerate intellects of weak kings, the bosses, political, financial, and industrial are befuddling and befooling our sovereign American citizenship; and— likewise—they are corrupting it.

14   And it is corruptible, this citizenship. "I know what Parks is doing," said a New York union workman, "but what do I care. He has raised my wages. Let him have his graft!" And the Philadelphia merchant says the same thing: "The party leaders may be getting more than they should out of the city, but that doesn't hurt me. It may raise taxes a little, but I can stand that. The party keeps up the protective tariff. If that were cut down, my business would be ruined. So long as the party stands pat on that, I stand pat on the party."

15   The people are not innocent. That is the only "news" in all the journalism of these articles, and no doubt that was not new to many observers. It was to me. When I set out to describe the corrupt systems of certain typical cities, I meant to show simply how the people were deceived and betrayed. But in the very first study—St. Louis—the startling truth lay bare that corruption was not merely political; it was financial, commercial, social; the ramifications of boodle were so complex, various, and far-reaching, that one mind could hardly grasp them. . . .

16   It was impossible in the space of a magazine article to cover in any one city all the phases of municipal government, so I chose cities that typified most strikingly some particular phase or phases. Thus as St. Louis exemplified boodle; Minneapolis, police graft; Pittsburg, a political and industrial machine; and Philadelphia, general civic corruption; so Chicago was an illustration of reform, and New York of good government. All these things occur in most of these places. There are, and long have been, reformers in St. Louis, and there is to-day police graft there. Minneapolis has had boodling and council reform, and boodling is breaking out there again. Pittsburg has general corruption, and

Philadelphia a very perfect political machine. Chicago has police graft and a low order of administrative and general corruption which permeates business, labor, and society generally. As for New York, the metropolis might exemplify almost anything that occurs anywhere in American cities, but no city has had for many years such a good administration as was that of Mayor Seth Low.

17   That which I have made each city stand for, is that which it had most highly developed. It would be absurd to seek for organized reform in St. Louis, for example, with Chicago next door; or for graft in Chicago with Minneapolis so near. After Minneapolis, a description of administrative corruption in Chicago would have seemed like a repetition. Perhaps it was not just to treat only the conspicuous element in each situation. But why should I be just? I was not judging; I arrogated to myself no such function. I was not writing about Chicago for Chicago, but for the other cities, so I picked out what light each had for the instruction of the others. But, if I was never complete, I never exaggerated. Every one of those articles was an understatement, especially where the conditions were bad, and the proof thereof is that while each article seemed to astonish other cities, it disappointed the city which was its subject. . . .

18   They are not such bad fellows, these practical politicians. I wish I could tell more about them: how they have helped me; how candidly and unselfishly they have assisted me to facts and an understanding of the facts, which, as I warned them, as they knew well, were to be used against them. If I could—and I will some day—I should show that one of the surest hopes we have is the politician himself. Ask him for good politics; punish him when he gives bad, and reward him when he gives good; make politics pay. Now, he says, you don't know and you don't care, and that you must be flattered and fooled—and there, I say, he is wrong. I did not flatter anybody; I told the truth as near as I could get it, and instead of resentment there was encouragement. After "The Shame of Minneapolis," and "The Shamelessness of St. Louis," not only did citizens of these cities approve, but citizens of other cities, individuals, groups, and organizations, sent in invitations, hundreds of them, "to come and show us up; we're worse than they are."

19   We Americans may have failed. We may be mercenary and selfish. Democracy with us may be impossible and corruption inevitable, but these articles, if they have proved nothing else, have demonstrated beyond doubt that we can stand the truth; that there is pride in the character of American citizenship; and that this pride may be a power in the land. So this little volume, a record of shame and yet of self-respect, a disgraceful confession, yet a declaration of honor, is dedicated, in all good faith, to the accused—to all the citizens of all the cities in the United States.

From THE AMERICAN SCHOLAR
by Ralph Waldo Emerson (1837)

1   . . . I have dwelt perhaps tediously upon this abstraction of the Scholar. I ought not to delay longer to add what I have to say, of nearer reference to the time and to this country.

2   Historically, there is thought to be a difference in the ideas which predominate over successive epochs, and there are data for marking the genius of the Classic, of the Romantic, and now of the Reflective or Philosophical age. With the views I have intimated of the oneness or the identity of the mind through all individuals, I do not much dwell on these differences. In fact, I believe each individual passes through all three. The boy is a Greek; the youth, romantic; the adult, reflective. I deny not, however, that a revolution in the leading idea may be distinctly enough traced.

3   Our age is bewailed as the age of Introversion. Must that needs be evil? We, it seems, are critical. We are embarrassed with second thoughts. We cannot enjoy any thing for hankering to know whereof the pleasure consists. We are lined with eyes. We see with our feet. The time is infected with Hamlet's unhappiness, —

"Sicklied o'er with the pale cast of thought."

4   Is it so bad then? Sight is the last thing to be pitied. Would we be blind? Do we fear lest we should outsee nature and God, and drink truth dry? I look upon the discontent of the literary class as a mere announcement of the fact that they find themselves not in the state of mind of their fathers, and regret the coming state as untried; as a boy dreads the water before he has learned that he can swim. If there is any period one would desire to be born in, — is it not the age of Revolution; when the old and the new stand side by side, and admit of being compared; when the energies of all men are searched by fear and by hope; when the historic glories of the old, can be compensated by the rich possibilities of the new era? This time, like all times, is a very good one, if we but know what to do with it.

5   I read with joy some of the auspicious signs of the coming days as they glimmer already through poetry and art, through philosophy and science, through church and state.

6   One of these signs is the fact that the same movement which effected the elevation of what was called the lowest class in the state, assumed in literature a very marked and as benign an aspect. Instead of the sublime and beautiful, the near, the low, the common, was explored and poetized. That which had been negligently trodden under foot by those who were harnessing and provisioning themselves for long journeys into far countries, is suddenly found to be richer than

all foreign parts. The literature of the poor, the feelings of the child, the philosophy of the street, the meaning of household life, are the topics of the time. It is a great stride. It is a sign—is it not? of new vigor, when the extremities are made active, when currents of warm life run into the hands and the feet. I ask not for the great, the remote, the romantic; what is doing in Italy or Arabia; what is Greek art, or Provencal Minstrelsy; I embrace the common, I explore and sit at the feet of the familiar, the low. Give me insight into to-day, and you may have the antique and future worlds. What would we really know the meaning of? The meal in the firkin; the milk in the pan; the ballad in the street; the news of the boat; the glance of the eye; the form and the gait of the body;—show me the ultimate reason of these matters;—show me the sublime presence of the highest spiritual cause lurking, as always it does lurk, in these suburbs and extremities of nature; let me see every trifle bristling with the polarity that ranges it instantly on an eternal law; and the shop, the plough, and the leger, referred to the like cause by which light undulates and poets sing;—and the world lies no longer a dull miscellany and lumber room, but has form and order; there is no trifle; there is no puzzle; but one design unites and animates the farthest pinnacle and the lowest trench.

7   This idea has inspired the genius of Goldsmith, Burns, Cowper, and, in a newer time, of Goethe, Wordsworth, and Carlyle. This idea they have differently followed and with various success. In contrast with their writing, the style of Pope, of Johnson, of Gibbon, looks cold and pedantic. This writing is blood-warm. Man is surprised to find that things near are not less beautiful and wondrous than things remote. The near explains the far. The drop is a small ocean. A man is related to all nature. This perception of the worth of the vulgar, is fruitful in discoveries. Goethe, in this very thing the most modern of the moderns, has shown us, as none ever did, the genius of the ancients.

8   There is one man of genius who has done much for this philosophy of life, whose literary value has never yet been rightly estimated;—I mean Emanuel Swedenborg. The most imaginative of men, yet writing with the precision of a mathematician, he endeavored to engraft a purely philosophical Ethics on the popular Christianity of his time. Such an attempt, of course, must have difficulty which no genius could surmount. But he saw and showed the connexion between nature and the affections of the soul. He pierced the emblematic or spiritual character of the visible, audible, tangible world. Especially did his shade-loving muse hover over and interpret the lower parts of nature; he showed the mysterious bond that allies moral evil to the foul material forms, and has given in epical parables a theory of insanity, of beasts, of unclean and fearful things.

9   Another sign of our times, also marked by an analogous political movement is, the new importance given to the single person. Every thing that tends to insulate the individual,—to surround him with barriers of natural respect, so that each man shall feel the world is his, and man shall treat with man as a sovereign state with a sovereign state;—tends to true union as well as greatness.

"I learned," said the melancholy Pestalozzi, "that no man in God's wide earth is either willing or able to help any other man." Help must come from the bosom alone. The scholar is that man who must take up into himself all the ability of the time, all the contributions of the past, all the hopes of the future. He must be an university of knowledges. If there be one lesson more than another which should pierce his ear, it is, The world is nothing, the man is all; in yourself is the law of all nature, and you know not yet how a globule of sap ascends; in yourself lumbers the whole of Reason; it is for you to know all, it is for you to dare all. Mr. President and Gentlemen, this confidence in the unsearched might of man, belongs by all motives, by all prophecy, by all preparation, to the American Scholar. We have listened too long to the courtly muses of Europe. The spirit of the American freeman is already suspected to be timid, imitative, tame. Public and private avarice make the air we breathe thick and fat. The scholar is decent, indolent, complaisant. See already the tragic consequence. The mind of this country taught to aim at low objects, eats upon itself. There is no work for any but the decorous and the complaisant. Young men of the fairest promise, who begin life upon our shores, inflated by the mountain winds, shined upon by all the stars of God, find the earth below not in unison with these,—but are hindered from action by the disgust which the principles on which business is managed inspire, and turn drudges, or die of disgust,—some of them suicides. What is the remedy? They did not yet see, and thousands of young men as hopeful now crowding to the barriers for the career, do not yet see, that if the single man plant himself indomitably on his instincts, and there abide, the huge world will come round to him. Patience—patience;—with the shades of all the good and great for company; and for solace, the perspective of your own infinite life; and for work, the study and the communication of principles, the making those instincts prevalent, the conversion of the world. Is it not the chief disgrace in the world, not to be an unit;—not to be reckoned one character;—not to yield that peculiar fruit which each man was created to bear, but to be reckoned in the gross, in the hundred, or the thousand, of the party, the section, to which we belong; and our opinion predicted geographically, as the north, or the south. Not so, brothers and friends,—please God, ours shall not be so. We will walk on our own feet; we will work with our own hands; we will speak our own minds. The study of letters shall be no longer a name for pity, for doubt, and for sensual indulgence. The dread of man and the love of man shall be a wall of defence and a wreath of joy around all. A nation of men will for the first time exist, because each believes himself inspired by the Divine Soul which also inspires all men.

WRITING ASSIGNMENTS

Write a persuasive essay on one of the following topics. Be sure to support your position and show the weakness of the alternative(s). Feel free to draw on the readings and your previous essays, to appeal to authority or emotion, and even to try your hand at irony and satire.

1. What should be the function of the news media?

2. Does television have a moral responsibility to the public?

3. Should the government ban offensive stereotypes from the entertainment media?

4. Should schools teach values?

5. What should be the purpose of college education?

6. Does the United States have a special mission?

7. Should English be the official language of the United States?

8. Should the United States be a "melting pot" or a "tossed salad"?

9. Prove one side of an issue that emerged from the discussions for Making Connections.

10. Propose a solution to a problem or inequity that exists at your school.

11. Propose a solution to a problem or inequity that exists at your job.

12. Propose a solution to a problem or inequity that exists in the United States.

13. In 1987 the average cost of a formal wedding was $10,000 nationally and $35,000 in large cities. Do you approve or disapprove of such expensive weddings?

14. In *Miseducation: Preschoolers at Risk,* David Elkind suggests that expensive clothes, toys, and schools for children are the current forms of conspicuous consumption. What do you think?

15. William Faulkner once said: "You can't eat for eight hours a day nor drink for eight hours a day nor make love for eight hours a day—all you can do for eight hours is work. Which is the reason why man makes himself and everybody else so miserable and unhappy." Do you agree or disagree?

16. Writing in the *Dallas Times Herald* (September 5, 1982), Drew Jubera said: ". . . work has become such an integral part of modern civilization's self-esteem that most people find not working to be much too difficult a thing to pursue, at least for very long." Do you agree or disagree?

17. In *Abortion and Divorce in Western Law,* Mary Ann Glendon suggests that abortion on demand and no-fault divorce are extreme expressions of the American commitment to individualism. Paul Robinson says in the *New York Times* Book Review (February 14, 1988) that abortion on demand and no-fault divorce may reflect "the puritanism and sexism endemic to our culture" by relieving men of responsibility. What do you think?

C·H·A·P·T·E·R E·I·G·H·T

RESEARCHED WRITING

Researched writing differs from other essays more in purpose than in form. Research papers in school usually focus on a small aspect of a course, most often for the purpose of proving that you can apply the concepts and showing what you can do on your own. Business or political research reports frequently supply the background for a proposed action or the philosophy underlying a program. To accomplish these goals, researched writing is somewhat more formal in tone than other essays, incorporates sources, and often contains documentation.

Because a research paper is the final assignment in many courses, it frightens students more than it should. You must remember that a research paper is really just another essay. Depending upon what your teacher assigns, it can take the form of an analysis, evaluation, argument, or proposal; it can grow out of papers you have already written; and it can present either original observations, the results of interviews and questionnaires, or summaries of authoritative sources. The same is true of all the essays you have written as assignments from this textbook. The only additional requirements in a research paper are finding the information by yourself and documenting it according to certain conventions.

A research paper, therefore, should have

a manageable topic
adequate analysis and evaluation
a sense of authority

a clear purpose and audience

documentation of any sources used

· CHOOSING AND NARROWING A TOPIC

You have already experienced taking an idea from prewriting to completed essay and you may have revised one or two early essays for later assignments. In addition, you have been practicing critical reading and have thus built a body of knowledge about several topics or issues in the American experience. Specifically, starting with personal decisions, you have examined your values and tried to see where they fit into the larger society; you have learned about other people's values and experiences; and you have read several major historical documents and several famous analyses of American culture.

Now you are asked to write a research paper. Where do you start? You could start from scratch, but that would not be the wisest course. A better approach is to examine what you have read and written so far and see if there is anything that you are interested in learning more about. You may, for example, want a deeper understanding of American values. But this is a field of study which you could explore for years; it is too large to be a topic for a paper. You must analyze a field of study in order to find a topic that is both manageable and worth doing. You can reduce the general field to its specific components: family values, interpersonal values, economic values, contemporary American values, American values during the colonial period. You can compare American values to German values, or nineteenth century- to twentieth-century values. You can examine causation, for instance the influence of immigration on American values. You can evaluate whether American values are or were what they should be.

We have been emphasizing that looking for connections is the key to knowledge. Likewise, worthwhile topics are found where two or more fields cross paths. Sample topics that would produce good papers are American values as portrayed on television, the interaction of values and education, or the role of religion or the frontier in shaping economic values. Trying to make connections in this way helps you formulate a goal that will guide your research and may evolve into a thesis for a paper. Saying, "I would like to learn more about how values are portrayed on television" will suggest that you ought to watch at least some television with this purpose in mind. The limits on your time will make you narrow your viewing to a specific kind of show, perhaps soap operas or news. And what you find as you watch may lead to a thesis statement such as "News shows portray American values in a more positive way than Asian values."

The following paper was motivated by the student's interest in previous class discussions about television images and class consciousness in America. In the paper, the student evaluates what she has observed by watching commercials carefully.

Language and Image in TV Commercials

by Margaret Carfagno

1   By presenting an image based on preconceived stereotypes, television commercials reflect the advertiser's aim to sell an image rather than a product.

2   The French people, for instance, are popularly regarded as worldly and refined. As a result, commercials promoting fashionable clothing feature a French accent as well. Similarly, Americans credit the French with skillfulness in the culinary arts. A French style yogurt is advertised on television by various people speaking that language in the hope that viewers will react to the obvious connection made between the French nationality and good food.

3   Indeed, the French language often implies a higher level of social breeding. A Warner Brothers cartoon perpetuates this stereotype in its portrayal of a skunk named Pepe le Pew who woos various female characters with his unmistakably French accent and his sophisticated manners. The French have acquired a reputation as superior in the social graces and very successful in romance.

4   In addition to the French accent, native Spanish speakers may give rise to feelings of passion in some viewers. Ricardo Montalban describes the luxury car Cordoba in his heavy Spanish accent. His manner of speaking is rather sensual in tone, and his audience, it is hoped, will respond to this by associating the Cordoba with the feelings stimulated by his accent. He promotes not only the car, but also the image of prestige and romance very closely related to the car.

5   In contrast to the portrayal of the fashionable upper-class promoting such merchandise as luxury cars, many advertisers depict unsophisticated members of the middle- or lower-class. In general, these advertisements call the public back to a simpler, more down-to-earth lifestyle. Loretta Lynn, Don Meredith, and Minnie Pearl, for example, all share a similar reputation in their respective commercials. Each celebrity is readily understood as unrefined but by no means disagreeable. Loretta Lynn in a natural Southern dialect promotes Crisco shortening. Before she mentions the product itself, however, she describes in some detail her family parties which include square dancing and traditional Southern foods, such as fried chicken and apple tarts. The viewer immediately receives the impression that she lives in a rural environment, uncomplicated by extravagance or a dependence on modern

conveniences. The manner in which Loretta Lynn expresses her easily-remembered slogan ("Crisco'll do
ya proud ev'ry time") reflects the entire theme of the
commercial. Her speech pattern is characteristic of an
unsophisticated person.

6   Similarly, Don Meredith, in his Lipton tea commercials, speaks very plainly; he is portrayed as a
rustic man who enjoys the simple pleasures in life,
especially a cup of Lipton tea. He too employs a catchy
phrase ("dandy-tastin' ") which informs the viewer
that this man is probably not very worldly or cultivated. The advertisement is presented in such a way
that the viewer easily recalls his words and associates
them with the tea. Minnie Pearl likewise praises Spic
and Span in an exaggerated Southern accent. Her gram-
matically-incorrect slogan ("the right clean at the
right price") adds to her characterization of a simple
person from the country.

7   Television commercials of this sort featuring
non-celebrities include the Ivory soap advertisement
in which a very plain-looking couple speaking a Midwestern dialect shares its feeling about this pure
soap. The description of what the soap does not contain actually refers to what modern technology has developed, namely additives, and what members of the
upper-class frequently use and enjoy, fancy perfumes.

The couple prefers the "natural clean" which Ivory soap gives, and in a sense rejects modern technology and the materialism associated with the upper-class through the rejection of unnatural additions to soap. The dialogue is very convincing because the couple's dialect immediately gives rise to an image of a natural and unaffected lifestyle, compatible with the natural and unaffected composition of Ivory soap.

8   Television commercials manipulate viewers by promoting not only products but also images which are often an integral part of the products. The viewer is aware that he is being informed about a specific item, but he may not be aware that he is being presented with an image to associate with the item. Advertisers employ a number of devices to create and sell such images. In featuring a speaker with a foreign accent or regional dialect, the advertiser promotes his product with words but also more significantly with a subtler and perhaps more effective technique, a particular manner in which the words are spoken.

The preceding paper has a manageable topic: not language on television, not image in commercials, but language and image in television commercials. The student has collected and analyzed a sufficient number of examples to make her point. Her moral standards motivating the evaluation, as well as the competent organization and sentence structure, give the essay a tone of authority. There are no references to articles or books, so we can assume that the assignment did not require them and the writer did not find them necessary.

To gather the information for her report, the student had to watch television purposefully. It is possible that she began by watching television with an open mind, waiting to see what data would emerge, but it is more likely that at this point in the semester, after the reading selections and class discussions, she already had a thesis idea—perhaps something like "Commercials sell an image rather than a product." She then presumably kept a pad or index cards with her while she watched television and noted the kinds of speech associated with a specific product. After collecting ten or a dozen examples, she tried to classify and analyze them: Did they fall into certain patterns? Was there an explanation for these patterns? Then she evaluated what she found: Does the explanation reveal something good or bad about the way dialects are used in commercials? Her analysis is that certain foreign accents—European Spanish and French—are considered attractive and are therefore attached to luxury items, and that certain regional dialects—Southern and Midwestern—are considered unsophisticated and therefore used to sell "down-to-earth" products. Her evaluation is that this practice is a form of manipulation and therefore not completely honest.

· WORKING WITH SECONDARY SOURCES

Another type of research paper can arise from something that you have already written about in a brief essay and now want to investigate further. The additional investigation may involve rereading a poem or story or reexamining previously collected data, or it may require finding outside help. The data in the paper we just read came from *primary* sources, that is, the student's observation and analysis of the television commercials themselves. The data in the next essay comes from *secondary* sources, what others have said or written about the topic.

After examining the personal values that motivated her to take the job she now has and then reading Max Weber's analysis of the rise of capitalism, Margaret M. Degano wondered why the Japanese—who apparently do not have the Protestant work ethic—were better workers than Americans. To answer this question, she had to find information in the library and interview people at her company.

LESSONS TO BE LEARNED FROM JAPAN
by Margaret M. Degano

1   People have recently been suggesting that the United States adopt the policies and procedures in use

by Japanese companies, and how the operations of Japanese companies differ from those of companies in the West has been the subject of many recent books. Because Japan, like the United States, has a democratic system of government and a free market economy, there is the hope that we might somehow be able to adopt some of their successful business practices.

2   We can indeed learn something from studying Japanese business policy. Three of the most important areas that Western companies can emulate are lifetime employment, management by consensus, and fair compensation practices.

3   Background. For nearly forty years the Japanese have run one of the world's most dynamic economies, and Japan's unemployment rate of 2.7% is one of the lowest in the world. The approach Japanese manufacturing firms are taking to increasing productivity and reducing costs in the manufacture of a wide range of products is a good example of development that Western competitors can adopt. For, "at present the Japanese approach to manufacturing is yielding 30 percent over Western competitors," according to James C. Abegglen and George Stalk, Jr., in Kaisha: The Japanese Corporation.

4   Just as there are important lessons to be learned in the area of manufacturing, so too many Western firms can study Japanese financial methods for a competitive

advantage. Japanese companies reinvest most of their earnings for capital gains and growth. Dividend policy affects a firm's ability to fund growth at a relatively low cost for capital. Japanese levels of dividend payments are possible here in the West without damaging share price levels, and a number of fast-growing U.S. companies pay little or no dividends. Western companies tend to pay high dividends instead of reinvesting their earnings, and in this respect they can learn a lesson from the Japanese.

5   The West can learn many lessons from studying the structure of the very successful Japanese companies. The "money game" acquisition activities of the West, with asset stripping and forced, massive reductions in employment, are unlikely to become an issue with Japanese companies. There is only a small-scale merger and acquisition activity, and companies in trouble find affiliation with a more successful company to their advantage, and that affiliation offers improved prospects of continued job security to the labor force. Japan's companies are survivors. They have survived the most rapid and far-reaching changes in economic history, the move of the Japanese economy to world levels of output and competitiveness. They are highly competent and highly competitive.

6   If there is one prevailing belief in Japan, it is

in the centuries old Confucian work ethic, which is founded on respect for harmony in personal relationships and the hierarchy of classes. Confucianism discourages individualism, rejecting the mysticism common to many organized religions. The end result is the accommodating personality of most Japanese people.

7   In contrast to Japan's consensus approach to decision making, which requires ideas to percolate through the system from the bottom up, Western capitalism, where power comes from the top down, is based on the Protestant Work Ethic, and Max Weber in his book The Protestant Ethic and the Spirit of Capitalism focused on what was meant by the system of "rational bourgeois capitalism." Weber, for understandable reasons, like others, emphasized a profit-making business enterprise, but he was careful to point out that it was not orientation to profit alone which was the crucial criterion, but such orientation in the context of careful, systematic rational planning and discipline, which connected profit-making with "bureaucratic" organization of the economy and with high technology which eventually, for the most part after he wrote, developed a scientific base.

8   Lifetime Employment. The social commitment to full employment is absolute in Japan. Not only is the

economy expected to provide work for 20–60 year olds, it also has to find jobs for them again once they have supposedly retired. Because social security is rudimentary, one in four Japanese over 65 works. It is a well-known tradition in Japan for large companies and government bureaus to employ their workers for life. Actually, only about one-quarter of the work force are employed for life, but it has been a national ideal, the notion of company as family.

9   Large Japanese companies hire people right out of college into entry-level positions. These people work in groups, carrying out group assignments under the supervision of a senior. They then move through an automatic system of promotions and pay raises until they retire around 55 or 60. For this reason, age and seniority are usually synonymous. The Japanese like the security this system offers and they find that it attracts dedicated workers. Japanese companies often move their employees within a company through various departments and even other branch offices every two to five years. This exposes workers to a wide variety of experiences, allowing them to meet many different people and giving them an understanding of how their company functions.

10   When the Japanese go to their office or factory they act as if they were with their family. Japan pre-

fers the rule that you cooperate closely with who ever happens to be in the group situation with you. They believe in more "instinctive" incentives, starting with the natural cooperativeness of the group then creating emotional challenges, real or artificial, to motivate the group. The positive aspects of the more "instinctive," or family approach of the Japanese include political stability, low rates of individual crime, a lack of litigiousness, and openness to outside ideas and applied technology.

11   Japanese companies are dramatic testimony to the power of an organization that does in fact consider and treat its workers as its most important asset. The strength of these corporations argues that Western firms must give substance to what to them has become an empty phrase.

12   James Abegglen, in his book Kaisha, makes the following observations about Japanese traits dealing with the corporate sector. "There is a rational and generally nonhostile labor-management relationship; a vigorous entrepreneurial spirit; a group loyalty nurtured through lifetime employment, virtually without the practice of layoffs; and most important in contrast to the American practice, the ability of corporate managers to take long-term strategic investment decisions free from the pressure of outside shareholders. Japa-

nese management consists of successful career employees free from pressure by shareholders to achieve
quick profits on investments. Firmly committed to the
company and its employees, management is able to take a
long-term strategic view of its investment programs to
secure a successful future at the expense of short-term
profits."

13   <u>Management by Consensus</u>. The Japanese system of
group work assignments and vague job descriptions per-
mits those of greater skill within the group to compen-
sate for those of lesser skill. Those who make it to the
top in Japanese companies are those who have the best
interpersonal skills. A top manager is more of a human
relations leader than a decision maker or a goal set-
ter. Top managers in the Japanese system are good listeners and harmonizers. They know how to orchestrate
the "right" environment and boost workers' morale.
Harmony is very important in the Japanese view. As
abilities become apparent, people are given tougher
job assignments and put on the track that will move them
properly through the right departments to prepare them
for top management.

14   Japanese companies are conscious that their employees are their most important resource. Accordingly, business leaders tend to look after the physical
needs of their employees. Companies offer free lessons

in practically everything, and company and group parties are regular events. More workers are employed in a Japanese company than in a comparable American or European company. One reason for this is that Japanese managers believe that their people build their markets. Even Japanese law seems to uphold this by requiring companies to employ people in what would appear to be superfluous positions.

15   Most work assignments are carried out by groups of workers. The group is headed by a chief, usually someone who has been with the company for at least 15 years. Individual roles and assignments to accomplish a project are not well defined within the group. One of the differences between Japanese and Western companies is the formalized structure the Japanese have for a from-the-bottom-up method of making proposals and participating in decisions. Of course, the ultimate authority for approving an important decision lies at the top. All levels of management are involved in the process of proposals and a good point is that in the end no single person must take sole responsibility for a mistake or a bad decision. Japan is famous for its consensus approach to decision making, which requires ideas to percolate through the system from the bottom up.

16   An important concept to bear in mind is that peo-

ple are more productive when working in groups than
they are when spending a lot of energy competing with
one another as is the habit in many large U.S. companies. In Japan there is a respect for all forms of
labor, a viable work ethic, and a high level of education which is constantly improving the capabilities of
people.

17   In contrast to Western systems, the Japanese labor system's features—career employment in the big
companies, promotion by seniority, company trade
unions, a chunk of pay by profit-related bonuses, and
labor transfers—speed the pace at which Japanese companies can cut their costs. It thereby allows them to
buy time to redesign products to lower break-even
points and to move to higher value new products. The
flexibility of the system means that the supply of labor can be reallocated quickly to where it can be best
used. There is never an attitude of "this is not my
job." The contract between the employee and employer is
that the employee allows himself/herself to be shunted
around in return for being guaranteed a paycheck for
life. Employers go to extraordinary lengths to cut
their work forces only through intra-group transfers,
early retirements, and cutbacks on new hirings rather
than to let someone go.

18   An example of a Western company that uses Japa-

nese strategy very successfully is Goldman Sachs, &
Co., a major investment banker in New York City. It
calls itself "The Dallas Cowboys of Investment Banking" and says "The other players play their positions
very well, so when you come aboard you will be taxed to
become an accepted member of the organization. But you
know you are playing on the best team." Many others see
Goldman Sachs as the best team. Financial World magazine named Goldman Wall Street's "best broker" for
seven straight years. Part of the reason for this harmony can be traced to Goldman's chairman. He takes a
dim personal view of internal politics and rewards
people well for working within groups. No one person
ever gets credit for a job well done, only the group as a
whole. Those who work well within those groups
achieve favor, and the financial incentive is to do it
together as a group. Goldman's staff, even clerical
workers, are paid an average of 15 percent more than
others in the investment banking industry, according
to Michael H. Merrill, a personnel vice-president. In
addition, they receive a bonus: in 1986 employees got
25 percent of their salary and this year they got 22
percent. On top of the salary and bonuses, Goldman employees also share in the profits of the company. In
recent years, the partners have set aside the equivalent of 15 percent of an employee's salary and bonus

into his or her profit-sharing retirement account. The
employee can match the company's contribution with
nontaxable income.

19   The vast majority of Goldman Sachs professional
employees are hired directly out of business schools
and stay with the firm for their entire careers. The
company believes in promotion from within. Once hired,
Goldman expects their people to work hard.

20   Obviously, the management of the largest bank in
Japan, Sumitomo Bank, approves of the management policy at Goldman Sachs & Co. as they recently invested
approximately $1 billion in the company.

21   Fair Compensation. Compensation contingent on
organization performance is widely practiced in Japan,
and there is a more uniform level of compensation in
Japanese companies than in Western companies. Salaries
for CEOs of Japanese companies are considerably lower
than those for their American counterparts, and there
is no such thing as "golden parachutes."

22   Today, the difference in compensation in the
average Japanese corporation between the new employee
and the CEO is only about eight times more for the CEO.
This relatively narrow disparity in salary between
management and employees makes it easier for managers
and employees alike to attain unity.

23   Goldman, Sachs & Co. is an excellent example of a

Western company that successfully uses group consensus
and compensation practices to motivate its employees.
Also, it is a company where the majority of its employees have lifetime employment.

24   The West believes that most of these policies and
procedures would not work in the United States, because
the distinctiveness of the Japanese is based on a
culture that cannot be learned, or even adapted. However, it would appear that practices similar to those
used in Japan are working very well for Goldman Sachs &
Co.

25   While the U.S. has spent vast fortunes on military buildup, the Vietnam War, worldwide policing actions, and the race to the moon, Japan has concentrated
all her resources, human and financial, on economic
competition and the exchange of ideas. This tiny, over-
crowded island nation boasts the world's largest bank,
the biggest blast furnaces and cargo ships, and the
fastest trains. She ranks first in the manufacture of
electronic equipment and many other products.

26   Japan has developed its technology on foreign
scientific achievements, most of it from the U.S.; they
take the best of the knowledge from other countries,
then make things cheaper and faster in Japan. In a new
high-rise building being constructed in New York City,
it is not unusual to see a team of Japanese filming the

workmen using new products and questioning them as to what they think about the products and procedures being used.

27   I believe that Western nations should be more interested in learning why most Japanese companies are successful.

Although "Lessons to Be Learned from Japan" incorporates research, it is not a so-called cut and paste job; that is, it is not a collection of quotations and footnotes held together by a few original words from the student. The information that the student gathered has been absorbed, summarized, paraphrased, and reshaped to serve the purpose of her paper. The paper impresses the reader with the value of the content, not with the number of footnotes or size of the bibliography.

You may also have noticed that Degano's report is longer than the previous paper we read, perhaps because the assigned length was greater or perhaps because the student simply felt that this is what the topic required. Whatever the reason, the student was wise to include subheadings that help the reader keep track of the major points. These subheads, in fact, summarize the "lessons to be learned from Japanese corporations" that are promised in the title: lifetime employment, management by consensus, fair compensation.

· WRITING THE TRADITIONAL LIBRARY PAPER

Sometimes, of course, the assignment will require that you use secondary sources, either to compare and contrast what several authorities say about an issue or to support your own interpretation. In this case the report still must have a clear topic, analysis, and evaluation, but now you also have to weave documented references neatly into the discussion.

After reading the selections from Henry Adams's *History of the United States*, Nathan Jacobs decided to examine the work itself and came upon Adams's belief that nations have a social energy governed by natural laws similar to those that control physical energy. Jacobs became intrigued with the significance of this concept and the question of how Adams had devised it. But it was not a subject he could write about from his own experience or using his own resources. He

needed secondary sources. What he discovered in these sources and his evaluation of the theory are presented in the report.

HENRY ADAMS IN HIS TIME

by Nathan Jacobs

1   "No historian cared to hasten the coming of an

epoch when man should study his own history in the same

spirit and by the same methods with which he studied

the formation of a crystal. Yet history had its scien-

tific as well as its human side, and in American his-

tory the scientific interest was greater than the

human."

2   With these words from his History of the United

States (IX, 224–225), published in 1890, Henry Adams

unconsciously outlined the major problem in his aca-

demic and professional life. For, while he did not

"care" to see himself, as part of humanity, in the

terms he saw crystals and other natural phenomena, he

did not have an alternative if he wanted to remain loyal

to the ideals of his discipline at a time when the

historical method he cherished was becoming lost in

the rush for the popular prestige associated with

science.

3   Defrauded of prestige in a science-conscious

world, the adherents of the liberal arts attempted to

show that they too had a place of importance. And their

solution was to apply the scientific method to work in the humanities. "The black-letter man may be the man of the present," said Justice Oliver Wendell Holmes, "but the man of the future is the man of statistics and the master of economics" (Lerner 83).

4   And thus it is that in a world that demanded scientific proof for all theories, Henry Adams tried to formulate a science of history. That the attempt had to be made was clear, since as Adams wrote in "The Tendency of History" (Degradation 126), "science itself would admit its own failure if it admitted that man, the most important of its subjects, could not be brought within its range."

5   Adams could not prove that the tendency he sought in history existed, for the only proof of a scientific hypothesis is to predict the result of a controlled experiment, an obvious impossibility for a historian. The best that Adams could do was to draw analogies between social energy and cosmic energy, and, by explaining the past as a redistribution of energy, predict that social energy was subject to the same dissipation as cosmic energy was, according to Lord Kelvin and other contemporary authorities. The problem, as Van Wyck Brooks (263) suggested, was that Adams and a whole school of historians theorized that "the

laws of history paralleled the laws of physics, obviously and strictly," though in their historical
writings they paid no attention to these "fanciful
laws." In fact, Levenson (127) argues that Adams did
not believe history really followed scientific laws
but "used these concepts for the fruitful doubt they
raised about the mode of historical writing he actually
practiced."

6   The problem that plagues Adams in his historical
works is that he seems to have known that historical
"energy" could not be reduced to a chemical process,
but he felt obliged to explain events as if it could.
Then, when the fiction proved untenable, he would abandon the metaphor without acknowledgement. This explains why Adams is at his best when giving free rein to
personal reveries and interpretation. Adams wrote several such personal books, including The Education of
Henry Adams, which won the Pulitzer Prize in 1919 and in
which he "sought to explore himself in order to discover
the cosmos" (Spiller 1081). And according to Adams's
biographer Elizabeth Stevenson, even the History was
"an act of self-exploration" that "quivers with
Adams's own beliefs, doubts, struggles" (137).

7   Because of his intensely personal approach,
Adams realized the difficulty of a scientific theory of

history. And in "A Letter to American Teachers of History" (Degradation 230–231) he wrote: "Man refuses to be degraded in self-esteem. . . . The contradiction between science and instinct is so radical that, though science should prove twenty times over . . . that man is a thermodynamic mechanism, instinct would reject the proof."

8   Adams knew that his science was false. Yet he clung to his theory and surrendered it piece by piece through qualifications and exceptions. Thus, he admitted in the "Letter" that if his theory had been correct, if social energy were slowly dissipating, then "nothing remains for the historian to describe or develop except the history of a more or less mechanical dissolution" (206). And, being unwilling to do this, he instead determined that "for human history the essential was to convince itself that social energy, though a true energy, was governed by laws of its own" (147).

9   Thus, no matter how many times he professed to be approaching history with a blank, unemotional mind, Adams could never quite accept that method in practice. As Spiller (1096–1097) says, "Adams was primarily a man of feeling, and his ultimate strength lay in his long delayed but overwhelming discovery of that fact."

Works Cited

Adams, Henry. The Degradation of the Democratic Dogma. New York: Peter Smith, 1919.

_____. History of the United States during the Administrations of Jefferson and Madison. Washington, D.C.: Gordon, 1980. (Originally published, 1889–1891.)

Brooks, Van Wyck. New England: Indian Summer. Chicago: University Press, 1984.

Lerner, Max. The Mind and Faith of Justice Holmes. Boston: Houghton-Mifflin, 1943.

Levenson, J. C. The Mind and Art of Henry Adams. Stanford: University Press, 1957.

Spiller, Robert E., Willard Thorpe, Thomas H. Johnson, eds. Literary History of the United States. New York: Macmillan: 1953.

Stevenson, Elizabeth. Henry Adams: A Biography. New York: Octagon, 1977.

"Henry Adams in His Time" is a traditional research paper. The writer isolated a limited topic, found several authorities who discussed it, summarized and evaluated the relevant sections of their works, and arrived at a conclusion.

Also in the traditional style, the writing is a little too formal and stilted, perhaps because the student thought it was expected. But there can be no doubt that the writer has demonstrated his ability to investigate a topic independently and show its relevance to the semester's work.

· BACKGROUND REPORTS

A final type of researched writing presents the background for a proposal. It is common in business or politics to have a philosophical statement to support a plan of action. For example, you may say to your boss, "Why don't we screen our workers with lie detectors to reduce pilfering?" If the boss seems interested, you may be told, "Give me a report on that." Now you will have to find out which other companies have adopted the technique and what the result has been.

A background report frequently begins with a brief summary of the problem and proposed solution on a separate cover page and then follows normal essay format. The following report illustrates the approach.

SHOULD XYZ CORP. INSTITUTE THE USE OF POLYGRAPHS?

by Silvia Lee Roberts

Problem

1   At my supervisor's request I have looked into the feasibility of instituting the use of polygraphs at XYZ Corp. Even though XYZ does not manufacture finished dosage forms, we do have active drug ingredients that are used for research purposes. In the wrong hands these drugs can be detrimental. Hence, we have to be sure to hire honest staff. Polygraph tests were suggested in the belief that they are cheaper, quicker, and more reliable than conventional background checks. However, when the question was researched, the answer proved otherwise. Polygraph

tests are neither cheaper nor more reliable than background checks.

Recommendations

2   The polygraph is not the answer to employee
screening problems. Unfortunately, right now there is
really no simple, quick, inexpensive, and reliable re-
placement for the conventional background check, sound
management practices, and the judgment of those in personnel management. At this point I recommend that XYZ
Corp. continue to use the conventional methods of employee screening.

Rationale

3   All attempts at lie detection from ancient times
to the present have relied upon the same basic principle—the measurement of physiological changes presumed
to accompany the psychological stress of telling a
lie. For instance, the ancient Chinese believed that
the stress of lying inhibits the flow of saliva, making
it difficult to chew or swallow dried matter. Hence,
suspected liars were tested by making them chew rice
powder and then spit it out. If the powder remained dry—
presumably because the stress of being dishonest had
inhibited the flow of saliva—the suspect was deemed
guilty.

4   The modern polygraph, developed in the 1920s, is
merely a more sophisticated, complex machine. About

the size of an attaché case and equally portable, the polygraph instrument or lie detector machine is now widely used as a means of screening employees for honesty. The device monitors changes in breathing, blood pressure, pulse rate, perspiration, and electrical conductivity of the skin as the subject is asked a succession of questions by the polygraph operator.

5   Even though in these respects the modern lie detector seems to be nothing more than a sophisticated version of an ancient concept, polygraph operators claim that the key to their technique is in the form and mix of questions. But this itself can cause difficulty.

6   The standard format, known as the Control Question Test, involves interspersing "relevant" questions with "control" questions. Relevant questions relate directly to the critical matter, such as, "Did you steal the $1,000 that is missing from the safe?" Control questions, on the other hand, are less precise, such as, "In your lifetime, have you ever taken something that didn't belong to you?" The assumption underlying the Control Question Test is that the truthful subject will display a stronger physiological reaction to the control questions, whereas a deceptive subject will react more strongly to the relevant questions. For example, pursuing the control question above, most

people are likely to have taken something that did not belong to them at some stage in their lives. Yet fear of embarrassment may lead the subjects to deny misdeeds and therefore to answer the control questions dishonestly.

7   Since the polygraph merely records general emotional arousal, it cannot distinguish anxiety or indignation from guilt. When it comes to verifying the truthfulness of innocent subjects, both David Raskin, psychophysiologist of the University of Utah, and David Lykken, psychologist of the University of Minnesota, agree that the lie detector turns up more innocent people found guilty—false positives—than guilty people found innocent. For example, Floyd Fay in Ohio failed a lie detector test and was convicted of murder. But he had volunteered to take the test because he knew he was innocent. Typically, he was asked relevant questions like, "Did you do it?" along with control questions like, "Is today Tuesday?" Because Fay responded more strongly to the "Did you do it?" questions than to "controls," he failed. He served two years in prison before the real killers were found.

8   Moreover, not every question can be answered effectively and meaningfully by simply answering yes or no only. For instance, if the examiner were to ask if you have any unpaid debts you will reply positively

because your home mortgage and/or car loan may immediately come to mind. This monosyllable answer may not be in your favor on the polygraph chart. However, with a detective you could say that you do owe money but you have an excellent credit history, and the detective will check it out for him or herself. This, on the contrary, will be a good point for you as an excellent credit history indicates that you are a reliable, trustworthy, and responsible person.

9   A second problem is that there are numerous causes for emotional stress. Polygraph instruments do not measure physiological states that accompany lying specifically, but rather physiological changes generated by all kinds of emotional stress. Fear, guilt, anger, physical conditions such as heart trouble, headache, and fatigue, and even tension created by the test itself can all distort the accuracy of the polygraph. Studies have also shown that in some people lying produces no physical symptoms of stress at all. Criminals, for example, generally do what they do because they think that they are not doing anything wrong. Such people can escape the lie detector test and go free. Additionally, it has been contended by Lykken that with some preparation, it is possible to defeat the test. Countermeasures like biting your tongue or rubbing your foot against a tack hidden in your shoes

during the control questioning can make the polygraph
needles jump. In my opinion, these inconsistencies
should raise serious doubts concerning the polygraph's
validity and effectiveness of its use in personnel ap-
plications. Conventionally, such inconsistencies do
not arise. No countermeasures can be taken against
background checks. The detective simply asks many people about you. Background checks do not have to rely on
physiological changes for final results, thus elim-
inating a very variable factor.

10   A third problem to be considered is that the operator is a major component of the polygraph test.
Although no mandatory requirements mandate the educational and professional training of polygraph operators, the sellers of polygraph machines generally
agree that a lie detector test is no better than the
examiner giving it. The instrument itself accounts for
only an approximate ten percent of the total examination effectiveness—it only records. The qualifications and necessary specialized training of the examiner are an estimated ninety percent responsible
for a successful test conclusion. In many states no
licensing requirements prevent anyone from purchas-
ing and operating the polygraph machine. A person who
merely passed a six-week polygraph course can be hired
as a polygraph operator. Such inadequately trained

operators, and improper questioning methods or interpretation of measured responses, may result in
misleading test results. Many people lose their jobs
and go through life branded as a liar or thief due to
the inaccuracy of the polygraph. Also, the polygraph
examiner's responsibility to himself and his profession is based on learning, ability, tact, talk, temperance, talent, thoroughness, and conscience. The
examiner should never approach a test when he is overly
tired, or emotionally upset; under the influence of
intoxicants, drugs or their after-effects, or while
suffering from any serious physical ailment. He also
must not permit himself to be subjected to political,
religious, or any other pressures that might consciously or unconsciously influence the outcome of an
examination. There is definitely no guarantee that a
polygraph operator, who is only human, can have all
these variables under complete control all the time.
Hence, a subject will always be faced with such threats
like: what if the examiner is a racist, what if he has
skin color preference, what if he is against a certain
religion, what if he disliked you on first impression,
what if he is moody due to personal reasons? The list
goes on. These variables, if not controlled, can cause
the examiner to use an improper tone of voice which will
effect the subject tremendously and may cause him to

respond to the questions wrongly. Here, the individual being tested has little chance to refute the results of the machine. The polygraph test generates a situation where the machine and an operator of perhaps questionable ability will be primary witnesses. Disproving the charts could be difficult if not impossible. The employer has to accept the examiner's interpretation of the test results. Since a detective hired to do background checks will ask as many people as he can about you, chances are that those who dislike you will be balanced out by those who like you. Additionally, a detective will also be able to present recommendations. Any employer of average intelligence will be able to understand and evaluate all the findings of the detective and then make his final decision. He will not be presented with long sheets of incomprehensible graphs. Besides, the polygraph being relatively new as compared to the conventional background checks and operated unlicensed, it will be very difficult to find a good and reliable operator. But a detective must be licensed, and it is easier for an employer to sort out a good and well-known detective to do background checks and hence be expected to come up with reliable and valid information.

11   A fourth drawback is that even if the polygraph test were accurate and reliable, employers may be

subjected to legal action for invasion of privacy. A
polygraph test often forces a subject to reveal information of a sensitive and personal nature not particularly relevant to the employment situation. A study
found, for example, that the following questions were
asked on standard pre-employment tests: Have you ever
been questioned in connection with a felony? Do you
have any lawsuits pending against you? Do you owe more
debts than you indicated in your application? Do you
drink, take drugs, or gamble excessively? Is there
anything in your background that, if known, would
cause embarrassment to the company? Companies have
also been known to question employees about their sex
life, political activities, and involvement with
labor unions. The polygraph has yet to gain the legiti-
macy of legal recognition. The detectors are accepted
as evidence in criminal cases in only about twenty
states, and then only when both sides agree in advance. Lawyers, public figures, and others involved
in the legal aspects of our civil rights claimed that
polygraph is infringing the Fourth Amendment's protection of privacy, as cited in "The Polygraph: A
Questionable Personnel Tool," by John Belt. Even
though this privacy protection is not yet directly
concerning the polygraph per se, there are strong
signs indicating the great possibility of the in-

stitution of such a law to protect the subjects of
polygraph tests. Then, not only can an employer be
sued for wrongly branding a potential employee or an
employee a liar simply because he failed the unrelia-
ble polygraph test, the employer can also be sued for
the invasion of an individual's privacy. Normally
only highly trained psychiatrists and psychologists
are allowed to enter this personal territory to help
those with emotional problems. The polygraph operator charged with administering a pre-employment
test hardly seems a necessary reason for such an intrusion. A detective, on the other hand, can be told by
the employer to only look into the relevant areas of the
potential employee and omit any intimate personal
information.

12   A fifth problem is possible abuse. Some employers have been using the polygraph as a continuing
check on employee loyalty and honesty, often requiring an employee to answer questions concerning not
only his own behavior, but that of fellow employees as
well. This was mentioned in "The Polygraph: A Questionable Personnel Tool," by John Belt. That, in my
opinion, is poor business practice. By instituting
the use of the polygraph, the company management will
create a climate of distrust and suspicion. Besides,
not only will the employees feel that they are under

constant suspicion by management, but they may resent the pressure of being asked to report on their fellow employees as well. The atmosphere may degenerate to one of self-interest and a low degree of company loyalty. Also, cooperation among employees may be hindered.

13   Finally, one of the primary arguments for the use of the polygraph is its low cost—typically $35 to $150 per test versus an average of $350 for background checks. But this is misleading. The real cost must include the costs associated with legal issues, and the long-term costs of employee-employer relations must be included if the cost is to be a realistic estimate.

14   In conclusion, as a matter of sound business management, an employer should be able to hire trustworthy people. But the use of the polygraph to "detect" lies is inappropriate and impractical.

Works Consulted

Belt, John A. "The Polygraph: A Questionable Personnel Tool." Personnel Administration Aug. 1983: 65.

Dreyfack, Raymond. "Can Employee Refuse Lie Detector Test?" Plant Engineering 4 Feb. 1982: 76.

Lykken, David. "The Truth about Lie Detectors Is They Can't Detect a Lie." People 11 May 1981: 75.

Matusewitch, Eric P. "Fear of Lying: Polygraphs in

Employment." Technology Review Jan. 1981: 10—11.

Meyer, Alfred. "Do Lie Detectors Lie?" Science 82.3

(1982): 24—27.

The report addresses the question of whether polygraphs—lie detectors—are a good way for a particular company to screen job applicants. The student points out that as a drug manufacturer the company has moral and legal obligations and therefore must have trustworthy employees. Polygraph testing has been suggested because of the scientific guarantee it seems to offer. In the first paragraph the writer rejects this tool, and the remainder of the report explains why.

The student begins with a brief history of lie detection in general and polygraphs in particular. The juxtaposition of the latest scientific tool with the ancient Chinese test for a dry mouth is especially clever because it makes the reader question just how far the technology has really come; it also sets the tone for the subsequent point-by-point analysis of the supposed strengths of the polygraph and the comparison/contrast with the current method of background investigation. The systematic, step-by-step analysis establishes the writer's knowledge and is further supported by the occasional mention of an authority she has consulted, as well as by the bibliography of works consulted but not mentioned. By the end of the essay the reader is convinced that the recommendation is based on careful consideration.

You may also have noticed that without the first two paragraphs, which limits the recommendation to a particular company, the remainder of the essay could have been an academic term paper. With minor adjustments, the presentation could become a report on the reliability of polygraphs, the advisability of using polygraphs to screen employees, or the place of polygraphs in a democracy.

· GATHERING INFORMATION SYSTEMATICALLY

Regardless of the form in which you present your research, you will need to gather information. You will make your work easier and more efficient by approaching the task systematically.

The paper about television commercials, for example, is based entirely on personal observation. The thoughtful way to gather information for such a report is by keeping a stack of index cards and a few pens or pencils next to the television set at all times, even when you are not "officially" working on the paper. Then, if a relevant commercial appears you can immediately note the important details. You might even have prepared the index cards beforehand with short headings:

product:
speech pattern:
intended audience:
description of ad:
famous person (if any):

This system is better than trying to find a scrap of paper to write on while the advertisement is on the air or trying to remember the content later. In addition, when the time comes to organize and classify your findings you will have chunks of information that are convenient to work with, not odds and ends scribbled on candy wrappers and backs of old magazines.

Assuming that the student made her entries on index cards as we have suggested, she could now sort them according to speech pattern, making separate stacks for French, Spanish, Southern English, and Midwestern English. Then she could subdivide these stacks further and discover that French appears in advertisements for expensive clothing and yogurt, Spanish in ads for expensive cars, Southern dialect in ads for food and household cleanser, and Midwestern dialect in ads for soap. These findings seem rather mixed, so she may want to try a different set of classes, with labels like "expensive products" and "inexpensive products." Then she could see what each new stack contains and try to subdivide further, for example into groups labeled "foreign accents," "regional dialects," "respected speech," "nonstandard speech." She might then discover that foreign accents are used in commercials for luxury items and certain foods, and regional dialects appear in commercials for foods, household cleanser, and soap. She would now ask herself why these particular foreign accents would motivate viewers to buy these particular items and why these particular dialects are attached to these particular products. In this way, by trying different sets of classes, she will finally arrive at the classification that makes sense to her.

Now she has to write the paper. Since the bulk of the essay will be the examples she has found, the sets of index cards will determine the organization. That is, she can state her evaluation of the findings in the introduction— commercials sell images not products—and then prove her thesis by presenting classes of advertisements that use particular kinds of speech to create the image required for particular products. Because the information was gathered and organized systematically, all she needs for each section of the essay is a topic sentence that explains what she wants us to see in the samples that follow. Thus "The French people, for instance, are popularly regarded as worldly and refined" introduces one set of commercials, and "In general, these advertisements call the public back to a simpler, more down-to-earth lifestyle" introduces another.

Interviews

A systematic approach will also help you if your information comes from interviews. If you interviewed someone for the paper about how values reflect or conflict with one's background, you may have found that people do not always talk about what you need to know. You have your purpose in interviewing them; they have their purpose in talking to you. And the two are not always the same. You have to learn to control the interview so that it serves your purpose, but you also do not want to offend your subject or lose the chance of discovering a whole new area that the subject may be able to teach you.

The key, again, is having a system. You should go into the interview with a clear grasp of your own purpose, aided by a written list of questions—one to an index card. The questions should cover the points that you need to know for your essay. There should be specific facts that establish the person's authority or relevance. For a paper on values and background you need the subject's age, country of birth, religion, years in the United States, and similar facts. For a paper on a technical topic you need to know the subject's job title, previous jobs, training, schooling, as well as honors and awards the subject has won, titles of books and articles the subject has written, and the like. There should be questions that allow the subject to talk freely about opinions and experiences. A good interviewer listens carefully to these responses and asks for elaborations of points that seem promising. But you should not lose sight of your own essential questions.

When arranging for the interview you should ask for permission to bring a tape recorder, as this will allow you to give full attention to the conversation without the interference of telling your subject to speak slowly or stop while you are writing notes. But you must transcribe these tapes onto index cards—or directly into a file in your word processor—immediately after the interview, while the discussion is still fresh in your mind. And you should put in new batteries and a clean tape right before the meeting.

When it is time to write, the information will be readily available, as we saw in the previous section. If direct quotations are already in a computer file, they can be copied into your working file without additional transcription.

Questionnaires

If your topic requires similar information from a large number of subjects, a questionnaire is a valuable tool. But, as before, it must be carefully thought out beforehand. The time spent in preparing the questionnaire correctly will be rewarded by allowing you to collate the answers quickly and interpret them accurately.

Certain kinds of information can be collected through questionnaires: for example, the age of students in a class or school, the income of residents in a neighborhood, or preferences about specific products or proposals. Questionnaires cannot supply other information, for example, the truth or falsehood of specific facts. Asking high school seniors when the Civil War took place can tell us what percentage of them know and don't know, but it can't tell us the correct date by majority vote.

Each question must ask for only one piece of information, and the answers offered as choices must not overlap, that is, they must be mutually exclusive.

good: "Where were you born?"
poor: "Where and when were you born?"
good: "I buy imported foods. Yes _____ No _____ "
poor: "I prefer: American cars _____ foreign cars _____ other _____ "

The wording of the questions must not be ambiguous or prejudicial.

good: "I allow my children to watch television: less than one hour a day
         _____ more than one hour a day _____ "
poor: "I allow my children to watch television: a little _____ a lot _____ "
good: "Do you support the welfare policy of the current administration?
         Yes _____ No _____ "
poor: "Do you approve of the American way of life? Yes _____ No _____ "

The questionnaire on page 433 asks writing teachers whether they think their department should require a standard format for work submitted by students and, if so, what the format should be.

When you write the report, you should include a copy of the questionnaire and an explanation of why you believe the specific questions address the issue you are discussing.

Using the Library

Of course, there is some information that you will find only in the library. Regardless of your major in college or the job you eventually take, you will need books or reference material that you don't own. For most serious research, in both college and business, the local library will probably not be adequate, and you will have to go to the reference room at your college library, to special collections at museums, corporations, and historical societies, or to a friend with an on-line database.

FACULTY ATTITUDES TOWARD REQUIRING STANDARD FORMAT

Do you believe the English Department should require a standard format for work submitted by students?   Yes _____ No _____

In case a standard format is adopted, please rate the importance of the following:

	require	suggest	unimportant
typing	_____	_____	_____
8½ × 11 paper	_____	_____	_____
double-space	_____	_____	_____
white paper	_____	_____	_____
no onion skin	_____	_____	_____
no erasable bond	_____	_____	_____
elite or pica type	_____	_____	_____
handwritten (if allowed)			
print	_____	_____	_____
blue or black ink	_____	_____	_____
one side of a page	_____	_____	_____
8½ × 11 paper	_____	_____	_____
lined paper	_____	_____	_____
no spiral notebook paper	_____	_____	_____
skip lines	_____	_____	_____
cover sheet	_____	_____	_____
binder	_____	_____	_____
clip	_____	_____	_____
staple	_____	_____	_____

Comments: _____

The Card Catalogue

The **card catalogue,** which in many libraries is now a computer terminal, lists every book the library owns or, sometimes, what material it can borrow for you. Card catalogues and computerized files usually have three entries for each book, under the author, title, and subject. If you want to see what a particular author has written, check the entries under that person's name. If you need a particular book, the title card will tell you if the library has it. If you want an overview of a topic, so that you can get ideas about what would make a manageable essay, the subject entries are the place to begin.

The **call number** assigned to each book gives its location. On catalogue cards this code appears in the upper left-hand corner; on computer entries it is often the first line, but as yet there is no standardized system used by all libraries. In most libraries you find a book by following the numbers on the shelves or referring to a map of the floors and rooms.

```
973.4
Ada
          Adams, Henry; 1838 - 1918
            History of the United States of America during
          the administrations of Thomas Jefferson &
          James Madison. 2 Vols.
          N.Y., N.Y., Literary classics of United States,
          c. 1986, Vol. 1.
            1308p. (The Library of America)

            1. United States - Politics and government,
          --1801 - 1809
          I. Title
          II. The Library of America
```

Author card for a book by Henry Adams.

```
973.0992      ADAMS, HENRY, 1838 - 1918
S          Shepherd, Jack
            The Adams Chronicles, 1750 - 1900. Four
          generations of greatness.
          Boston: Little, Brown & Co., 1975
          448 p. illus.
            1. Adams family
            2. Adams, John, Pres. U.S., 1735 - 1826
            3. Adams, John Quincy, Pres. U.S., 1767 - 1848
            4. Adams, Charles Francis, 1807 - 1886
            5. Adams, Henry, 1838 - 1918
            I. Title
```

Subject card for a book about Henry Adams.

Since books on a topic are shelved together, it is not always necessary to make an exhaustive search of the catalogue; instead, if you note a few call numbers and then browse in the relevant sections, you will often find useful books you did not see listed. In libraries where you submit a request form and an attendant gets the book for you, a more thorough catalogue search is needed. A new aid, however, is available in many libraries: a computerized author and subject search. You type in what you are looking for and receive a list of all the relevant books the library owns or can borrow through interlibrary loan. Again, several competing systems exist, so you must ask the librarian for assistance.

ADAMS, HENRY, 1838–1918.

Adams, Henry, 1838–1918. Degradation of the democratic dogma. 1949.

MCC, SBE, VGO, ZWP

Adams, Henry, 1838–1918. Education of Henry Adams. 1907.

CLC, GBL, LMR, TPL

Adams, Henry, 1838–1918. Education of Henry Adams. 1942.

SBE, ZWP

Auchincloss, Louis. Henry Adams. 1971.

NCL, RCC, WNM

Blackmur, R.P., 1904– Henry Adams. 1980.

RCC, SBE

Chalfant, Edward, 1921– Both sides of the ocean: a biography of. 1982.

SBE, VRR, ZLM

Sample computer search for books by and about Henry Adams, listing call number, author, and abbreviated title. Codes identify libraries with the book which participate in the interlibrary loan program.

```
E    302.1    .A2    1962

Adams, Henry, 1838-1918.

History of the United States of America.

New York: Antiquarian Press, 1962.

9 vols.; maps.

Reprint  of  New  York:  Charles  Scribner's  Sons,
   1891-1896.

Vols.  1-2:  The  first  administration  of  Jeffer-
   son.

Vols.  3-4:  The  second  administration  of  Jeffer-
   son.

Vols.  5-6: The first administration of Madison.

Vols.  7-9: The second administration of Madison.
```

Sample on-line catalogue screen showing complete information.

Readers' Guides

Books are not the only source of information at a library; for most college writing they are not even the major resource. Current and specialized data are found in newspapers, magazines, and journals. To help you locate what you need there are a variety of **readers' guides.**

For current events and records of history as it unfolded, newspapers are indispensable. *Facts on File* is a general guide to reportage since 1941. The *New York Times Index,* with its alphabetical listing of people, places, and topics, will tell you when the newspaper published any article since 1851. The *London Times Index* goes back to 1785. The *Wall Street Journal* and *Christian Science Monitor* also have indexes. *Readers' Guide to Periodical Literature* and *Magazine Index* provide similar information for popular and general magazines.

In addition, there are guides to the journals in many fields, for instance, *Applied Science and Technology Index, Business Periodicals Index, Education Index, Index to Legal Periodicals, MLA International Bibliography* (for language and literature), *Public Affairs Information Service Bulletin, Social Science Index,* and *Statistical Abstracts of the United States.*

The numerous publications of the federal government since 1895 are listed in *The Monthly Index to the United States Government Publications.* The work of international organizations appears in *United Nations Documents Index* and *International Bibliography, Information, Documentation.*

If you are researching Henry Adams, for example, you can find his name in the subject index of the 1982 *MLA International Bibliography,* with a note telling you to check the entries beginning with number 5799 under "American Literature 1800–1899." There, among other titles, you will find the following information:

Elder, Gaye Elissa. "Henry Adams on the American Presidency." *DAI.* 1982 June; 42(12): 5120A.

Lesser, Wayne. "Criticism, Literary History, and the Paradigm: *The Education of Henry Adams." PMLA.* 1982 May; 97(3): 378–394.

White, Hayden. "Method and Ideology in Intellectual History: The Case of Henry Adams." 280–310 in LaCapra, Dominick, ed.; Kaplan, Steven L., ed. *Modern European Intellectual History: Reappraisals and New Perspectives.* Ithaca: Cornell UP; 1982. 317 pp.

The Guide in the front of the book explains the format of the entries; the List of Periodicals spells out the abbreviations. Thus, the first entry is a dissertation that is summarized in the June 1982 issue of *Dissertation Abstracts International,* volume 42, number 12; the third is an essay on pages 280–310 of a book edited by Dominick LaCapra and Steven L. Kaplan, published by Cornell University Press in 1982. If these articles seem promising, you then see whether the library has these sources or can get them for you through interlibrary loan.

Abstracts

Whereas an index or bibliography simply lists authors, titles, and subjects, an **abstract** also includes a brief summary that helps you decide whether an article is as valuable to you as its promising title suggests. Some important abstracts are *Biological Abstracts, Chemical Abstracts, Community Development Abstracts, Language Teaching and Linguistics: Abstracts,* and *Sociological Abstracts.*

Abstrax, which is available on microfiche or through on-line database, summarizes articles from over two hundred general and widely quoted specialized periodicals, such as *Newsweek, Fortune, Psychology Today, Black Enterprise, Harvard Business Review,* and the *New England Journal of Medicine.* The *Social Issues Resource Series* assembles and reprints selected articles in separate volumes; some current examples are "Alcohol," "Consumerism," "Crime," "Drugs," "Ethnic Groups," "Family," "Human Rights," "Population," "Technology," "Women," and "Youth."

For a paper on multiethnic societies, for instance, you might browse in *Language Teaching and Linguistics: Abstracts.* In the July 1977 issue, the following entry appears:

> Hasan, Ruqaiya. Socialisation and cross-cultural education. *International Journal of the Sociology of Language* (The Hague), 8 (1976), 7–25.
>
> It is argued, following Bernstein, that educational systems are intricately related to the culture in which they are embedded. Socialisation through the family and the educational institutions on the Indo-Pakistani subcontinent creates a particular sense of identity which is challenged when the student is brought into the English educational system at university level. This conflict gives rise to many intangible problems for the foreign student.

Based on the abstract we can expect the article in question to be useful for a paper on multicultural societies, the melting pot ideal, education of minorities, education and politics, and several other topics we have been discussing. In addition, it gives us a new lead: the name Bernstein. Who is this Bernstein who is mentioned in passing as if we are supposed to know his or her theories? Finding the answer—by checking the author list in an index—will obviously open new leads. Clearly, the summary tells us much more than a mere title does. We have a very good idea of the content of the article and, therefore, whether it will serve our purpose.

Two additional sources that help you discover whether a particular author or book is worth reading are *Index to Book Reviews in the Humanities* and *Technical Book Review Index.*

The Librarian

Finally, do not underestimate the help available from the librarian. The resources mentioned here are only a small hint of the kinds of aids offered by a library. Librarians will know of special collections in your area, interlibrary loan services, and numerous other resources—and they are always eager to help.

· ACKNOWLEDGING SOURCES

In researched writing you necessarily draw on ideas and information that are not your own. Whether you quote directly or paraphrase your sources you must give them credit, or **acknowledgment.** The only exceptions are facts that are general knowledge and familiar expressions that have become part of the common heritage. Thus, you do not have to explain where you found the dates of the Civil War or the Supreme Court case abolishing segregation in public schools. You can, if you wish, mention the author of a famous quotation: "As Thomas Jefferson said in the Declaration of Independence, 'all men are created equal.'" However, you should not give a source for uncontested facts; it would actually make you look foolish to write "According to the *Encyclopaedia Britannica,* John Kennedy was president from 1961 to 1963."

As we said in Chapter 3, the simplest way to acknowledge your source is to mention it in the sentence where the information occurs.

```
According to the article "What Makes Mario Run?"

(Newsweek, March 24, 1986), Governor Cuomo was very

much influenced by his family.
```

In addition to placing the name of the article and the magazine it appeared in where the reader sees them immediately, the sample sentence paraphrases the thesis of the article because there is no especially catchy sentence or phrase worth quoting. We already explained in Chapter 3 that paraphrasing shows your grasp of what you have read, whereas extensive quotations create a pastiche that suggests only a superficial understanding. You should therefore paraphrase everything except those ideas that the author has captured in a few brilliant words.

When you must quote, the quotation should follow the exact wording of the original and still read smoothly as part of your sentence; a quotation is identified by quotation marks, not distorted word order.

```
His role model was his father, whom Frank Cuomo calls

"a Catholic, family-type guy."
```

In case you are still unsure about incorporating quotations into your essays, we will briefly review the pointers given in Chapter 3; you can refer to the full discussion which begins on page 117 for more details.

1. Use double quotation marks at the beginning and end of any words that you take from a source.
2. Use a comma to separate the source from a quoted sentence.
3. Use a colon to make a quotation more emphatic or to introduce a long quotation.
4. Indent, without quotation marks, quotations longer than five lines or fifty words.
5. Use three spaced periods to show ellipsis—that is, omitted words—in the body of the quotation.
6. Use four spaced periods to indicate ellipsis at the end of a quoted sentence, or the omission of an entire intervening sentence.
7. Use square brackets to indicate an addition to or change in the quotation.
8. Use parentheses after the quotation to indicate a change within the quotation.
9. Put a comma or period required by your sentence inside the quotation marks.
10. Put all other punctuation required by your sentence outside the quotation marks.
11. Omit your own punctuation when the sentence ends with punctuation in the quotation.
12. Avoid sentence organizations that require strings of end punctuation.
13. Use single quotation marks to indicate a quotation within the quotation.

· DOCUMENTING SOURCES

On occasion you will have to acknowledge sources in a more elaborate style than the one we have suggested. Some publications present such **documentation** in footnotes or endnotes, as in "The Role of the Media during a Terrorist Incident" (p. 363) and "Fourth Amendment Rights of Law Enforcement Employees" (p. 466). But the most widely used stylebooks recommend using notes only for comments that you do not want to include in the running text.

For formal documentation, many writers follow the styles of the Modern

Language Association (MLA) or the American Psychological Association (APA).

MLA documentation calls for a list of sources labeled *Works Cited* at the end of the essay.
You cite these works in the text by author and page.

Adams theorized that "the laws of history paralleled
the laws of physics" (Brooks 263).

If the author is mentioned in the sentence, give the page in parentheses.

Levenson (127) argues that Adams did not believe history really followed scientific laws.

When your list contains more than one work by an author, add a brief title.

As Adams (<u>Degradation</u> 126) wrote, "science itself
would admit its own failure. . . ."

The list of Works Cited is arranged alphabetically by author. The works of each author are also alphabetized.

Adams, Henry. <u>The Degradation of the Democratic Dogma</u>.
    New York: Peter Smith, 1919.

————————. <u>History of the United States during the</u>
    <u>Administrations of Jefferson and Madison</u>. Washing-

ton, D.C.: Gordon, 1980. (Originally published, 1889–1891.)

Brooks, Van Wyck. New England: Indian Summer. Chicago: University Press, 1984.

Levenson, J. C. The Mind and Art of Henry Adams. Stanford: University Press, 1957.

The format for an article is the following:

Sledd, James. "Bi-Dialectalism: The Language of White Supremacy." English Journal 58 (1969): 1307–1315.

APA Style

The APA lists sources at the end of the essay under the heading *References.* You cite the sources in the text within parentheses, including the author, year of publication, and page, with a comma before and after the year, and *p.* before the page number.

Adams theorized that "the laws of history paralleled the laws of physics" (Brooks, 1984, p. 263).

If the author is mentioned in the sentence, give the year in parentheses immediately after the author's name, and the page at the end of the sentence, before the period.

Levenson (1957) argues that Adams did not believe history really followed scientific laws (127).

When your list contains more than one work by an author, no additional identification is needed because APA style already cites the date of publication. But if two or more works by an author have the same date, the APA labels them, for example, 1985a and 1985b.

Like Works Cited in MLA documentation, the APA list of References is arranged alphabetically by author. However, APA style differs in several ways:

1. It places the date immediately after the author.
2. It capitalizes only the first word and proper nouns in a title.
3. It lists the works of each author from earliest to latest.

In APA format the first two titles in the previous list therefore look like this:

Adams, Henry. (1919). <u>The degradation of the democratic dogma</u>. New York: Peter Smith.

_____. (1980). <u>History of the United States during the administrations of Jefferson and Madison</u>. Washington, DC: Gordon. (Originally published, 1889—1891.)

The APA format for an article is the following:

Sledd, James. (1969). "Bi-dialectalism: The language of white supremacy." <u>English Journal</u>, <u>58</u>, 1307—1315.

The preceding examples, of course, are only a brief guide for the most common sources. For complete details you should consult a writing handbook or style manual.

CHECKLIST FOR RESEARCHED WRITING

A report should have

a manageable topic
adequate analysis and evaluation
a sense of authority
a clear purpose and audience
documentation of any sources used.

· ESSAYS FOR CRITICAL READING

For most of the twentieth century, immigration to the United States was determined by quotas. As explained in the Commissioner-General's Report, under the "per centum limit act"—or "quota law"—of 1921,

> The number of aliens of any nationality who may be admitted to the United States in any fiscal year shall not exceed 3 per cent of the number of persons of such nationality who were resident in the United States according to the census of 1910.
> Monthly quotas are limited to 20 per cent of the annual quota.
> For the purposes of the act, "nationality" is determined by country of birth.

Since quotas were a rejection of America's earlier open door philosophy, the introduction to the annual report gives the background of the law.

From ANNUAL REPORT OF THE COMMISSIONER-GENERAL OF IMMIGRATION, 1923

1   It is not very generally realized that the per centum limit law marked the beginning of actual restriction or limitation of immigration to the United States from Europe, Africa, Australia, and a considerable part of Asia. The Chinese exclusion act of 1882, the passport agreement with Japan which became effective in 1908, and the "barred zone" provision in the general immigration law of 1917 had already stopped or greatly reduced the influx of oriental peoples, but so far as others, and particularly Europeans, were concerned, all applicants who met the various tests prescribed in the general law were admitted. This general law, first enacted in 1882 and several times revised and strengthened, was and still is based on the principle of selection rather than numerical restriction. It is probably true that the provision barring illiterate aliens from admission, which was added to the general law in 1917, was intended as a restrictive measure rather than a quality test, but in its practical effect it was only another addition to the already numerous class of alleged undesirables who were denied admission, and obviously could not be relied upon to actually limit the volume of immigration.

2   The immigration act of 1882, which, as already indicated, was the first general law upon the subject, provided for the exclusion from the United States of the following classes only: Convicts, lunatics, idiots, and persons likely to become a public charge. This law underwent more or less important revisions in 1891, 1893, 1902, 1907, and 1917, until the last-mentioned act, which is the present general immigration law, denies admission to many classes of aliens,

including the following: Idiots, imbeciles, feeble-minded persons, epileptics, insane persons; persons who have had one or more attacks of insanity at any time previously; persons of constitutional psychopathic inferiority; persons with chronic alcoholism; paupers; professional beggars; vagrants; persons afflicted with tuberculosis in any form or with a loathsome or dangerous contagious disease; persons certified by the examining physician as being mentally or physically defective, such physical defect being of a nature which may affect the ability of the alien to earn a living; persons who have been convicted of or admit having committed a felony or other crime or misdemeanor involving moral turpitude; polygamists, or persons who practice or believe in or advocate the practice of polygamy; anarchists and similar classes; immoral persons and persons coming for an immoral purpose; contract laborers; persons likely to become a public charge; persons seeking admission within one year of date of previous debarment or deportation; persons whose ticket or passage is paid for with the money of another or who are assisted by others to come, unless it is affirmatively shown that such persons do not belong to one of the foregoing excluded classes; persons whose ticket or passage is paid for by any corporation, association, society, municipality, or foreign government, either directly or indirectly; stowaways; children under 16 years of age unless accompanied by one or both of their parents; persons who are natives of certain geographically defined territory; aliens over 16 years of age who are unable to read some language or dialect; certain accompanying aliens, as described in the last proviso of section 18 of the act; and persons who have arrived in Canada or Mexico by certain steamship lines. Persons who failed to meet certain passport requirements were added to the excluded classes in subsequent legislation.

3   Obviously it would be difficult to find, or even invent, many other terms denoting individual undesirability which might add to the foregoing list, but, as already pointed out, the general law is essentially selective in theory, for even its most rigid application with respect to the excludable classes above enumerated could not be depended upon to prevent the coming of unlimited numbers of aliens who were able to meet the tests imposed.

4   Even a casual survey of congressional discussions of the immigration problem during the past quarter of a century demonstrates very clearly that while the law makers were deeply concerned with the mental, moral, and physical quality of immigrants, there developed as time went on an even greater concern as to the fundamental racial character of the constantly increasing numbers who came. The record of alien arrivals year by year had shown a gradual falling off in the immigration of northwest European peoples, representing racial stocks which were common to America even in colonial days, and a rapid and remarkably large increase in the movement from southern and eastern European countries and Asiatic Turkey. Immigration from the last-named sources reached an annual

average of about 750,000 and in some years nearly a million came, and there seems to have been a general belief in Congress that it would increase rather than diminish. At the same time no one seems to have anticipated a revival of the formerly large influx from the "old sources," as the countries of northwest Europe came to be known.

5   This remarkable change in the sources and racial character of our immigrants led to an almost continuous agitation of the immigration problem both in and out of Congress, and there was a steadily growing demand for restriction, particularly of the newer movement from the south and east of Europe. During the greater part of this period of agitation the so-called literacy test for aliens was the favorite weapon of the restrictionists, and its widespread popularity appears to have been based quite largely on a belief, or at least a hope, that it would reduce to some extent the stream of "new" immigrants, about one-third of which was illiterate, without seriously interfering with the coming of the older type, among whom illiteracy was at a minimum.

6   Presidents Cleveland and Taft vetoed immigration bills because they contained a literacy test provision, and President Wilson vetoed two bills largely for the same reason. In 1917, however, Congress passed a general immigration bill which included the literacy provision over the President's veto, and, with certain exceptions, aliens who are unable to read are no longer admitted to the United States. At the same time, however, the World War had already had the effect of reducing immigration from Europe to a low level, and our own entry into the conflict a few days before the law in question went into effect practically stopped it altogether. Consequently, the value of the literacy provision as a means of restricting European immigration was never fairly tested under normal conditions.

7   The Congress, however, seemingly realized that even the comprehensive immigration act of 1917 would afford only a frail barrier against the promised rush from the war-stricken countries of Europe, and in December, 1920, the House of Representatives, with little opposition, passed a bill to suspend practically all immigration for the time being. The per centum limit plan was substituted by the Senate, however, and the substitute prevailed in Congress, but it failed to become law at the time because President Wilson withheld executive approval. Nevertheless, favorable action was not long delayed, for at a special session called at the beginning of the present administration the measure was quickly enacted, and, with President Harding's approval, became a law on May 19, 1921.

FUTURE USE

Summarize the selection, showing how it is relevant to your previous essay topic(s). Be sure to point out four or five significant passages.

From *FIRST LESSONS: A REPORT ON ELEMENTARY EDUCATION IN AMERICA* by William J. Bennett, Secretary of Education (1986)

1   . . . After studying elementary schools, visiting them, discussing them, and consulting with some of the country's leading educators, I conclude that American elementary education is not menaced by a "rising tide of mediocrity." It is, overall, in pretty good shape. By some measures, elementary schools are doing better now than they have in years. Yet elementary education in the United States could be better still. Indeed, it will need to be better in the years ahead because we depend so much on it, because not all schools are yet as good as they ought to be—and because it is not in our nature as a society to settle for less than excellence for all.

2   In the remainder of this report I go into some detail about the condition and direction of elementary education in America. Let me here set forth certain general observations and recommendations:

   1. The principal goals of elementary education are to build for every child a strong foundation for further education, for democratic citizenship, and for eventual entry into responsible adulthood.

   2. Parents have the central role in children's education and must be empowered to play it successfully.

   3. Children do not just "grow up." They must be raised by the community of adults—all adults. The community should accept as its solemn responsibility—as a covenant—the nurture, care, and education of the coming generation. . . .

3   What should a child know?

4   In an address at the National Press Club, shortly after becoming Secretary of Education, thinking mainly about high schools, I tried to answer that question as follows:

   We should want every student to know how mountains are made, and that for most actions there is an equal and opposite reaction. They should know who said 'I am the state' and who said 'I have a dream.' They should know about subjects and predicates, about isosceles triangles and ellipses. They should know where the Amazon flows and what the First Amendment means. They should know about the Donner Party and slavery, and Shylock, Hercules, and Abigail Adams, where Ethiopia is, and why there is a Berlin Wall. . . .

5   I refer back to this litany because in our examination of elementary education we asked much the same question and received a closely related answer. While we do not expect sixth-graders to understand the geopolitical implications of the Berlin Wall, we hope that they can locate the divided city on a map. While elementary graduates cannot be expected to give a sophisticated analysis of the slavery issue, we can reasonably believe that they will have heard about Dred Scott, and will know that slavery was a major cause of the Civil War.

6   In other words, we may plausibly expect that elementary school will give our children the basic facts and understandings of our civilization, and that it will equip them with the skills to apprehend more complex knowledge, thus awakening the appetite for further learning. . . .

7   Parents belong at the center of a young child's education. The single best way to improve elementary education is to strengthen parents' role in it, both by reinforcing their relationship with the school and by helping and encouraging them in their own critical job of teaching the young. Not all teachers are parents, but all parents are teachers.

8   Parents' oversight of their children's education ought not to be limited to the margins. We already expect parents to make a wide array of choices: whether to start a child in preschool or kindergarten; whether to accept or contest a recommendation for retention, and so on. We expect—and should expect—parents to engage themselves directly in their children's education: to read to them if they can, to ask others to read to them if they cannot, to encourage children to read on their own, to meet with teachers, to ensure that homework gets done, to furnish necessary supplies and materials, perhaps above all to convey to their children—not just once, but incessantly—the immense value that they, the parents, assign to a good education.

9   I propose that we acknowledge parents' right to choose their children's schools as the norm, not the exception, and that we extend it to as many parents as possible—not just to those fortunate enough to live in particular communities or wealthy enough to change their place of residence. . . .

10   The primary requisites for parental cooperation in the enterprise of education, for two parents or one, are attitude and commitment. As Ken Levine, a Baltimore mathematics teacher, wrote, "Children coming from a home where one or both parents come to school, meet the teacher, and know the curriculum, come from a home with a message: 'We value what you do. Your success is important to us'. . . . And children coming from a home where the parents do not get involved get an equally clear message: 'You're on your own. Let us know how things work out.'"

11   . . . [T]hese are the first lessons of living in a democracy. We take turns; we follow and lead; we solve disputes by appealing to reason, not fists; we help others when they are in danger; we stand up for what's right. These simple lessons learned in home and school resonate through the great decisions of our national life.

12   Reciprocity between parents and school implies a significant commitment on parents' part. Here are some specific parental practices that may help a child's progress:

>   Establishing a quiet place where children can read and do homework; giving assistance when needed; looking over homework, helping with it when necessary, but encouraging children to manage it on their own;
>   Setting limits on play time and television watching;
>   Staying in touch with the teacher; meeting with the teacher several times a year to examine the child's problems and successes in school;
>   Checking report cards, talking with the child about problems and progress in various subjects; commenting on the child's work, providing positive reinforcement for good work;
>   Taking part in PTA and school board meetings; chaperoning school trips; perhaps volunteering in the school itself.

13   Parents are the central figures, captains of the vessel on which children voyage to maturity. But they are not the entire crew. Even as a ship captain must be able to rely on expert navigators, engine-room technicians, and cargo handlers, so must parents be able to draw on the expertise, the caring, the energies, the support, the example of other adults: of family members, neighbors, church members, friends, teachers, doctors, policemen, television writers, social workers, advertisers, clergy, legislators, professors, and coaches. What is more, when parents are absent, inept or irresponsible, though it is folly to suppose that others can truly replace them, it is nevertheless imperative that the community of adults do all within its power to fill in for them. It matters not whether the child is rich or poor, black or white, brilliant or slow. Children who tomorrow will join the community of adults should be the foremost concern of that community today.

14   Though only 27 percent of American households include school-age children, we cannot afford to regard elementary education as the exclusive concern of parents and professional educators. If our institutions, values, and knowledge are to make it into the next century in good shape, we must come to regard the education of young children as a task shared by all adults. We must see it as a covenant with the family firmly at its center; with the adult community supporting—not supplanting—the family; and with elementary schools as a fundamental expression of the community's values and aspirations.

15   When we form this covenant, what is the task to which we mutually agree? What, in other words, is the goal of American elementary education? I believe its highest purposes are to prepare children well for further education and to lay the groundwork for their own eventual entry into the community of responsible adults and democratic citizens. In our time, in this land, democratic citizenship requires an array of knowledge and skills: a common language through which we

all can communicate; an understanding of our civilization and its institutions; knowledge of our national symbols; a grasp of America's unique cultural pluralism; and respect for the values and precepts that enable people from different backgrounds to live together as Americans.

16   The specific purpose of schools within this covenant is to provide a foundation—to teach the grammar and syntax through which our many American voices speak to one another. This means, of course, the basic skills of reading, writing, and math. But it also means historical, scientific, geographic, and civic literacy; it means art and music, and all the tools with which our children can build lives of independence, virtue, and wisdom.

17   Since elementary schools are virtually the only institution in our society in which attendance is compulsory for everyone, we have asked them to perform all sorts of functions unrelated to their instructional mission. Study Group member Leanna Landsmann writes: "Our schools are asked to do a lot more than they can, and rather than say 'no,' schools try. They are considered the tool to achieve widespread integration, to teach children health, to feed the hungry, to help counsel children of divorce. Now it's time to encourage supportive partnerships that relieve schools of noninstructional services." . . .

FUTURE USE

Summarize the selection, showing how it is relevant to your previous essay topic(s). Be sure to point out four or five significant passages.

In the early 1970s several investigations revealed misconduct on the part of the Central Intelligence Agency. This discovery led to a national debate about the morality of covert operations and their place in a democracy. The following selection is the summary of the report of the Senate Select Committee to Study Governmental Operations with Respect to Intelligence Activities, released in 1976.

From REPORT ON FOREIGN AND MILITARY INTELLIGENCE ACTIVITIES OF THE UNITED STATES

General Findings

1   The committee finds that United States foreign and military intelligence agencies have made important contributions to the nation's security, and generally have performed their missions with dedication and distinction. The committee further finds that the individual men and women serving America in difficult and dangerous intelligence assignments deserve the respect and gratitude of the nation.

2   The committee finds that there is a continuing need for an effective system of foreign and military intelligence. United States interests and responsibilities in the world will be challenged, for the foreseeable future, by strong and potentially hostile powers. This requires the maintenance of an effective American intelligence system. The committee has found that the Soviet KGB and other hostile intelligence services maintain extensive foreign intelligence operations, for both intelligence collection and covert operational purposes. These activities pose a threat to the intelligence activities and interests of the United States and its allies.

3   The committee finds that Congress has failed to provide the necessary statutory guidelines to insure that intelligence agencies carry out their missions in accord with constitutional processes. Mechanisms for and the practice of congressional oversight have not been adequate. Further, Congress has not devised appropriate means to effectively use the valuable information developed by the intelligence agencies. Intelligence information and analysis that exist within the Executive branch clearly would contribute to sound judgments and more effective legislation in the areas of foreign policy and national security.

4   The committee finds that covert action operations have not been an exceptional instrument used only in rare instances when the vital interests of the United States have been at stake. On the contrary, Presidents and Administrations have made excessive, and at times self-defeating, use of covert action. In addition, covert action has become a routine program with a bureaucratic mo-

mentum of its own. The long-term impact, at home and abroad, of repeated disclosure of US covert action never appears to have been assessed. The cumulative effect of covert actions has been increasingly costly to America's interests and reputation. The committee believes that covert action must be employed only in the most extraordinary circumstances.

5   Although there is a question concerning the extent to which the Constitution requires publication of intelligence expenditures information, the committee finds that the Constitution at least requires public disclosure and public authorization of an annual aggregate figure for US national intelligence activities. Congress' failure as a whole to monitor the intelligence agencies' expenditures has been a major element in the ineffective legislative oversight of the intelligence community. The permanent intelligence oversight committee(s) of Congress should give further consideration to the question of the extent to which further public disclosure of intelligence budget information is prudent and constitutionally necessary.

6   At the same time, the committee finds that the operation of an extensive and necessarily secret intelligence system places severe strains on the nation's constitutional government. The committee is convinced, however, that the competing demands of secrecy and the requirements of the democratic process—our Constitution and our laws—can be reconciled. The need to protect secrets must be balanced with the assurance that secrecy is not used as a mean to hide the abuse of power or the failures and mistakes of policy. Means must and can be provided for lawful disclosure of unneeded or unlawful secrets.

7   The committee finds that intelligence activities should not be regarded as ends in themselves. Rather, the nation's intelligence functions should be organized and directed to assure that they serve the needs of those in the executive and legislative branches who have responsibility for formulating or carrying out foreign and national security policy.

8   The committee finds that Congress has failed to provide the necessary statutory guidelines to insure that intelligence agencies carry out their necessary missions in accord with constitutional process.

9   In order to provide firm direction for the intelligence agencies, the committee finds that new statutory charters for these agencies must be written which take account of the experience of the past three and a half decades. Further, the committee finds that the relationship among the various intelligence agencies and between them and the director of Central Intelligence should be restructured in order to achieve better accountability, coordination and more efficient use of resources.

10   These tasks are urgent. They should be undertaken by the Congress in consultation with the Executive branch in the coming year. The recent proposals and executive actions by the President are most welcome. However, further action by Congress is necessary.

Recommendations

11   1. The National Security Act should be recast by omnibus legislation which would set forth the basic purposes of national intelligence activities, and define the relationship between the Congress and the intelligence agencies of the Executive branch. This revision should be given the highest priority by the intelligence oversight committee of Congress, acting in consultation with the Executive branch.

12   2. The new legislation should define the charter of the organization and entities in the US intelligence community. It should establish charters for the National Security Council, the director of Central Intelligence, the Central Intelligence Agency, the national intelligence components of the Department of Defense, including the National Security Agency and the Defense Intelligence Agency, and all other elements of the intelligence community, including joint organizations of two or more agencies.

13   3. This legislation should set forth the general structure and procedures of the intelligence community and the roles and responsibilities of the agencies which comprise it.

14   4. The legislation should contain specific and clearly defined prohibitions or limitations on various activities carried out by the respective components of the intelligence community.

FUTURE USE

Summarize the selection, showing how it is relevant to your previous essay topic(s). Be sure to point out four or five significant passages.

Political scientist Jeane J. Kirkpatrick has taught at Georgetown University in Washington, D.C., and served as U.S. Ambassador to the United Nations. Identified as a "neoconservative," she is strongly anticommunist in foreign policy but closer to liberal thinkers on domestic issues. In 1974 she published Political Woman, *an important study of women's achievements in public life. The present selection appeared in 1980 in* Reflections of America, *published by the U.S. Department of Commerce.*

From WOMEN IN THE SEVENTIES: CHANGING GOALS, CHANGING ROLES
by Jeane J. Kirkpatrick

1   During the seventies important changes occurred in popular rhetoric concerning women. One heard on radio and television and read in newspapers about women's revolution, women's liberation, International Women's Year, equal opportunity, affirmative action—all proclaiming the demand that women get a larger share of the basic values of the society and participate more fully in all social domains. What really happened to women in that decade? Did the flamboyant rhetoric reflect a swift or dramatic change in the reality of women's lives and their place in society, or was it merely media hype announcing changing fashions in "liberation" much as it hawks changing hemlines and hair styles?

2   Without doubt, important changes occurred in the education, attitudes, and roles of women during the past decade. Most of these changes were an extension and acceleration of trends in progress since the aftermath of World War II. The percentage of women in the population continues to rise, as do median and average life expectancies. Marriage and birth rates are down, the divorce rate up. The number of families headed by women continues its steady rise and the percentage of children living with both parents declines. Probably the most dramatic objective changes in women's lives relate to the employment of progressively larger numbers of women for progressively longer periods of time. In 1950, women comprised 29.6 percent of the American work force, in 1978 they comprised 41.8 percent.

3   This dramatic increase, described by a recent Labor Department study as "the most significant phenomenon of the last 30 years," has altered the character of the American work force and the experience of American women (table 1). Changes in the sexual composition of the work force were, however, only the proverbial tip of a proverbial iceberg.

4   In 1978 multiple trends reflected changing expectations about women's ap-

Reprinted from Reflections of America, *Bureau of the Census, U.S. Department of Commerce.*

Table 1.   Percent of Female Population in the Labor Force

Year	All women	Single	Married	Married, husband present	Widowed/ divorced
1940	27.4	48.1	16.7	14.7	32.0
1950	31.4	50.5	24.8	23.8	36.0
1960	34.8	44.1	31.7	30.5	37.1
1970	42.6	53.0	41.4	40.8	36.2
1978	49.1	60.5	48.1	47.6	40.0

Note: The percentage of women who work has gone up sharply since 1940 in all categories except widowed/divorced.

Source: *Statistical Abstract*, 1979, table 660.

titudes and possible futures. More girls were seeking and receiving education in fields previously regarded as appropriate only for males. More women held nontraditional jobs and performed traditional roles in nontraditional ways. More women worked after they were married and had had children. Each of these trends reflected changes in women's conceptions of themselves and of femininity. Each reflected changes in the attitudes and expectations of the men who educated their daughters and acquiesced in their wives' employment.

5   The gradual movement of women from private domains to greater participation in the public life of the society can be viewed as part of two historical trends. On the one hand, the changes affecting women incorporate them into the liberating, egalitarian trends that have been so powerful in shaping Western societies in this century. On the other hand, the evolution of women's roles can be seen as part of an equally broad trend that involves the transfer of ever more functions from what is ambiguously termed the private to the public sector. In this essay I am concerned with both these processes.

6   To see where we are going, it is always necessary to remind ourselves of where we are coming from. Traditional sex roles, as they actually existed in the lives of most women, constitute the baseline. In the United States, as in most other societies, those traditional roles required that women concentrate on "affection" values and prepare themselves for nurturant roles, most of which were carried on inside the home. The institution specializing in the pursuit of affection is, above all, the family, which features the roles of daughter, wife, and mother, and requires the skills of homemaking, nursing, child care, educating the young, and aiding a husband. Satisfactory performance of these roles has been regarded as incompatible with other roles. The traditional expectation in this and other cultures has been that these roles were appropriate for all women and would be performed within the family. The few alternative roles traditionally available to women outside the family—nursing, elementary school teaching—require similar skills and feelings as those required by family roles. The distinguishing characteristic of roles that have been widely available to women in Western societies during this century is the centrality of *empathy* to their performance. In

Table 2. Women in Educational and Health Professions

(Thousands)

Occupation	Male	Female
Education, total (1976)	1,278	2,321
Administration	37	7
Principal, assistant principal	93	17
Classroom teacher	701	1,345
Elementary	169	823
Secondary	493	415
Other professional	78	161
Teacher's aide	18	218
Clerical, secretarial	5	231
Service workers	346	340
Health, total (1978)	1,205.1	3,429.9
Health administrators	99.0	85.0
Physicians	376.1	47.9
Registered nurses	36.7	1,075.3
Health technologists and technicians	144.9	353.1

Source: *Statistical Abstract*, 1979, tables 162 and 248.

education they have been teachers rather than principals; in medicine they have been nurses rather than physicians or administrators (table 2).

7   Of course, women have always cultivated other skills and worked at a wide variety of occupations, but most of these activities have been carried out within the home, within the context of the family, or under conditions of dire economic need. Women's share of other values, including wealth, status, and power, have been derived from the activities of husbands, fathers, and, occasionally, brothers. Thus the wife of a rich man is rich, the daughter of an important man, important, and so forth. The notion that women could or should compete in the public arena directly and independently for an independent share of values is a revolutionary idea that is a prerequisite even to noting that women as a class do not fare very well in the allocation of values in the society.

8   But it is clear that in this and most other societies, the traditional expectation was that unless dire economic need forced women into the marketplace, they would take the responsibility for home and family, looking after aged parents and growing children and making a house a home. Pursuit of other values and occupations would be left to men. The range of activities and jobs open to men has been wide; traditionally men have been excluded only from specializing in roles concerned mainly with nurturing. . . .

9   In a reasonably stable society, the goals and identities of each person are roughly consistent with those of all, and their roles are complementary. "Male"

and "female" roles thus reinforce one another. Boys and girls learn and internalize the norms and behavior recommended for males and females and prepare themselves through education, training, and practice to fill the roles "appropriate" to their sex. In the United States rapid cultural and social change are altering traditional patterns of ways of feeling, being, and interacting. In consequence, growing numbers of women doubt that their participation in contemporary values is all that it might be. . . .

10   The fact is that more women than ever are participating in more institutional processes. Politics is a microcosm of the changes that have occurred in most domains. Even though a constitutional amendment enfranchised women on an equal basis with men, decades passed before the percent of women who actually voted equalled the percent of male voters. Eventually, however, women decided that voting was an appropriate activity for people like themselves. In the 1978 congressional elections, equal proportions of women and men cast ballots.[1]

11   Slowly women have moved into other political roles. The first page of *Political Woman*, completed in 1973, commented:

> Half a century after the ratification of the nineteenth amendment, no woman has been nominated to be president or vice-president, no woman has served on the Supreme Court. Today there is no woman in the Cabinet, no woman in the Senate, no woman serving as Governor of a major State, no woman mayor of a major city, no woman in the top leadership of either major party.

12   The first three of these statements remained true 5 years later. No woman has been nominated to be President or Vice President and no woman had been appointed to the Supreme Court. By 1980, however, women headed the Department of Health and Human Services and the new Department of Education; Nancy Kassebaum, Republican of Kansas, was elected to the Senate in 1978; women served as governors of Connecticut and Washington and as mayors of a dozen major cities including Chicago, San Francisco, Houston, and Oklahoma city;[2] and in both parties there are women such as Anne Armstrong, Mary Louise Smith, and Anne Wexler who have achieved national influence. These changes in women's political role signal real if undramatic changes in the attitudes of those in a position to appoint women to high positions and broad if undramatic changes in the attitudes of voters who elect women to statehouses and city halls. At no level in any branch of Government are women present in

[1] Although women's turnout has dropped during the past decade, so has that of men. Between the 1968 and 1976 Presidential elections, the proportions of women voting declined 7 percent and that of men 10 percent. (U.S. Department of Commerce, Bureau of the Census, *Statistical Portrait of Women: 1978*, p. 84.)

[2] Also, Raleigh, North Carolina; Austin, Texas; San Jose, California; Phoenix, Arizona; San Antonio, Texas; Lincoln, Nebraska; St. Petersburg, Florida; Cincinnati, Ohio. (*U.S. News & World Report*, July 16, 1979.)

numbers remotely proportionate to their numbers in the population or in the relevant age or educational level. Moreover, in the Congress, women have declined in numbers and influence. But at lower levels of the political system the number of women candidates—for State legislatures, city councils, school boards, and dozens of other offices—has increased more markedly (table 3).

13 Changes in the sexual composition of the Nation's political class is made more significant because of its relation to changes elsewhere in the society. In a democracy, the tenure of officeholders depends on popular approval; therefore women can succeed in politics only with the permission of majorities of voters. A woman can succeed brilliantly in business or journalism or science without any broad changes in the attitudes of others. But a woman can be elected governor only when and if a majority of voters in her State believe that a woman is, in principle, competent to serve in that office and that the candidate, in particular, is as capable, as reasonable, and as judicious as her male opponent.

14 The slow but significant increase in the number of women who seek and win public office is then one measure of broad secular change in feelings and expectations concerning women's natures and women's roles. One measure of this change is provided by four decades of public opinion polls of attitudes toward a woman as President. Those polled in 1937 indicated that 31 percent would accept a woman, 65 percent would not, and 4 percent had no opinion. By July 1978, after a steady change over the years, the figures were 76 percent accepting and only 19 percent not.

15 Since roles are anchored in self-conceptions and self-systems, changing women's share of values will not be easy or quickly accomplished. Significant change in the value position of a group occurs as the last step in a complex process that involves changes in both the subjective and objective aspects of society. It entails changes in modal character, in skill acquisition, and in role definitions.

Table 3. Number of Women Candidates for Public Office: 1974 and 1978

Public office	1974	1978
Federal Government	47	47
Senate	3	2
House of Representatives	44	45
State government	1,177	1,395
Governor	3	1
House	989	1,170
Senate	137	178
Statewide offices[1]	48	46

[1]Excluding governor.

Source: *A Statistical Portrait of Women in the United States: 1978*, Current Population Reports, series P–23, no. 100, 1980, table 10–3, p. 86; National Women's Educational Fund.

This is another way of saying that women's position in society can change significantly only as women change and society changes. If more women desire public office or good jobs and acquire the skills needed to fill these jobs and are permitted to compete for them, then—and only then—will women gain a larger share of power, wealth, and other values.

16   In a society in which individuals define their goals and choose their careers, changes in the distributions of values reflect changes in the goals of persons and in the rules governing access to the institutional processes through which the values in question are available. Significant changes in value distribution as between the sexes can occur only (1) as the goals of women change, as, for example, when significant numbers of women are motivated to seek higher income and more status rather than the pleasures of affectional relations; (2) when significant numbers of women acquire the resources and skills needed to effectively compete for the values in question; and (3) when the rules of access to institutional processes through which the desired goods are distributed permit women to compete. The available evidence suggests that trends toward the diversification of women's roles are already well established.

17   One indicator of the goals of women are responses to a question: Now if you were free to do either, would you prefer to have a job outside the home or would you prefer to stay home and take care of a house and family? In the 6 years between 1974 and 1980, the percent of women who avowed a preference for taking a job rose from 35 to 46 percent. Moreover, sharp differences between the preferences of women under 30 and those over 50 foreshadow still greater changes to come.[3] Even more striking are generational differences in expectations of women who do not work. The Virginia Slims Poll reports that:

> Nearly three-quarters (73 percent) of non-working women under 30 years of age plan to work in the future. More than three-fifths (62 percent) of the non-working women now in their 30's intend to get full time jobs eventually.[4]

18   Another study showed that among 1st-year college students in 4-year institutions, the percents agreeing that it was better for women to devote themselves to the home was still lower—only 18.3 percent in nonselective public universities and 6.5 percent in highly selective private universities held these views.[5] Changing patterns of behavior also testify to these changing attitudes. Today

---

[3]*The 1980 Virginia Slims American Women's Opinion Poll: A Survey of Contemporary Attitudes,* conducted by the Roper Organization, p. 44.

[4]1980 Virginia Slims Poll, p. 34.

[5]Alexander Astin, Margo R. King, and Gerald T. Richardson, *The American Freshman: National Norms for Fall 1979,* Cooperative Institutional Research Program, American Council on Education, University of California at Los Angeles, p. 71.

Table 4. Degrees Received by Women: Academic Years 1969–70 and 1976–77

(Percent)

Degree	1969–70	1976–77
Bachelor's	43.1	46.1
Master's	39.7	47.1
Doctorate	13.3	24.3
Biological science	14.3	21.4
Business management	1.7	6.3
Education	20.3	34.8
Engineering	.7	2.8
Fine and applied arts	19.3	32.5
Foreign languages	33.4	51.5
Health professions	16.2	32.0
Physical sciences	5.4	9.5
Social sciences	13.0	22.1

Source: U.S. Department of Commerce, Bureau of the Census, A *Statistical Portrait of Women in the United States:* 1978, Current Population Reports, series P-23, no. 100, 1980, table 5–3, p. 39.

even larger numbers of women finish high school, finish college, and pursue postgraduate studies (table 4).

19   The progressive penetration of all fields by women is illustrated by their growing share of doctoral degrees in all fields, including such male bastions as engineering and business. A recent study of college students reported that women's interest in the four careers traditionally considered male domains—business, engineering, law, and medicine—has more than quadrupled since 1966 (from 5.9 to 25.9 percent from 1966 to 1979). Moreover this has occurred during a period when men's interests in these fields has remained stable.[6]

20   The steady growth in the proportion of women in the labor force itself constitutes further indirect evidence on women's changing goals. Since the overwhelming majority of employed women say the need for money is the primary reason they work (as compared to only 14 percent who say they work for something interesting to do), it has been suggested that high rates of employment reflect the pressures of inflation rather than changing goals and self-conception. Altogether, however, the data strongly support a conclusion that changes in priorities—and therefore in values and self-conceptions—underlie the mass entrance of women into the work force. Note first that this occurred during a period of rising affluence. Note second that income is roughly correlated with education, and over half of college-educated women prefer a job to

[6]The University of California, Office of Public Information, press release January 20, 1980 for Astin, King, Richardson, *The American Freshman* (see footnote 5).

staying home as compared to 40 percent of the less educated. Rising material appetites would appear to be a more important spur to employment than economic needs as more traditionally conceived, especially since the median percent of family income accounted for by wives' earnings was only 26.1 in 1977 and the median income of married couples in which the wife is in the paid labor force ($20,268) is substantially above the median for all married-couple families ($17,616).[7]

21   None of this implies that women's work experience is like that of men or that it is likely to become so in the foreseeable future. To the contrary, the jobs, hours, and wages of women continue to be very different from those of men. Through the seventies, women worked fewer hours, at lower rates of pay then men. They were twice as likely as men to work part-time and substantially less likely to have held a full-time job for at least 40 weeks. There was, moreover, almost no change in this pattern during the decade.

22   Neither the present nor the future of America's women conforms to the expectation of those who would like women to pattern their lives on men's. No more do they conform to the hopes of those who would like a return to traditional sex roles. The fact is that all of us—male and female—are involved in relatively slow but sweeping changes in sex-role distributions that have already transformed the lives of many of us and our children. I see no grounds to expect a brave new unisex world just over the horizon but good reason for thinking that by the beginning of the next century, young women will have more choices, more freedom, and problems quite different from the ones confronting those who came of age at the beginning of this century.

[7]U.S. Department of Commerce, Bureau of the Census, *Statistical Portrait of Women: 1978*, p. 79.

FUTURE USE

Summarize the selection, showing how it is relevant to your previous essay topic(s). Be sure to point out four or five significant passages.

· MAKING CONNECTIONS

1. Why do you think attempts to limit immigration (p. 445) began when they did? What was happening in the United States at the turn of the tieth century that affected attitudes toward foreigners and immigration? What was the effect of the closing of the frontier? The rise of labor unions? The agitation for women's rights? What was Booker T. Washington's attitude toward immigrants (p. 244)? Did the various underclasses see each other as allies or competitors? Why do think this was so? Is the situation still the same? What research topic(s) can emerge from this discussion?

2. What does William Bennett (p. 448) believe is the purpose of elementary schools? What is the role of parents? Of the adult community in general? How does the curriculum he outlines produce the results that he wants? How do his ideas compare and contrast with other selections you have read this term? What research topic(s) can emerge from this discussion?

3. What values are assumed in the Senate report on intelligence gathering (p. 452)? How do these values compare and contrast with the values taught in school? How does the behavior of the American government compare with the values that America espouses, for example those of President Carter (p. 373) or Senator Beveridge (p. 370)? Is there a place in a democracy for covert activities? Is it sufficient or moral to say "everyone does it"? What is the function of covert activity? What is the alternative? What research topic(s) can emerge from this discussion?

4. To what extent do Jeane Kirkpatrick's training and political views influence her analysis of women's achievements? Would a career politician use the data in the same way? Would a traditional liberal or conservative reach the same conclusions she does? How does this essay compare in purpose and content with the selection by Feinstein (p. 368)? The selection by Veblen (p. 134)? How does the data compare with the present situation? What research topic(s) can emerge from this discussion?

5. To what extent do the selections by Bennett and Kirkpatrick reflect American values? What would be different if these studies had been done by a foreigner examining life in the United States? What if an American were studying schools and women in Russia or Japan? What research topic(s) can emerge from this discussion?

· ADDITIONAL ESSAYS FOR DISCUSSION

SMALL TOWN VALUES IN THE BIG CITY: AN INTERVIEW WITH DA TOM SULLIVAN
by Harvey Minkoff (1981)

1   "There are many reasons to change a law, but the worst is because people are breaking it. When you start letting the numbers control morality, society is in danger."

2   The speaker is Thomas Sullivan, for the past 25 years with the office of the District Attorney of Staten Island and for the last six years the DA, and in a wide-ranging interview he is describing law enforcement in a borough that has kept its small town values in the midst of the Big Apple.

3   "Law must come from the people," DA Sullivan says. "It's the job of the Legislature to understand what laws people want, and it's the job of the police and courts to enforce those laws. The trouble arises when you make changes not because of social standards but because of the numbers. On Staten Island, we still make arrests for pornography and bust dirty book stores. But more often than not, public pressure forces adult bookstores to close." In one recent case, which the DA cites, there were 200 parents picketing by the time the police arrived with the summons.

4   But isn't pornography a victimless crime? "There is no such thing as a victimless crime," DA Sullivan insists. "When certain types of behavior are allowed, society as a whole is the victim."

5   The reason the police can go after such crimes on Staten Island, the DA believes, is that people there still have a sense of community and local pride. For example, though the borough's 400,000 people would make it one of the forty largest cities in the country, there is a close—and often personal—relationship between the police and the DA's staff because all the assistant DAs and most of the area's 800 police officers live in the borough. "There's no feeling among the public that this is an occupying army. These are all hometown people protecting their families and homes," he explains.

6   But on the question of whether a residency law would provide the rest of New York City with a similar positive feeling, DA Sullivan has his doubts. "I don't support a citywide residency law because there would be monumental problems in some areas of Manhattan and the Bronx," he says. "Where it's possible, it works very well, but it isn't always possible. And having it in those instances would do more harm than good."

7   In other ways also DA Sullivan is wary of extrapolating from the experience

of his jurisdiction to the rest of the city and other areas. For this reason, while he acknowledges the importance of responding to the needs of his constituency, he believes that city-wide or state-wide officials cannot do the same thing as easily. "It would be an error to look at Staten Island and then say that there could be a uniform standard or approach for the whole city," he says. "Manhattan has prostitution. Brooklyn has racial friction. These problems don't exist on Staten Island. If you tried to establish uniform goals, most of them would not be relevant here, and the problems that we feel strongly about would be considered unimportant. A uniform standard for a city as large as New York would have to be a lowest common denominator. And I don't think we should reduce Staten Island to the standards of the rest of the city."

8   Nevertheless, the DA feels that the public officials have an important role to play in law enforcement. "When Mayor Koch, for example, tells the media that the law enforcement system is not doing its job properly, he is not putting pressure on the DA's office. As a matter of fact, he is mirroring what we ourselves are saying," he says.

9   And on the issue of political pressure on law enforcement in general, he adds: "The DA's office must be political in the sense that we are elected and have to respond to the concerns of our constituents. This in itself is not bad, since the laws that we enforce must derive from the will of the people. But politicians should be careful not to meddle in the actual workings of the judicial system. They pass the laws, but we enforce them."

10   In practice, what this means is that the police and DA's office work together to get the criminals off the streets, not to make headlines or please political leaders. "The police here are not concerned with just making a collar. They want to get a conviction and often ask our advice about what they ought to do before an arrest to make sure it leads to a conviction. And for their part, my assistant DAs avoid puffing up charges. When they get an indictment, they want to be sure it sticks."

11   In addition, DA Sullivan is proud of the way his staff handles the cases that come to them. From beginning to end, each case is the responsibility of a single assistant DA, who interviews witnesses, assesses the evidence, decides on the indictment and only then goes to the grand jury. Moreover, victims of a crime have only one assistant DA to deal with and are not discouraged by being sent from person to person and having to retell their story over and over again. "In fact," says the DA with a certain satisfaction, "they come to see the assistant DA as 'their lawyer' in a sense."

12   All of this leads to the kind of success that is evident even in bare statistics: the court backlog is the lowest of any county in the city, with fewer than 5% of the cases more than six terms old—and even these all have valid explanations such as defense requests and psychiatric study.

13   "We are definitely in control of the situation here," says DA Sullivan proudly. "The system has not broken down."

From FOURTH AMENDMENT RIGHTS OF LAW ENFORCEMENT EMPLOYEES AGAINST SEARCHES OF THEIR WORKSPACE
By Daniel L. Schofield, S.J.D. (1987)

1   Public employees are not, by virtue of their employment, deprived of the protection of the U.S. Constitution, and the Supreme Court has ruled that police officers "are not relegated to a watered-down version of constitutional rights."[1]

2   However, the government has an interest in the integrity of its law enforcement officers which may justify some intrusions on the privacy of officers which the fourth amendment would not otherwise tolerate.[2] Recently, in the case of O'Connor v. Ortega,[3] the Court examined the constitutionality of workplace searches of a public employee's office, desk, and file cabinet and concluded that public employers must be given wide latitude to search employee workspace for work-related reasons. Lower courts have also addressed that issue in the context of law enforcement employment. These decisions set forth the legal principles that govern such searches and are of obvious interest to administrators and employees in law enforcement organizations. This article examines those decisions and offers some recommendations to assist in the development of organizational policy and procedures that are consistent with fourth amendment requirements and also meet legitimate law enforcement objectives.

FOURTH AMENDMENT
PROTECTION IN THE WORKPLACE

3   The fourth amendment protects "the right of the people to be secure in their persons, houses, papers, and effects, against unreasonable searches and seizures," and searches and seizures by government employers or supervisors of the private property of their employees are subject to the restraints of the fourth amendment.[4] The strictures of the fourth amendment have been applied to the conduct of government officials in various civil activities, including searches of

[1]*Garrity v. New Jersey,* 87 S.Ct. 616, 620 (1967).
[2]*Kirkpatrick v. City of Los Angeles,* 803 F.2d 485 (9th Cir. 1986).
[3]107 S.Ct. 1492 (1987).
[4]*Id.* at 1497.

Reprinted from FBI Law Enforcement Bulletin.

employee workspace by government employers for the purpose of determining whether any administrative or personnel action is warranted or for other reasons. Fourth amendment protection is not limited to only investigations of criminal behavior but can also protect public employees when a workplace search infringes their reasonable expectation of privacy.

4   For definitional purposes, the terms "workplace" or "workspace" in this article include those areas and items related to work and generally within the employer's control, such as offices, desks, file cabinets, and lockers. These areas remain part of the "workplace" even if an employee places personal items in them. However, an item does not necessarily become part of the "workplace" merely because it passes through the confines of a government facility. For example, an employee may bring closed luggage, a handbag, or a briefcase to the office. Such items do not necessarily become part of the "workplace" for purposes of determining whether the employee has a reasonable expectation of privacy in their contents.

Supreme Court Decision

5   On March 31, 1987, the Supreme Court announced its decision in O'Connor v. Ortega, which addresses two issues of importance to public employers and employees. First, under what circumstances do public employees have a reasonable expectation of privacy in their workspace? Second, where an expectation of privacy exists in a particular workspace area, when and under what conditions may public employers search such areas? A proper understanding of the O'Connor decision and its implications for law enforcement organizations requires a careful review of the facts.

Facts and Procedural History

6   Dr. Ortega was an employee of a State hospital and had primary responsibility for training physicians in the psychiatric residency program. Hospital officials became concerned about possible improprieties in his management of the program, particularly with respect to his acquisition of a computer and charges against him concerning sexual harassment of female hospital employees and inappropriate disciplinary action against a resident. While he was on administrative leave pending investigation of the charges, hospital officials, allegedly in order to inventory and secure State property, searched his office and seized personal items from his desk and file cabinets that were used in administrative proceedings resulting in his discharge. No formal inventory of the property in the office was ever made, and all other papers in the office were merely placed in boxes for storage. In a subsequent civil suit against hospital officials, Dr. Ortega alleged that the search of his office violated the fourth amendment. The U.S. Court of Appeals for the Ninth Circuit concluded that the search unconstitu-

tionally intruded on his reasonable expectation of privacy because the office had a locked door, contained confidential and personal files, and had been occupied by Dr. Ortega for 17 years.[5]

7   The Supreme Court unanimously concluded that Dr. Ortega had a reasonable expectation of privacy in his desk and file cabinets, and five Justices agreed he had a similar expectation in his office. Disagreement on the Court centered on the appropriate standard of reasonableness that should govern workplace searches. A plurality of four Justices, in an opinion authored by Justice O'Connor, voted to remand the case to the district court to determine whether hospital officials were justified by legitimate work-related reasons to enter Dr. Ortega's office and also to evaluate the reasonableness of both the inception of the search and its scope.[6] Justice Scalia concurred, but disagreed with the plurality's reasonableness analysis. Four dissenting Justices concluded that the search of Dr. Ortega's office violated the fourth amendment because there was no justification to dispense with the warrant and probable cause requirements.[7]

Expectation of Privacy Analysis

8   The Court unanimously rejected the argument that public employees lose their fourth amendment rights as a condition of public employment and can never have a reasonable expectation of privacy in workspace.[8] An employee's expectation of privacy in workspace may be reduced by actual business practices and procedures or be so open to fellow employees or the public that no expectation of privacy is reasonable.[9] The great variety of work environments requires a case-by-case analysis to determine whether an expectation of privacy in workspace is reasonable in light of a particular employment relationship. The Court concluded that Dr. Ortega has a reasonable expectation of privacy because he had occupied his office for 17 years, did not share his desk or file cabinets with any other employee, and the hospital had not established any reasonable regulation or policy discouraging employees from storing personal papers and effects in their desks or file cabinets.[10]

Reasonableness Determination

9   The warrantless search of Dr. Ortega's office must meet the reasonableness test of the fourth amendment. The appropriate standard of reasonableness depends on the context within which a search takes place and is determined by

[5]*Ortega v. O'Connor*, 764 F.2d 703 (9th Cir. 1985).

[6]Joining Justice O'Connor were the Chief Justice and Justices White and Powell.

[7]Justice Blackmun wrote the dissenting opinion and was joined by Justices Brennan, Marshall, and Stevens.

[8]107 S.Ct. at 1498.

[9]*Id.* . . .

[10]*Id.* at 1499.

balancing ". . . the invasion of the employees' legitimate expectations of privacy against the government's need for supervision, control and the efficient operation of the workplace."[11] In that regard, a majority of the Court concluded that ". . . requiring an employer to obtain a warrant whenever the employer wished to enter an employee's office, desk, or file cabinets for a work-related purpose would seriously disrupt the routine conduct of business and would be unduly burdensome."[12] A probable cause requirement for such work-related searches was also rejected as an inappropriate standard because it ". . . would impose intolerable burdens on public employers."[13] Instead, the plurality adopted the lesser standard of reasonableness (also referred to as reasonable suspicion)[14] to regulate employer workspace searches:

> "Ordinarily, a search of an employee's office by a supervisor will be justified at its inception when there are reasonable grounds for suspecting that the search will turn up evidence that the employee is guilty of work-related misconduct, or that the search is necessary for a noninvestigatory work-related purpose such as to retrieve a needed file."[15]

Justice Scalia expressed somewhat differently his understanding of the appropriate standard to govern such searches:

> "Government searches to retrieve work-related materials or to investigate violations of workplace rules—searches of the sort that are regarded as reasonable and normal in the private-employer context—do not violate the Fourth Amendment."[16]

Despite these differing formulations of the appropriate standard of reasonableness, a majority of the Court would probably reach the same result in most cases and uphold employer workspace searches that are reasonably employment-related.

10   It is important to note that the Court's determination of a reasonableness standard in *O'Connor* is limited to certain types of employer searches. The Court acknowledges ". . . the plethora of contexts in which employers will have an

---

[11]*Id.*

[12]*Id.* at 1502.

[13]*Id.* at 1501.

[14]The plurality used interchangeably the terms "reasonable grounds" and "reasonable suspicion." In that regard, Justice O'Connor wrote that ". . . the delay in correcting the employee misconduct caused by the need for probable cause rather than reasonable suspicion will be translated into tangible and often irreparable damage to the agency's work, and ultimately to the public interest." *Id.* at 1502.

[15]*Id.* at 1503.

[16]*Id.* at 1506 (Justice Scalia concurring).

occasion to intrude to some extent on an employee's expectation of privacy"[17] and restricts the precedental value of its reasonableness determination in O'Connor to ". . . either a noninvestigatory work-related intrusion or an investigatory search for evidence of suspected work-related employee misfeasance. . . ."[18] In that regard, the Court offered the following three examples of legitimate work-related reasons for employers to search employee workspace: (1) The need for correspondence or a file or report available only in an employee's office while the employee is away from the office; (2) the need to safeguard or identify State property or records in an office in connection with a pending investigation into suspected employee misfeasance; and (3) a routine inventory conducted for the purpose of securing government property. Finally, it is important to note that the Court in O'Connor declined to address the appropriate reasonableness standards for situations where ". . . an employee is being investigated for criminal misconduct or breaches of other nonwork-related statutory or regulatory standards. . . ."[19]

What Constitutes a Reasonable Search?

11   The fourth amendment guarantees freedom from unreasonable searches and seizures. It does not protect against all governmental intrusions but only those that are unreasonable. If a particular intrusion into employee workspace does not invade an employee's reasonable expectation of privacy, the fourth amendment is not implicated. The preceding discussion illustrates how an inspection policy and other workplace realities can defeat an employee's privacy claim. However, where employees retain a reasonable expectation of privacy—albeit diminished—in a particular workspace area, the fourth amendment requires that employer intrusions meet the test of reasonableness.

12   A reasonableness analysis determines whether probable cause or some lesser standard should govern a particular workplace search. Determining the appropriate standard of reasonableness depends on the context within which a search takes place and requires a case-by-case balancing of competing interests. With respect to workplace searches, courts balance the invasion of an employee's legitimate expectations of privacy against the government's need for supervision, control, and the efficient operation of the workplace. The nature of the employment is a relevant factor in this balancing process.[31]

13   In law enforcement organizations, the reasonableness of workplace searches depends on the nature of law enforcement and the responsibilities of the em-

[17]Id. at 1501.
[18]Id.
[19]Id. at 1504.
[31]See, e.g., Commonwealth v. Gabrielle, 409 A.2d 1173 (Pa. Super 1979).

ployee involved.[32] In that regard, employee discipline and obedience to rules and regulations is essential in the quasi-military environs of a law enforcement organization; supervisors must have the flexibility to move swiftly and decisively to search employee workspace to prevent and/or detect any transgressions. Law enforcement employees are also given access, by virtue of their employment, to classified and confidential information, and supervisors need wide latitude to search employee workspace to uncover any breaches of security and to retrieve pertinent files and papers. Government also has a heightened interest in police integrity. Law enforcement officers interact with the public in ways that require a high degree of trust and confidence. The public rightly expects that officers who work to enforce the law will also obey the law, and the ability of law enforcement officers to offer credible testimony is dependent on their integrity which must be above reproach.

14   The purpose or reason for a particular workspace search is another relevant factor in determining reasonableness. Workplace searches in law enforcement organizations occur for a variety of reasons, including: (1) The need to secure government property, such as a gun or badge; (2) the need to retrieve a file or government documents believed to be in an officer's locker or desk; (3) the need to seize evidence of work-related misconduct or improper performance; and (4) the need to gather evidence of criminal misconduct. A majority of the Court in *O'Connor* recognized that ". . . employers most frequently need to enter the offices and desks of their employees for legitimate work-related reasons wholly unrelated to illegal conduct."[33] By implication, the Court suggests that a different standard of reasonableness might govern workplace searches for evidence of criminal activity unrelated to employment.

15   Lower courts have also suggested that the appropriate standard of reasonableness depends on whether a particular workplace search was administrative in nature and work-related or aimed at uncovering evidence of criminal misconduct unrelated to public employment.[34] That distinction has less significance for workspace searches in law enforcement organizations where suspected criminal

[32]The U.S. Courts of Appeals for the Fifth and Ninth Circuits have suggested that searches of postal employees' lockers by postal inspectors based on a suspicion of theft are reasonable because of the heightened governmental interest in protecting the safety of the mail and the need to prevent and discover theft of the mails. *United States v. Sanders*, 568 F.2d 1175 (5th Cir. 1978); *United States v. Bunkers*, 521 F.2d 1217 (9th Cir. 1975), *cert. denied*, 96 S.Ct. 400 (1975).

[33]107 S.Ct. at 1500.

[34]In *United States v. Collins*, 349 F.2d 863 (2d Cir. 1985), *cert. denied*, 86 S.Ct 1228 (1966), the court upheld the search of a work jacket belonging to a clerical employee of the Customs Service that hung in the supervisor's outer office; the court concluded the employer was not investigating a crime unconnected with the performance of a Customs employee whose job included handling valuable mail. See also, *State v. Ferrari*, 357 A.2d 286 (N.J. Super, 1976) where the court ruled that the warrantless search of the locked desk of the deputy chief of police was unreasonable because it was not necessary to the day-to-day business but part of a criminal investigation.

activity by employees frequently constitutes a legitimate work-related reason for conducting a search. Workspace searches in law enforcement organizations, even for the sole purpose of discovering evidence of criminal activity, may be related to law enforcement employment because of a heightened governmental need for officer integrity and credibility. The U.S. Court of Appeals for the Fifth Circuit held that the search of a Federal employee's office and desk was reasonable because the employer's investigation of suspected employee misconduct ". . . was within the outer perimeter of . . ." the employer's line of duty.[35] Suspected criminal activity by a law enforcement employee is arguably always related to and within the outer perimeter of law enforcement responsibilities. Courts have applied a similar rationale to justify strip searches of law enforcement employees on a reasonable suspicion standard, even though such searches would probably not be reasonable for public employees whose employment responsibilities did not involve a heightened need for integrity and credibility.[36]

CONCLUSION

16   The divided vote of the Court in O'Connor complicates the task of interpreting the decision and offering advice to law enforcement organizations regarding the constitutionality of workplace searches. Language in the opinions regarding the appropriate fourth amendment standard of reasonableness to govern workplace searches is specifically limited to ". . . either a noninvestigatory work-related intrusion or an investigatory search for evidence of suspected work-related employee misfeasance. . . ." While the Court did not address the fourth amendment standards governing searches for evidence of criminal misconduct or the validity of inspection policies, lower court decisions discussed in this article establish several general principles that are applicable to workspace searches in law enforcement organizations. First, law enforcement employees can acquire a reasonable expectation of privacy in their workspace areas. Second, workspace searches that invade an employee's reasonable expectation of privacy are constitutionally reasonable if based on a reasonable work-related justification. Third, workspace searches conducted pursuant to a valid organizational inspection policy are constitutionally reasonable. In that regard, law enforcement organizations should promulgate a written policy that clearly forewarns employees of the possibility of work place searches and provides clear notice of their privacy rights regarding personal effects carried into the workplace and in workspace such as offices, desks,

[35]*Williams v. Collins*, 728 F.2d 721, 728 (5th Cir. 1984).

[36]In *Kirkpatrick v. City of Los Angeles*, 803 F.2d 485 (9th Cir. 1986), the court held that ". . . in spite of the government's interest in police integrity, strip searches of police officers for investigative purposes must be supported by a reasonable suspicion that evidence will be uncovered." *Id.* at 488. The court did not decide whether evidence uncovered in an investigative search without a warrant or probable cause would later be admissible against an officer in a criminal proceeding. See also, *Security and Law Enforcement Employees v. Carey*, 737 F.2d 187 (2d Cir. 1984).

lockers, and file cabinets. A valid inspection policy provides necessary guidance to administrators, promotes consistent treatment, and helps insure that workplace searches are based on legitimate governmental interests that are consistent with the reasonableness requirements of the fourth amendment.

WRITING ASSIGNMENT

Write a research paper on a topic that has emerged from the semester's discussions. The topic can be philosophical or practical, academic or job-related. But be sure it is manageable. Feel free to collect information through observation, interviews, questionnaires, and library research.

A·P·P·E·N·D·I·X

REVIEW
Checklists for Critical Reading and Writing

CHECKLIST FOR CRITIQUING

For free writing and essays ask

What did I find interesting?
What does it look like I can learn from this?
What insights caught my attention?
What sentence or section seemed best?
What sentence or section seemed weakest?
What parts would I like to see explained more?
What parts should be omitted?
What parts seemed real?
What parts seemed phony?
What parts did the author really care about?
What parts seemed worth writing an essay about?
What idea held the whole piece together?
What was the most important idea?
What idea might tie the different points together?

For essays ask

What is the point of the essay? Why is the writer telling us this? What is the idea that holds the essay together?

What is the purpose of the first paragraph? Does the opening catch our interest and make us want to continue? How does it prepare us for what we found in the rest of the essay?

What is the point of each example or story? Why is each example where it is? Why aren't there additional examples, or fewer ones?

How does the essay flow from one idea to the next? Are the ideas connected logically? What is the point of each paragraph? Why are the paragraphs arranged in this particular sequence?

Why does the essay end the way it does? Is this how we thought it would end? Is the ending justified by what went before, or does it seem tacked on as an afterthought? Does it resolve the discussion or raise new questions? Does the ending satisfy us or make us feel cheated?

CHECKLIST FOR CRITICAL READING

When previewing ask
   Who is the author?
   What are the author's qualifications?
   When and why was this written?
   What type of writing is it?
   What kind of publication was it in?
   What is the significance of the title?
   What do the headings or other graphics call attention to?

Underline (or highlight) phrases and passages that
   capture the author's point
   serve your purpose in reading and writing
   require further study

Write notes that
   state the significance of the underlining (or highlighting)
   show the logic of the passage
   give your reactions
   explain difficult points
   suggest how you might use this information

Condense
   the essay into a brief summary
   the thesis statement into a short title
   significant passages into a few key words

Outline the work by listing
   the thesis statement
   subheads of major divisions
   secondary thesis statements
   topic sentences
   important supporting details

Evaluate
the meaning by asking
   What is the overall point?
   How is this point conveyed?
   What are the secondary or supporting points?

the organization by asking
   Why is this passage included?
   Why is it in this particular place?
   What does it add to the whole?

the authority by asking
   Is the author a recognized authority?
   Is the evidence from authoritative sources?
   Is the evidence convincing?
   Is the logic valid?
   Is the author's use of the evidence reasonable?

the usefulness to you by asking
   Do I agree with this?
   If not, can I refute it?
   Are there particularly good examples?
   Is there a striking turn of phrase?
   What have I learned from this?
   How is this connected to other topics?

CHECKLIST FOR QUOTING AND PARAPHRASING

1. Paraphrase wherever possible.
2. Quote only phrases or short passages that cannot be presented as well through paraphrase.
3. Quote the author's exact words.
4. Structure your sentence so that it accommodates the quotation smoothly.
5. Use double quotation marks at the beginning and end of any words that you take from a source.
6. Use a comma to separate the source from a quoted sentence.
7. Use a colon to make a quotation more emphatic or to introduce a long quotation.
8. Indent, without quotation marks, quotations longer than five lines or fifty words.
9. Use three spaced periods to show ellipsis—that is, omitted words—in the body of the quotation.

10. Use four spaced periods to indicate ellipsis at the end of a quoted sentence, or the omission of an entire intervening sentence.
11. Use square brackets to indicate an addition to or change in the quotation.
12. Use parentheses after the quotation to indicate a change such as emphasis within the quotation.
13. Put a comma or period required by your sentence inside the quotation marks.
14. Put all other punctuation required by your sentence outside the quotation marks.
15. Omit your own punctuation when the sentence ends with punctuation in the quotation.
16. Avoid sentence organizations that require strings of end punctuation.
17. Use single quotation marks to indicate a quotation within the quotation.

CHECKLIST FOR EXPOSITORY ESSAYS

An expository, or objective, essay has
   an introduction, development, conclusion
   a thesis statement for the main idea of the essay
   topic sentences for the main idea of paragraphs
   paragraphs organized around a single idea

CHECKLIST FOR DEVELOPING THE ESSAY

Ideas are logically connected in terms of
   place
   time
   similarity
   contrast
   condition
   causation

Methods of developing an essay are
   definition
   comparison/contrast
   classification
   analogy
   causation
   narration
   description

Showing Logical Connections

There are six categories of logical transition. Each is divided into two structural groups.

	Group I	Group II
	1. Take semicolon or period between ideas. 2. Connected idea stands second. 3. Move within their idea. 4. May be set off within idea by commas.	1. Take comma between ideas. 2. Included idea may be first or second. 3. Begin their idea. 4. May not be set off within idea by commas.
Place	in these/such places	where, anywhere, everywhere, wherever
Time	afterward, later, next, subsequently, thereafter, thereupon, then, finally, earlier, before this, formerly, now, meanwhile, still, at this/that time	after, before, while, until, since, when, whenever, as soon as, as long as, just as
Similarity	again, also, besides, further, indeed, likewise, furthermore, moreover, so too, still more, in other words, in addition, in fact, for example, for instance	as well as, just as, in the same way as/that
Contrast	conversely, however, still, nevertheless, nonetheless, rather, in contrast, on the other hand	although, (even) though, whereas, while, even if, despite the fact that, less than, more than
Condition	if so, if not, in that case	if, unless, whether, lest
Reason	accordingly, consequently, hence, therefore, thus, as a result, for this reason, it follows that, that's why	because, since, inasmuch as, insofar as, whereas, due to the fact that

CHECKLIST FOR EVALUATION

An evaluation must have

an analysis of the issue
a clear set of values
a sense of authority

When examining the evidence for a conclusion we ask

Is it relevant?
Is it adequate?
Is it necessary and sufficient?

Is it representative?
Is it complete?
Is it current?
Is it from a trustworthy source?
Is it in agreement with the experience of others?

Among the common logical fallacies are

Ad hominem: attacking the person instead of the point.
Begging the question (circular reasoning): taking for granted what you are supposed to be proving.
Dominoes: assuming the first step in a process must lead to the last.
Everyone does it: two wrongs make a right.
False analogy: similarity in one respect assumes similarity in others.
False authority: quoting famous people out of their field.
False dilemma: setting up unreal either/or choice.
Non sequitur: "it does not follow."
Overgeneralization: stretching the evidence too far.
Overlooked alternative: ignoring other possible answers.
Post hoc ergo propter hoc: confusing sequence with causation.
Straw man: drawing attention away from the real issue.

CHECKLIST FOR PERSUASION

An essay to persuade must
address an arguable issue
analyze the problem
evaluate alternative solutions
prove one choice
reject the other choices

When evaluating a persuasive essay we ask
Is the problem clearly defined?
Is it arguable?
Is it analyzed adequately?
Is the proposed solution clear?
Is it reasonable?
Is it supported convincingly?
Are alternative solutions offered?
Are they presented fairly?
Are they convincingly disproven?

CHECKLIST FOR RESEARCHED WRITING

A researched paper should have
a manageable topic

adequate analysis and evaluation
a sense of authority
a clear purpose and audience
documentation of any sources used

You must acknowledge any idea that is

not your own
not general knowledge
quoted or paraphrased

You should follow an accepted style manual for documentation.

INDEX

B

Begging the question, as a logical fallacy, 285
"Belief in Things Unseen, A" (Patricia Cleary Graham), 104–7
Bennett, William J., 448–51, 463
Bethel School District v. *Fraser* (1986), 176–78, 191, 313
  future use, 178
  significance, 178
Beveridge, Sen. Albert J., 370–72, 375, 376, 463
Biological Abstracts, 437
Brainstorming, personal experience essay, 13–14
Brown v. *Board of Education* (1954), 224–25, 303–6, 313
  future use, 307
  significance, 306
Burger, Warren, 274–75
Business Periodicals Index, 437
Byrd, William, 223–24

C

Card catalogue, 433–36
  call number, 433
Carfango, Margaret, 396–99
Carnegie, Andrew, 180–83, 191–92, 204, 312, 376
Carter, Jimmy, 373–74, 375, 376, 463
Causation, 209, 221–24
  conditionality of, 222
Charles, Edlyne, 335–41
Checklists:
  critical reading, 61–62, 475–76
  critiquing, 28–29, 474–75
  development, 232, 477
  evaluation, 293, 477–78
  expository essays, 175, 477
  paraphrasing, 119–22, 476–77
  personal writing, critiquing of, 28–29
  persuasion, 362, 478–79
  quotes, 119–22, 476–77
  researched writing, 444, 479
Chemical Abstracts, 438
"Choosing Your Own Way of Life" (Maria Martinez), 228–32
Christian Science Monitor, 436
Circular reasoning, 285

"Civil Disobedience" (Henry David Thoreau), 381–84
Classification, 219–21, 251
  visual aids and, 220–21
"Classism, Sexism, Racism and the Situational Comedy" (K. Edgington), 129–32, 138, 220, 375
  facts, 132–33
  future use, 133
  significance, 133
  vocabulary, 132
Comma, in quotes, 122
Community Development Abstracts, 437
Comparison/contrast, 216–19
Complete evidence, 284
Conclusions, 159–62
  drawing, 283–85
Condensing, 51–52, 61
Connections, 4–5, 78, 137–39, 191–92, 212, 251–52, 312–13, 375–76, 462–63, 480
  evaluation, 312–13
  importance to reading/writing, 4–5
  persuasion, 375–76
  researched writing, 462–63
"Content Counts" (Paul Gagnon), 319–22
Conventions, used to clarify main idea, 167–74
Cooper, James Fenimore, 196–98, 204, 312
Crèvecoeur, Hector St. John de, 188–90, 192, 204, 215–16, 312, 376
Critical reading/writing, 1–29
  major benefit of, 22
Critical reviews, 278–79
Critical thinking, developing habit of, 2
Current evidence, 284

D

Darrow, Clarence, 222–23
"Defining Socialist Womanhood: The Women's Page of the *Jewish Daily Forward* in 1919" (Maxine S. Seller), 199–204
Definition, 214–16
Degano, Margaret M., 400–412
Description, 225–26
Development:
  analogy, 221–22
  causation, 209, 221–24
  checklist, 232